W9-CHN-156

DISCARDED
From the Nashville Public Library

Star of Empire

Star of Empire

A Study of

BRITAIN

AS A WORLD POWER

1485–1945

WILLIAM B. WILLCOX

NEW YORK
ALFRED A. KNOPF
1950

CARNEGIE LIBRARY
OF
NASHVILLE

942
W69

THIS IS A BORZOI BOOK,
PUBLISHED BY ALFRED A. KNOPF, INC.

COPYRIGHT *1950* by William B. Willcox. All rights reserved. No part of this book may be reproduced in any form without permission in writing from the publisher, except by a reviewer who may quote brief passages in a review to be printed in a magazine or newspaper. Manufactured in the United States of America. Published simultaneously in Canada by McClelland & Stewart Limited.

FIRST EDITION

CARNEGIE LIBRARY
OF
NASHVILLE

TO

A E W

Whose Zest Extends to History

213207

INTRODUCTION

THE PAGES that follow are an attempt to interpret the story of modern Britain. They are not primarily an attempt to tell the story; that has been done in a number of excellent textbooks. The salient facts must of course be given in order to be interpreted, but my interest is in the meaning behind them. They were produced by complex forces — of ideas or personality, economics or geography — and the significance of the story lies in the forces. These were seldom clear to any particular generation that had to deal with them; they are not yet wholly clear, and the effort to read their meaning becomes progressively more difficult as the story advances toward the present. But meaning is there, and it is important.

Although I am not attempting to prove any thesis about British history, I am attempting to develop certain ideas that I believe are fundamental to it. They explain the emphases throughout the book, and the reader ought in fairness to know of them in advance. One idea is that religion had a profound influence on British development at least into the nineteenth century; hence my stress in the first chapter on the nature of the Tudor church as the matrix of the future. A second is that until the Victorian era the English system of local government by amateurs conditioned the functioning of national government. A third (which should be a truism) is that Britain has developed in response to outside stimuli, especially European, and that in consequence her history is inseparable from the history of Europe. A fourth, derivative from the third, is that her policy has in the long run been governed by the strategic demands of her peculiar and highly specialized forms of power. A fifth is that since the time of the American Revolution — which was a much more superficial schism than it seemed to be — Britain and the United States have been drawing together again toward the entente of the present day. None of these ideas is original. But in sum they will explain, I hope, why the book seemed worth writing.

I do not believe that all historical periods are of equal importance for the present, and I have made no attempt to treat them equally. The crucial nature of the Puritan Revolution explains why the

early Stuarts and Cromwell receive as much attention as the whole
Tudor era, or as the hundred years after the Restoration. The chronological pace of the book is slower in the nineteenth century than
in the eighteenth, and slower still in the twentieth, because the story
becomes more relevant as it approaches our time.

It also becomes more difficult to interpret. The characters in its
most recent chapters have not yet entered what Lord Curzon called
"the cold dissecting chamber of history" — where historians, he
might have added, perform their post-mortems under the lamp of
hindsight. Causes are harder to discern in the immediate than in the
more distant past, and when it comes to results — to describing how
the causes will work into the future — the historian has nothing to
say as historian. If the study of the past impels him to look ahead,
he sees no more clearly than any other observer of the unknown.
But I cannot help trying to look, and in my final pages I have consciously departed from the historian's role to advance some tentative
conclusions about the crisis into which we are moving.

One ingredient of the crisis, and one that particularly concerns
the United States, is the decline in Britain's position. The troubles of
the present Labour government are the result not of socialism, but
of history: the currents of change that produced the Victorian *Pax
Britannica* have now ended it, and to blame the ending on a particular regime is to confuse effects with causes. Confusion befuddles
American thinking about Britain at a time when clear thinking is
vital. Since the first settlement at Jamestown, American history has
been intimately associated with British. For a time after 1783 the
association was hidden, but in the twentieth century it has become
increasingly evident as British power has ebbed. I believe that we
have now reached the point where the survival of western civilization depends in large measure on the closeness of Anglo-American
collaboration. Collaboration depends in turn upon mutual understanding, and understanding upon a sense of perspective — a sense
of forces working through time to make the two nations what they
are. History, if it cannot help to provide this perspective, is the salt
of events that has lost its savor.

For this reason the writing of interpretative history is needed. But
it is a dangerous occupation. In the first place its results cannot be
documented according to the rigid standards of the profession. As
soon as a writer tries to go beyond what facts meant for the men

who experienced them, he is beyond the range of documentation. His findings can be no more than provisional, and they are peculiarly open to his own subjective bias — the bias that is the historian's equivalent of original sin, something he deplores in himself but knows he will never be rid of. Bias expresses itself not only in the handling of topics but in the choice of them. Why do I discuss Burke and not Jeremy Bentham, or the Whiggism of 1688 without mentioning Locke? My only answer is that I feel free from the text-book-writer's obligation to touch on virtually everything, and that free selection is necessarily arbitrary.

Another and more serious danger of interpretative history is that the writer does not know enough. In order to interpret soundly he ought to be familiar with every aspect of an enormous subject. Ought he therefore to resemble that fabulous British scholar "whose field was history and whose foible was omniscience"? If so, this book should never have been written, for it has led me into areas where I am all too conscious of my ignorance. I have done what I could to remedy it. For the rest I can only plead that the professional conscience, if given free rein, makes cowards of us all.

I am indebted to the editors of the *American Historical Review* and the *Yale Review* for allowing me to incorporate material from articles of mine, and to Professor Edward Mead Earle for reading the last two chapters of my manuscript and making many valuable suggestions. I am grateful to my publishers, first for inducing me to write the book, and then for helpfulness and encouragement during its composition; and to the University of Michigan for accelerating its progress by granting me a sabbatical leave of absence. Lastly I am under a deep obligation to my wife. Her patience is equaled by her critical sense, and she has contributed so much to these pages that they are in effect a joint enterprise.

W. B. W.

Ann Arbor, Michigan
October 3, 1949

CONTENTS

CHAPTER ONE: SEEDS OF GREATNESS
1485–1603

I	The Island Peoples	3
II	The Tudor Setting	7
III	The Two Henrys	15
IV	Catholic and Protestant	23
V	The Religious Seesaw	29
VI	The Elizabethan Defensive	38
VII	"Confident from Foreign Purposes"	45

CHAPTER TWO: THE PASSING OF TUDOR ENGLAND
1603–1660

I	The Advent of the Stuarts	50
II	The Pedantic King	53
III	The Breach with Parliament	61
IV	The King Alone	68
V	The Fall of the Monarchy	75
VI	"Sword Government"	87

CHAPTER THREE: THE TRIUMPH OF THE OLIGARCHY
1660–1763

I	The Merry Monarch	98
II	Tory and Whig	104
III	The Conservative Revolution	109
IV	The Duel with Louis XIV	116
V	The Duel of Tory and Whig	122
VI	The Whig Ascendancy	127
VII	The Second Phase of the Duel with France	133
VIII	Victory Overseas	137

Contents

CHAPTER FOUR: THE DEFENSIVE AGAINST REVOLUTION

1763–1815

I	Rationalism and Reform	145
II	The Emergence of the King	151
III	Civil War in the Empire	156
IV	The Repercussions of Defeat	161
V	Economic Revolution	170
VI	War against the French Revolution	176
VII	Crisis in Ireland	185
VIII	Victory at Sea	188
IX	Victory on Land	193
X	The Aftermath	200

CHAPTER FIVE: REVOLUTION BY CONSENT

1815–1867

I	The Vienna Settlement	202
II	Great Britain and the Concert of Europe	205
III	The Genesis of Reform	212
IV	Liberalism and the Reform Bill	217
V	The Fruits of Liberalism	222
VI	Liberalism and the Empire	230
VII	Threats to Liberalism	238
VIII	The New Toryism	245
IX	The Beginning of Democracy	251

CHAPTER SIX: THE VICTORIAN TWILIGHT

1867–1906

I	Major Themes	255
II	Domestic Reform	257
III	The Irish Question	261
IV	The New Europe	268
V	The Renascence of Imperialism	276

Contents

VI	Conquest in Africa	286
VII	Forces of Reform	296
VIII	The Diplomatic Revolution	300

CHAPTER SEVEN: GEORGIAN BRITAIN
1906–1932

I	The Socialist Experiment	307
II	The Road to War	312
III	From Blitzkrieg to Deadlock	320
IV	Victory and Versailles	330
V	London, Geneva, and Washington	338
VI	The British Commonwealth	343
VII	Domestic Change	347

CHAPTER EIGHT: SLEEP AND WAKING
1932–1945

I	The Background of Foreign Policy	352
II	The Undeclared War	361
III	The Nazi Offensive in the West	367
IV	Counteroffensive	373
V	The New World	378
VI	Crystal-Gazing	387

| Bibliographical Note | 395 |
| Index | *follows page* 399 |

Star of Empire

Chapter One

SEEDS OF GREATNESS

1485–1603

I The Island Peoples

THE SIXTEENTH century was a turning point in the destiny of the British peoples. In 1500 they were torn by dissension; Scotland was aligned with France, Wales was only partially subjugated to England, and Ireland was almost entirely beyond the Pale. England herself was still suffering from the aftermath of foreign defeat and civil war. Her new dynasty was insecure upon the throne, and her weight was slight in the scales of European power. In 1600 England and Scotland were being drawn together against their will, England and Wales were at least a governmental unit, and the English had made strides on the long, grim path of conquering Ireland. England was not yet recognized in Europe as a power of the first rank, but she had made a place for herself as a champion of Protestantism, the David to the Spanish Goliath. Her sailors had learned the taste of the seven seas and had opened new horizons for the adventurous, and she was on the verge of the greatest expansion of power in history.

At the beginning of the sixteenth century no signs of this future appeared. The British Isles were then little more than an appendage off the coast of Europe — and off a coast remote from the heart of European life. The economy of the Continent was still focused upon the Mediterranean, and Italy was still the trading center of Christendom. From Italian ports the routes of supply ran eastward, by ship and caravan, to the riches of India and China; from Italy the routes of distribution radiated through western Europe. The British

Isles were far removed from this commerce, and its main rewards were denied to British merchants by the facts of geography supplemented by the sea power of Spain and Portugal. The lucrative if less important trade routes of the Baltic were also denied to them by the strength of the Hanseatic League. The only possible outlet for expansion was westward into the Atlantic, where the gains were at best problematical and the dangers obvious. The British peoples seemed confined by nature to the economic periphery of Europe.

In 1500 they were also on its cultural periphery. Their development varied in direct proportion to their nearness to the Continent: the English, at least politically, were far more mature than the Scots, Welsh, or Irish, and the English of the southeastern counties were generations ahead of those in the north and west. But even the most civilized segments of society were behind the times by Continental standards. The Renaissance, germinating in fifteenth-century Italy, had spread northward into France and westward into the Iberian peninsula; as yet it had scarcely crossed the Channel. A great part of the reason lies in political developments that had cut England off from Europe, turned her energies inward, dammed them up, and so prepared the way for their subsequent outburst overseas. England's past lay in Europe; her future lay in all the other continents.

During the Middle Ages England and France had grown toward nationhood by struggling with each other. The struggle had its roots in the Norman Conquest, whereby the Duke of Normandy, the most powerful vassal of the King of France, became in his own right king of England. For almost four hundred years his descendants labored to increase their possessions in France, and for a time they aimed at the French throne itself. The climax of their efforts was the Hundred Years' War; when it ended in 1453, nothing remained of their great French holdings except the Channel port of Calais. Their successes had been sometimes grandiose and always transient; their failure was complete and final.

That failure was a landmark in English history. It ended the dream of Continental expansion once and for all, and began an era that was isolationist in the literal sense. For the next century and a half the inhabitants of the British Isles developed as islanders, and their expansion, when it came, reached almost every part of the globe except Europe. They alone, among the great powers of European history, have had no major territorial ambitions on the Conti-

4

nent; they alone have been free to devote their full energies to commercial development, emigration, and conquest overseas. Their imperial greatness, in short, derives in large part from the fact that the English were thrown back upon their island in the fifteenth century by the power of France.

When the House of Tudor came to the English throne in 1485, this blessing was still in disguise. Defeat in war abroad had been followed by war at home — a vicious series of feuds that history has sweetly disguised as the Wars of the Roses. The aftermath was such demoralization of people and government as England had not seen since the twelfth century. The legal and political system seemed to be breaking down, and public order to be giving way to chaos. The English were at loggerheads with the other British peoples, and a unified state for the island of Great Britain — let alone for Great Britain and Ireland — was a still-distant dream. Little chance appeared that the islanders would compose their own differences, and less that they had in them the strength for expansion.

The great future problem in the interrelations of the British peoples was already taking form. The Tudors claimed sovereignty over Ireland, as their predecessors had done, by virtue of a conquest in the Norman period. But despite four centuries of intermittent effort English authority scarcely extended beyond the narrow limits of the Pale, with its capital at Dublin. The reason was part of the enduring tragedy of Anglo-Irish relations. The English world was so different from the Irish, not only in race and language, but in law and economics, that the average English administrator had no more understanding of the Irish clans and their system of land tenure than he did of their language; to him they were in every sense beyond the Pale. They retaliated with a hostility that scarcely disposed their overlords to know them better, and that would have thrown the English back into the sea years before if the chieftains had not hated each other more than they hated the foreigner. Because they were unable to combine, the English had little difficulty in carrying out the first half of the Roman maxim, divide and rule.

The second half was another matter. Ireland was geographically too near England to be ignored, but it was too far away to be conquered and held with the means available to the English state of that period. Governmental resources were, by modern standards, unbelievably meager. The machinery of power was correspondingly primitive, and its force was attenuated by mere distance; the farther an area was from the capital, the less susceptible it was to royal control. This factor operated in the border regions of England itself, and far more strongly in the hills of Connaught. The only basis for effective Tudor rule in Ireland was English armies, which were depleted by wholesale desertions on the journey and could not be increased without a prohibitive drain on the treasury. The Pale was therefore a liability. It caused a dispersion of the scanty power available to the Tudors without bringing them any compensating advantage.

Their power was barely adequate for other demands made upon it nearer home. The small northern kingdom of Scotland had been a problem and a temptation for English monarchs since the shadowy days of Macbeth and Malcolm. The Scots hated the English as much as the Irish did, and had resisted English aggression far more successfully. They could combine in moments of crisis, as the Irish could not, and they had a source of help abroad. Medieval English kings had twice reduced Scotland to the status of a fief, but she had twice freed herself. The liberation on the field of Bannockburn in 1314 proved to be final, because soon afterward the English turned their backs on the Scots to follow the will-o'-the-wisp of conquering France in the Hundred Years' War.

The Scots used their opportunity to consolidate a working arrangement with France, which endured as a political tie until 1560. It was a *mariage de convenance,* common in the power politics of any age, and it increased the difficulties of the English in their French wars by creating a Scottish threat from behind. It was also dangerous for the Scots. Their land had been divided by geography and history into two parts, the Celtic highlands of the north and the Teutonic lowlands, and the center of political power had long been in the latter, exposed to the invasion of both English armies and English culture; now the magnetism of French ideas was being felt with increasing strength, and it seemed that Scotland might save herself from England only to become an appanage of France. For the Scots that possibility, however unwelcome, might be the lesser of two evils. For the English it threatened disaster.

The problem of the fourth British people, the Welsh, was already well on the way to settlement. The English conquest of Wales in the thirteenth century had proved more enduring than similar ven-

6

tures in Ireland and Scotland. The conquerors held their new principality much as the Romans had done, by a series of castles along the border and the coasts, and left the tribesmen of the interior largely unmolested in their mountains. The highlanders periodically swept eastward on raids into the Vale of Severn, to loot the fatness of its farming lands, and life on the Welsh Marches was as precarious as on the Scottish. But rebellion, as distinct from raids, had ended more than half a century before the Tudor era, when Henry IV and his warrior son had stamped out the rising of Owen Glendower. Since then English influence had expanded steadily in Wales, until the moment was nearly ripe for a political fusion of the two. The actual fusion was achieved in 1536 by the great-grandson of a Welsh country gentleman, Henry VIII of the House of Tudor.

II   The Tudor Setting

AT its accession the position of the new dynasty seemed far from promising. The Tudor right to the throne was questionable; in law it rested on a devious descent from Edward III through a female line, and in fact it rested on success in war. The last of the House of York, Richard III, had governed more despotically than even the Yorkists could endure, and within two years he had been defeated and killed in battle by the only pretender strong enough to challenge him, Henry Tudor. Henry was thereupon accepted by the nation, less of right than of necessity, and the Wars of the Roses were over. But the new king was confronted with an enormous task of reconstruction. Within England the people were exhausted by fighting abroad and at home; private quarrels were rife and rebellion endemic; the prestige and power of central government were at low ebb. Elsewhere in the islands the Irish were unsubdued, and the Scots maintained their menacing independence. From abroad the great powers of Europe eyed the troubled waters shrewdly, calculating when and where they could fish to best advantage.

Henry's England, however, had deep sources of strength on which to draw. The people, whatever their surface difficulties, were well equipped by history and geography for the new age dawning in Europe. Their island home had molded their society, which was both elastic and tough, and their insularity had largely freed them from the threat of overseas invasion. They had consequently needed the military less than their Continental neighbors, and their feudalism had developed no such warrior caste as in France or Germany. The profoundly civilian character of their society, in other words, derived at bottom from geography.

The preceding century of warfare had threatened to make a serious alteration. During the Hundred Years' War the old feudality, a poor weapon for fighting abroad, had been largely superseded by a new nobility of the sword. Almost as soon as the fighting in France had ended, fighting in England had begun; the mercenary captains had supported one or the other claimant to the throne, and many of them had been eliminated in the battles and proscriptions of the Wars of the Roses. At the same time the people at large had learned to think of an armed nobility as synonymous with rapine and oppression. The nobles had acquired much the same reputation as their modern prototype, the large-scale gangster, and the rest of society was as eager to be quit of them. The monarchy, on the other hand, had been strengthened by the wars. It was immortal, unlike the monarch, and with the victory of first one faction, then the other, the royal treasury had gained by confiscation much of the land and wealth of the vanquished. The bulk of the nation, furthermore, looked to the throne for relief from the curse of the military, and a tacit alliance of king and people against the nobility was taking form.

"People" is a confusing word at any time, and particularly so when applied to Tudor England. The great mass of the people counted for next to nothing in national affairs; only a small minority had the wherewithal for political influence. The aristocrats were the most conspicuous members of this minority, but far from the most numerous. Below them was the middle class of town and country: the burgesses, who ranged from small shopkeepers to merchant princes; the gentry, who owned much of the land and had it cultivated for them. These two groups are worth some attention, because they were the most important constituents of English society for centuries to come.

Neither the gentry nor the burgesses were a closed group. A family of yeomen farmers might achieve gentility within a few generations by acquiring enough wealth to emancipate them from the working of their land. The aristocracy, on the other side, was constantly adding new blood to the gentry because of the law of primo-

8

geniture: the eldest son of a peer inherited the title and the lands, while his younger brothers, who remained commoners at law, were likely to grow up as country gentlemen. The burgesses were an equally undefined group, recruited from above and below, and they were also closely tied to the gentry. The tie was in great part economic, although it had its social side. The mainspring of the national economy in the late Middle Ages was the wool trade. Sheep-raising was the most lucrative use to which land could be put in many parts of England, and the marketing of wool brought wealth to the towns. Inevitably, therefore, the landowner and the merchant were brought together by a community of interest, and their business relations were often cemented by a marriage alliance. The English middle class was much more than a bourgeoisie. Some of its roots were urban, others deeply planted in the land, and it derived its vitality in equal measure from both.

Its political importance was already out of all proportion to its size. The monarchy had long been attempting to weaken the power of the aristocracy by transferring the work of local government to the gentry and burgesses. Much was still to be done by the Tudors, but already the principal royal agents in the counties and towns were unpaid amateurs of the middle class. Because they were amateurs they had to acquire their administrative experience and knowledge of the law as they went along. Because they were unpaid they had to work for the king in such time as they could spare from supervising the tenantry or managing the shop. Behind them stood no tangible force — no police or army worth the name, nothing but the prestige of a distant king. On that and on their own skill depended their capacity to get obedience from neighbors whom they could not coerce. Whenever local opinion was solidly opposed to the policy of the crown, that policy could not be carried out. The royal agent, whether squire or townsman, could not flout the feeling of the community even if he would; the attempt would be hopeless from the start, and he was usually dependent on the community for his livelihood. He did the king's work free of charge, and did it reasonably well. But the king paid for the saving to his treasury in terms of a real if implicit limitation on his power: he could not enforce a policy opposed to the wishes of the middle class.

The political strength of that class had its base in local government and its apex in the House of Commons. The "commons" of

England were the gentry and burgesses, and their interests were mirrored in the House that they elected. The peers of the realm, who sat by hereditary right in the House of Lords, had encouraged the Lower House in its adolescence because it was amenable to their influence; a merchant or a squire did not shake off his awe of the titled magnate in his locality when his neighbors sent him to Westminster. For this reason, among others, the House of Commons had thrived inconspicuously on the chaos of the fifteenth century. Its members were often a flock of scared sheep, but the House as an institution gained strength for the future. It was used to legalize one factional victory after another; although the victories were evanescent, the use was growing into a habit with great implications.

By 1485 the implications were not fully apparent. The House of Commons had participated, as of right, in the making and unmaking of kings; it had assumed control of a large part of the royal revenue; it had tried unsuccessfully to encroach on the executive sphere of policy-making. But in the modern sense there was no House of Commons. The group of men who sat in St. Stephen's Chapel was at most a debating society concerned with ways and means of petitioning its betters — crown and lords — for redress of outstanding grievances. The members had been thrown together hugger-mugger by the chance of the last election; they did not know each other, their betters, or the Londoners among whom they had to live, and they had small desire to. Their attendance at Parliament still had much of its medieval character, of a burden foisted upon them by their neighbors through the electoral process. Their aim was to secure the redress of a maximum of grievances in return for voting a minimum of taxes, and to complete this bargain and go home as quickly as possible. Shakespeare's later gibe at "the wavering commons" might equally well have been aimed at them: "their love lies in their purses." [1] In their eyes a good session was a short one, and a good king was one who governed for years without needing to summon a parliament. If such a king did not create grievances or require parliamentary subsidies on a large scale, the middle class was more than willing to leave the mysteries of state in his hands, and to see parliaments become few and far between. The House of Commons, despite its privileges and potential power, was an expensive luxury for those whom it represented and taxed. Whether or not

---

[1] *Richard II,* II, ii, 129–30.

they would dispense with it depended on the Crown. A dynasty that alienated them would bring the House to life; a dynasty that pleased them could, if it chose, reduce the House to a constitutional ornament.

The political importance of the middle class, in local and central government, was equaled by its financial importance. "The people in these latter ages . . . are no less to be pleased than the peers; for, as the latter are become less, so . . . the commons have all the weapons in their hands." ² The principal weapon was money. The wealth of the country was rapidly coming into the hands of the most enterprising among the gentry and burgesses, and the leaven of this new capitalism was destined to remake English society.

The leaven first appeared in the wool trade, which since the fourteenth century had been both expanding and changing its character. The emphasis was shifting, with the growth of domestic manufacture, from the export of raw wool to that of finished cloth. Wool was a rural as much as an urban industry, and the new capitalism was not only cracking the craft guilds in the towns, but beginning to transform the countryside through the agrarian revolution known as enclosure. The fields of one manor after another were being turned into sheepfolds; the manorial structure was shattered, and the tenants were turned out to fend for themselves. Although the climax was still to come — and to be paid for in mass unemployment — the enclosure movement was already increasing the supply of fluid capital, which was helping in turn to stimulate other phases of the national economy. The export trade in wool, for example, had hitherto been largely in the hands of foreigners. Now, with the capital at hand and the need to expand the selling market, English merchants looked forward to the day when the carrying trade would be in English bottoms, and the farsighted dreamed of mercantile expansion on a far greater scale.

These capitalists, of ship and sheep-run, looked to the new dynasty to further their ambitions. They had little interest in the legality of Henry Tudor's claim to the throne, and none in his being a romantic king. Romance had hitherto usually meant a profitless war in France, with its Agincourt or its Poitiers, for which the king had had the glory and the taxpayer the bill. What the capitalists asked

---

² Sir Walter Raleigh, quoted by C. H. McIlwain: *The High Court of Parliament and Its Supremacy* (New Haven and London, 1910), p. 339.

of Henry VII was that he should be a good businessman with an eye for trade rather than for the Crown of France. If he satisfied them, they would support him. If they supported him, his House would be on firm foundations regardless of the grumblings of lawyers and aristocrats.

The first prerequisite of a businessman-king in 1485 was that he should re-establish public order. Trade, whether by sea, by river, or by the narrow and muddy paths that were called the king's highways, could not expand under the constant menace of pirates and robbers, and civil war was a catastrophe for business. The middle class therefore had economic as well as social reasons for demanding that the king should enforce the king's peace.

The demand was universal. The demoralization of the preceding period had bred a craving for strong government; the English had reached one of those moments in the life of a people when order is preferable to liberty. Order could not be despotism. The fate of Richard III was an object lesson for his successors, and none of the Tudors was a despot in the usual sense. Order meant rather an increasing emphasis upon the Crown as executive, and upon the means for exercising its authority within the amorphous limits of the constitution. Beyond a point authority could not go, but the point would be determined by practice rather than by law — determined after the fact by a breakdown of the machinery of government or by a successful rebellion. The power of the Tudors was limited by a nice calculation, revised from moment to moment, of what the market would bear. If their power seems from a distance to have been absolute, it is because no sovereigns of modern history have been shrewder calculators.

Equal shrewdness, of a different sort, was needed to guide English foreign relations. Some members of the dynasty were adept at working their way through the maze of European politics; others were not. The winding path they took is no longer important in itself, but the problem confronting them is. While their difficulties can be understood only in terms of their period, the essence of their problem has remained from that day to this. It is at the core of England's policy toward the states of Europe.

At the opening of the sixteenth century the House of Valois was shaking the uneasy equilibrium of the Continent by attempting to consolidate and expand the French state. The attempt created a co-alition of enemies, as aggression has done ever since. The principal opponents of France were the Hapsburg House of Burgundy-Austria and the shrewd pair whose marriage had made one kingdom out of Aragon and Castile. These two dynasties, Austrian and Spanish, were brought together by their fear of France, and soon another marriage paved the way for their union. The situation in the making was one that endured in substance till the reign of Louis XIV: a balance of power between France and the Austro-Spanish combine. The state of that balance was a major determinant of English foreign policy.

"Balance of power" is a phrase in bad repute today. It cannot be used intelligibly, even about the Europe of 1500, without clearing away the nonsense attached to it. The balance was not created by England or by any other country; it came into existence automatically as Europe emerged from medievalism into the era of nation-states, and it derived from the nature of international relations in that era just as a balance scale derives from the nature of the laws of gravity; one kind of balance is no more good or evil than the other. "Balance-of-power politics" is not a phrase of reproach, though it is often used as one. With politics what they are and have been since the days of Henry VII, it is mere redundancy.

This does not imply that a balance of power in Europe was something Englishmen could take for granted. Quite the contrary. It was a condition from which they drew enormous advantages; it was periodically shifting, and at some moments it ceased to exist. If the advantages were to be enjoyed, the balance had to be maintained and, when necessary, restored. Otherwise — if a single power over-shadowed the Continent — English commercial and imperial interests overseas would be jeopardized and the British Isles threatened with invasion. Hence the consistent opposition of England, and later of Great Britain, to everyone who has attempted to unify Europe by dominating it.

Great Britain has fought these attempts, as her critics point out. But they usually fail to point out that she has fought them successfully only because she has had allies: other states have shared her interest in the balance to the point of fighting for it. This is neither accident nor the result of British shrewdness. The age of sovereign states is at bottom an age of anarchy; in an anarchic world the only defense against aggression, though a poor one, is some form of balance of power.

English foreign policy has oscillated between intervention in Europe and isolation from it. Intervention was never complete until the wars of the twentieth century; isolation was even less complete because of the constant need to safeguard multifarious English Continental interests, political and economic. When all exceptions are made, however, it remains true that over the centuries English attention has swung like a pendulum, now toward Europe and now away from it: toward, when the European balance was upset; away, when it was temporarily restored. The sixteenth century is an example in point. For its first six decades the Continent was absorbed by the struggle between France and the Austro-Spanish power of the Hapsburgs. England was not fundamentally involved because her small weight was not needed, and the occasional involvements into which her sovereigns forced her were neither deep nor lasting. Then France was torn apart by civil wars, from the 1560's to the 1590's, and the Spain of Philip II threatened to bestride the world. England, reluctantly but inevitably, was drawn into a fight for life against the colossus — drawn partly for reasons of religion and trade, but also because the balance of power had been destroyed. By 1600 the fight was over. Spain had made and lost her bid for hegemony, France had recovered her strength, Europe was again in equilibrium, and England was at the beginning of another sixty years of isolation.

So much for the Tudor setting. The England of which Henry VII possessed himself was far from being a great power by the standards of Paris, Madrid, or Vienna. A kingdom of Great Britain, control of the sea lanes, a British empire overseas — these were far in the future. But there were sources of power in the geography of England, both in relation to the rest of the Islands and to continental Europe; in English society and government; in English economy and in the hardy class that dominated it. These seeds of greatness would not thrive by themselves; they needed astute and laborious tending. The middle class could not tend them because it lacked the constitutional means to take the initiative and the political maturity to desire it. The nobility could not tend them; its ineptitude had been abundantly proved. Only one guardian was left, the Crown.

The future of English power depended to a great extent on the skill of four persons, successive sovereigns of the Tudor House, in protecting their country against disaster from abroad and tending the growth of its resources at home. Strong monarchs were needed, and strong monarchs were forthcoming. The different members of the family had their failings, but weakness was not in them.

III   The Two Henrys

THE FOUNDING father of the dynasty is one of its least-known members. Henry Tudor became Henry VII by the grace of God and the virtue of his sword-arm. But he was not a soldier-king, and he sadly lacked flamboyance of other sorts. Posterity has almost forgotten him. His contemporaries did not, at least if they were wise, and his memory lingered for several generations; his best epitaph was the phrase of a biographer born in his granddaughter's reign. "What he minded," said Sir Francis Bacon, "that he compassed."

There could be no better summary of Henry's reign. What he minded, or purposed, was modest by the standards of an Edward III or Henry V. The Crown of France was no temptation for this self-made king; his aims were practical and adapted to the situation. Security for his House; prosperity for his people, so that the middle class might identify its interests with the dynasty and leave to it the affairs of state with little parliamentary surveillance; recognition of England, and of himself as her parvenu leader, by the powers of Europe. These were what he minded, and these in great measure he compassed. He made himself secure at home, superficially by eliminating two pretenders to the throne, basically by showing their supporters among the nobility that the Crown was no longer to be trifled with by gangsters. He promoted English trade in every feasible way — a treaty here, pressure there — and opened to his subjects one commercial road after another; in the long story of British mercantile expansion, Henry's role is of key importance. He won acceptance abroad partly by his hard-driving skill in trade treaties, even more by his tortuous foreign policy. The intricacies of the latter were worthy of the Cinquecento, but its underlying design was simple.

Henry's purpose abroad was to fill his coffers and enhance his prestige, and his principal means were foreign wars and marriages.

The wars were financial and political ventures rather than military; they produced cash or concessions from one side for making war, cash or concessions from the other for making peace. Such unromantic conduct must have made several of his chivalric predecessors turn over in their graves. But it was good business and good politics, based on a sound estimate of the European situation: the struggle between France and Spain gave England a high nuisance value, so that Spain was willing to pay well for her assistance and France for her neutrality. Henry managed to pocket both payments.

His marital policy was equally impartial and businesslike, although its results were of far greater consequence. Eligible children were chips in the game of statecraft, and the King had been blessed with two sons and two daughters. One daughter, Mary, was too young to be more than betrothed during the reign. The other, Margaret, was married to the King of Scotland, James IV, of the House of Stuart; she bore a son, through whom the Stuarts acquired a residual claim to the English throne. The claim would materialize only if the male Tudor line died out, and Henry's two sons made the chance appear slim. Their marriages were a matter of higher politics and more immediate importance than those of their sisters, and one to which Henry devoted all his gifts for diplomacy.

He was determined that the heir to the throne, Prince Arthur, should find a Spanish bride among the daughters of Ferdinand and Isabella. This match would further the prestige of the upstart Tudor dynasty, but it was dangerous. Through it England might be subordinated to Spain and drawn into her wars with France. Henry was clever enough to cope with the danger while he lived; the difficulties to come, with a dynasty half Tudor and half Spanish, Arthur would have to cope with for himself. Negotiations were accordingly opened with Madrid. They dragged on for years; the blood royal might repent at leisure, but it rarely married in haste. At last a proper dowry was settled upon the bride, Katharine of Aragon; she reached England and was married in 1501. Five months later, just when the King was negotiating the Scottish marriage as a counterweight to his Spanish commitment, Prince Arthur died.

Henry's diplomacy was not to be deflected. The marriage had been fruitless: there were no children, and most of Katharine's dowry was still unpaid. The King proposed as a substitute husband

Arthur's younger brother Henry, now Prince of Wales. Canon law forbade a man's marrying his brother's widow. But the Pope was prevailed upon to grant a dispensation, and the court of Madrid was equally agreeable. Katharine was accordingly provided with a second bridegroom, although the arrangements took so long that he was king before she married him. The wedding, arranged out of frugality and common sense, affected the whole subsequent history of the Tudors and their subjects.

Henry VII died in 1509. He was unlamented, because he had neither minded nor compassed the love of his subjects. But he had compelled respect from them and from Europe. He left to his son an established dynasty, an ordered country, and the largest cash reserve of any king in Christendom. He also left him the opportunity to be singularly popular by contrast. Young Henry was equipped for popularity — charming, handsome, a good athlete, and (so the courtiers said) a scholar and a gentleman. He inherited his father's uncanny sense of public opinion and his iron will, but he lacked one major gift: a sense of humor. Underneath his sometimes boisterous gaiety, Henry VIII regarded himself with great seriousness. He was an egoist whom power slowly corrupted.

The first decade of the new reign was more romantic than important in itself. A war against France in conjunction with Henry's father-in-law, King Ferdinand, served the interests of Spain rather than of England, and Ferdinand blithely deserted when it suited his turn. Simultaneously the traditional invasion from the north ended in disaster for the Scots on Flodden Field. Hoodwinked by his father-in-law, attacked by his brother-in-law, Henry had little reason to trust in marriage alliances.

He was not yet cured of his taste for foreign adventures, and neither was his confidant and minister, Cardinal Wolsey. The two seemed intent on involving England against her will in the maze of Continental politics. Those politics depended in great part, by 1519, on the relationship of three young men. Henry was the least of the three in power, if not in ambition; the others were Francis I of France and Charles of Hapsburg — Charles of Austria, of Burgundy, of Spain. The three men competed for election as Holy Roman Emperor, which reveals the depth of nonsense to which Henry's romantic ambition could lead him. Fortunately for England, Charles was elected. His dominions now virtually surrounded France, and the most bitter phase of the Hapsburg-Valois struggle was beginning. The wars broke out in 1521 and lasted for almost forty years.

What was England's role to be? Wolsey seems to have glimpsed, if faintly, what it should be — to maintain the balance by aiding whichever contestant was being worsted. Henry detested Francis and dreamed of renewing the Hundred Years' War; he aligned himself with Charles. His assistance was not on a scale to evoke gratitude, for the English were apathetic; the House of Commons would not vote taxes, and those levied without its consent could not be collected. Henry was learning the limitations of his power. In 1525 his education was advanced by a French disaster in Italy, which left Charles dominant in the peninsula and for the time master of Europe, with Francis his prisoner in Madrid. This shift in the scales of power boded trouble for England.

By this time Henry had more than foreign affairs to trouble him. The future of the dynasty was in danger. Katharine, despite frequent pregnancies, had borne him only one child who lived, a girl named Mary. Although girls were useful adjuncts to a royal house, leaving the throne to a daughter invited disaster. England had not been ruled by a woman since the twelfth century, and the precedent was scarcely heartening: that Queen's accession had touched off two decades of civil war. If Mary died, the nearest heir would be the King of Scotland; his claim could be established only by another civil war, backed in all likelihood by a French invasion. If Mary gained and held the crown, she would have to marry in order to carry on the line. But marry whom? Her only peer would be a foreign sovereign, and kings had a way of annexing their wives' domains for their own side of the family. Within the past generation single women had come to the thrones of Brittany, Burgundy, and Castile; they had all married, and now Brittany was part of the French kingdom, Burgundy and Castile parts of the Hapsburg empire. Precedent, old or new, was not encouraging. The House of Tudor had been established for only forty years, and Mary's accession might well be the signal for its disappearance.

This was the crux of Henry's problem. It was simple but imperative; delay could only make it more dangerous. Katharine was not going to produce a son, Mary's health was precarious, and at any

18

time Henry might die as abruptly as his brother had done. Only one solution was possible. A male heir would have to be born in wedlock, since no bastard could have a secure title. The King must therefore marry again in hopes of a son. Katharine had failed to fulfill the basic function of a queen, and Katharine must go.

The idea of getting rid of her was not new. Henry considered her as an agent of Spain, and his anger at Spanish duplicity had led him years before to threaten her with separation. But that would not now serve his purpose, because it would not leave him free to remarry. Divorce in the modern sense did not exist in the sixteenth century. Nothing remained except to have the marriage annulled — to have the Church declare that Henry and Katharine had never been legally man and wife, and that Princess Mary was illegitimate. This would be a scandal to rock Europe. It would also be a gamble on physiological accident: the living child would be disinherited for a son not yet conceived. But the only alternative was risking everything on Mary, and this was even more of a gamble.

As Henry struggled with his dilemma, his eyes fell on Anne Boleyn. The more he saw of her, the more convinced he became that he was living in sin with Katharine. His marriage had been authorized by a dispensation from Pope Julius, but did even the Pope have the power to dispense with the law of God? That law had been declared to Moses in no uncertain terms. "If a man shall take his brother's wife, it is an unclean thing: he hath uncovered his brother's nakedness; they shall be childless." Although the last phrase was difficult to reconcile with the existence of Mary, the death of Katharine's other children before or soon after birth did suggest divine anger at the union. Henry became convinced that Julius had exceeded the authority even of God's vicegerent on earth, and that the error should be rectified at once by his successor. Whether such reasoning was hypocrisy is a matter of definition. Sincere religious scruples, in a man without humor, may further the conviction that he should have his own way.

These were the ingredients of Henry's decision. Although religion played its part, as did the charms of Anne, the dominant factor was dynastic. Henry was primarily a great politician; he was only secondarily devout and sensual. But the Book of Leviticus was there for the reading, and Anne was to be had for the asking — provided she was asked to be queen. In the spring of 1527 Henry revealed the intention to have his marriage declared null from the beginning. This could be done in a number of ways, but all of them led sooner or later to Rome. One pope had made the wedding possible, and only another could undo it.

Henry's proposal — and with it the future of England — rested in the hands of a wily and worldly scion of the Medici, Clement VII. In normal times Clement would probably have been glad to oblige, for Henry had been a good enough servant of the church to receive the title of Defender of the Faith. But times were not normal; for the papacy, as an institution, they were sadly out of joint. The revolt begun by Martin Luther ten years before was making alarming headway in the Germanies. It could be suppressed, if at all, only by the strongest exertion of papal authority, which must therefore be preserved in its plenitude. Yet Henry was asking, at bottom, for its curtailment. He wanted Clement to admit to the world that Julius had exceeded the powers of his office — that there was a law of God which even Christ's Vicar could not set aside. However well the issue might be concealed in technicalities, there it was. If Clement granted this request, he would be creating a breach in the medieval edifice of the *plenitudo potestatis* just when the heretics were storming it.

The times were also out of joint for the papacy as a secular power. Military developments in Italy reduced Clement, as sovereign of the Papal States, to greater and greater dependence on the Emperor, who became in effect the power behind the papal throne. Katharine was Charles's aunt, and the Pope felt that the moment was not opportune for reducing her to the status of a concubine. Henry's request could not be granted, in short, because of religious developments in the Germanies and military developments in Italy.

Clement, however, was not the man to say so. He evaded and delayed, while the King's patience wore thin. In 1529 it snapped, and Henry decided to coerce the Pope by threats of secession. For this purpose he took the momentous step of calling Parliament. Hitherto he had followed the policy of his father, of having as little as possible to do with Parliament, and it seemed conceivable that the institution might wither away as the monarchy grew stronger. Now, however, Henry broke with Tudor tradition. He summoned Parliament, took it into his confidence, and kept it in session for seven years. By the time it was dissolved a revolution had been made in

England. The structure of church and state had been drastically revised by statute, and the participation of Parliament had enormously strengthened its constitutional role.

The reason, as always in the growth of parliament, was eminently practical. Henry's aims gave focus to unformulated desires of lords and commons; he found that this Parliament would do his bidding with little need of threats or cajoleries, and he used it to give his will the sanction of national approval. Whether the nation approved can never be known because the nation was inarticulate. But the aristocracy and middle class approved, and they purported to speak in Parliament for all Englishmen.

What were Henry's aims, and why did they have such support? His original objective seems to have been to exert pressure on the papacy by increasing royal as opposed to papal control of the English church. The move was popular not only in Parliament but also in sections of the English clergy. Papal control was unpopular in an age of rising nationalism, and the popes of recent years had been more concerned with feeding condottieri than with feeding Christ's flock. The English church, furthermore, was in serious need of reform. Wolsey had attempted to reform it by use of his legatine authority, but the attempt had stirred anti-papal feeling in clergy and laity alike. Reformation could come only through the King in Parliament.

For three years the assault on papal jurisdiction continued, until by 1532 Henry had virtually replaced Clement as head of the English church. Still no sign came from Rome of a more amenable attitude on the basic problem. The Pope did make one concession of future consequence: he concurred in the appointment of Thomas Cranmer as Archbishop of Canterbury. But on the issue of the annulment he stood firm because he had to. He was still in the Hapsburg shadow, and he could not bargain. Henry's policy of intimidation had failed; it left him with an enormous increment of power, but Katharine was still his wife. The logic of what he had already done compelled him to go on.

By this time it was clear that he would not go on unaided. He had support for a reform so drastic that it would necessarily entail a complete breach with Rome — the abolition of the monasteries. The regular clergy were at this time in a peculiarly vulnerable position. Through the centuries they had acquired vast wealth, until monasteries, priories, and nunneries owned roughly one-sixth of the land of England. In return for this endowment the religious houses performed no commensurate service, or at least none that appealed to a Tudor capitalist. To him prayers and meditations, unlike lands, were of doubtful value to society; the monasteries were inefficient as educational and charitable agencies; their agrarian policy was even more inefficient because they were unwilling to move with the times and enclose their lands for sheepfolds. Would it not be better, he argued, for all concerned — or at least for all who mattered — if the regular clergy were eliminated, and their wealth turned over to businessmen who knew how to put it to productive use?

The answer was as obvious to the King as to his greediest subject. Confiscation would be an easy move because the monks had virtually no political power. It would be a wise move because the regular clergy had always been more closely tied to Rome than the secular clergy. It would be an enormously lucrative move for the King, who would possess himself of the land and sell what he chose. Last but not least, confiscation would give the new church edifice a foundation in the soil of England. Henry was about to make a momentous change, and he had at hand one of the best methods of ensuring its permanence — the method subsequently used in France, in Russia, in Mexico, of associating a revolution with a widespread transference of land, and thereby creating a vested interest in preserving the new order. Ruin of the monasteries would set the seal on royal headship of the Church.

The rising star of Anne Boleyn thus became allied with the new capitalism, and the setting star of Katharine with religious and economic conservatism. Because the King and the majority of Parliament favored the change, the outcome was not in doubt. Katharine's marriage was annulled in 1533 by an English ecclesiastical court, shortly after Henry had married Anne. By the end of the following year Parliament had completed the repudiation of papal authority, had made the King the head of the Church, and had given him such power against recalcitrants as none of his predecessors had exercised. The attack on the monasteries was begun in Parliament shortly before it was dissolved in 1536, and was completed within a decade by royal fiat. A new nobility of the middle class was built — as many of its houses were built — out of the monasteries, and self-interest made the new peers loyal to the King and distrustful of the Pope.

Henry succeeded in his objectives, but the one with which he had started gave him the most trouble. Although Anne bore him a child with scandalous alacrity, it was only another girl, christened Elizabeth. He was less patient than he had been with Katharine; time and his temper were getting shorter. In 1536 he had Anne beheaded on a variety of unsavory and unproved charges, and a few days later married again. This shadow-wife, Jane Seymour, produced the long-awaited son and then died. Henry went on to three more marriages, but they were unimportant because they were childless. His progeny now consisted of two girls and a boy, each by a different mother. In order of age they were Mary, Elizabeth, and Edward, but in order of succession the last took precedence over his half-sisters. Henry drew a will and had it given statutory form; it left the crown to the lines successively of Edward, of Mary, and of Elizabeth, and then, in default of issue of any of these three, to the line of his own sister Mary. The succession at last seemed reasonably secure.

IV   Catholic and Protestant

HENRY left to his children a legacy of troubles. There were the ruins of the Spanish match and the hostility of Rome. There was the Franco-Scots menace, complicated by the Stuart claim to the throne. There was the rising strength of the middle class, because of which Tudor society could never achieve more than a transient equilibrium. Greatest of all, and interwoven with the others, was trouble in the Church. The difficulties of Henry's children, and of the Stuarts who followed them, are intelligible only in terms of the church that Henry established.

Within that church were powerful opposing forces, and it was only a question of time before their opposition appeared. The obvious force in Henry's day was that of tradition, discipline, authority; the latent force clashing with it was the impulsion of individual Englishmen to find God for themselves. The clash did not come out during Henry's lifetime. But after his death it shattered his religious settlement, undermined Mary's attempt to return to Rome, and eventually destroyed even the idea of a national church. Out of the wreckage came on the one hand the modern establishment, with its liturgy, its traditionalism, its sense of order, and on the other hand the nonconformist sects, with their emphasis on individual liberty. The story is long and intricate. Its details are largely irrelevant, but its kernel is not. The religious development of the British peoples cannot be separated from the political, or the exercise of British power at any period from the moral and spiritual context of that period.

In the sixteenth and seventeenth centuries the people of the British Isles went through religious experiences that left their mark on the subsequent character of the nation. In the sixteen decades between the breach from Rome and the Toleration Act of 1689 religion was at the core of domestic politics, of Anglo-Scots and Anglo-Irish relations, of foreign affairs, even to some extent of economic growth. The questions raised about the doctrine and structure of the church brought into dispute the basic nature of Christianity, and were so fundamental that they could not be settled by reason, let alone by force. They were implicit at the beginning of the period, and they were the reason why it was important that Henry set the church on a new path.

He had no such intention. His breach from Rome was a political act to achieve a political end. He was determined to change the headship of the Church, but equally determined to make no other religious change if he could help it. He considered himself always as Defender of the Faith, and by his own lights he was; Protestants were as much heretics to him as to Clement. If one Englishman, such as Sir Thomas More, insisted on papal headship of the Church, he was executed for the political crime of treason; if another Englishman insisted that the seven sacraments were nonsense, he was executed for the religious crime of heresy. Henry's logic was excellent, if narrow. His church reflected his narrowness, for in doctrine it was thoroughly Catholic, though no longer Roman.

Catholic doctrine rested on the belief that Christ founded a church to continue His redemptive work through all time. His authority was passed on to the apostles and from them to their successors, the bishops; from the bishops of each generation it passed outward to the priests. This theory of apostolic succession meant that the cleric was distinct from the layman by virtue of a God-given power, and the distinction accounts for the enormous historical influence of any Catholic church. Its clergy monopolized the means of salvation, which were the sacraments of the Church. This statement is theoretically untrue, because theologians did not contend that those outside the Church would be universally damned. But it is historically sound. The man in the medieval street, whether of London or Byzantium or Kiev, believed that he would be saved not through his own efforts alone, but also through having his sins periodically wiped away by the absolution of a priest. God acted through the priest, rather than directly, because the priesthood had been divinely instituted for the purpose.

> "Who hath not heard it spoken
> How deep you were within the books of God?
> To us, the speaker in His parliament;
> To us the imagin'd voice of God Himself;
> The very opener and intelligencer
> Between the grace, the sanctities of heaven,
> And our dull workings." [3]

The keys of heaven and hell were with the Church. The Pope laid particular claim to them for a further reason. Because he was Bishop of Rome, the argument ran, he was the successor of St. Peter; he was therefore possessed of Petrine supremacy, the same authority over other bishops that Peter had had over other apostles. The pope derived from Christ his headship of Christ's church; he was the rock, as Peter had been. The papal position thus rested on the general theory of apostolic succession and the particular theory of Petrine supremacy. The latter carried with it the claim that the papacy had the sole right to determine true doctrine; it was the divine purpose that the final arbiter of faith should be the Bishop of Rome, whom Christ Himself had designated as His vicar, or agent.

The papal claims had never been universally accepted, and the claim to determine doctrine had been opposed with particular stubbornness. The Eastern Orthodox Church had broken away in the eleventh century, largely on this issue, but the schism had not secured papal victory even in western Europe. Anti-papal writers had advanced the argument that the faith should be determined by the *universitas fidelium,* the body of the faithful, and had appealed from the authority of Rome to that of an ecumenical council representing both clergy and laity. In the fifteenth century the papacy had triumphed at last, but the opposition was silenced rather than

---

[3] Shakespeare: *Henry IV*, Part 2, IV, ii, 16–20.

convinced. Soon it was playing its part in the great revolt of Protestantism.

That revolt rapidly developed into an attack on the concept of an authoritarian church. "The Christian who has true repentance," said Luther, "has already received pardon from God." In that sentence he touched the essence of Protestantism. If an individual can secure absolution through his own direct relationship with God, what is the role of the priest? It is not to administer a sacrament in the Catholic sense; priestly mediation is not required when God absolves directly. The power inherent in the priesthood through apostolic succession evaporated as the logic of Protestantism developed; the sacraments changed from a priestly rite to an inner experience, and the change revolutionized the older conception of the church.

The priest became the minister, or agent, and in practice he was at least as much the agent of the congregation as of the Almighty — the teacher and counselor, with no more authority than his human learning and wisdom might give him. The Protestant ministry slowly abandoned its claim to determine doctrine. That right rested in the last analysis with the individual Christian, who depended for salvation on his own contact with deity. He might depute his right to the community of the faithful — by which he meant the group of those who believed as he did — but he never surrendered it. For the final sanction of pope or metropolitan he substituted that of his own conscience.

A tremendous centrifugal force was thus innate in Protestantism. Since the days of Luther there has not been *a* Protestant church, but more and more sects and divisions of sects. This disruptive process has gone on despite appeals to the authority of the state, despite the efforts of religious leaders and the rigid centralization of some groups, such as the Presbyterians. It has gone on because the logic of Protestantism approaches as its limit religious anarchy, where there are as many churches as individuals.

The Catholic, in summary, emphasized the church. It was a human institution divinely ordained, and the power and authority derived from its origin were vested in its priesthood; the priests were instruments of salvation for the laity, whose duty was faith and obedience. The Protestant emphasis was on the other extreme, the individual, whose duty was to recognize and maintain his own relationship with God. Whatever help he might derive from his minister and his church, none of the awful responsibility could be transferred to them. If they or any other authority, secular or religious, permitted him to do what his conscience told him was sinful, he faced the alternatives of revolt or damnation. It was not accident that the Reformation began an era of civil wars and revolutions.

Henry VIII, as a king, had no patience with revolutionaries, and as a Catholic he had no patience with Protestants. His breach with Rome was a denial of *papal* authority, not of authority; he repudiated the theory of Petrine supremacy, but he retained in full the theory of apostolic succession. His bishops were heirs of the Twelve, and by virtue of that inheritance his priesthood administered the sacraments. He himself was not in theory the spiritual head of the church; he could not be, since he was not in holy orders, and nominal headship was vested in the archbishop of Canterbury. Final doctrinal authority was vested in the source of all other law, the king in parliament.

Although these were major changes, they were in the long antipapal tradition. The Orthodox Church had accepted a large measure of state control, and in the west the Holy Roman Emperors had advanced — and occasionally made good — a claim to surveillance of the papacy. The conciliar movement of the previous century had derived from the premise that authority rested not with Christ's vicar but with His flock. The same premise might apply to a national segment of the flock; the English equivalent of the ecumenical council was Parliament, where the bishops and archbishops in the House of Lords represented the high clergy, and the secular peers and commons the laity. The first major statement of doctrine after the breach from Rome was approved by Parliament in the Six Articles of 1539; ever since then the final word on the faith of the established church has been by statute.

Thus at the beginning of its separate existence the Church of England had in it an element of paradox. It was Catholic, authoritarian, and episcopal. Yet its bishops, while they had the aura of apostolic power, depended on the legislature for their dogma and on the Crown for their policy. This meant in practice, under Henry, dependence on the Crown. He would not brook the interference of Parliament any more than of the prelates, and used both as instru-

ments of royal control. He would not allow his subjects the dangerous freedom to argue points of religion, for that way Protestantism
lay.

> "And what follows then?
> Commotions, uproars, with a general taint
> Of the whole state: as, of late days, our neighbours,
> The upper Germany, can dearly witness,
> Yet freshly pitied in our memories." [4]

Henry's position was strong because he was strong. Logically,
however, it was weak in two fundamentals, and its weakness boded
trouble for his successors. The passage of the Six Articles established that the source of doctrine was the king in parliament. This
legal phrase had meaning at the time, because Crown and Parliament were virtually a single, fused power. But what would happen
if one of the constituent elements went one way, one another? Authority had passed from the priesthood to the laity, but where in the
laity did it reside — in the body of the faithful, represented in Parliament, or in the layman who wore the crown?

The second weakness was in the king's control of ecclesiastical
administration. Church affairs had traditionally been the field of
papal and royal prerogative rather than of statute, and in it Henry
was now more absolute than in secular government; his absolutism,
political and temporal in origin, was exercised in the spiritual sphere.
This was Erastianism, state control of the Church, in its baldest
form. It would be accepted only as long as divinity hedged the king,
as long as the people accepted the principle of authority in religion
without inquiring into its genesis or logic. Once the government of
the Church began to gall a significant group of laymen, royal control through the bishops would come into question. That question
would lead, as surely as the doctrinal question, to the issue of where
ecclesiastical sovereignty resided. The authoritarianism of Henry's
church was not founded on the rock of theory. He had good reason
to extirpate his few Protestant subjects.

He did two things, however, that paved the way for the spread of
Protestantism. In the first place he had the Bible translated into
English and a copy put in every parish church, so that the laity —
or rather the minority of laymen who were literate — could explore
for themselves the written basis of the faith. In the second place he

---

[4] Shakespeare: *Henry VIII*, V, iii, 27–31.

retained Thomas Cranmer as Archbishop of Canterbury, little real-
izing how that good servant would refashion his master's work.
Cranmer's subservience was deceptive. He was a convinced Erastian, who felt it his duty to implement the royal will; at the same
time he was a devout Christian, whose belief was developing more
and more toward Protestantism. His public duty took precedence
over his private inclinations as long as Henry lived, partly because
he was too timid to be a ready martyr, partly because he was loyal
to the man who had raised him from obscurity. Henry therefore underestimated him. The spirit that seemed so pliable was in fact a
spring that could be wound but not broken. It was loosed in 1547
by the King's death.

V   The Religious Seesaw

THE SUCCEEDING reigns were bound to be a period of rapid developments. One man had dominated the scene for almost four decades. For the first two he had ruled, by and large, according to time-
honored formulæ; in the third he had broken with Spain, with the
Pope, and with some of the deepest-rooted traditions of the country; the fourth he had devoted primarily to solidifying his revolution and preventing its further progress. But revolutions are more
easily begun than halted; they gain an impetus that their initiators
can, at most, delay or divert. Henry's had threatened to get out of
hand even during his lifetime, and at his death plunged England
into a welter of dissension.

He was succeeded by his son, the one nonentity in the Tudor
House. Edward VI, for whose birth his father had overturned so
much, was a nine-year-old at the time of his accession. His health
was precarious and rapidly grew worse, and at the age of fifteen he
died. During his reign he was almost as shadowy a king as his
mother had been a queen. The power of the Crown devolved upon
two successive Regents, and Edward did not seriously disobey either of them except once, by dying.

The history of the reign is important only as it bears on the
Church. For the rest it is an unedifying story of intrigue and judicial murder. The kingdom was governed at first by Edward's mater-
nal uncle, the Duke of Somerset, an idealist before his time. His enlightened social policy ended in disaster, and he was ousted and

executed. His successor, the Duke of Northumberland, had as much idealism as the worst ward politician, but both he and Somerset favored, for different reasons, the new religious doctrines. With that favor and the guidance of Cranmer, the Church first moved toward Protestantism.

Henry had seen to it that the services were not translated into English. Laymen were unlikely to question the content of the liturgy as long as it remained in a Latin that was both familiar and incomprehensible. The linguistic barrier between the priest and the congregation, furthermore, was like the physical barrier of the rood screen between them in church, the symbol of an inner distinction.[5] Two years after Henry's death the services were rendered into English. The work was directed by Cranmer and was in places his own; it is still his greatest memorial. With the exception of the Bible, nothing in English literature has exercised a deeper influence than the Book of Common Prayer.

The book was more Protestant than Henry would have countenanced, particularly in its handling of the sacrament of communion. This sacrament was from the start the touchstone of Catholicism. The whole theory of apostolic succession hinged on what happened at the moment when the bread and wine were consecrated. Did they become in essence the flesh and blood of Christ, or did they remain merely bread and wine? If the former, the change was achieved by virtue of a power transmitted through the priesthood; if the latter, there was no such power, and communion was no more than a memorial service. On this crucial point the first edition of the prayer book was ambiguous. But in the "black rubric" of the second edition, of 1552, communion was explicitly pronounced to be a memorial.

The doctrinal change reflected a rapid increase of Protestantism in the government. This was due only in part to the development of Cranmer's thought. Somerset was a liberal in religion, with an idea scandalous and sinful to most of his age — that diversity of belief should be tolerated within the national church. Toleration could be achieved only by a statement of doctrine, like that in the prayer book of 1549, so ambiguous that the layman could interpret it to

---

[5] One office of the Church minimized that distinction: the litany was recited in the fields by priest and people together, in common supplication for the crops, and the litany alone was translated before the old King died.

suit himself. But toleration was almost as unpopular as social reform, and Somerset gave place to Northumberland. The latter
feared that a return to Henrician Catholicism would mean surrendering power to Henry's conservative nobility; he accordingly embarked on a new course, less tolerant and more Protestant than his
predecessor's. The result was the prayer book of 1552.

Northumberland and Cranmer were moving too fast for the people. Protestant extremists were committing excesses, and iconoclasm
did not add to the popularity of the new ideas but toughened the
roots of the old; Catholicism was deeply planted in nobility and
peasantry alike. The changes were borne because they were made
in the name of the King, and the Church was still the King's business. But when Edward lay dying and Northumberland tried to alter the succession, ostensibly to save Protestantism and actually to
save his own skin, he and his schemes were tossed aside. The crown
went as Henry had willed it, to his daughter Mary.

Her accession meant a return to Rome. As the daughter of Katharine of Aragon, Mary had suffered for the faith; she had been declared illegitimate, had been forced into obscurity, and at last had
succeeded to the crown in defiance of Protestant machinations. She
was resolved to bring England back into the papal fold, and she had
a Tudor confidence in her power to do so for her lifetime. But what
would happen when she died? Her legal successor was Elizabeth,
under whom England would in all likelihood drift again into heresy.
This could be avoided only if Mary barred her half-sister by producing an heir herself. She was faced with the necessity of marrying, as her father had foreseen, and she had to marry quickly. She
had no doubt about where to turn for a husband; her Spanish blood
and loyalties made the choice obvious. Henry VIII's marriage alliance with Spain, in abeyance for almost thirty years, was promptly
revived by his daughter.

Those thirty years had been a period of relative isolation from
the affairs of Europe. But by 1553 England could no longer remain
aloof. The Queen's marriage was merely the occasion for involvement; the underlying causes were the rise of Spain and the resurgence of Roman Catholicism. Charles V, the old and tired Emperor,
was on the verge of abdicating and completing the partition of his
vast inheritance into two parts — the imperial title and the Austrian
dominions to the line of his brother, and to his son the Low Coun-

tries, Italy, Spain, and the Spanish possessions in America. The son, Philip II, had great resources at his command. The New World provided bullion, at first gold and then silver, to finance his empire; the great money markets of the Low Countries provided the means for converting bullion into power; Spain provided the finest armies in Christendom. And the Church provided the dynamic of crusade.

The papacy was setting its citadel in order and turning to the attack. The Council of Trent was eliminating some of the worst abuses on which the Protestant revolt had fed, and was reiterating the dogma of the Church with uncompromising clarity. The Society of Jesus, disciplined like the Spanish armies in which its founder had been trained, was carrying that dogma into the strongholds of Protestantism. But the counteroffensive was not only ideological warfare; it was waged also with the military force of Spain. Spanish nationalism had been nurtured on the long struggle to oust the Moors from the peninsula, and crusading zeal was in the marrow of the Spanish bone. Now the nation was called again to its destiny of defending the faith, and it responded with a will — a will that to the Spaniard was one with the will of God. The spearhead of the Catholic Reformation was forged of Toledo steel.

The progress of that reformation was inseparable from the Spanish bid for political hegemony. England was vitally concerned with both. She could be returned to Rome only by being subordinated to Madrid, as Mary's policy soon made clear. The Queen moved by stages, each of which aroused greater opposition than the preceding. Henrician Catholicism was restored by her first parliament, but beyond that point Parliament would not go. Mary momentarily abandoned the effort, in order to arrange her marriage with Philip. In this she finally succeeded, after crushing a rebellion that had for a time endangered her throne. Success blinded her to the fact that she was squandering her popularity, and she next turned to completing the religious reaction. Parliamentary opposition was overborne, papal headship re-established (though only on the assurance that the former monastic lands would not be touched), and the nation formally absolved of the sin of schism. Mary was in sight of her objectives.

But she had not yet secured them. The few English Protestants were covert rebels, waiting to undo her work, and large numbers of Catholics were anti-papal and anti-Spanish. Mary resolved to eliminate all shades of opposition by striking at the extremists. She disregarded her Spanish advisers, who knew when persecution was impolitic, and in 1555 she began the series of trials and burnings for heresy that have given her the name of bloody. The martyrs came from all walks of life, but Mary, like her father, preferred to strike at the prominent for the sake of the object lesson. The greatest of her victims was Thomas Cranmer — Cranmer the vacillating, caught in his old struggle between loyalty and conscience, recanting and retracting and recanting again, then going at last to the fire with steadfast courage. The nation looked on appalled. Such things might happen abroad; at home wholesale burnings were unheard of. They turned the stomachs even of sixteenth-century Englishmen, scarcely a squeamish lot, and incited riots that verged on rebellions. Mary's policy was discrediting not Protestantism, but the principle of persecution and the Queen who implemented it.

Mary's foreign policy further sapped her prestige. She sent English troops to aid her husband against France, and as a result lost Calais; England was subordinated to Spain and paid in humiliation. Mary's achievement was to associate, in the minds of her people, the Spanish alliance and the return to Rome with persecution at home and failure abroad. Out of this association grew the nationalism of the coming age — a spirit neither Catholic nor Protestant, but anti-Spanish and anti-papal. When the Queen died in 1558, without the child she had so desperately hoped for, her subjects were ready to be quit of everything for which she had stood.

The new sovereign, a red-headed girl of twenty-five, was an unknown quantity. As Anne Boleyn's daughter Elizabeth could scarcely be partial to Spain and the Pope. She had proved her dexterity by staying alive: during Mary's reign she had been the hope of the opposition as heiress presumptive, and a false step might have led her to the block. But dexterity was not enough to meet the enormous problems confronting her. The prestige of the Crown was at lower ebb than at any other time in the century. Government was impoverished; unemployment, pauperism, and social unrest were increasing; the people were divided and confused on the issue of the church. England was in a poor state to defend herself, and she would be without a friend in Europe if she broke with Spain.

Elizabeth was undismayed by the prospect. She had self-confidence and a deep, abiding love for her job; she knew even better than her father how to win the affection of her subjects, and had inherited his uncanny sense of public opinion. At home her leadership was less aggressive than his because she did not have his power; her position was increasingly circumscribed as the middle class grew toward maturity. In Europe she faced a danger more serious than anything in Henry's reign, and handled it with a cunning and sagacious courage. For forty-five years she played an essentially defensive game, in domestic policy guarding the church she had established and the prerogative she had inherited; in foreign policy guarding England against the menace of Spain and Rome. The game was to her taste. She played it brilliantly, if by rules of her own, and she had a great measure of success.

At Elizabeth's accession the most immediate problem was the church. In the preceding generation her people had been through bewildering alterations, from Roman to Henrician Catholicism, then to the Protestantism of Cranmer and Northumberland, then back to Rome again. By 1558 each position had its embattled adherents; discord threatened to split the country and open it to foreign domination. The problem, as the Queen saw it, was less one of doctrine than of politics — to reach a quick and broad settlement, which would isolate the die-hards of right and left by satisfying the great bulk of the nation. If the result were puzzling to theologians, that would be a small price to pay for the good of the realm. The good was for Elizabeth much what it had been for Machiavelli, "that with which the majority is content."

The Queen's settlement of the Church was thus a political act, even more than Henry's had been, and the establishment still bears her hallmark. The authoritarian element was preserved in theory by emphasizing the priesthood and the bishops, in practice by exerting the power of the Crown. Elizabeth did not call herself head of the Church, but she allowed no one to question that she was. Her control was exercised in part through the hierarchy, in part through prerogative courts outside the purview of the common law. Parliament might suggest, if it did so tactfully, but it might never command. Its function was to legalize the basic structure and doctrine of the Church as formulated by the government, and then to refrain from interference in matters ecclesiastical. "I see many over-bold with God Almighty," she told Parliament, "making too many subtle scannings of His blessed will, as lawyers do with human testaments.

The presumption is so great as I may not suffer it . . . nor tolerate newfangledness."

The structure of the Church was substantially what it had been in Henry's day. The novelty was in doctrine, as determined by the Thirty-Nine Articles of 1571. These articles were so ambiguous that they have provoked theological controversy ever since, and ambiguity was their political virtue. Elizabeth, even more than Somerset before her, grasped the fact that the only way to keep the majority content within a national church was to enforce an ambiguous dogma. The articles provided it. They were strongly anti-Roman, but on key points of controversy between Catholic and Protestant, such as the nature of communion, they were so skillfully phrased that they gave great latitude to individual interpretation. The prayer book of 1552, with its unequivocally Protestant passages modified, provided the guide for uniform worship, and the Queen provided the enforcement. Pastors who led their flocks from the designated path of salvation were sternly recalled to it. The path was broad enough for Catholics and Protestants to walk it together. But its boundaries were fixed, and guarded by the powers of church and state.

The boundaries excluded both extremes. The Roman Catholic — the recusant, as he was then called — might be tolerated in practice if he kept his religion to himself, but he could not assert Petrine supremacy without running the risk of a traitor's death. The thoroughgoing Protestant might believe virtually what he pleased, but he had to accept the authority of his bishop; behind it stood the coercive force of the Crown. Both extremists were dissatisfied, and hence were potential dangers. Yet for the moment neither could gain adherents. The mass of Englishmen still associated Rome with the dark days of Mary and radical Protestantism with the discord of Edward's reign. They turned to the new compromise with relief if not with enthusiasm.

The first danger to materialize was from the recusants. But it was the result of foreign developments more than of domestic, and can best be considered later as part of the great struggle against Spain. The danger from left-wing Protestants was an internal matter. It gave the Queen more and more trouble as the reign wore on, and by the time of her death was preparing an explosion.

The short-lived Protestantism of Edward's reign had been largely

Lutheran. If it had remained so, Elizabeth's difficulties would have been less than they were. Whatever the Lutheran's intransigence on matters of faith, he was slow to question the Erastian principle when it provided a congenial form of worship. But English Protestantism had been transformed during Mary's reign. Some of its adherents had been martyred; others, less courageous or more nimble, had escaped to the Continent, and many of them had gone not to the Germany of Luther but to the Geneva of John Calvin. When they were allowed to return after Elizabeth's accession, they brought home with them the germs of the Puritan movement.

Few words in English history are harder to define than the word "Puritan," unless possibly the word "liberal" today. The dictionary is little help; a Puritan is more than one who wishes to purify the church, just as a Protestant is more than one who protests against abuses. In the one case, as in the other, accurate definition is less important than the connotation that the name has acquired from the men who bore it. In this sense a Puritan might be a squire or a pauper, a member of the Church of England or an Anabaptist; but whatever his class or sect he was strongly tinged with Calvinism.

His faith rested on the hard rock of predestination — the belief that God had chosen some for salvation, some for hell, and that no man's conduct in this life could alter his foreordained fate. The Puritan bent his will, nevertheless, to achieving a rigid standard of conduct, the righteousness fitting for one elected by God to the company of the saints. His motive was not to *win* election, which was impossible, and not primarily to convince his neighbors of his election, but at bottom to convince himself. This motive, more psychological than logical, was the dynamic of Puritanism.

The Puritan's attitude toward the state was an outgrowth of his attitude toward heaven. He had no respect for temporal authority as such. No government might command his obedience for long unless he was convinced that it was a government of the elect. His conviction was a fragile thing; in practice it might be shattered as effectively by an attack on his economic as on his religious interests. Because no government can endure without trespassing on some interests, the Puritan was from the beginning a potential revolutionary.

His attitude toward the church was even more uncompromising.

Religious authority did not rest in a monarch or in bishops, but in the body of the elect. That body might depute its authority to a representative council or synod; the synod might then govern the church, even with a rod of iron, but only by virtue of a power delegated by the governed. This element of democracy found its first expression in Calvinist churches of the late sixteenth century, among the French Huguenots, for example, and in the Scottish Kirk. The influence of the Scottish experiment in particular was soon felt in England, where the Puritan touched a match to the kindling of ideas.

No one in Elizabethan England could have foreseen the resultant conflagration. But Puritan hostility to the church settlement was soon apparent; as Calvinism spread, from the returning Marian exiles and other sources, the hostility grew stronger and more vocal. It was not directed so much against dogma, because the Thirty-Nine Articles might be read in a Calvinist sense, as it was against the bishops, the crux of church organization. A bishop, in his dual capacity as successor of an apostle and agent of the Crown, represented the principle of human authority devolving from the top downward. The Puritan represented the principle of authority devolving from the body of the elect upward. The two principles were irreconcilable, and even Elizabeth could not frame an ecclesiastical organization to comprehend them both.

She made no attempt to do so. For years the Puritans seemed to be lonely voices, crying aimlessly, but in the 1580's they emerged as an effective and well-knit group. Although their numbers were still small, their influence was disproportionately large. They came in great part from the urban middle class, the group that was growing most rapidly in wealth, political maturity, and ambition. The House of Commons was aghast when one of its members, the Puritan Peter Wentworth, lectured the Queen on her shortcomings, and the House committed him to the Tower for his pains. But a number of his fellow-members were beginning to wonder in their hearts whether he might not be right in his major premise, that the royal prerogative was more ubiquitous than need be. Might not the Church be more godly if the House were allowed a hand in amending it? As for the self-important agents of prerogative, the bishops, might not a curtailment of their power improve their Christian humility? The times were unhealthy for such thoughts, and they were uttered only by extremists. But moderate men listened with an increasing interest that boded trouble once Elizabeth was gone.

She herself evaded serious trouble. She did so partly because of her skill and popularity, partly because the opposition still lacked a coherent program, and above all because the country could not afford religious dissension. England was engaged in a struggle for national existence, and one of the cardinal aspects of existence was the national church. When survival is at stake, reform is likely to go by the board. So the Elizabethan Puritans found. They had to bide their time, and meanwhile to fight for Queen and Church.

VI   The Elizabethan Defensive

THE GREAT struggle against the Catholic Reformation was to a large degree inherent in Elizabeth's accession. She was bound to renew the breach with Rome, if not because of her birth, then because of the lesson of Mary's reign. Once the breach was reaffirmed and the Spanish tie finally renounced, only one factor could save England from a desperate war against the Pope and Philip. That factor was France. If the Valois monarchy continued as a prime obstacle to Spanish ambition, England might not be deeply involved. But France at this juncture was paralyzed by thirty years of civil wars, during which her power in Europe sank to the negligible. England was thus forced, for the first time in the century, into a key position. She was the leading anti-Roman state, and she was an obvious target for Spanish hostility. Sooner or later she would have to fight for her life.

Elizabeth greatly preferred later to sooner. Although she had her share of the family courage, it was of the sort that accepts dangers, and juggles them until they wear away. She hated nothing more than irrevocable decisions, and her skill in postponing them brought gray hairs to her councilors. But in some cases it also brought great gains to her people, and in none more patently than in her dealings with Spain. For thirty years — two-thirds of her reign — she avoided an open breach. While France was apparently falling apart, the cause of Protestantism going into eclipse, and Philip's power spreading across the world from the Netherlands to the Pacific and the Indian Ocean, England remained nominally at peace. When the Spanish blow finally came, the English had had ample time to make ready and had used it well.

In the first year of Elizabeth's reign she was a godsend to Philip. The Dauphin of France was married to Mary Stuart, who was herself at once queen of Scots, daughter of the great French House of Guise, and claimant to the throne of England. The marriage paved the way for a dynastic union of France and Scotland, to which England might be added if Elizabeth died or a French invasion dethroned her. Such a state would jeopardize Philip's empire, and he was solicitous for Elizabeth's health.

The tightening of the Stuart-Valois tie was no more to Elizabeth's taste than to Philip's; it placed her between the Spanish frying pan and the Franco-Scottish fire. But soon the Scots themselves took a hand. Their nationalism, aroused by French predominance in the government, had been given a religious impetus by the rapid spread of Calvinism. The chief object of their discontent was the Regent, Mary Stuart's mother, who was a Frenchwoman and a Catholic. A rebellion broke out against her, and the rebels asked aid from England. Elizabeth had no love for rebels or Calvinists, but her scruples rarely took precedence over her interests. She sent help, and the Scots government agreed to send home its French troops. This agreement, the Treaty of Edinburgh of 1560, marked the beginning of the end of French influence in Scotland.

In a decade the Scots broke the tie that English policy and force had failed to break in three centuries. Their reasons were religious and political: their shift from Catholicism to their own brand of Calvinism had weakened the pull of France, and the grandiose ambition of the House of Guise had made it seem a greater menace to their independence than the House of Tudor. A more basic reason was strategic: France was useful to them only as long as she could assist them in time of need, either by direct intervention or by absorbing English energies in Europe; by 1560 England's sea power in home waters was a barrier to direct intervention, and the English had long since abandoned their tradition of large-scale military adventures on the Continent. The Franco-Scots accord was dissolved, in other words, because the factors that had occasioned it ceased to operate. Scotland was thereby condemned to an isolation from which she could escape only by drawing closer to England.

The Treaty of Edinburgh was merely the first stage in Elizabeth's deliverance. A few months later Mary Stuart's husband, who had recently become King of France, died without issue. Mary soon tired of being a dowager queen in Paris, and returned to try to be a real one in Edinburgh. Her chance at best was slim. She was as much a Catholic as her mother and almost as French, and the Scots were ill-disposed toward another female ruler; the Crown had little prestige or force, at a time when rebellion had become a habit. Mary destroyed what little chance she had. She remarried to carry on the line, and soon bore a son — James, the future king of Scotland and England. But she had chosen to marry a fool; she became involved in his murder and then eloped with his murderer. Such conduct was political lunacy. However much it has appealed to subsequent romanticists, it outraged the moral sense of the Scots, Catholic and Calvinist alike. Rebellion germinated almost spontaneously. Mary abdicated in favor of her son and escaped to England, where her fellow queen promptly imprisoned her.

Elizabeth was acting not generously, but sensibly. Mary, from the day she crossed the border to the day of her death, was the most dangerous person in the kingdom. She had lost Scotland, it is true, but she was not dangerous as Queen of Scots. In Protestant eyes she was heiress presumptive to the English throne, because Elizabeth was the last Tudor, and unmarried. In Catholic eyes Mary was the rightful queen of England, because Elizabeth was illegitimate and therefore a usurper. Extremists among the recusants turned to Mary as their hope, and so did Elizabeth's foreign enemies. France had shot her bolt and was crippled with civil wars, but Philip was observing with interest. Mary without her French backing could be invaluable to Mother Church and to Spain. If the disaffected recusants were stiffened with a Spanish army, and Elizabeth conveniently assassinated, Queen Mary II might again return England to the fold, this time as a complete Spanish satellite. Philip's design matured over the years, and it insured that Mary remained in confinement; Elizabeth dared not allow her at large. One plot after another was made to release her, but they all miscarried.

Philip might have been more effective if he had not been distracted elsewhere. He was involved in the Mediterranean and in the French civil wars. In 1566 his subjects in the Low Countries, his richest dominion, rose against him. The struggle dragged on for years; he eventually succeeded in winning back the southern Neth-

erlands, but the Dutch continued to defy him. He was playing a
chess game with a continent for board, simultaneously attacking
and defending, and Mary Stuart was only one of his many pieces.

England was greatly concerned in the revolt of the Netherlands.
She had long had with them a close economic connection, that between the sheep and the loom, and she quickly felt anything that
affected their industrial health. The Dutch, furthermore, were Calvinists, fighting against the common enemy of all Protestants. For
economic and religious reasons their struggle concerned the English
middle class. Elizabeth shared the concern, but her position was delicate. She still had no love for rebels, however useful; besides, what
if she embroiled herself with Philip for their sake, and they then
made peace? Yet she wished to prevent their defeat, because they
occupied Spanish armies that might otherwise be turned against
England. Prudence dictated official neutrality, combined with a covert harrying of Philip's resources in any way that came to hand.

The Elizabethans evolved a popular and profitable technique for
waging this undeclared war. English trade had been increasing rapidly during the preceding decades, and the traders had been pushing farther and farther afield. Their ships were warships, for the
navy had not yet been differentiated from the merchant marine;
these privately owned vessels began to prey on Spanish commerce
from the New World. Elizabeth denied responsibility for her subjects' piracy, while she put some money in secret into their specula-
tive ventures. Success meant profit and a weakening of Spanish
resources; failure merely meant death or prison for the ships' companies and a washing of official hands. In such an informal war the
sea dogs were a most convenient weapon.

The loot was gratifying, but the important result was the effect
on the looters. Large numbers of Englishmen acquired a knowledge
of the high seas, of how to sail them anywhere and in all weather,
and learned to fight as resourcefully as they sailed; soon they knew
every weakness of the galleons they hunted. They went out for
plunder, but they brought back with it the beginnings of a naval tradition unsurpassed in history.

The Spaniards were vulnerable to attack. Their sea power had
grown in areas of relatively calm water and reliable winds: first the
Mediterranean, then the southern Atlantic, finally the western edge
of the Pacific. Their ships, designed to sail with the trades and to

carry cargoes rather than guns, were larger, less maneuverable, and weaker in fire-power than the English ships; the latter were designed for the choppy seas and changeable winds off the British Isles, and they carried tiers of guns on the lower decks. The Spaniards were not only at a tactical disadvantage; they had also been lulled into a false security. American waters had long been their preserve, primarily because no enemy had been strong enough and near enough to attack, and the appearance of the English was a rude shock. In America itself no effective defense was possible. The Spanish government could not protect every valuable cargo or garrison every tempting coastal town without squandering its last resources. Either the raids would continue indefinitely, or the raiders would be stopped at their base. The best defense of the American empire was to invade England.

By the 1580's more pressing developments led Philip to decide on invasion. In 1584 the Dutch leader, William the Silent, was assassinated, and the rebellion threatened to fall apart without his guiding hand; Elizabeth was at last forced to active intervention. At the same time she took a step that was even more open defiance of Spain. As tension grew, the danger from Mary Stuart and the English recusants increased. In 1586 the Queen of Scots embarked on her last plot, which was conducted as usual under the surveillance — almost the auspices — of the English government. It was exposed, and Mary was tried and convicted. By now, even Elizabeth's scruples had worn thin; she signed the death warrant, and in February 1587 Mary was beheaded.

Her execution was tantamount to a declaration of war on Spain, and was so accepted; Philip determined to attack. The problem before him was that which has subsequently confronted every master of western Europe from Louis XIV through Hitler: he had an overwhelmingly superior land force, but how was he to get it across the narrow waters of the Channel? The Spanish answer was simple — to assemble in Spain the largest fleet that the world had yet seen, and with this armada to sweep the Channel as far as the Low Countries; then to ferry the Duke of Parma's veterans from the Netherlands to England. Elizabeth's army was a rabble of civilians, Parma's the finest in Europe. Once the Spaniards landed, the issue would be settled.

The few Englishmen who understood the situation sensed that

the odds were heavily in their favor. The legendary picture of Sir Francis Drake finishing his game of bowls after the enemy had been sighted symbolizes the self-assurance of the expert. Drake, like all the other competent sea dogs, knew that the tactical advantages of the English ships would be even greater in home waters than they had been in the South Atlantic. The Armada was composed of fair-weather sailers and fair-weather fighters, and the English Channel is not noted for fair weather.

The Spaniards were also at a mental disadvantage. Naval doctrine was not yet born; a fleet engagement was a mere mêlée. But the English prepared for battle as sailors, whereas soldiers dominated Spanish planning. The Armada was commanded by a general with little experience of the sea. His primary objective was not to destroy the English fleet but to brush it aside, in order to reach Parma's force and carry it to Kent. The ships were more ferries than units of fire-power; in action the Spaniards hoped to grapple and board and win at sword's point. They were planning, in other words, for a land battle fought on the water.

On July 19, 1588, the Armada was sighted off the Lizard. The English swarmed out to engage it, and for a week the fight raged up the Channel. The Spaniards found themselves battered by an enemy they could not reach; trying to board a faster and well-armed ship, manned by sailors and gunners who knew their business, was like trying to wrestle with a striking rattlesnake. When the Spaniards took refuge in the neutral port of Calais, the English loosed upon them fireships, the terrifying predecessor of the torpedo, and they fled again in confusion. By the time they cleared the Channel their rendezvous with Parma was forgotten; their objective had changed from invasion to getting home alive. For the majority this proved impossible. The fleet rounded Scotland rather than brave the Channel once more, and storms completed the work of English guns. The wreckage of Spanish power was strewn along the Scottish and Irish coasts; less than half of the Armada ever saw Spain again. The great crusade had ended in disaster, and the Spaniards' faith in their destiny had had a blow from which they never recovered. God, they said, had forsaken them.

Philip refused to agree. For the next ten years, until his death in 1598, he carried on the war with every means at hand. Although he dreamed of new armadas, they did not materialize. He therefore

turned to the weakest outwork of England's defenses, the point at
which the French later struck repeatedly. This was Ireland. Philip's
attempt failed to achieve his ends, but it further embittered Anglo-
Irish relations.

Ireland was for Elizabeth much what the disaffected Netherlands
were for Philip, a drain on governmental resources and an opportunity for foreign intervention. The native Irish outside the Pale had
been restive ever since Mary's day, when the English had begun
planting settlers on land confiscated from rebellious chieftains; during Elizabeth's reign the Anglo-Irish of the Pale grew resentful of
the taxation imposed by her governors. These grievances were subordinate, however, to religious friction: the attempt to impose on
the Irish an English church, and even a liturgy in English, created
an explosive situation within and without the Pale. As Scottish nationalism was becoming tied to a new faith, Irish was becoming tied
to an old, and the effect on the two countries was opposite. Calvinism was pulling Scotland away from France and toward England;
Roman Catholicism was pulling Ireland away from England and toward whatever Continental enemy the English might have.

For the moment that enemy was Spain, and the agents of the Pope
and Philip were quick to seize the opportunity. Within three years
of Elizabeth's accession, papal emissaries had begun their work in
Ireland. A series of rebellions reached its climax in the rising of
1598, a nearer approach to a national movement than anything with
which the English had had to contend. As in almost all Irish bids
for freedom, the timing was bad: the rebels' momentum spent itself
before a Spanish army came to the rescue, and the English disposed
of the two threats separately. Although Elizabeth's resources were
strained to the breaking point, peace was virtually restored by the
time of her death.

Like so many other aspects of the Queen's great defensive, the
struggle in Ireland brought troubles to come. It taught different lessons on the two sides of St. George's Channel. The Irish began to
learn that their only hope of shaking off the foreign yoke was to rebel when England was involved in a crisis of her own; the English
began to learn the Irish aptitude for what they considered treach-
ery in a dark hour, and they retaliated ruthlessly. The aftermath was
bitterness on both sides. The suppression of the rising also left a
momentous question to Elizabeth's successor. Now that Ireland was

more nearly conquered than ever before, how was the conquest to be utilized — as a step toward union, like the thirteenth-century conquest of Wales, or as a chance to exploit the conquered?

VII   "Confident from Foreign Purposes"

THE IRISH problem, grim as it was, amounted to only a small cloud in the Elizabethan sunset. The dominant consideration was Spain, not Ireland, and in the last years of Elizabeth the dominant fact was victory over Spain. The fact was apprehended only gradually, yet its impact was enormous. As defeat brought the Spaniards a sense that God had deserted them, victory brought the English a complex elation. Part of it was religious, the feeling that the Lord of Hosts had set upon the nation the seal of His approval. Part was secular pride, focused in loyalty to the Crown. Part was a dawning awareness that England's ships enabled her to defy the world. These were the ingredients of the Elizabethans' legacy to their descendants.

The established church was finally separated from Rome. Philip, the two Marys, the Armada had done their work beyond undoing, and the Almighty seemed to have sanctioned the breach. Hatred of the Pope had become an even more basic tenet of patriotism than hatred of Spain. In the next century France rose to be the great political enemy, but enmity to Rome remained inveterate; the suspicion that the sovereign had papal leanings contributed to one revolution, and the certainty precipitated another. A minority of recusants continued to worship in private, but even they slowly lost hope of returning England to the fold. Elizabeth's Church had become the church of the nation, and the struggle to defend it had engendered a love for it.

What had been defended, and what was loved? The answer was no clearer than it had been, but the question was in abeyance as long as national survival was in doubt. The crisis, or at least the sense of crisis, persisted until the end of the century. This fact, more than the efforts of government, circumscribed Puritan criticism of the Church. Fundamental problems were tacitly postponed for the duration, which meant until the last few years of the reign. By 1600 the crisis was over; Philip was dead, the France of Henry of Navarre was recovering with phenomenal speed from the ravages of civil war, the Dutch had made good their independence. The

solidarity of wartime England began to be marred by the bickerings of peace, but serious trouble did not develop as long as Elizabeth lived.

The Queen was loved by her people, probably more than any
other sovereign in their history. They loved her partly for herself
(most of them never saw the mean side of her) and partly as the
embodiment of England. Also they feared her. She was Tudor to
her marrow, and age impaired the Tudor temper but not the Tudor
will. She retained to her dying day the gift of using love and fear
for the defense of her own prerogative, and so for the defense of
the status quo. Why, after all, should the Puritan vent his grievances when he could get a glow of loyalty from postponing what he
was afraid to do? He had all the more reason to wait until the awe-
some old woman was dead, because he expected that then his chance
would come.

It would come, he thought, in the person of a Calvinist king. Elizabeth had juggled for years with the issue of the succession, flirting
with one suitor after another while Parliament begged her to settle
the question — to marry someone, almost anyone, in order to carry
on the dynasty. Whether she ever intended to is still her secret; only
the outcome is apparent. In the early decades of the reign she used
flirtation as a diplomatic weapon; it served her as a smoke screen to
keep the courts of Europe guessing what her course would be. By
the later 1570's the marital problem became separated from the dynastic because the Queen was beyond the age of child-bearing. But
she still encouraged suitors and refused to discuss her successor.

Well she might refuse; the dilemma seemed too hopeless to discuss. The heir by statute was the descendant of Henry VIII's
younger sister, Mary, but this line had sunk into political insignificance. The heir by heredity was the Queen of Scots, who could gain
the throne only through civil war and Spanish invasion. This Gor-
dian knot was cut by the axe that beheaded Mary Stuart. Thereafter
there was an heir, her son, whose claim rested both on heredity and
on common sense. James was a foreigner like his mother, but he
was neither a Roman Catholic nor a puppet of Catholic powers.
The shadow of the Kirk had been over him since birth. The English
Puritans therefore assumed that he was a good Calvinist, and they
awaited his accession as the dawn of a new era. Until the dawn
came, they were willing to delay their awkward questions.

Many other Englishmen, at the turn of the century, were antici-
pating a new era. England was not yet a power of the first rank,
but for the first time since the Hundred Years' War she had intervened decisively in European affairs. She had done so, moreover, on
the sea; it had long been the Elizabethans' habitat, and the hum-
bling of Spain brought home to them its importance. The realization
was exhilarating, although only a few had a clear idea of its implications.

Among the few was Sir Walter Raleigh. He glimpsed, before his
time, one of the elements that later determined the growth of English sea power — colonial expansion. He emphasized colonies primarily as weapons against Spain, means of impairing the trade and
security of Philip's empire. According to the best-known publicist of
his circle, Richard Hakluyt, English settlements within reach of the
Caribbean would be "a great bridle to the Indies of the king of
Spain." "If you touch him in the Indies, you touch the apple of his
eye; for take away his treasure, which is *nervus belli*, . . . his old
bands of soldiers will soon be dissolved, his purposes defeated, his
power and strength diminished, his pride abated, and his tyranny
utterly suppressed." [6]

This concept found little favor. At court the view prevailed that a
degree of Spanish power was a necessary counterweight to France.
The mercantile interests considered a company chartered to colonize as a slow and risky investment; colonists sucked up money like
a sponge, and the return was likely to be in fool's gold. Businessmen
were possessed by the immediate excitement of cash returns from
plunder and trade, and they were as deaf as the Queen's government to the plea for a long, weary struggle with the wilderness.

The Elizabethans' excitement over gold was not a mere outburst
of avarice. Gold was pouring in upon them because a fundamental
change had taken place in the geography of trade. In the late fifteenth century England had been on the fringe of European commerce; in the late sixteenth she was at the heart of it. As a result of
the Spanish and Portuguese discoveries the great trade routes had
shifted from the eastern Mediterranean and the Near East to the

---

[6] "A Particular Discourse concerning the Great Necessity and Manifold
Commodities that are Like to Grow to This Realm of England by the Western
Discoveries lately Attempted," 1584: William H. Dunham and Stanley Pargel-
lis (eds.), *Complaint and Reform in England, 1436–1714* (New York: Oxford
University Press; 1938), pp. 313, 321.

open Atlantic, through which they ran around Africa to the Orient and westward to the New World. Their European terminus was no longer Italy, but the Iberian peninsula. Both Spain and Portugal, however, were poor countries without the financial resources to exploit their opportunities, the domestic market to absorb their imports, or the domestic manufactures to satisfy colonial demands and to trade for the riches of the East. By the late sixteenth century their capital and exports came in large part from the Low Countries and the Germanies; consequently their imports from overseas, in commensurate part, passed through the great entrepôts of the peninsula back to northern Europe. Because transport was infinitely cheaper by water than by land, one of the busiest trade routes in the world was that which ran through the Bay of Biscay, the Channel, and the North Sea.

This shift in trade revolutionized England's economic position. Tudor capitalists found new horizons opening before them; manufactures were in increasing demand, traders and investors had opportunities thrown in their path at every turn. The English business world was being pulled into closer contact with its counterpart across the Channel, and was putting out tentative feelers into the darkness beyond Europe. English society, which might have become spiritually isolated and ingrowing after the break with Rome, was beginning to have cosmopolitanism forced upon it through trade.

The new geography of commerce made possible the emergence of England as a major power. The sea dogs had demonstrated that Spain was vulnerable in the New World, and the temporary merger of the Spanish and Portuguese empires in 1580 opened still greater vistas of freebooting. But it was in Europe that the weight of England, as a state, was being felt most markedly. The defeat of the Armada suggested that where Spain had failed no other naval power might hope to succeed — that England could, if she exerted herself, clamp a tourniquet on the artery of trade that ran through the narrow seas. Any state that artery fed had to reckon with her.

The English alone were focusing all their energies on a single form of power, their ships. They had no real standing army — despite a so-called system for raising one — because they had been unwilling to bear the burden of what they had hoped was unnecessary. The Armada put their hope to the crucial test and fulfilled it. They

were saved by what were later famous as their walls of oak, and
victory perpetuated their concentration on naval force.

The timing of their victory was of cardinal importance. It came
just when forces of change were turning their energies seaward. The
drama of the great fight, with its overtones of divine intervention,
fired the national consciousness and stimulated an outburst of energy. Through the smoke of gunfire in the Channel a vague glimpse
of her future came to

> "England, hedg'd in with the main,
> That water-walled bulwark, still secure
> And confident from foreign purposes." [7]

The Elizabethans were confident, ebulliently so, because they had
proved their security from foreign purposes — security for their
land, their church, their monarch. But the blend of confidence and
security led their descendants to question the nature of what had
been secured. The questioning revealed paradoxes, ecclesiastical
and constitutional, and in the atmosphere of peace dissension throve.
Within forty years of Elizabeth's death the land had become a bat-
tlefield, and the Elizabethan structure of church and monarchy lay
in ruins. The winning of security from without, in short, contributed
to its destruction from within.

---

[7] Shakespeare: *King John,* II, i, 26–8.

Chapter Two

THE PASSING OF TUDOR ENGLAND

1603–1660

I   The Advent of the Stuarts

WHEN Queen Elizabeth lay dying, in March of 1603, Tudor statecraft was dying with her. Its ghost lingered for another generation, but its life was disappearing with the conditions that had brought it into existence. The Crown and the middle class had once been in tacit alliance against the relics of the aristocracy and the vested power of the Church. Now the alliance had been dissolved by success. The nobles had been shorn of authority and the Church reduced to a department of the state; the political ambition of the middle class was increasing with its wealth and experience. The Tudors, for all their acumen, had made the job of kingship progressively more difficult. They had forced the people who mattered — those of substance — into the work of local and national government, generation after generation, and had thereby bred into them a sense of their own importance.

The mirror of change was the House of Commons. Its members were no longer the same breed who had listened in awe to Cardinal Wolsey; their temper was now too tough to bend even before Elizabeth. She had kept government going by a judicious blend of feminine and royal prerogative, of cajolery and concession, and she had been supported by the prestige of victory and of her own longevity. Hers had been a personal and intuitive technique, not a theory of sovereignty, and it was inimitable. Whoever followed her would inherit her problems, grown worse with her passing, and could not inherit her solutions.

If changing conditions made the task of any successor difficult, that of James Stuart was peculiarly so. He was a foreigner, come to rule a people seething with nationalism. He believed in peace, and England for a generation had thrived on war with Spain. For all his intelligence he was a poor judge of men, both in the mass and as individuals competing for his favor. He was a theorist where Elizabeth had been an artist in sovereignty, and the work of art that she left him was not a fit subject for his rationalism. Last, and worst of all, his particular theories were sure to upset the delicate Tudor equilibrium.

James had been nurtured in Scotland on a three-cornered struggle between the Crown, the nobility, and the Church. The nobility represented a dying order of feudalism that had little effect on the King's theories of his office, but the Church represented a dynamic principle: that authority in doctrine and government derives from all the faithful. Calvinism in Scotland had taken a Presbyterian form, expressed in a hierarchy of bodies chosen by laymen and clergy and culminating in the general assembly of the Kirk. The bishops, although they had not been permanently eradicated, were largely submerged in this wave of popularism. The real leaders were the elders and presbyters, whose duty was to bring home the word of God to every Scot, especially to "God's silly vassal" on the throne. This was theocracy. The end of it, as James was well aware, would be the transference of sovereignty from the Crown to the Kirk. "Some small, fiery-spirited men in the ministry," he complained, "got such a guiding of the people . . . that, finding the gust of government sweet, they began to fancy a democratic form."

James himself had a glutton's fondness for "the gust of government." He had no intention of remaining in tutelage to the clergy or of abandoning sovereignty to them. As a Christian he was a Calvinist; as a king he was the inveterate enemy of Presbyterians. His years of controversy with the clergy raised more and more sweeping claims to authority on both sides. As the Kirk advanced its pretensions in the name of God, so did the King. Against the divine right of the presbytery he asserted the divine right of monarchy — a right inherent in him by heredity, derived not from men but from God, and not to be curtailed by subject or sovereign. His prerogative was for him the earthly will of the Almighty, to which all human authority was subordinate. The proud claims of God's elect were matched by the equally proud claims of God's anointed.

James's theory was not a mere outgrowth of Scottish quarrels. Its roots were in the Middle Ages, and its full flowering was still to come on the Continent. There the old authoritarian principle of the papacy was growing weaker in practice, and the new pretensions of Protestant sects were producing civil chaos; men were turning more and more to the solace of secular authority, and their emphasis on kingship was rising. James's notions were not peculiar to him, but were signs of a new age in Europe.

That age was not for Britain. The Scots were unready for it: they did not want secular authority at the price of their turbulent freedom. The English were beyond it: the monarchy that had saved them from social and religious chaos had outlasted the reasons for its emergency powers. James and his son attempted to elevate those powers to the status of a divine commandment. The attempt was resisted as an innovation by the Scots, as an anachronism by the English.

England was the testing ground for James. He knew his Scots too well to press them, and his pretensions at home were limited by an almost Tudor consciousness of what the market would bear. In England he was on strange ground. He never learned his new subjects' way of speech or thought, and he mistook his position as their king. His problems called for a maximum of adaptability, tact, and forbearance; what he saw was a heaven-sent opportunity for putting his theories into effect. The misjudgment is not surprising, for the English constitution seemed to be ideal material for a reforming monarch. The independence of the Crown was limited, it is true, by parliamentary control of finances and by a common law entrenched in largely autonomous courts; but the Tudors had shown that these restrictions could be to a great degree circumvented, and a wise king might improve on their example. The government was woefully untidy. It challenged James, with his logician's sense of neatness, to reform it into an ordered system.

If the challenge of civil government was alluring, that offered by the Church was dazzling. To a king who had struggled for years in the Scottish wilderness, the episcopal establishment seemed like the promised land. Here the power of the Crown had already been exalted. The king ruled through the bishops and the ecclesiastical courts; Parliament, representing the laity, had at most the right to approve a fundamental change in doctrine. James had no wish to meddle with doctrine; the laity, in return, he expected not to meddle with administration. The reality of Stuart power might then rise to the height of Stuart theory.

II The Pedantic King

JAMES'S hopes were illusory. Disillusionment came first in the Church, where he had expected the most, and it naturally came from those who had expected the most from him. The English Puritans petitioned him for a number of minor changes in church ritual and government, and he agreed to a conference with them at Hampton Court. Among their requests was a suggestion that the bishop of each diocese should be advised by a synod of the lower clergy. This point, moderate as it seemed, stung the King to fury. He accused the petitioners of desiring a Presbyterian system, which to his mind — filled with memories of his mother's dethronement and his own humiliations — meant that they were rebels. He virtually told them so, and ended his tirade with a final blast: "no bishop, no king."

Those four words brought into the open an issue that had long been latent. James was not a diplomat; his volcanic temper boiled over, unlike Elizabeth's, at the most inopportune moments. But even in a rage he made sense. Thanks to his Scottish experience he saw the heart of the issue more clearly than the Puritans did themselves. His control of the Church through the bishops was rooted in the Tudor tradition; consequently the Puritans were challenging the accepted nature of prerogative. James took up the challenge at once, and stated it with a logic his opponents did not yet dare to accept. Whether he was wise to be logical is beside the point. His action identified the Crown with the episcopacy; the two stood together through the storms of the next forty years, and they fell together.

The Puritans at Hampton Court were appalled by the royal blast. Their expectations, cherished for years, had been shattered in a matter of minutes: they were no better off under the new King than under the old Queen. Three hundred of them were expelled from holy orders because they would not conform, and a few left the country; but the great majority reconciled themselves once more to biding their time. Their party was not yet bold or numerous enough to join battle on the lines the King had drawn. His position behind the wall of prescriptive authority was almost impregnable, and few Englishmen were ready to assail it in earnest. As long as authority was not used to narrow the doctrine of the broad Elizabethan settlement, the Puritan's resentment of the bishops drew only sporadic support from the bulk of the squires and burgesses.

But other sources of resentment were appearing, with which the Puritans as such had no concern. As James's reign progressed, his policy engendered discontent on financial, legal, economic, and political grounds as well as on religious. These disparate grievances had a single focus in the House of Commons, where they were slowly fused into one. Grievance, unredressed, generated a demand for power by the Lower House, and raised the ultimate problem of where sovereignty resided. This problem, like all constitutional ultimates, transcended settlement by constitutional means. The only possible arbiter was force.

At the beginning of the reign such a development was as far from the King's thoughts as from his subjects'. James merely intended to rationalize certain aspects of the Tudor regime. Public finance was a jumble; the legal system required overhauling; the nation needed a wise directing hand for its economy and a logical framework for its foreign policy. These were the types of reform that the King had in mind. Much can be said for each of them, and in some he was wiser than his opponents. What vitiated his plans was not their aim but their premise, that his wisdom exceeded that of all others. The premise made discussion difficult and compromise almost impossible, and tied the prestige of monarchy to the outcome of the monarch's experiments.

James's handling of the financial crisis is a case in point. The problem of revenue was fundamental to the Stuarts because the traditional methods of financing the state were becoming progressively less adequate. The needs of an increasingly complex society had to be met by increasing the activities, and therefore the cost, of government; and the buying power of money was declining as more and more bullion came into circulation. The ordinary revenues of the Crown, derived from royal lands, feudal dues, court fines, etc., were relatively fixed and inelastic. The extraordinary revenues — the taxes granted by Parliament — were lump sums set by tradition and virtually unrelated to the nation's taxable wealth; the number of taxes granted could be increased, but not the yield from any one.

The King had the choice between two alternatives to bankruptcy: either to ask for more and more grants or to find other sources of income.

The first alternative was out of the question. The underlying causes of the problem were not clearly perceived either at court or in Parliament, and misunderstanding bred resentment; courtiers muttered about a niggardly legislature, the legislators about an extravagant court. The commons were averse to voting money at the best of times, and their reluctance grew in proportion to their grievances. James could not look to them for any major increase in supply unless he was willing to abandon, in return, those aspects of the prerogative to which they objected. This he could not do; his prerogative was part of him. He was therefore forced to the second alternative, the search for other sources of revenue.

First he tried to fill his coffers by collecting import duties. The courts upheld him, but the commons grew restive. Next he offered to surrender a multitude of archaic feudal obligations owed to the Crown, in return for a permanent parliamentary grant of £200,000 a year. This reasonable proposal, known as the Great Contract, foundered on an extraneous issue: Parliament began to criticize the bishops, and James sacrificed the chance of stabilizing his income to the protection of his Church. Early in 1611 he dissolved the Houses. For the next decade, with one brief exception, he ruled by prerogative alone.

The breach with Parliament necessitated increasing the ordinary revenue by hook or crook. The King's expedients strained the limits of legality, and thereby brought to the fore another issue implicit since the reign began — the role of the law courts in the state. Would the judges adopt the King's view that he was the interpreter of the law, and acquiesce in any innovation, financial or otherwise, for which his legal staff could spin an argument? Or would they stand out in the absence of Parliament as the guardians of the subject against the Crown? On the answer hinged much more than the continuance of James's personal rule.

Magna Carta had established the principle that the will of the king was subordinate to the fundamental law of the land. The principle had subsequently been dramatized by the deposition of two monarchs — one on the charge, among others, that he had claimed to have the law in his own breast. But if it was not there, where was it? In practice, it had resided wherever there had been the power to declare and enforce it — in the medieval Crown or baronage, in the Lancastrian Parliaments as tools of a new aristocracy, in the Tudor synthesis of the Crown in Parliament. Now that this synthesis was disappearing, and King and commons were drifting apart, what institution had a better claim than the Crown to interpret law?

Parliament by itself had no claim; it possessed authority only in conjunction with the sovereign. The prerogative courts, which had been growing in number and prestige during the Tudor period, could not by their nature be a brake on the prerogative. The only remaining possibility, and a faint one, was the courts of common law. Their judges were conservatives, dyed in the wool of precedent, and they were royal servants who held office at the king's will; consequently they were weak strings with which to bind royal pretensions. The wonder is not that they failed to do so, but that one of them was bold enough to make the attempt.

In Sir Edward Coke, chief justice successively of Common Pleas and King's Bench, James met his match in self-assurance. Coke refused to be influenced or intimidated. In the face of divine right he advanced the claim that law is supreme, above king or parliament or judge. His claim had more sweeping implications than he or his contemporaries could realize. Its logical conclusion was that fundamental law is superior to both prerogative and statute, and that the judges as interpreters of law take precedence over the executive and legislature. A development of this idea became possible two centuries later in the United States, with its written constitution, but such a concept of the judiciary remained permanently alien to the British tradition.

Neither Coke nor James was interested in the implications of the argument. What mattered to them was that the majesty of law had been asserted in the teeth of Stuart majesty. The assertion, however much it impressed that legalistic age, was impracticable while the substance of power remained with the King. James triumphed, as he was bound to do in such an unequal struggle; Coke was dismissed, and for the next two decades the courts offered little hindrance to the prerogative. But the triumph was dearly bought. A generation of Englishmen lost the chance for legal redress of their grievances, which grew until they became explosive.

The triumph also failed to solve the financial problem. All the

King's expedients, whether archaisms or innovations, failed to fill his coffers; and his need for cash soon led him into a disastrous experiment with the wool trade. The bulk of English cloth was exported for finishing abroad, so that domestic manufacturers were losing, it seemed, a profit in which the Crown might share. In 1615, accordingly, the export of unfinished cloth was stopped, and a single private company was entrusted with finishing and dyeing it at home. The results were that foreign merchants refused to buy, the finished cloth piled up in London, and unemployment spread through the clothing districts. Within two years the experiment collapsed, but by then the harm had been done. In 1618 the economy of Europe began to be disrupted by the Thirty Years' War, and England's Continental market could not be restored; the wool trade remained in the doldrums for years. Lasting depression, in any era of planned economy, injures the prestige of the government by discrediting its planners.

Most men weathered the hard times with no more than grumbling, as most Puritans bore their religious grievances. But poverty and failure drove some, as conscience drove others, to seek a new life overseas. Few went to the Continent; economic conditions there were as uninviting as at home, and the average Englishman or Scot of the period was too parochial to adjust to a foreign society. The emigrants turned instead to the two areas that the Elizabethans had dreamed of colonizing, Ireland and the coast of North America. The government permitted them to go; they were often troublesome elements in the population, and no one could foresee that they carried with them seeds of greater trouble.

The exodus to Ireland was made possible by the rebellion of 1598. The lands of rebel chieftains, particularly in the northern province of Ulster, were considered forfeit to the Crown and were largely allocated to settlers from Britain; the Irish were reduced to tenants, who thirsted for revenge on their new landlords. Now that England and Scotland were joined in a dynastic union, Scots were quick to take advantage of the opportunity opened to them in the plantation of Ulster, where they soon became the predominant group. This Calvinist invasion in the north alarmed the Anglo-Irish gentry of the Pale, and their old loyalty to the Crown began to give place to a sense of solidarity with the rest of Catholic Ireland. Thus the policy of plantation split the island in two. Southern Ireland was largely Celtic in blood and speech, devoutly Roman Catholic, and embittered by British conquest and exploitation. Ulster was ruled by English-speaking Scots, Presbyterians in religion, who looked to Britain for the support on which their position depended. These two Irelands, existing side by side and hating each other, grew from the dragon's teeth that the Jacobeans sowed.

The emigration to North America, like that to Ireland, was closely connected with hard times at home. The Pilgrims had been toughened against the rigors of the New World, as William Bradford testified, by the rigors of life in England; "it was the Lord which . . . had beforehand prepared them, many having long borne the yoke, yea, from their youth." Others, less conscious that they were upheld by the Almighty, were driven to the adventure by sheer desperation. "God send me to go," wrote one who was leaving for Virginia. "If His will be, I shall die, for I had rather die with credit than live with shame." [1] In such a mood the settlers fought the Indians and nature. Many died, but the settlements lived.

The dangers were not only from Indians and nature. The Spaniards were already in Florida, the French on the St. Lawrence; soon the Dutch occupied the Hudson valley and, with the Swedes, established themselves on the Delaware. As these and the British holdings expanded toward each other, friction was bound to develop in America and between the home governments. Britain could never consolidate her position on the Atlantic coast until the Dutch had been ousted from the Delaware and the Hudson, or secure the northern flank of New England without a struggle against the French. Political and commercial rivalries in Europe, conversely, were sure to kindle sooner or later the fires of colonial war. A struggle for empire was implicit in the building of the first houses at Plymouth and Jamestown.

During the first half of the century Britain was unready for such a struggle. She was torn by domestic quarrels and little interested in empire, and the Stuart navy was pitiably weak; her rivals in America might well have been able to wrest her colonies from her. Instead France and Spain, the Netherlands, and Sweden turned their attention to central Europe. While they were fighting the Thirty Years' War, British settlements grew and prospered along the Chesa-

---

[1] From a private letter of 1620, Gloucester (England) Public Library MS. 16,531, fol. 64.

peake and the New England coast. That war gave Britain a breathing spell, between the waning of the Spanish menace and the rising of the French, during which she laid the foundations of empire and, at the end, of a navy in the modern sense.

The Jacobeans, like their contemporaries on the Continent, were far more concerned with the Thirty Years' War than with events in America. But their concern was relatively superficial, unlike that in France or Sweden, because the war did not touch the core of their interests. They could therefore afford the luxury of a quarrel. Although King James and his subjects agreed on the need for intervention, they disagreed on the method. The upshot was a long and angry debate, which produced negligible results in Europe but had major results at home.

James's daughter had married Frederick, Elector Palatine, a leading German Calvinist, and in the first storm of the Thirty Years' War Spanish troops drove the Elector and his wife into exile. The honor of the Stuart House and the cause of Protestantism were alike involved in restoring Frederick to the Palatinate, and James and his subjects for once had a common objective. But their disagreement on how to attain it appeared soon after Parliament met in 1621.

The real issue lay between two concepts of foreign policy. The commons, as so often in their struggle with the Stuarts, looked to the past for guidance: in order to coerce Spain they advocated a naval war in the Elizabethan manner. James differed, and with reason. The object was no longer Elizabethan, to defend the British Isles or relieve pressure on the Dutch, but to secure Spanish withdrawal from the Palatinate — from an inland region out of reach of a navy. How to do it? The method of later generations was to use Britain's sea power in conjunction with the land power of a European ally. Although James did not grasp this possibility, he saw that naval war alone was wide of the mark. It might enrich the English merchants, but it would leave Frederick and his wife to a lifetime of exile. The King believed that he had a better solution. If the wind could not blow the cloak off the Spaniard, the sun might warm it off.

He revived an old project for a marriage alliance between the Infanta and the Prince of Wales, now conditioned on Spanish evacuation of the Palatinate and with war as an alternative. British friendship was valuable to Spain: France was sure to oppose, sooner or

later, an Austro-Spanish attempt to dominate the Germanies, and
the Hapsburgs would need what allies they could get. Spanish
friendship was valuable to Britain as a counterweight to France in
the west. On this logical basis negotiations were opened with
Madrid.

Logic ignored two factors: English nationalism and Spanish acumen. The long crusade against Philip II had bred in the English
people a hatred of Spain and of the Pope. Now the King was pro-
posing to ally his dynasty with both — to insure a succession of Roman Catholic, pro-Spanish sovereigns, under whom the Jesuits
might work to subvert the Church, England become a Hapsburg
pawn, and the wealth of Spanish America be closed forever to English adventurers. The arguments that had roused the Elizabethans
against Philip now roused the Jacobeans against their own king.

The Spanish government was well informed. It knew that James
could not offer a real alliance, and that Prince Charles by himself
was worth little; it consequently had no intention of accepting the
proposal. But the continuance of negotiations averted war and embroiled James with Parliament; negotiations therefore continued. At
last the would-be bridegroom took a hand: Charles went courting
to Madrid, where he and his companions found a cold welcome, and
whence he soon returned a bachelor. London greeted him with the
one and only ovation of his life. The Spanish match had failed, and
the cheers of the crowd marked the end of James's scheme and virtually of his reign. He lingered on until 1625, discouraged and sick,
but the government passed to younger hands.

For more than twenty years James unconsciously sowed the
wind. The problems he met at his accession were serious; those he
passed on to his son would have baffled the wisdom of Solomon.
The change was the measure of the reign, but the King was only in
part responsible. He was faced by pressures before which even Elizabeth had had to give ground; his choice, at bottom, was between
submitting voluntarily to a further diminution of the prerogative or
clinging to it and precipitating conflict. For him this was no choice.
God had made him a king, in an age when kings were in the ascendant, and duty impelled him to uphold the rights of his calling.

James was miscast as royalty. As a don of an Oxford or Cambridge
college he might have busied himself in writing tomes on statecraft,
wrangling with a few colleagues, and lecturing students who dared

not disagree. He was no fool, not even a wise one, and in many ways he was more intelligent than most of his subjects. But his intelligence was not political. It was inelastic, without room for even the humility of doubt. He could never foresee, like Louis XV, that a deluge was impending, and this intellectual arrogance made him as bad a judge of measures as of men. He welcomed the forthright course, and if necessary the open breach, as much as Elizabeth had dreaded them; he trusted flatterers where she had only delighted in flattery. He passed on to his son, in consequence, a legacy of grievances and a pernicious favorite.

III   The Breach with Parliament

GEORGE VILLIERS, Duke of Buckingham, was a charming young man from Leicestershire, the most successful of the upstarts who had replaced Elizabeth's counselors. She would have found a place for him; he was decorative and amusing, and his manners made up for what he lacked in lineage and morals. But she would never have given him power. James did, and Charles gave him — as he gave no one else — the friendship of a brother. The Duke accompanied the Prince to Madrid, and the two returned to become virtually joint rulers. Their combined statesmanship did not equal that of James alone. For four years they guided Britain deeper and deeper into the morass of foreign adventures, while at home they followed a policy that completed their fiascoes abroad. By the time the Duke died, in 1628, the breach between monarchy and people had grown beyond bridging.

The pair assumed power on a wave of popularity. They were the champions of nationalism against Spain, and for the first time in years the executive could reasonably expect support from Parliament. But support was lost by one of the first acts of the new regime. Because a Spanish war put a premium upon the friendship of France, a marriage was concluded between Charles and Henrietta Maria, the sister of Louis XIII. The rebound from the Spanish match precipitated a French one, which was equally impolitic.

The Bourbon alliance was built on misunderstandings. Louis' new minister, Cardinal Richelieu, expected the British government to adopt a more tolerant attitude toward recusants, and to stand by while he settled accounts with the rebellious French Huguenots;

then and only then did he plan to co-operate against the Spaniards. Charles could not befriend Catholics at home and at the same time abandon the Protestants of France, who for half a century had looked to England for support; he expected Richelieu to attack the Palatinate forthwith and leave the Huguenots alone. Friction mounted rapidly, and soon Charles and Buckingham drifted into the incredible folly of a war with France. The Hapsburgs and the Bourbons were inveterate enemies, yet Britain was fighting them both at once. This was the nadir of statesmanship.

Buckingham, who had blundered egregiously in the Spanish war, hoped to regain his popularity. He decided to open the new war by an expedition to aid the Huguenot stronghold of La Rochelle. No money, it was patent, would be forthcoming from Parliament; the Duke had too many failures to his credit. Raising the money strained the King's resources to the breaking point. Charles had already experimented with a free gift, and had found that his subjects were stingy givers. He now tried what was called a forced loan, and was almost universally defied. A few prominent defaulters were arbitrarily imprisoned, to encourage the others, but the King gained far more hostility than cash.

The failure of the loan led to difficulty in collecting the troops. The government, unable to pay for their keep, was forced to billet them in private homes on their way to the port of embarkation. The Tommy Atkins of the period was far from an ideal guest. He had been forced into service by the press gang, which usually took from any community the men whom the magistrates wished to be rid of. He was likely to be a criminal and almost sure to be rowdy; "he will be his own carver of whatsoever he likes best and can lay his hands on, to the great damage and impoverishing of the country." [2] The householders subjected to this damage were for the most part men of substance, and billeting soon became an acute grievance.

By the time Buckingham sailed for La Rochelle, England was seething with anger. The one thing needed to turn anger to fury was a military disaster, and this he supplied. His generalship was on a par with his statecraft; after three months he was chased home with less than half of his soldiers. The army was now a wreck, the government bankrupt, but Charles was still in honor bound to aid

---

[2] Quoted in my *Gloucestershire: a Study in Local Government, 1590–1640* (New Haven, 1940), p. 99.

the Huguenots. The only possible hope was from Parliament, and a new one assembled in March 1628.

The shame and anger of the past years found immediate voice. In May the Petition of Right was submitted to the King, with the promise of handsome subsidies if he signed it. It declared illegal four main instruments of his prerogative: martial law in time of peace, billeting, arbitrary taxation, and arbitrary imprisonment. He hesitated, and considered dissolving Parliament. But his word was pledged to the Rochellais, and he could not help them without cash. He surrendered, and the petition became law.

Like other landmarks in British constitutional history, the Petition of Right was a specific remedy for the grievances of a particular moment. It was an answer to the domestic crisis precipitated by the attempt to aid the Huguenots; its effect was not on those unfortunate rebels but on the structure of royal government. The ban on arbitrary taxation and imprisonment was subsequently evaded (Charles was as ingenious in thwarting the purpose of a law as he was scrupulous in observing its letter), but the military clauses of the great petition he could not evade. Those clauses, combined with his poverty, made it impossible to hold together an army worth the name. His government henceforth had to rest solely on consent, and that base was already beginning to crack.

Parliament turned at once to attack Buckingham, in words which revealed its anger and humiliation. Charles was asked "whether the miserable disasters and ill success that hath accompanied all your late designs and actions . . . have not extremely wasted that stock of honor that was left unto this kingdom, sometimes terrible to all other nations and now declining to contempt beneath the meanest." The Duke was named as the cause of failure, and his dismissal was requested. Charles curtly refused. Soon afterward Buckingham was assassinated. It was a cruel blow to the King; the one friend of his life was gone, and his people went wild with rejoicing. The Londoners welcomed the dead Duke even more enthusiastically than they had the live one five years before on his return from Spain; the trained bands escorting the funeral procession beat their drums for joy.

Buckingham was the last outstanding exemplar of the Jacobean era. His world went with him, drummed joyfully through the London streets; there was no longer a place for the political frivolity of "the young courtier of the king's" whom the ballad-maker had satirized.[3] The men who buried the Duke were even then on the road to civil war, and he had done his share to set them on it. Fourteen years later the drums of the trained bands were beating again in London, but not for joy.

The murder made the struggle between Charles and Parliament all the more patent. As long as Buckingham had lived, it had been possible to pretend that he was misleading crown and people. Once he was dead, responsibility devolved inescapably upon the King, and the throne itself became the focus of the nation's resentment. Charles was alone in the center of the stage.

By contrast with his father, Charles looked like a king. He was not tall, but he had the bearing of a patrician; his dignity became almost heroic as the world darkened around him. He was isolated from the run of men by the awful concept of the kingly office that he had inherited from his father, and his natural shyness gave his manner toward strangers or opponents the frosty aloofness of an iceberg. The Puritans were incomprehensible to him. He was devout, but he had none of James's Calvinism; the church that he loved was the ritualistic, sacramental church that the Puritans detested. To that church, to his family, and to his idea of kingship he was deeply loyal. Out of his loyalties grew the later, legendary picture of Charles the Martyr.

But he had another side. He could be vindictive to his enemies and an ingrate to his ablest servants; above all his pledged word was unreliable. Bad faith might have been useful if a Machiavellian mind had guided it, but Charles's intelligence was meager. His judgment of people was no better than his father's — as witness Buckingham — and his judgment of policy was far worse. At bottom he was an obstinate little man, wandering in dignified bewilderment through an earthquake.

By the time of Buckingham's death the first tremors of the earthquake were perceptible. King and commons were fighting each other rather than the foreigner. Parliament controlled the wherewithal for policy because it alone could provide the necessary cash; the King alone controlled the making of policy, and he would not surrender his prerogative. This constitutional deadlock had pro-

---

[3] See *Percy's Reliques of Ancient English Poetry* (Everyman ed., 2 vols., London and New York, 1906), II, 128–30.

duced a vicious circle of disaster abroad and discord at home, which had indeed reduced Britain "to contempt beneath the meanest."

While the wars against France and Spain continued only in name, the war at Westminster grew fiercer. The major questions in dispute were no longer military, but financial and religious. The King was continuing to collect import duties; his legal grounds may have been sound, but to the House of Commons he seemed to be violating the Petition of Right by arbitrary taxation. The issue was particularly serious for another reason: most members of the House felt that the Church was being subverted — that the king who had abandoned the Protestant cause in Europe was now betraying it at home, and that only Parliament remained as defender of the faith. Defense would be impossible if the Crown obtained an independent revenue. Hence the struggle over import duties was only the surface of a struggle over religion.

What alarmed the commons was the fact that Charles was promoting to control of the Church a group of clergy with Catholic beliefs. These men preached, in effect, a return to Henrician Catholicism. They emphasized the apostolic power of the bishops, the distinction between priesthood and laity, the vital importance of the sacraments; to the Puritan claim that the Bible contained the full word of God they opposed the authority of a church derived from Christ. They also taught that obedience to the Crown was a religious duty, and that whoever resisted or even questioned the King's actions risked damnation. They had no practical alternative to this Erastian position. Ever since Henry VIII had substituted King for Pope, the ecclesiastical prerogative had been inseparable from the secular. Church and state were two aspects of a single community, and the Stuart emphasis on authoritarian monarchy inevitably revived the tradition of an authoritarian church under the royal aegis. To good Protestants this tradition, long dormant, seemed a shocking innovation that smelled of popery. If the King accepted it, he would extend the struggle with his subjects from the halls of Westminster into every parish church.

James had been saved from the attempt by his Calvinism and acumen. Because he had kept Elizabeth's broad doctrinal settlement the Puritans had not obtained widespread support for their attack on Church government; the majority had remained content. In his declining years, however, new men came forward to upset his work.

Chief among them was William Laud, with whom the Catholic movement has become synonymous. Laud was in high favor with Buckingham and Charles, and the new King's accession brought him rapid advancement; in 1628 he was made Bishop of London, whence his eyes turned toward the pinnacle of Canterbury. His progress was proof that the new King embraced his ideas.

Charles could scarcely help himself. His incomprehension and dislike of Puritanism, his devotion to the beauty of ritual, predisposed him to favor the Laudians; their deference to him on details of Church government flattered his sense of guiding his people. He was oblivious of danger because he did not know his subjects. He had no way of knowing them except by observing the barometer of the House of Commons, and he was even less able than his father to read that delicate instrument. In consequence he adopted a course that shattered the Elizabethan Church and did more than any other single factor to bring down the monarchy.

The immediate effect was a breach with Parliament. The financial quarrel was insoluble because it involved the vital issue of the Church. Tension mounted rapidly, and in the spring of 1629 the climax came in three resolutions of the House of Commons. They declared that anyone who advocated new doctrines in the Church, or had any part in the collection or payment of customs duties without the consent of Parliament, was a capital enemy of the kingdom. Obedience to the King, in other words, was treason to the kingdom. This was verbal rebellion, and Charles replied by dissolving Parliament.

The dissolution marked the end of the Tudor system. The delicate balance of forces that had made possible a government by Crown, lords, and commons had given place to a conflict of the two strongest forces in the state, the King and the Lower House. In the days of Peter Wentworth this conflict had been foreshadowed in religion, and in James's reign it had spread rapidly to issues of law, economics, and diplomacy. The crisis came when Charles began to remodel the Church at a moment when his fiscal and foreign policy had already stirred the commons to fury. The result was the end of parliamentary government as Englishmen had known it.

Such government was possible only on a basis of co-operation, for neither side could force its will on the other. The King could not coerce the House of Commons; he could only dissolve it. The commons could hamstring his policy by refusing supplies, but they could not force him to adopt their policy. He had the initiative, both in law and in practice; once he had embarked on a course of which they disapproved, the most they could do was to bring his government to a standstill. This they had virtually achieved by the spring of 1629.

From Charles's viewpoint the achievement was the work of wilful trouble-makers, who had turned his best intentions into grievances. The commons had cried for war with Spain in 1624; he had gone to war. They had cursed the French marriage and called for help to the Huguenots; he had sent help at the cost of the Bourbon alliance. They had refused the money needed to make the army effective, and then had blamed the Duke for failure. They had utilized the crisis caused by their parsimony to limit the secular prerogative in the Petition of Right, and had gone on to assail the ecclesiastical prerogative. What was the end to be, the King might have asked with some reason, except anarchy in Church and state? The commons were, in fact, trying to deprive him of powers essential to government — control of the armed forces, of foreign policy, of the Church. Yet they were not assuming those powers themselves because they had no means of doing so.

Charles saw only one solution. The Crown in Parliament had become the negation of government, but government had to go on; hence it had to be government by the King alone. He would rule — for the rest of his life if God were good — without summoning another parliament. Sovereigns before him had tried this experiment for long periods, but since the days of Henry VIII none had attempted to erect it into a permanent system. Charles made the attempt; the old regime had collapsed, and the King substituted a new regime of prerogative. It lasted for eleven years, which were the seed time of revolution. Then it collapsed in turn, and gave place to a more obviously revolutionary phase, dominated at the end by the men who gave their name to the whole movement. But the Puritan Revolution was far more than a rising of the Puritans. The forces that made it had been at work before 1629, and they were still at work long after the monarchy was restored in 1660. What Charles achieved by his personal rule was to bring the forces temporarily together, in overwhelming opposition to the principles for which he stood.

IV The King Alone

DURING the years of personal government British foreign policy was in abeyance. Money was lacking, and the energies of the King's councillors were taxed to the uttermost to keep the wheels of domestic administration turning. While the grim drama of the Thirty Years' War unfolded, England and Scotland looked on; their influence in Europe was negligible, and their military force was a laughingstock. But the great powers fighting each other for dominance in the Germanies turned their backs on the British Isles. The English and Scots were left free, unlike their German contemporaries or the French or Dutch before them, to settle their own problems in their own way. The Jacobeans had used that freedom for the luxury of debate; their sons used it for revolution.

The European situation was more than a setting for the troubles to come. It was a factor in the collapse of personal rule because it had a subtle but pervasive effect on the King's administrative machinery. By dissolving Parliament Charles had dispersed his quarrel with his subjects into every county, borough, and parish; there, and not in London courts and councils, his experiment had its final test. The working of prerogative depended upon a host of local officials throughout the kingdom, and could be only as effective as they were. In a period of national security their effectiveness declined.

Local magistrates had long tended to resist the demands of the central government. The Tudors, in the process of uprooting the feudal magnates, had deputed more and more authority to middle-class officials, and by the seventeenth century these new recipients of power had become a vested interest, almost as tenacious of their right to govern and as restive under control from London as the barons before them. For a time their restiveness had been curbed by the Spanish crisis, during which the exactions of government had had the grudging consent of the governed. Once the crisis passed, the administrative machinery grew less workable as its human cogs became absorbed in their own affairs and impatient of interference from London. The process culminated in Charles's personal rule, which failed in great part because it ran counter to vested local interests.

The King, in summary, ruled through a governing class to which his predecessors had taught a sense of its own importance. It would co-operate with the Crown in emergencies, but in tranquil times it had the will and means to assert its autonomy. In this sense it was analogous with the House of Commons; it could paralyze government more slowly, less dramatically, but with greater finality. Charles's only way to avert paralysis — centralization — was also the surest way to outrage the self-importance of the local magistrates. For eleven years he tried to control the country through the prerogative courts, through royal proclamations, through letters, commands, and messengers from the privy council. His paternalistic program had three salient parts: economic interference, a new scheme of taxation, and Laudianism in the Church. One or more of these parts antagonized almost every Englishman of importance, and so bred resistance to the Crown in its own agents. By 1640 the wheels of government had almost ceased to turn.

The King's economic interference was benevolently meant and in the long mercantilist tradition. But it was carried into new fields, and beyond the traditional limits in old ones; the government stepped on a multitude of toes. Native-grown tobacco, for example, was competing with Virginian; the Crown's attempt to suppress the domestic industry conflicted with the interests of rural producers and consumers, and therefore of rural magistrates, and the Crown failed. An effort to improve the wool trade by regulating the minutiae of the manufacturing process aroused protest and passive resistance, and came to nothing. Endeavors to curtail enclosure, to limit unemployment, to regulate wages, were equally unavailing. The King's planners were frustrated and his subjects annoyed. Even a seventeenth-century businessman disliked having his business run for him. He rarely expressed himself; the weight of custom was on the side of a planned economy. But his feeling was one of the many centrifugal forces in English localism.

If Charles's economic policies were the climax of an old paternalism, his scheme of taxation was new. His lawyers were ingenious in hiding his fiscal experiments under a cloak of precedent, but they could not long hide the unprecedented purpose — to establish prerogative government on a base of taxes levied without benefit of parliament. The purpose was defeated not by the courts or Parliament, but by the passive resistance of tax-collectors and taxpayers. As they withdrew their obedience the prerogative grew weaker, until in 1640 it was brought down by a breath of rebellion.

After a few unsuccessful experiments the lawyers hit upon a really promising plan. Elizabeth had occasionally asked the seaports to contribute to the navy, on the ground that their commerce was protected by the royal ships; however questionable the logic, the money had been paid. In 1634 Charles made a similar request, and the response of the ports was so gratifying that within two years the levy was extended to all England. But opposition spread with the tax. If ship money became established, it meant the permanent substitution of royal for parliamentary government. The taxpayer's only question was how to avoid paying.

The obvious recourse was to the law, and this way was taken by John Hampden. His famous case came to trial in 1637, the last moment when the courts might have resolved the impending conflict. But the spirit of Coke had been dead for a generation, and the Crown's argument was cogent. Elizabethan precedents showed that ship money was legal in a moment of emergency, and the King had decided that this was such a moment. The right to decide, not the correctness of the decision, was the issue before the court; a verdict against the Crown would have denied to it an essential attribute of sovereignty, the power to provide for national defense. The judges found for the King. However sound their law, they brought revolution closer. Like the Dred Scott decision, more than two centuries later, the verdict precluded legal redress for a grievance that was bringing men's tempers to the boil. Once the way of the law is closed, only the way of force remains.

By the time the judges upheld the King's experiment it was already beginning to collapse. Assessors of ship money were refusing to assess, collectors to collect; if a sheriff impounded cattle in default of a man's tax, the beasts were released in the night, or no one came forward to buy them. The King had transgressed the limits of consent, and the results were obvious at Whitehall: as the stream of receipts shrank to a trickle, the whole system of prerogative began to totter. But it did not fall of its own weight, like the Bourbon regime in 1789. It was destroyed by a blow from outside, which it had not the strength to resist.

The blow had been preparing for years. It was the outcome of the religious factor that had helped to launch Charles upon his experiment. He had advanced Laud to the see of Canterbury in 1633, and for the next seven years the Archbishop's concept of the Church was rigorously enforced. A communion that had remained national only because it had been undefined was now receiving a narrow, Catholic definition. Between the Puritan left wing of the Church and the Catholic right wing was a great group of moderates, clergy and laity alike, whom Laud was driving into alliance with the left — not because they opposed the Elizabethan settlement but because they loved it. Laud, they felt, was destroying it through the power of the Crown. Reluctantly they faced the alternatives of conforming to a ritual they detested or of attacking the prerogative itself.

Another factor alarmed them. James had been friendly with Catholic Spain, his son was married to a Roman Catholic, Laud was busy introducing what seemed like Roman practices. Were these the signs of a Stuart plot to return the country to the papal fold? They were not; one of the few feelings that Charles and his Archbishop shared with the most rabid Puritan was a hatred of Rome. But all Catholics were papists to the average Englishman, who understood doctrine in terms of what he saw with his own eyes. The faith he had known was changing to something strange and monstrous, and the change was forced on him every Sunday in the parish church.

The parochial clergy were taking on new ways. They wore elaborate vestments instead of sober black, and they interlarded the service with bowings at the name of Christ. Their sermons, although unquestionably learned, smacked of the church fathers more than of Calvin and Melancthon; their favorite texts emphasized obedience. A preacher might not dare to say explicitly, under the eagle eye of the squire, that Bible-reading was dangerous, but he would probably tell stories of heretics who had misinterpreted God's word. Worst of all, the new trend had been symbolized in a physical alteration in the church. The communion table had been moved from the entrance of the chancel to the east end, decked with damask and a cross, and cut off from the congregation by a rail. Where previously a minister and his people had communicated together in fellowship at a table, now laymen knelt at the rail while a priest brought the elements to them from an altar. The change expressed in a form no man could ignore the shift from a Protestant to a Catholic concept of the relationship between clergy and laity. If this was not Roman, what was?

The innovations could not be resisted. Laymen had to acquiesce because they had no alternative to worshiping by the forms of the established church; nonattendance was both illegal and, to the majority of a devout generation, unthinkable. The clergy also had to acquiesce or stand alone against the power of Church and state. Laud made diocesan visitations to ferret out any who dared deviate from his requirements; the government used the prerogative courts to enforce uniformity, until men forgot the routine and valuable functions of those courts and regarded them only as engines of tyranny. The Church was gradually made to conform to the pattern set by the privy council. "In all state alterations, be they never so bad," as Thomas Fuller put it, "the pulpit will be of the same wood as the council board." [4]

The anger of the country simmered under the surface. Criticism was not aimed in general at the parish clergy, who had to obey or lose their pulpits, or primarily at the Crown, which to most men was remote and somewhat unreal; it was aimed at the bishops, the heirs of the apostles and the henchmen of prerogative. Hatred of them spread from the Puritans to many moderates, who came to agree with the extremists in desiring not only the removal of the Laudian prelates but the abolition of the whole episcopacy. In trying to pull out the tares of Puritanism Charles and Laud had disseminated them.

Still nothing happened. Discontent that would have roused rebellion a century before was now endured; generations of domestic peace had made obedience an English habit. In the seventy years since the last armed rising the Crown had become synonymous in men's minds with the principle of social order, and the church had taken root in their hearts as the way of salvation. They were appalled to watch the King twist the law and his bishops twist the ritual, but their grievances were still local and disconnected. Only Parliament could link them. Until the Houses met again the English might refuse to pay the King's taxes, but they would keep his peace.

Not so the Scots. They were a tumultuous people, as James had known to his cost, and little divinity hedged their sovereign. They had dethroned Mary and had given James no peace until he exchanged Holyrood for Hampton Court; Charles, the stranger, they tolerated only because he had left them largely alone. The monar-

---

[4] Quoted by G. P. Gooch, *The History of English Democratic Ideas in the Seventeenth Century* (Cambridge, 1898), p. 62.

chy had conquered neither of the forces that opposed it: the nobles were still a power in the land, and the Kirk combined the political dynamic of popularism with the ruthlessness of the aroused Calvinist conscience. The Englishman's respect for authority, civil and ecclesiastical, was little regarded north of Tweed.

James had been aware of this fact. He had succeeded in reimposing an episcopacy upon the Kirk, but he had been wise enough to ride the Scots with a light rein. Bishops were unpopular. To some they represented the earlier age of papal supremacy, to others the subversive influence of England; the noble distrusted their increasing role in government, and to the presbyter they were scouts for the host of Midian. James's success had been more apparent than real.

Charles could not distinguish appearance from reality. He blundered in handling the Scots as his father never would have done, partly because he lacked James's shrewdness and partly because his upbringing had divorced him from the Scottish background of his House. By 1636 he convinced himself that all was going smoothly in England, and that the Kirk should be fitted to the Laudian pattern. A new order of service for Scotland was accordingly drawn up in London. The Scots were not consulted. The prayer book was to be imposed upon them by royal fiat operating through the bishops, and Charles assumed obedience.

The assumption was gross folly. To introduce a Laudian discipline into the Kirk was to thrust a torch into a powder-barrel. Nobles and presbyters were united in their jealousy of the bishops; patriots resented English interference; Calvinists saw behind the prelates and Laud the satanic face of Rome. On the Sunday in 1637 when the new service was to be read from every pulpit, Scotland exploded in revolt. The King's authority collapsed, and the repercussions in England were fatal to his rule.

Charles governed essentially by prestige, which is fragile. He could not maintain the prerogative of divine right in one kingdom while he capitulated to defiance in the other; he had to suppress the rebellion. But he could not. Long negotiations only revealed the gulf of misunderstanding between him and the Scots, and he was powerless to fight them. They were united and belligerent, led by veterans of the German wars; he had no army worth the name and no means of improvising one. He dared not risk a battle. Neither did the Scots, for fear that success would rouse against them the old hostility of the English. But the King's position could not be maintained by the forbearance of rebels. With the energy of the doomed he struggled to find military force.

In the emergency he called upon his ablest servant. Thomas Wentworth, now created Earl of Strafford, had been a champion of parliamentary liberties in the early years of the reign. But he had also defended the prerogative, particularly against the Puritans; his experience of the House of Commons had convinced him that law and order could never be fashioned by that debating society, and he had turned to the Crown — sacrificing his regard for liberty, like the fascist of a later day, to his craving for strong government. In 1632 Charles had sent him to govern Ireland, into which his policy of "thorough" had brought a semblance of order. When he returned in 1639, his ruthlessness had been sharpened by cutting through the tangles of Irish politics. "Black Tom Tyrant" was as competent as he was arrogant, and his arrival meant the end of half measures. If anyone could give new life to a dying prerogative, he was the man.

No one could. The Scottish crisis had gone too far to be settled by the means at hand, and the loyalty of the English — who alone could provide new means — had been drowned in their grievances. Strafford saw the first half of this dilemma but not the second; the Irish had accustomed him to a legislature that could be bullied into voting supplies. He advised the summoning of Parliament, and the desperate King agreed; the houses met in April 1640. It was apparent at once that the Earl had miscalculated. The commons refused supplies until they had considered England's ills, and they insisted on immediate peace with the Scots. Neither Charles nor Strafford was ready to surrender on such terms. After twenty-four days the Short Parliament was dissolved.

For the next months Black Tom held the center of the stage. He was making his last bid to save the monarchy, and all his enormous vigor and resource were thrown into the effort. He hoped to wring money from Irish and English taxpayers, and to bring over an Irish army as his answer to rebellion. But Ireland was drifting toward chaos now that his strong hand was removed, and neither taxes nor troops were forthcoming. As for England, the will and energy of a demon could not have extracted ship money in the summer of 1640.

While Strafford schemed and labored, the Scots sat quiet in the north. They had advanced as far as Newcastle, forced the King to accept their terms, and agreed to retire when he furnished them with a large indemnity; until then they demanded their expenses. This arrangement was shrewd business and shrewder statecraft. After the meeting of the Short Parliament the invaders knew that the House of Commons was their ally against prerogative, and they wished to force Charles to call Parliament again. This could be done more efficiently by appropriating the remnants of his cash than by attacking his tatterdemalion army. So the Scots remained.

The King was in check, and he had only one move. His writs went out, and in November his last Parliament met — the Long Parliament, which destroyed the monarchy, the church, and then itself. The game was up, as Charles had played it for eleven years. He could not dissolve the Houses again because the Scots at Newcastle guarded the members at Westminster. The situation was out of his control, and the initiative passed inevitably to the commons.

V The Fall of the Monarchy

THE LONG Parliament, when it met, was united against everything for which the King stood. Nobility, gentry, and burgesses were determined to curb the prerogative, whether in taxation, the courts, or the Church, and the outstanding agents of prerogative stood in danger of their lives. At that moment civil war was impossible; virtually everyone was against the King. This opposition disintegrated, during the next eighteen years, into many warring factions, and the process is the central fact in the history of the revolution. First the ranks of Parliament were split in two, and civil war ensued. The victors then fought each other over the fruits of victory, and one group triumphed only to break apart. In the end a small minority was ruling the islands by military force. Thus government by the sole prerogative of the Crown led, through revolution, to government by the sole prerogative of the sword. The sequence was so instructive that the British never needed another lesson.

At the beginning the vast majority of the members of Parliament were moderate royalists, who thought and spoke in terms of precedent, not of revolution. Their basic aim was little different from that of their predecessors in 1629: to establish a balanced constitution.

But the King had meanwhile unbalanced it, and their methods were more drastic. They were less interested in asserting rights than in manipulating power. The Scottish army, the London mob, the control of the purse, were means to the great end of insuring that the King should never again govern on his own.

Charles had been forced onto the defensive, but he was far from surrender. The supine fatalism of a Louis XVI or a Nicholas II was not in him; he was a fighter in a way of his own, and the fact that his way antagonized even his supporters reflects on his intelligence rather than his spirit. At times he tried the bold attack, usually when patience would have been wiser, and more often he used devious intrigue. As the leaders of the commons progressed from distrust to a conviction of his bad faith, their own actions became more high-handed and less legal. So the last hope of peace faded. When neither side believed in the other's respect for law, the constitutional struggle could no longer be waged by constitutional means.

The session opened with an attack on the two great agents of the Crown. Laud was impeached for high treason and committed to the Tower, where he remained until his execution in 1645. The cause for which he stood was lost before he entered prison; he had attempted to play the part of an ecclesiastical Procrustes, and his fate was not unlike that forthright reformer's. His ideas, however, survived as one element in the Church. He would have forced the establishment into a narrow Catholic frame; his enemies would have forced it into the equally narrow frame of their Calvinism. If, in the long run, either side had had its way, Anglicanism would have lost its essential character. Instead it retained the dualism of its Elizabethan origin, and in the periodic conflict of its elements, Catholic and Protestant, it continued to renew its vitality. This conflict was Laud's unintended but enduring legacy.

Legacies were no concern of the hurried and fearful men in the House of Commons. At the same time that they were ridding themselves of the Archbishop they were faced with an even more pressing danger. They could not breathe freely as long as Strafford lived, because he was the King's military adviser and his brain; as the Earl of Essex put it, "stone dead hath no fellow." Strafford had been impeached and imprisoned eight days after Parliament convened, and soon he was brought to trial before the House of Lords. At once the inadequacy of the law was revealed. The charge was treason —

by definition a crime against the King. In this case Charles had patently sanctioned the acts of his servant, which therefore could not be treasonable. The prosecution endeavored to establish that treason to the nation was a crime, but this legal innovation the peers refused to accept. At bottom Charles, not Strafford, was on trial, and the law took no cognizance of wrongs done to the state by the head of state.

The peers intended to act as judges, not as politicians who feared and detested the Earl. Time was pressing; at court a plot was under way to use the nondescript army for a coup d'état. The commons therefore dropped the impeachment and substituted a bill of attainder, which was in effect a joint resolution of both Houses condemning the accused to death without trial. Such legislative murder had not been perpetrated for almost a century; but news of the army plot alarmed the lords, and the bill went through. The last hurdle was the King. An attainder, unlike an impeachment, required his signature. This could be extorted only by force, and for the first time force was used. The palace was besieged by the mob, howling for the head of the Queen — the foreigner, the papist, the instigator of the army plot. Charles at last gave way, out of fear for his wife, and the next day Strafford died.

His death may have been necessary. But many moderates were disturbed at the revival of attainder and deeply shocked at coercion of the King. They felt revolution in the air, and instinctively they moved closer to the court. Strafford thus left his master a parting gift, the beginnings of a royalist party. As the great pendulum of change swung leftward, this party grew into an army.

Parliament was destroying the institutions as well as the agents of Charles's personal rule. The prerogative courts were abolished, and the tenure of the remaining judges made dependent solely on their good behavior; ship money was outlawed, customs duties brought under parliamentary control, and the ordinary revenue reduced to a shadow; frequent parliaments were made obligatory, and the Crown even lost for a time its power of dissolution without consent of both Houses. These reforms were passed with virtual unanimity; moderates joined with radicals in clipping the wings of secular prerogative once and for all.

The Church was another matter. Here a cleavage developed that did more than any other factor to prepare the way for civil war.

The radicals wished to abolish the whole episcopacy, root and branch, although they were far from clear what should replace it. As their position was expressed by a country member named Oliver Cromwell, they knew what they did not want but not what they did. The policy of root and branch shocked the conservatives. They might dislike the bishops as individuals, but they were defenders of the episcopal office. The Church was a tree of great age. Almost everyone agreed that its branches had recently been bearing poor fruit and needed pruning. But the trunk was sound Elizabethan wood, and the roots went deep — deeper than Henry VIII, than Becket and Lanfranc and St. Augustine. Root and branch was a policy of revolution, of sweeping away the known on the chance that the unknown would be better. Conservatives, much as they wished for reform, were appalled at this prospect of destruction.

Defense of the episcopacy lay with the Crown, and on this issue Charles would not capitulate. The one thing needed to bring waverers to his side was that Parliament should try to assume his legal powers — should advance from coercion to usurpation. England would then be on the road to parliamentary absolutism, a concept more alien to her tradition than the King's personal rule. Yet to the leaders of the commons usurpation soon appeared as the only way to protect everything they held dear, including their own heads. In self-defense they laid hold of an authority not theirs by any stretch of the law.

They were impelled by a military crisis in Ireland. The resentment that Strafford had been sent to suppress broke into flame on his removal, and by the autumn of 1641 the end of British authority seemed in sight. To Englishmen, whose contempt for the Irish was tinged with bigotry and fear, this challenge called for immediate action. Troops were needed, but who would command them? The King had the right, in law and practice, to appoint their officers. If he were voted the money and allowed to organize the army, however, it was more likely to be used against the English than the Irish. Either Parliament would control the military, or the military would destroy Parliament. The commons demanded control, and the demand was as necessary as it was illegal.

Charles countered with illegality of his own. In January 1642 he invaded the House with an armed band to seize five leaders of the opposition. He thus violated a basic privilege of the commons, the freedom of members from arrest; here was the long-dreaded coup d'état. It failed ignominiously because the men had escaped, but it showed that the King had no more scruples than his enemies about the use of violence. A committee of the commons took refuge in the city, which called out its trained bands for their defense; a week later Charles fled to the country. The weapons of legal process had broken, and only the sword remained.

During the following months a majority of the peers and a minority of the commons withdrew from Parliament to join the King. Most of those who went and those who stayed were moderates, for whom the coming war was a calamity. They all had a common aim — to rebuild the old constitution and define a sphere for both the Crown and Parliament. The quarrel at this stage was about the definition, not the principle, of limited monarchy, but the principle itself was jeopardized once fighting started. If the King won, monarchy would scarcely be limited; if the commons won, it would be reduced to impotence. This dilemma bred the half-heartedness reflected in the early campaigns. The combatants lacked the will to total victory.

Half-heartedness does not imply that the differences at issue were minor. They derived, on the contrary, from a divergence so fundamental that it endured through many transmutations into the nineteenth century. The essence of the first Civil War was not a dispute over methods or men, but a conflict of two instinctive attitudes toward government. From those attitudes grew the later political parties, Whig and Tory, Liberal and Conservative, which fought each other down the years. The questions at issue in any period were symptoms; below them was the clash of instincts that had drawn blood in the days of King Charles.

Party labels had not been invented in the 1640's, and the period is confused with names. Among them Puritan predominates, but the Puritans were not the only revolutionaries. The supporters of parliament, known generically as Roundheads, ranged from episcopalians to Christian communists, although a majority was tinged with some form of Puritanism. Among the royalists the most numerous group was the Anglican Cavaliers; by their side fought Roman and Laudian Catholics, and Puritans who loved the Crown more than they hated bishops. Then where is the conflict of instinctive attitudes? In the two most numerous groups, where it can be shown only by hypothecating, for contrast, two men who did not exist — the typical Puritan and the typical Cavalier.

The Puritan was a rebel against traditional authority. In religion he substituted for apostolic tradition the voice of his own conscience; "he would have me believe him," as John Selden put it, "before a whole church that has read the word of God as well as he." That word, for him, was not primarily love but righteousness; his God was the God of Sinai more than of Calvary, and he went to war with the psalms for battle-hymns. "I will smite down his foes before his face, and plague them that hate him." His grim earnestness cut him off from ordinary men, and they often disliked him cordially — above all when he had an official position. The complaint of some villagers about their policeman had its echoes all over England: he was accused of "arrogating to himself a singularity of sanctity." [5]

The same earnest individualism colored the Puritan's politics. In principle he was willing to be ruled by the elect, but in practice he was quick to doubt the predestined salvation of any rulers. The doubt was less a matter of belief than of instinct; he distrusted government as such. For this reason his cause found adherents for a time among those who cared little for his religious views. The tenant whose cattle had gone for his landlord's ship money, the disgruntled clothier, the sheriff bullied by the privy council, the countryman who had lost his tobacco — such men, for secular reasons, shared the Puritan's resentment of royal interference and identified the cause of Parliament with their desire to be let alone. Puritanism and localism both drew their power, in different ways, from the self-importance of the individual, and at the outset both contributed to the great rebellion.

The self-importance of the Cavalier was as robust as that of his opponents. Its source, however, was the corporate strength of the community — a community that was not a thing of the moment but went back into the immemorial past. The institutions that embodied it for him were those with the prescriptive sanction of time. Among them two were paramount, the Church and the Crown. His abiding loyalty to both was untouched by his dislike of Laud and his annoyance with Charles. Prelates and kings came and went; prelacy and

---

[5] From manuscript testimony, *ca.* 1613, in the Public Record Office (London): St. Ch. 8/239/3.

kingship represented the continuity of the nation's past and present. In the authority exercised by those institutions he saw the cohesive force without which the nation dissolves.

He was acclimated to paternalism. In most cases he came from the gentry, a class that still dominated the communal life of the countryside, and he still thought in terms not far removed from the feudal. He was trained to social and political responsibility for the welfare of those below him, and he instinctively accepted the king's responsibility for the welfare of all. However much he might resent particular activities of the Crown, he did not, like the Puritan, distrust government in itself. Respect for the powers that be was the foundation on which his own power rested.

He had on his side the force of old loyalties. The country folk, for the most part, were indifferent to the theoretical claims of king and commons; their habit of obedience was ingrained, and the name of majesty was still one to conjure with. Their religion was not Puritanical but that of an earlier age, consonant both with superstition and with boisterous revels after Sunday service. The time was drawing to an end, as the ballad-maker realized,

> When Tom came home from labor,
> Or Ciss to milking rose,
> Then merrily went their tabor,
> And nimbly went their toes.[6]

But the end was not yet. Until it came, the Cavalier — with his sociability, his exuberance in living, his sense of authority — could touch the hearts of the common people as the Puritan never could. If the cause of Parliament drew on new forces, that of the King drew on the strength of Tudor England.

The Civil War was thus a struggle between two attitudes of mind. The Roundheads, who were largely Puritans, fought against the ubiquitous power of the Crown, whether exercised in religious, political, or economic terms; they agreed in emphasizing the freedom of the individual as against the prerogative, although they were not agreed on how much freedom to allow in a government dominated by themselves. The royalists, who were preponderantly Cavaliers, supported the Crown because they believed that prescriptive authority was the only protection from chaos. The issue was funda-

---

[6] *Percy's Reliques,* II, 320.

mental. On the one hand was the principle of freedom, which contained the seeds of anarchy; on the other hand was the principle of order, which contained the seeds of absolutism. Either side, in triumphing, would endanger the objects for which it fought.

Inevitably, therefore, the fighting was done by minorities. The bulk of the population remained aloof, out of either apathy or bafflement. "The people," said a discouraged Puritan leader, "care not what government they live under, so as they may plough and go to market." [7] They waited to have the outcome determined for them. They might not acquiesce in the verdict of arms, but they would resist, if at all, by their traditional method of passivity.

The Roundheads suffered at the beginning from serious handicaps. Officers and privates alike were civilians, unaccustomed to the requirements of army life, and Puritans were peculiarly difficult to discipline. "Our soldiers generally manifested their dislike to our lieutenant-colonel, who is a Goddam blade and doubtless hatched in hell; and we all desire that either the parliament would depose him, or God convert him, or the devil fetch him away quick." [8]

The King's officers had at least the habit of command, and the countryman turned foot soldier had the habit of obedience. The royalist cavalry was a terrifying force; the Cavalier squire, unlike the Roundhead burgess, had been virtually born to the saddle, and the King's young nephew, Prince Rupert, was a dashing commander of horse. But these tactical advantages could not be exploited because of other factors.

Royalist strength was drawn primarily from the north and west. These areas were not only far behind the south and east in social development; they were also poor. The wealth of London was the mainspring of rebellion, and the capture of London would mean victory for the King. But he lacked the wherewithal. He had not the money to hold his armies together for a long campaign, and the enthusiasm of his soldiers waned as they got farther from their native counties. After 1643, when his offensive against the capital bogged down, the initiative passed to his enemies.

By 1644 a dynamic factor was emerging among the Roundhead

---

[7] Quoted by Keith Eiling: *A History of the Tory Party, 1640–1714* (Oxford, 1924), p. 84, n. 1.

[8] Quoted by C. H. Firth: *Cromwell's Army: a History of the English Soldier during the Civil Wars, the Commonwealth and the Protectorate* (London and New York, 1902), p. 280.

forces. In the counties of East Anglia a new kind of army had been taking form under the hand of a local squire, Oliver Cromwell. His soldiers fused religious with military enthusiasm; their faith was so direct that they scorned the shackles of a church, and they were as impatient of Presbyterian rigidity as of Cavalier extravagance. Their discipline, the admiration of professionals, was largely self-enforced. Because of their beliefs they were known as Independents; because of their strength in battle they were known as Ironsides.

The importance of Cromwell rose with that of his army. Like most Roundhead leaders he was a reluctant revolutionary. For all his opposition to the episcopal system he had a gentleman's respect for monarchy; he was no more a democrat than a Laudian. But he saw no alternative to breaking the military power of the King, and he devoted himself to the task with the efficiency of a whole heart. Even though his humor saved him from the dourness so common among Puritans, none of them had a deeper sense of divine guidance. If he was called upon to destroy, he would search his soul and then destroy. The Lord was the designer and he the instrument.

By 1645 the instrument had shown its power. The King's forces were shattered beyond repair, and in the next year the war ended. Cromwell was not yet in titular command of the victors; that position was held — a revealing commentary on the rebellion — by a peer of the realm, Lord Fairfax. But Cromwell had made success possible, and it projected him inevitably into political prominence. He was no Bonaparte, forcing his way from the camp to the council table; like many of his fellow-officers he was an active member of Parliament between campaigns, for the line between generals and politicians had not yet been drawn in this most civilian of revolutions. Four years of campaigning, however, had left their mark on him. He was less patient and more authoritarian than the squire who had gone home from Westminster to raise Cambridgeshire against the King. Triumph in battle was a heady wine for the Puritan commander. It not only brought him prestige and political influence; it also meant that his enemies stood convicted of sin, and that he had been the agent of a judgment by the Lord of Hosts. "Because of those things cometh the wrath of God upon the children of disobedience." [9]

Cromwell and his comrades were flushed with the wine of suc-

---

[9] Ephesians 5. 6.

cess, but the problems before them demanded sobriety. Charles was still King; though he was shorn of power, he was the rallying point for the numerous factions of discontent. The Cavaliers, although their spirit was temporarily broken, were too large a segment of the nation to be ignored, and they would have to be either conciliated or held down by force. The Anglicans who had taken no part in the war would oppose any government that did not allow them the use of the prayer book and the familiar liturgy. The Scots wanted the whole island made safe for Presbyterianism, and they had many supporters south of Tweed. It is far easier, the victors were discovering, to make a revolution than to consolidate it.

The worst problem of the Puritan leaders was to agree among themselves. Their regime rested upon Parliament and the army, and these two were soon drifting apart. The composition of Parliament had greatly changed with the withdrawal of the royalist members: the peers had become negligible, and the Lower House had shrunk in size. The majority of the commons had taken little part in the fighting, and looked askance at the army. Strange religious and political ideas were fermenting there, and the troops cost money; for both reasons the House wished to be quit of its saviors, preferably without giving them their arrears of pay. The soldiers, on the other hand, had no intention of being disbanded; more than pay was at stake.

Presbyterianism dominated the commons. The members did not aim at a Scottish kirk, superior even to the legislature, but at a church run by the state — meaning themselves — on lines that permitted no deviation in doctrine and discipline. Such an establishment would be no more tolerant than Laud's had been, and for the Independents no more tolerable. For them, in Milton's words, "new presbyter is old priest writ large."

The commons reckoned without their host. They had achieved their position by virtue of the army, and the army was predominantly Independent. The soldiers desired a church so decentralized as scarcely to justify the name, with wide room for varieties of Protestant belief and practice; Parliament desired its own Erastian form of kirk. Two principles were at loggerheads, and neither side would give way. In the quarrel the King saw his opportunity. He was still unable to recognize defeat, and the past six years had only heightened his capacity for intrigue; he started negotiating with both sides, hoping that one or the other would restore him to a vestige of power in return for the use of his name. This time he was risking his life.

The common soldiers had little use for his name. Radicals were carrying their ideas of individual freedom from religion to politics: "the poorest he that is in England hath a life to live as the greatest he," and should therefore have a voice in choosing the government.[10] Such notions of democracy were anathema to many of the officers, Cromwell and Fairfax among them, but even their prestige could not reconcile the dissidents among the rank and file to negotiating with the King.

Many Presbyterians, in Scotland and to a lesser extent in England, were more responsive. They had never intended to create a republic, let alone a democracy, and the rise of radicalism scared them. The initiators of a revolution rarely finish it; as the focus shifts to the left, they become alarmed at what they have started and often end as counterrevolutionaries. So with these Presbyterians of 1648. They had achieved their ends only to find their church, their power, and even their property menaced by the radicals. They could keep what they had gained only by defending the monarchy that they themselves had shorn of its strength.

This split within the nucleus of the revolution led to another civil war. On one side were Scots, some English Presbyterians, the King, and a few indomitable Cavaliers; on the other was the army of Independents. Dissension split both camps. Charles had sacrificed one of his few remaining principles by agreeing to the temporary establishment of Presbyterianism in England, and so had alienated the Anglicans. The army leaders, for their part, had become involved most unwillingly; their hand had been forced in part by pressure from the ranks, in part by the King's double dealing. They stood between the devil of Presbyterian intolerance and the deep sea of radicalism in their followers. Their only course was to destroy the devil and then to build dikes against the sea.

The first task was easily accomplished. Their opponents had little military force south of Tweed, and a Scots invasion was crushed in a single battle; the English phase of the war collapsed at once. The victors had then to secure their victory. They did so in a mood quite

---

[10] Quoted by G. M. Trevelyan: *England under the Stuarts* (London and New York, 1928), p. 282.

different from that of two years before; their enemies, in fighting a second time, had defied the judgment of the Almighty. "It is the repetition of the same offense," declared Cromwell, "against all the witnesses that God hath borne." The vanquished must suffer for their contumely, and chief among them the "man of blood," Charles Stuart. But only Parliament could claim the authority to judge him, and instead it reopened negotiations with him. In December 1648, therefore, the Independents took a fateful step: soldiers unseated the Presbyterian members of the Commons. This was more than punishment of a faction, more even than preparation for attacking the King. It marked the emergence of the sword as the final political argument.

Worse was to come. The purge left a small group in the Lower House, known to history as the Rump — either because it was the last fragment of the remainder of the Long Parliament, or because it was the part which still sat. Its members were for the moment the tool of their creator, the army, and they moved rapidly to implement its will. They abolished the House of Lords and brought the King to trial for his life. The disappearance of the peers left only a ripple in the surge of revolution, but the Crown was another matter. Shakespeare, in this, had spoken for an England that still endured.

> Not all the waters of the rough rude sea
> Can wash the balm from an anointed king;
> The breath of worldly men cannot depose
> The deputy elected by the Lord.[11]

Charles had done little to win the love of his subjects. He had misused his power, squandered his prestige, abandoned his friends and even his Church. The bulk of the people might have accepted a drastic curtailment of his authority; but to them he was still the Lord's deputy, and killing him was sin. This feeling was so widespread that it extended even to many members of the court that the Rump created to try him, and the death sentence was pushed through with difficulty. Charles himself was superb. The darker his fortunes became, the more they revealed his courage and dignity. He refused to acknowledge the jurisdiction of the court, and appealed from it to the judgment of the world. His greatest moment came in his speech from the scaffold: "For the people, truly I desire

---

[11] *Richard II*, III, ii, 54–7.

their liberty and freedom as much as anybody whatsoever. But . . . their liberty and freedom consists in having government, those laws by which their lives and goods may be most their own. It is not their having a share in the government; that is nothing appertaining to them. A subject and a sovereign are clear different things."

The Cavalier feeling for sovereignty could not have been better put. Charles took his final stand not on prerogative but on the basic need for authority. The new democratic premise would make every subject a sovereign, and so would negate authority itself by producing a state of anarchy in which the rights of the individual would lose all meaning; "liberty and freedom consists in having government." This was the argument on which the King rested his defense, and at the time it was unanswerable. His enemies, soon after they had taken his life, were forced to appropriate his logic.

VI "Sword Government"

BY the King's execution the Independents crossed the Rubicon. Thereafter they had to go ahead because they had nowhere else to go; a regicide who falters or turns back pays with his head. Their road was appallingly difficult. They had to deal with the Scots and the still-rebellious Irish, regain colonial allegiance, and establish respect for themselves in Europe. This part of their task was not for the faint-hearted; it required force directed by a single, unrelenting will — required the army, the navy, and Cromwell. That new constitutional trinity achieved its purpose.

But much more was needed. A government for Great Britain, although it could be improvised by soldiers, could not rest permanently on them. It had to be made acceptable to the governed, and for that purpose force and will were insufficient; they might command respect, but not consent. The Puritan regime was coercive at its core, and for that reason it could not win consent. At the first sign that its strength was failing, the country would shake it off. This was Cromwell's greatest problem, and it was insoluble. The transience of his government was predetermined by the way it had come to power.

The steps by which the regime advanced to its fall are far less significant than the ways in which it used its force during the brief decade of its prime. Those ways left their mark on British history, for better or worse, long after the Ironsides were forgotten, for in that decade Britain began to assume her position as a great power. Cromwell's chief claim to her remembrance is not as her one republican ruler but as her first great imperialist.

The government of the Commonwealth, established after Charles's death, was confronted by the necessity of pacifying the British Isles. The most immediate problem was Ireland, where Protestants and Catholics had been momentarily united by a common horror of regicide. The task of dealing with them devolved upon Cromwell, who was now the pivot of the regime; his only competitor, Fairfax, had been brushed aside as too conservative. The course that Cromwell took in Ireland made Elizabethan and Jacobean policy seem like kindness itself. In the streets of Drogheda his veterans put the defenders to the sword without discrimination or pity, and soon the whole island learned the terror of these new Israelites. The grim work continued for several years, and "the curse of Cromwell" took hold of the Irish soul.

The settlement was equally ruthless. The government rejected the policy of plantation for a more drastic method. Irish landholders who could prove their loyalty were to be moved to the western province of Connaught; those who could not were to be dispossessed in favor of Englishmen. This grim design of "hell or Connaught" was modified because the bulk of the population refused to move and could not be exterminated. But in two-thirds of the island almost all the old landholding class was dispossessed, and its place taken by English adventurers and soldiers. The latter seldom kept for long what they had acquired so easily; if they were not murdered by their tenants, they were bought out by their officers or by speculators. The result, in the long run, was the creation of numerous large estates held by Englishmen and Scots who were divorced from the land, and whose chief interest in the peasantry was as a source of rents. Thus the curse of Cromwell developed into the more insidious curse of eighteenth-century Ireland, the absentee landlord.

The pacification of Scotland was in the same forceful terms, although the settlement was very different. The Scots rejected the judgment of the second Civil War, and in 1650 they proclaimed Charles's son as Charles II, their Presbyterian king. Cromwell struck them fast and hard. At Dunbar he confronted their army, the cream of Calvinist orthodoxy; the Kirk had weeded out the ungodly and left only some four thousand "sanctified creatures who hardly ever saw or heard of any sword but that of the spirit." [12] Yet these saints should have been victorious on military as well as theological grounds; instead they were overwhelmingly defeated. In 1651 the Scots took heart again and invaded England; their army was annihilated at Worcester. Cromwell had extinguished the royalist cause for his lifetime, and in the process he had dealt a lethal blow to the power of the Kirk. Dunbar and Worcester were a sign for Scotland, as the defeat of the Armada had been for Spain, that the God of Battles had withdrawn His support. To the practical Scot such desertion suggested that presbyters might not be the unique instrument of deity. He remembered and mused upon the warning which had come from Cromwell before Dunbar: "I beseech you in the bowels of Christ, think it possible that you may be mistaken."

The settlement of Scotland was wholly unlike that of Ireland. The Scots were no Canaanites to be exterminated, but erring brothers to be brought firmly back to the fold. The country was soon incorporated with England and Wales into a single state. The Scots received generous parliamentary representation, free trade with England, a good judicial system, and a limited freedom of worship; they thus had a new world forced upon them at sword's point, and for six years they were compelled to experience the benefits of collaborating with England. Those benefits were remembered half a century later, but at the time they were hated because they were imposed. No system dictated by a foreigner, whether Charles or Cromwell, could be acceptable north of Tweed.

Although force did not win consent, it achieved much. Ireland was pacified and shackled to England for more than two centuries to come; Scotland was driven into co-operation. Simultaneously the colonial empire was reduced to obedience, and Europe was taught respect for the regicide government. This was the work of the navy, which for the first time emerged as a major instrument of policy. The Elizabethans had learned to fight at sea, but they had not had the rudiments of an offensive fleet. The Puritans created one and demonstrated its uses. This achievement, far more than their victories on land, made their regime a milestone on the British road to power.

---

[12] Quoted by A. F. Pollard: *Factors in Modern History* (New York, 1907), p. 199.

The materials for a navy had been provided by Charles during his personal rule. He had spent considerable ship money on ships, but not on their crews. The men had consequently presented the fleet to Parliament, and it had played an important if inconspicuous role in the King's downfall. By the end of the wars the Commonwealth found itself with one of the finest navies in Europe, and promptly took measures to improve it further. The result was a fighting force such as the British had not seen before and were not to see again for generations.

The republicans learned the uses of sea power by necessity. At the end of the second Civil War Prince Rupert took to the ocean to prey on commerce, and the Channel and Scilly Islands became nests of royalist privateers; these ships without a country were pirates in the eyes of the government, but the other maritime powers were tempted to treat them as the last representatives of legitimacy. In America the colonists were inclined to use the King's death as an excuse for asserting their autonomy. The Commonwealth used its fleet to good purpose. Robert Blake, who had behind him a brilliant record as an army commander, chased Rupert to the Tagus and into the Mediterranean; Portugal, Spain, and France began at once to doubt the propriety of harboring commerce-raiders. Another squadron crossed the Atlantic; Barbados promptly returned to its allegiance, and the appearance of two ships off the Virginia coast brought that colony to heel. "The strong arm of England," as Palmerston called it two centuries later, was felt for the first time in areas far from her home waters.

Her immediate naval concern, however, was still with the narrow seas. Cromwell hoped to win the allegiance of the merchant classes by furthering British prosperity according to the precepts of mercantilism. The total of world trade was considered as a fixed quantity, so that one nation could increase its own share only at the cost of its rivals. This eventually meant war. The first stage in the struggle, for an ambitious power, was to monopolize its own carrying trade, in order to impoverish its competitors and build up the merchant marine from which its navy was manned. The second stage was naked force, used to destroy enemy fleets, cripple enemy commerce, and seize the colonies that fed commerce. Prosperity through trade was the end, according to this view, and war the principal means.

The Tudors and Stuarts had long labored over the first stage, to increase the nation's trade. But they had not had the strength for the second because the navy had been at best defensive. The Puritans had a fleet capable of assuming and sustaining the attack, and they were quick to use it. They inaugurated a series of wars that lasted for more than a century and a half, and extended British power into the farthest reaches of the world.

Mercantilism was no respecter of religious or political sympathies. The Navigation Act of 1651, which confined English imports to the ships of England, her colonies, or the country of origin, was aimed primarily at the Dutch Netherlands. The Elizabethan tie with the Dutch and the fact that they were now republicans and the leading Protestant power of the Continent were nothing, in the eyes of Parliament, beside the fact that they were the carriers of Europe. The act gave them the alternatives of surrendering a part of their trade or of fighting for it, and they chose to fight. The war was brief, fierce, and decisive. The Dutch began it with an unsurpassed fleet and merchant marine; twenty-two months later they sued for peace on Cromwell's terms. The tide of their power had turned, although the ebb was not fully apparent until after another generation and two more wars with England.

The triumph of the Commonwealth was not due primarily to its seamen. Blake was one of the great admirals of history, and he was ably seconded by another soldier, George Monk; but the two met their equals in Tromp and de Ruyter. The principal weakness of the Netherlands was her strategic position. To guard her land frontiers she required an army that diverted resources from the fleet; to reach the Atlantic her trade had to run the British gantlet, whereas she could not effectively blockade British trade. The war thus revealed the two basic factors at the root of British sea power, the freedom to concentrate on naval force and the favorable position of the home islands.

Victory left Cromwell's government, eager for prestige and profit, with a fleet that was an almost irresistible incentive to aggression. The victim selected was Spain, who had by now grown weak enough to be tempting. In 1655 an expedition to the Spanish West Indies captured Jamaica, and the British obtained their first major foothold in the central Caribbean. At the same time their fleets were patrolling the Mediterranean, where they had a gratifying effect on the policy of neutrals and the arrogance of the Barbary pirates. In these two respects the Spanish War, minor in itself, presaged momentous developments. On the one hand it began the long struggle for control of the Caribbean, first against Spain and then against France, a struggle that grew until it became the focus of imperial rivalries. On the other hand the war demonstrated the importance of dominating Mediterranean waters, and so was a prelude to the later extension of British power from Gibraltar eastward to Alexandria.

The Cromwellian use of the fleet, in summary, evolved through three successive stages. The first was an extension of the victory won on land — the elimination of royalism on the seas and in the colonies. The second was the offensive against the Dutch, waged for geographical reasons in home waters. The third was the assault on the Spanish empire, during which the focus shifted to distant oceans. In the Channel and North Sea, the Mediterranean, the Caribbean, Cromwell's sailors began constructing the edifice of modern British power.

His soldiers, on the other hand, constructed only a jerry-built edifice. It was imposing at first sight, but it rested on the sands of coercion. Only in Ireland, where the sands had been packed down by long usage, did parts of it survive for centuries. In Scotland the building scarcely outlasted the builder, and a later generation had to reconstruct it on another foundation. In England the fabric had its crucial test; if the English part had been solidly fashioned, the rest might have stood. Instead the whole structure collapsed as soon as Cromwell was out of the way.

He became a dictator in spite of himself. "That you have by force," he had said in 1647, "I look upon it as nothing. I do not know that force is to be used except we cannot get what is for the good of the kingdom without force." The exception is revealing. In what did the good of the kingdom consist? Subsequent events showed that it did not, for the revolutionaries, consist in a king, who was defeated and beheaded; nor in an established church, which was abolished; nor in the dualism of lords and commons, since the Upper House was eliminated and the Lower House purged by the army. It consisted in a republic, arrived at by consulting only those few who wielded power. Cromwell was almost as often the agent as the master of that small group, but he personified its will. That will determined what was or was not for the good of the governed, whose role was obedience. The revolution thus came full circle. It began as a movement against the narrow authoritarianism of the King; it culminated in an authoritarianism equally narrow, sanctioned by the sword instead of by prescription. For Cromwell in practice, as for Charles in practice and theory, "a subject and a sovereign are clear different things."

The inevitable result, for one man as for the other, was the isolation of his regime. Cromwell's power rested initially upon the Independents, but even this minority was soon torn by dissension. On the extreme left were the Diggers, who wished to substitute for the old social order an agrarian and Christian form of communism. Less radical but more dangerous were the Levellers, or democrats, who demanded government by the people instead of usurpation by the military. The Diggers were suppressed with little trouble; their ideas outraged the social instincts of the squirearchy, and monarchists for once saw eye to eye with republicans. The Levellers were a more thorny problem.

The logic of Independency, indeed of the whole Puritan movement, pointed to some form of democracy. In an age when religion and politics were still fused, the view that authority in a church derived from the individual suggested the same view about the state. This popularism was consonant with dictatorship, theocratic or Erastian, only if the dictatorial power were deputed to Kirk or Commonwealth by the governed. That condition could not be satisfied in practice; a free election would have destroyed the Cromwellian regime. Many of the original Independents, whose thinking was untrammeled by the responsibilities of office, were eager to implement their democratic theories and impatient of military control. "We were ruled before by king, lords, and commons," they said, "now by a general, court martial, and commons, and we pray you what is the difference?" [13] Such questions stripped the cloak of legality from the soldier's armor.

These Levellers had one outstanding spokesman. "Freeborn John" Lilburne was the embodiment of Puritan dissent, a man who opposed whatever government tried to rule him. He had suffered for defying the King's prerogative, but he was no more ready for that reason to accept Cromwell in place of Charles. In 1649 and 1653 he

---

[13] Quoted by Gooch: *History of Democratic Ideas,* p. 198.

was brought to trial for challenging the rule of the military; in both cases he was more than a match for his antagonists, and was acquitted in the face of law and evidence. He became the hero of the hour — not because his notion of democracy was understood by the people, but because he expressed a defiance they dared not imitate.

The army itself had been penetrated by the Levellers' propaganda. Pressure from the ranks for a new Parliament, democratically elected, became difficult for even Cromwell to withstand, and the attitude of the Rump increased his difficulty. Its members were a self-important lot, fond of power, loath to relinquish it, and distrustful of the military. They refused to have an election forced on them, and took up the alternative of perpetuating themselves by co-option. At that point Cromwell's patience snapped. Backed by a squad of soldiers, he first berated and then dissolved the Rump.

This coup d'état, in the spring of 1653, ended the Commonwealth. The Protectorate that followed was based on the first and only written constitution in British history, the Instrument of Government. It was drawn up by the army officers; it contained the act of union with Scotland, and provided for a Lord Protector, a permanent council, and occasional parliaments. But by now any legislature was sure to conflict with the executive. The first Parliament that Cromwell called as Lord Protector quarreled with him over control of the army, and he dissolved it.

The year that followed revealed the true foundation of the regime. The island was divided into military districts, in which order was maintained and taxes were collected by the troops. The slow evolution of a civilian society had given place to military dictatorship. In the long run this experience confirmed and perpetuated the British aversion to a standing army; in the short run it completed the ruin of the Protectorate. The traditional governing class, still influential in town and country, was as much opposed to the idea of centralization as it had been under the King, and Oliver's soldiers were more detested, because more efficient than Charles's messengers. The forces of localism had aided the Puritan cause; now they were turned against it. When Cromwell called another Parliament, it contained so many plotting malcontents that at the beginning of 1658 he was forced to another dissolution. Once more government rested on his influence over the army.

In September his death ushered in confusion. His son, who suc-

ceeded him, had the wits to recognize his own incompetence; he resigned, and the passing of "Tumbledown Dick" went almost unre-
garded in the mounting anarchy. The army officers quarreled among
themselves until at last George Monk, who had returned from sea to
command in Scotland, decided that the time had come "to see my
country freed from that intolerable slavery of a sword government."
He marched on London, reinstated the Rump, added the members
expelled in 1648, and then persuaded this ghost of the Long Parliament to dissolve itself. For the first time since 1640 a virtually free
election was held, and the result was foreordained. Soon after the
new Parliament met, King Charles II was publicly proclaimed.
Three weeks later he entered London.

The Restoration, unlike the revolution it ended, was not achieved
by force. The army had disintegrated, and the revolution with it;
Britain was faced with the alternatives of monarchy or chaos, and
the first had to be arranged hastily before the second supervened.
Haste precluded any attempt at a thorough, final settlement of the
questions raised in the past two decades. Charles was asked, and
agreed, to return on the basis of an amnesty to rebels and "a liberty
to tender consciences" in matters of religion; but the definition of
these terms — on which everything depended — was left to a future
parliament. At the moment of the Restoration the needs of the moment made a settlement impossible.

Only one phase of the revolution ended when Charles stepped
ashore, the phase that had begun in 1629 with government by prerogative and had led through civil war to government by force. During that phase ideas had come to the fore about almost every aspect
of religion, society, and government. Some, such as Laud's concept
of the church or the Diggers' views of common land, were never
tried again. Others, such as divine right, endured for generations to
come. Still others, such as the Levellers' notions of democracy or
the Independents' theories of religious freedom, burrowed under the
years and came to light in the nineteenth century. In one sense the
revolution never ended: the subsequent history of the British people, at home and overseas, has been a running commentary upon
the questions it raised.

Certain major points, however, had been settled by 1660, and
their settlement determined the future growth of the constitution,
of the Church, and of Britain's military power. Government by the

King alone had proved unworkable, and no monarch in his senses would repeat the experiment unless he could find some alternative to a parliamentary income. Government by Parliament alone had proved even more disastrous; once the Church and monarchy had been destroyed, lords and commons had soon vanished in their turn. The basic constitutional problem had been defined but not resolved. Government would have to be by the Crown in Parliament; although the two could no longer be a fused power, as in the days of the Tudors, each was patently indispensable. The remaining task was to work out a relationship between them that would change peacefully with changing conditions.

In the Church the revolution had shattered the principle of uniformity. Elizabeth's broad establishment had given place first to a narrow Laudianism and then to an equally narrow Presbyterianism; the presbyters had been succeeded by the Independents, with a theory of tolerance that broke down in practice. Their fall did not mean a return to the old system or a new age of toleration, but a struggle between embittered factions. That struggle the Anglicans were sure to win temporarily, because the forces of reaction fought for them; their Church was identified with the returning dynasty. But their victory would not recreate a national communion. The Puritans, whether Presbyterian or Independent, had had their day of power and had grown in numbers and confidence; they could be persecuted, but not driven back into the Anglican fold. The Church of England could never again be the church of all England, and it could purport to be so only at its peril – the peril of obdurate men, watching and waiting for the day when the Lord would once more deliver His saints. "I will bring my people again, as I did from Bashan; mine own will I bring again, as I did sometime from the deep of the sea." [14]

In the field of power the Puritans had made one of their most lasting contributions. Their army had a negative but important effect: it drove into the marrow of the British bone an antipathy to "sword government." As a result public opinion became consistently opposed to a large professional army, and at the beginning of each major war Britain has had to improvise a military machine. Improvisation has contributed to a series of disasters, from Klosterzeven to Dunkirk; it has also contributed incalculably to the growth of free-

---

[14] Psalm 68. 22.

dom at home. If James II, or even George III, had had at his disposal a large force of professionals, divorced from the population and trained to obey rather than think, the course of British history might have been diverted. But the work of Monk never needed to be done again. The nation reverted permanently to its old tradition, of a government that had to depend on consent because it lacked force.

The Puritan fleet was force of another kind. It could not, in its nature, overawe the landlubbing bulk of the population; it could and did excite their self-importance by coercing the foreigner. The maritime wars of the Commonwealth and Protectorate, unpopular as they were at times, established a new and popular concept of naval power. The empire was held together and expanded at the cost of Spain; British mercantilists saw gains to themselves in the losses of the Dutch; the Mediterranean and the Caribbean appeared as foci of future interest. The Puritans, in short, made the army an object of distrust for centuries to come, and thereby ensured the pre-eminence of the navy; at the same time they transformed the latter into an effective, professional force and demonstrated how to use it offensively. In these ways, intended and unintended, Cromwell and his fellows set an enduring pattern for the future.

Chapter Three

THE TRIUMPH OF THE OLIGARCHY

1660–1763

I   The Merry Monarch

THE RESTORATION brought Great Britain into touch with a
new world. Old problems and factions remained, but the key
figures at court were of a different stamp from the Puritans and Cavaliers. Exile, like war, leaves its mark. The returning émigrés had
endured a decade of poverty and ostracism, of stillborn plots and
hopes, and they brought back with them a craving for the fleshpots
of security. Their public and private morals had been impaired as
gravely as their fortunes. They had acquired instead a polished
scepticism and an awareness of Europe.

The most patent aspect of this cosmopolitanism was their admiration for Versailles. France was becoming the capital of European
manners and letters and the hub of European statecraft. The great
cardinals, Richelieu and Mazarin, had paved the way for the reign
of Louis XIV; when Mazarin died in 1661, Louis assumed control of
the best-integrated absolutism on the Continent. Spain had played
out her part, Austria and the Germanies were bled white by the
Thirty Years' War; France of the Sun King — ordered, sophisticated,
unified — was the dominant political fact of the west, and she cast
her spell over the English exiles. Her monarchy not only embodied,
with splendid trappings, the principle of prescriptive authority so
dear to their hearts; it also had a particular attraction for men who
had abandoned their country for the sake of their king. On their
loyalty to him they had staked everything, and his loyalties inevitably colored theirs.

Charles was half French in blood and first cousin to Louis. His mother, Henrietta Maria, had helped to make him more than half French in his way of thought and a Roman Catholic by secret inclination; he always admired the state that Louis personified and the church that he championed. Charles shared his cousin's taste for the pleasures of kingship but not for its hard work; he detested business. Partly because of his Gallic wit and his sense of humor, partly because his tenure of the British throne was insecure, he did not grow inflated with Louis' majestic self-importance. Although he made sporadic efforts to refashion his government on French absolutist lines, his one overriding purpose was to preserve his crown and enjoy it.

This "tall man, above two yards high," as the Puritans had described him during the man-hunt after Worcester, was as much a stranger to the British as his father had been. There the resemblance ends. Charles II had what his father and grandfather lacked, a superb political mind, although it was usually veiled by an indolence that his opponents were likely to mistake for incompetence. His private life was notorious, and his diplomacy sometimes bordered on the treasonable. But he retained his grip on power for a quarter of a century because, when he exerted himself, he was a match for the shrewdest politicians in Britain and Europe.

The problems confronting him on his return required a skillful and subtle hand. The acts of the Long Parliament that his father had signed — those passed before the breach of 1641 — were acknowledged as binding, and the acknowledgment stripped from the Crown much of its former prerogative. Its ordinary revenue was stabilized, at long last, by an agreement resembling the Great Contract of fifty years before: the King surrendered his feudal dues in return for a fixed grant, impressive on paper but actually insufficient for the routine needs of government. Charles remained financially dependent on the commons, and they soon developed techniques of scrutinizing his expenditure. They were groping half-consciously for control of the executive, but it eluded their grasp.

Much of the initiative in making policy, and the entire administration of it, remained perforce with the King. Until the commons developed an executive instrument to carry out their will, they could only block measures proposed by the Crown and occasionally force on it measures of their own. The principle of their supremacy, largely established by the revolution, had not been embodied in administrative practice. Without the routine of practice and the customary law that ripens out of it the principle itself was insecure. It could be reasserted against an aggressive king only by force, the antithesis of legal process.

For this reason the equilibrium of Restoration politics was inherently delicate. It could not be maintained unless Parliament and the sovereign treated each other with phenomenal tact, compromising difficulties and curtailing demands for the sake of stable government. In the early days such forbearance seemed possible. Many men shared the optimism of Lord Clarendon, the conservative Cavalier who was the King's chief minister, when he urged the members of Parliament to restore the country "to its old good manners, its old good humor, and its old good nature — good nature, a virtue so peculiar to you that it can be translated into no other language, and hardly practiced by any other people." [1]

The hope of this restoration was illusory. New issues added fuel to old hatreds, until good nature was consumed in the blaze. The unanimity with which the nation had welcomed its returning King soon gave place to the strife of factions, in which Charles could scarcely remain neutral. Inevitably some factions grouped themselves about him while others drew together in opposition, and out of this grouping developed two political parties. If the court party controlled a majority in the House of Commons, the constitutional problem of the relation between King and Parliament might remain in abeyance. But if the opposition gained control, or if the court lost the backing of its party, that problem would become the stuff of revolution.

During the 1660's no such danger was evident. The focus of politics was the religious question; the first election of the new reign had produced a legislature more intolerantly Anglican than Charles or Clarendon, and this Cavalier Parliament endured for eighteen years. Its members were determined to establish the predominance of the Church of England beyond future questioning, and they were ready, for all their loyalty, to force their program on a reluctant King. They did so in the legislation known collectively, if unfairly, as the Clarendon Code. It virtually denied to the Puritans the right to preach or teach, to hold municipal office, or to worship

---

[1] Quoted by Feiling: *History of the Tory Party*, p. 69.

by any but Anglican forms; if the outsiders were not forced back into a national communion, Parliament calculated, they would be condemned to political insignificance. Many men, Presbyterians and Independents alike, refused to be forced and paid the price in civil liberties. This minority came to be known as the dissenters. They were far from insignificant, and they were potential allies for anyone who opposed the regime. In cutting the church to its own narrow cloth the House of Commons laid up trouble for generations to come.

The dissenters were not the only ostracized minority. The recusants still survived, and they took hope from the return of the Stuarts at a moment when France was in the ascendant. Charles was not hostile to their faith, and his brother James, the heir presumptive, made no secret of his leaning toward it. The situation resembled in some ways that of a century before: Louis, like Philip, was the recusants' patron and the most powerful figure in Europe, and the heir to the throne was their co-religionist. If Charles was no Elizabeth, so much the better for their hopes.

By the late 1660's Charles was in fact considering a scheme to establish absolutism with his cousin's assistance. Louis would have to be paid, presumably by subordinating Britain both to Rome and Versailles, but the price deterred Charles less than the chance that his plans might misfire and destroy him. In order to weigh that chance, while he still had time to turn back, he experimented with the temper of his subjects.

Much of the material for his experiments was provided by international developments. In retrospect the cardinal development was the rising power of France, but at the time Charles's subjects were more intent on their feud with the Dutch. Britain and the Netherlands, the two powers that had cause and means to oppose French aggression, were reaching for each other's throats, and their quarrel came close to giving Louis the hegemony of Europe.

The second Anglo-Dutch War broke out in 1665 and lasted for two years. In North America the Dutch lost their settlements on the Delaware and Hudson Rivers, and New Amsterdam became New York; in Britain, however, the war seemed appallingly mismanaged, and Lord Clarendon was impeached and driven into exile. In Europe Louis seized his chance to attack the Spanish Netherlands (substantially modern Belgium), a sensitive point for both the Dutch and the British, and their interest in keeping him out brought them together against their will. He was forced to suspend his aggression until he had settled accounts with the Dutch, and for that purpose he had to break their new accord with Britain.

Here was Charles's opportunity — to experiment with selling British foreign policy in return for domestic power. He asked Louis for enough French money to free him from the leading strings of Parliament, and for French troops whenever the time was ripe to declare himself a Roman Catholic; in return he offered to assist in the destruction of the Netherlands. The cousins came to a secret agreement, and in 1672 they joined forces in the third Dutch War. Charles was playing a subtle game, masked by appearances. He seemed to be merely implementing his subjects' old antagonism against the Netherlands. Until they realized that anti-Dutch was pro-French, and that France was the great danger, they could scarcely suspect that he was betraying them.

Simultaneously Charles tried a bold course in domestic affairs. He had two oppressed minorities to work with, the dissenters and the recusants; much as they disliked each other, they and he had a common antipathy to the church established by Parliament, and he hoped to win their support for a prerogative that would deliver them from statutes. In 1672, by a declaration of indulgence, he suspended the Clarendon Code and the penal laws against Roman Catholics, and established freedom of worship throughout the kingdom. The declaration derived in law from an old claim that the sovereign might halt at will the operation of a statute. "General laws made publicly in Parliament," James I had asserted years before, "may . . . by his authority be mitigated and suspended upon causes only known to him." Charles confined his claim for the moment to the ecclesiastical sphere, but no one could tell how far it might go. If some acts of Parliament were at the mercy of the Crown, what were the limits of prerogative? The King had rubbed the ancient lamp of the constitution and had conjured up a demon.

These two experiments, in foreign and religious policy, were Charles's way of testing the national pulse. If it had remained normal, he would doubtless have gone on toward his coup d'état. Instead he raised such a fever of excitement that he was thrown onto the defensive for years to come. Even the dissenters rejected his indulgence; they rightly suspected a move toward Rome, which they detested even more than their former restrictions. The commons were up in arms. The constitutional issue of their relationship with the Crown was again fused, as in the 1620's, with issues of foreign policy and the Church. Parliament first forced the King to withdraw the declaration, then passed the Test Act, which was aimed at the recusants but struck equally at dissent: no one might hold civil or military office under the Crown unless he was a communicant of the Church of England. The disabilities of the Clarendon Code were thereby extended from local to national government, and the Anglican monopoly of power was completed.

The Test Act and the Code before it were the work of Parliament alone. The King opposed both, for different reasons, and in each case he was overborne. Thenceforth the Crown was only in name the head of a national church. In fact the establishment ceased to be either national or royal, and became the preserve of an Anglican squirearchy entrenched in the House of Commons. The old Cavaliers had fought for a system and a liturgy they loved, and their formula had been James's, "no bishop, no king." The new Cavaliers used the communion service as the shibboleth of a ruling class; their implicit formula became "no bishop, no squire," which for centuries remained an unspoken tenet of the oligarchy. Charles's experiment in toleration served only to strengthen Anglicanism against both dissent and the Crown.

His experiment in foreign policy met as rough a reception. The war was unpopular, and in 1674 Parliament forced the King to make peace; the two decades of Anglo-Dutch hostilities were over. Charles learned his lesson gracefully. He abandoned his earlier ambitions and contented himself with playing off Parliament against Louis as sources of revenue: from the former he asked for subsidies with which to build up Britain's military force, from the latter for subsidies to keep the military idle. The game was risky. The truth of his dealings with Versailles would goad his subjects to fury, and his cousin, if pressed too far, might at any time reveal the truth. But the game was also to Charles's taste because it gave him a measure of precarious independence.

Peace with the Netherlands was a far cry from hostility to France. By 1674 few Englishmen grasped the fact that Britain's security was a function of the Continental balance of power and was menaced by French expansion. During the next fourteen years awareness grew slowly, stimulated by many factors. Louis posed as the champion of Rome; his successes made all Protestants uneasy, whether they were Presbyterian Scots or English Cavaliers. The energies of France were also turning into commercial and imperial expansion, and her navy was growing. British mercantilists began to see in her a greater and more dangerous Netherlands, against whom the only defense might be war. Such factors give increasing weight to the foreign problem.

As the years went by, the question of friendship or war with France became more and more closely interwoven with internal questions, and they all grew more pressing. When they came to a head in 1688, three years after Charles's death, the nation was confronted with a choice between two courses. One involved a great war in Europe and the triumph of the oligarchs over prerogative at home; the other involved the continuance of neutrality at the price of a Roman-Catholic absolutism. Thus the three central themes of Restoration politics, the religious, the constitutional, and the diplomatic, came together and were settled together. This was the end of the process that began with Charles's experiments.

II   Tory and Whig

THE PRIMARY factor in bringing the three themes together was the dynastic problem. The key members of the House of Stuart, their characters, marriages, children or lack of children, were parts of a single question: who would succeed to the Crown, and how would he or she use its powers? On the answer depended in large measure the fate of the Church of England, the outcome of the struggle between Parliament and prerogative, and the role of Britain in Europe.

The dynastic crisis first exploded in 1678, and it can best be understood by an introduction to the Stuart family as it was at that time. Charles had no legitimate children, and refused to divorce his wife in order to produce one; among his bastards none was politically significant except the Duke of Monmouth, a young man who had inherited his father's charm without his brains. The King's legal successor was his brother James, the Duke of York, a declared recusant and married to a Roman Catholic. She had borne him no children, however, and by an earlier marriage he had two Protestant daughters, Mary and Anne. Mary had recently married William of Orange, Stadtholder of the Netherlands, who was the leader of the Protestant cause on the Continent and Louis' most dangerous enemy. William, himself half Stuart on his mother's side, was his wife's first cousin, and he and Mary were the presumptive successors after James.[2]

The nub of the problem was James's recusancy. Charles at least remained a nominal Anglican; James was either more honest or more stupid, depending on the point of view, and his accession carried with it the threat of popery at home and subordination to France abroad. His claim was upheld by the King and by a large group in Parliament, but the opposition was almost as strong and at least as determined.

The Duke's supporters argued that accepting him was a lesser evil than debarring him. He was already in his forties, and in all likelihood his reign would mean only a Roman-Catholic interlude in the dynasty before William and Mary restored it to Protestantism. The opposition argued that a papist king backed by France was too great a menace to countenance even temporarily, and that either the crown must be deprived of its prerogative when James received it or he must be deprived of the crown. Either course would amount to revolution. The defenders of the existing order rallied to the dynasty; they received and accepted the name of Tory, and James's opponents the name of Whig. Thus the issue of a recusant heir, gathering to itself many other issues, completed the split of the political world into the two great parties of modern British history.

The Tory's position owed much to the Cavaliers of a generation before. Monarchy for him was the symbol of social order, and a king's religious vagaries were insignificant beside the value of maintaining the legal succession. The Tory was no friend of the Jesuits

---

[2] In genealogical terms, the problem before the country in 1678 was as follows (immediate contenders for the succession are italicized):

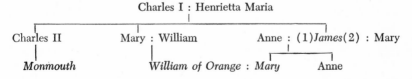

Charles I : Henrietta Maria

Charles II	Mary : William	Anne : (1)*James*(2) : Mary
Monmouth	*William of Orange* : *Mary*	Anne

or the French, but his royalism made him their reluctant apologist; he was forced to argue that a king's relations with his confessor and his cousin were a small price to pay for legitimacy. He was also forced to argue that the hereditary prerogative was indefeasible and immune to the authority of Parliament — in other words to resurrect the ghost of divine right. But he was a conservative, not a reactionary. He had little desire to restore the Crown's old authority, least of all in the church; he knew from experience that it would be used to succor the recusants and dissenters, whom he detested. His position was riddled with dilemmas. He was Anglican to the marrow, yet championed the cause of a Roman-Catholic heir; he had the true-born Englishman's dislike of the French, yet supported a monarchy that had obvious ties with Louis; he emphasized the prerogative, yet tried to lock the church against it.

The Whig position was less paradoxical. It derived much of its premise from the moderate Puritans of 1642 — the distrust of government, particularly royal government, and the emphasis upon the sovereignty of Parliament. Although the Whig was as much an Anglican as the Tory, he was far more tolerant of dissent. Divine right he considered an anachronism, and the legality of the succession concerned him far less than the danger from James's religion and his tie with France. The leading Whigs were beginning to suspect the pattern of Louis' design, and to realize vaguely — but less vaguely than the Tories — that it must be opposed while there was still time. Effective opposition was impossible while either of Louis' cousins was on the throne. Charles might be endured for the few years left to him, but the Whigs gradually concluded that they could not gamble on admitting his brother even conditionally. Parliament, which had beheaded one king and recalled a second, must now debar a third; woe to Charles if he stood in the way.

On whom, then, would the crown devolve? This question put the Whigs in a quandary. They advanced the cause of the Duke of Monmouth, even though the idea of a bastard king outraged the deepest political emotions of the people; the Whig leaders would scarcely have suggested him if the alternative had not been equally unwelcome. If James's daughter Mary was acceptable in herself, her husband was not. Collaborating with the Dutch against Louis was one thing; bringing in a Dutchman as prince consort, let alone as joint sovereign, was quite another. William, though half Stuart, was a foreigner and head of the state with which Britain had fought her three most recent wars, and as a candidate for the throne he would be a liability to the Whigs.

They were under another disadvantage. An attempt to change the succession was sure to be resisted by the King and the Tories to the point of war, and the fear of civil war had been bred into men's thoughts. A crisis would bring the timid, the cautious, and the undecided to the support of the Crown. They had seen what happened when fighting started and would dread repeating the experience; to many of them even a papist on the throne was better than another Cromwell and his major-generals. For several years the Whigs waited while their anxieties grew. Their fear of France was heightened by Louis' continuing war against the Dutch, their fear of Rome by rumors that the Jesuits were at work under the protection of the English court. The cause of Protestantism was under attack from within and without, and British liberties were staked upon it.

In 1678 the Whigs' fear spread suddenly to the people at large, and exploded in the frenzy of the Popish Plot. The plot existed primarily in the mind of an informer named Titus Oates, one of the outstanding liars of history. The "revelations" of his inventive brain convinced the timorous and credulous that the Jesuits intended to burn London, raise the Irish in revolt, murder the King, and impose their faith on Britain with the help of French bayonets. Oates was firing his arrows of suspicion almost at random. But some struck in a dangerous quarter, where the secrets of the court were hidden. James's secretary was found to have been in treasonable correspondence with France, and a magistrate with whom Oates had left his accusations was mysteriously murdered. These developments upset even the level-headed, and touched off a witch-hunt for Jesuits and recusants.

Charles was at last confronted with the results of his devious policy. He had entertained and abandoned a design little different from the Popish Plot, and bolder spirits had carried on when he turned back; reports of their strange doings had prepared the way for an outburst of hysteria. The charges that had actually provoked the outburst were a blend of fancy and distorted fact; they could neither be admitted nor circumstantially denied.

> Some truth there was, but dashed and brewed with lies,
> To please the fools, and puzzle all the wise,

Succeeding times did equal folly call,
Believing nothing, or believing all.[3]

The King and the Whigs were exceptions to Dryden's first statement. Charles was too wise to be puzzled, but he was powerless; he
could only lie low and hope that the storm would blow over without destroying the dynasty. The Whigs were pleased because they
were not fools: truth or lies, here was their opportunity. The Tory
majority in Parliament was aghast at the revelations, and the Whigs
at last had the chance of forcing through their program. Within six
weeks of Oates's bombshell, they brought into debate the question
of exclusion. Simultaneously they got wind of Charles's latest financial dealings with France, and promptly impeached his chief minister. The trial threatened to make the Crown as much the defend-
ant as in Strafford's case, and Charles was at last forced to dissolve
the Cavalier Parliament. The Whigs went to the electorate and were
returned in triumph. They believed that they had a mandate to save
the nation from popery, and if necessary from its King.

Charles was now forced into the open to meet the storm. The
commons were bent on exclusion, but he could determine whether
and when they met. For two years he frustrated them by proroga-
tions and dissolutions, until the Whig extremists were ready to destroy him along with his brother. They reckoned without two factors, Louis and the English squirearchy. The French King preferred
Tory isolationism to the Whigs' suspicious hostility, and he paid for
his preference by giving Charles another secret subsidy. The rural
gentry, appalled at the chaos the Whigs were precipitating, turned
instinctively to the Crown as the source of order. In 1681 Charles,
with the dual backing of French gold and Tory swords, dissolved
Parliament for the last time. The Whigs had overreached themselves in attempting their partisan revolution, and their cause was
shattered for the King's lifetime. It could be revived only if his
brother destroyed the elements of strength out of which Charles had
made his counterrevolution.

The remaining four years of the reign were the last Stuart experiment in personal rule. It rested on a broader base than that of
Charles I; the son had lost the father's instruments of prerogative,
but he had acquired a party. The Tories supported him and his

---

[3] John Dryden: *Absalom and Achitophel.*

brother as their safeguard against anarchy. Although their dislike of recusants was held in leash by their loyalty to James, they were allowed a vicious persecution of Whigs and dissenters. So they persuaded themselves that they were still defending the two great articles of the Cavalier faith, the monarchy and the Church.

This Indian summer of Toryism was ephemeral in its essence. Charles's position depended on French subsidies and the maintenance of neutrality. His supporters, at bottom, were little more friendly to France than the Whigs, and Louis' aggressions on the Continent were making neutrality more and more dangerous; the long era of British isolation was ending. Even the Tories accepted popery only on sufferance. If it became an open threat at home or from France, their allegiance to the throne would waver. Charles's rule, in short, taxed the skill of even that master politician. When he died in 1685, the skill vanished.

III   The Conservative Revolution

CHARLES had once referred to the time when he would leave the crown *"à la sottise de son frère."* The phrase would have shocked the reverential Tories; but it was the judgment of a keen observer, who knew his brother far better than they did. The new King was earnest, methodical, devout; he was also one of the most unintelligent sovereigns in English history. He resembled his Roman-Catholic predecessor, Mary Tudor, in his dogged pursuit of policy regardless of obstacles, and in his blindness to public opinion. But he was living in a far more critical world, in which opposition germinated overnight. Where Mary faced a rebellion and numerous riots during her five years on the throne, James took three years to produce a revolution.

He attempted to establish absolutism and Roman Catholicism — to do what his brother had tentatively tried and abandoned more than a decade before, and to do it without the active support of Louis. The possibility of success was so remote, the risk so obvious, that the attempt seems from a distance like madness. It was in fact merely the work of a stupid man deceived by adulation. When the Tories proclaimed in the press and pulpit the duty of nonresistance, of obedience to the will of God's anointed, James assumed that they meant what they said. By acting on the assumption he forced them

109

to examine it, to weigh their new principle against their loyalty to the state and church that he was attacking. The principle evaporated.

At the start James profited by an assault on municipal liberties that Charles had begun. The method was to coerce the boroughs by rescinding or threatening to rescind their charters, in order to secure docile burgesses in the House of Commons. The result was a packed Parliament, which turned out to be docile only within limits, and for which a price had been paid in the alienation of the local magistracy. From this Parliament James sought and obtained the wherewithal for a standing army.

His pretext was the rebellion of the Duke of Monmouth. That young man had had his head turned by the Whigs, and their fall had not taught him wisdom. His rising was crushed in a single battle; he was executed and his peasant followers proscribed. The King, like Mary before him, was deceived by his triumph into thinking that a loyal people would follow his lead in religion. He retained an army of thirty thousand and attempted to officer it with recusants (in defiance of the Test Act) while his priests converted the men. The attempt made little headway, but the troops encamped on the outskirts of London revived the dark fears of 1641.

The conversion of the government and church proceeded on similar lines. Those who would not change their religion were replaced by those who would; soon the Roman, not the Anglican, eucharist became the real test for office. In the Church a prerogative court was reconstituted in defiance of statute; the Crown, not content with this, reasserted its dispensing power by another declaration of indulgence. James's purpose, like Charles's, was to woo the dissenters, but again they refused to accept toleration in company with recusants. The King could not have undermined his position more effectively.

The Tories were in an impossible dilemma. They had expected James to keep his religion to himself; instead he was perverting the church and defying the law for the sake of popery. They had also expected to enjoy the fruits of office, but when they held to their faith they were dismissed to join the ostracized Whigs. The only consolation was that the King could not live forever, and that his successor was Mary. In June 1688, however, even this solace vanished: James's second wife finally bore him a son. The child took precedence over his half-sisters, and his birth meant that the legitimate Stuart line might continue Roman Catholic forever. The accident of a baby's sex had converted the Tory principle of heredity into a Tory nightmare. To rid the nation of this incubus the party at last joined hands with the Whigs.

Monmouth's death had greatly simplified the problem of replacing James. Mary and her husband were now the only possibility; William was no more popular than he had been, but his wife refused to be considered without him. A few weeks after the birth of the King's son Whig and Tory leaders invited the Prince of Orange to cross from Holland to England, ostensibly to discuss the new situation. Actually his coming meant revolution.

William was no Monmouth. He was a calculating politician, seasoned by crises at home, and for fifteen years he had been building coalitions against the power of France. In the summer of 1688 Louis was organizing a new and greater war of aggression that could only be checked by a new and greater alliance. William was playing for more than a crown. If he replaced James, the weight of Britain would be added for the first time to his Continental alignment against France. His crossing the Channel meant not merely an overturn in domestic British politics, but also a reversal of British foreign policy and a shift in the scales of European power.

The British themselves were at last ready for the reversal. Bourbon absolutism no longer had its admirers except at court. Louis' recent persecution of the French Huguenots, dramatized by the atrocity stories of refugees, waked slumbering memories. Mercantilists were alarmed by French commercial and colonial expansion, and politicians were coming to realize that Louis' ambition to achieve the "natural frontier" of the Rhine touched Britain's interests. These factors made war feasible; the domestic situation made it inevitable. William's coming, which necessitated intervention abroad, was the only way to preserve the church and constitution at home. Louis blundered badly. He might have kept William busy in the Netherlands or intercepted him at sea; instead he did nothing. He hoped that a civil war in England would leave the Dutch leaderless and the British impotent, but he miscalculated his cousin's fiber. James lacked the courage of his earlier days. Once William was ashore and marching on London, the King bolted for France like a scared rabbit. His arrival must have occasioned more surprise than pleas-ure at Versailles, but for the British it settled a number of awkward problems. Even the Tories admitted that a king who had decamped had in effect abdicated. After long argument and some legal leger-demain, William and Mary were recognized by Parliament as joint sovereigns. James and his infant son became pensioners of Louis. The revolution was accomplished, and France acquired the rival who fought her throughout the world until the Battle of Waterloo.

The Glorious Revolution differed from the Puritan in being virtu-ally unanimous. The Whigs and Tories who summoned William dis-liked each other as much as ever, but under the threat of civil dis-integration and foreign danger they dared not continue their old quarrels. The Whigs were forced to forget that the Tories had ar-gued for despotism. The Tories were forced to adopt the Whig can-didates for the throne, and simultaneously to come to terms with dissent. The dissenters had spurned James and supported his over-throw; in return they had been promised toleration by the Whigs and even by leading churchmen, and the Tories were obliged to ac-quiesce in fulfilling the promise. The party lost at one stroke the di-vinity that had hedged its king and its church.

The Glorious Revolution also differed from the Puritan in being carried through by conservatives. The oligarchs wished to retain what they had already won; when the Crown attacked their liber-ties and power, they defended them by changing the wearer of the crown so quickly that no crack appeared in the social crust for the lava of radicalism. They did not wish to change the nature of mon-archy but to conserve what they understood it to be, and the bounds they set upon it were intended to define rather than curtail its scope.

Curtailment, however, was implicit in the act of definition. James had violated the law as his subjects conceived it, by exercising royal powers that they thought had lapsed. Despite all the work of the Roundheads and of the Restoration Cavaliers the prerogative had turned out to be elastic, and had been stretched beyond the nation's endurance. Its boundaries had to be set again, and this time they were set explicitly and permanently. The outstanding act was the Bill of Rights in 1689, but it was supplemented by a series of statutes over the next twelve years. In their entirety they constitute the rev-olutionary settlement, the basis on which the modern British con-stitution has been built.

The settlement, although bipartisan, was a triumph of Whig ideas.

The rights and privileges of Parliament were confirmed, and precautions were taken against royal packing or corruption of the Lower House. The King's power to suspend or dispense with statute was abolished. The consent of Parliament was thenceforth necessary to remove a judge or to maintain a standing army in time of peace. The Tory doctrine of nonresistance was outlawed. The principle was recognized that the descent of the crown depended not upon accidents of heredity but upon the decision of Parliament. Thus the center of power was shifted, once and for all, from the sovereign to the legislature. No king thereafter could defy the will of the commons and retain his throne.

The revolution also stopped, until the nineteenth century, the encroachment of central power upon local autonomy. James's effort to dominate the boroughs had produced much the same reaction as his father's attempted paternalism, and this time the burgesses and their cousins the squires secured a more sweeping victory. The King's dethronement confirmed their power in the localities and vastly strengthened their role at Westminster. In the eighteenth century, when that role became predominant and one class controlled almost the whole of government, localism triumphed over centralization.

On its religious side the revolutionary settlement contained a principle new to the constitution — a declaration of the rights of dissent known as the Toleration Act. This statute was passed in 1689, over Tory opposition, by the combined efforts of the Whigs and King William. It was in part a payment to the dissenters for refusing the blandishments of James. It was also a reflection, within narrow limits, of a fundamental change in the climate of opinion.

The Independents' ideal of toleration had been the hallmark of a minority. The Presbyterians had rejected it as vehemently as the Anglicans, and the Cromwellian regime had been unable to apply it fully; tolerance of intolerance leads only to trouble. The ideal seemed to have been extinguished by the acts of the Cavalier Parliament, but under the surface of politics it was being carried forward by the intellectual current of the times — a current that Cromwell and Milton, Charles I and Laud, would have regarded as diabolic, yet which was forming the modern mind. The Clarendon Code and the Test Act were the expressions of an older way of thought; the Toleration Act was the first harbinger of a new.

The new attitude had diverse causes. One was weariness. In the generation between 1660 and 1689 intolerance had kept the country teetering on the edge of civil war, until temperate men were ready to cry plague on the contentions of Anglicans, recusants, and dissenters. A second cause was the need for unity. Britain could no longer afford domestic turmoil; Protestants of whatever breed had to hang together in the face of France, and wisdom suggested making even the lot of the recusants bearable before desperation drove them to treason. Thus the new spirit was compounded in part of attrition and expediency.

It was compounded also of logic. Religious persecution had rested on the premise that some body of men, whether an apostolic church or the regiment of the elect, possessed a monopoly of God's truth and the only way of salvation; those who thought differently had to be converted or exterminated because they were pestilential: they carried a contagious heresy of which the faithful would sicken and be damned, and God might pour His wrath upon the society that harbored them. This was the logic of intolerance. The British had never accepted it in its full implication, but it had played its part in their history from the autos-da-fé of Queen Mary to the frenzies of the Popish Plot. Now its premise was being undermined by experience and reason.

Experience suggested that no faith incurred the particular wrath of the Almighty. The great testing ground for religious diversity was the coast of North America, which by now had settlements ranging from Roman Catholic to Quaker; no colony, whatever its complexion, had been marked out for particular divine displeasure. Reason suggested that in God's house there might be mansions for many creeds. If this were so, persecution rested on an error that the Christian must reject as sinful and the rationalist as absurd.

> Of all the tyrannies on human kind,
> The worst is that which persecutes the mind.
> Let us but weigh at what offense we strike;
> 'Tis but because we cannot think alike.
> In punishing of this, we overthrow
> The laws of nations and of nature too.[4]

The leaven of rationalism was at work in the upper classes, preparing the way for great intellectual changes. The Restoration appears in retrospect as a transitional period between two worlds of

---

[4] John Dryden: *The Hind and the Panther.*

thought, one passionately religious and therefore explosive, and the other skeptical and self-contained. The last great outpourings of the Puritan soul, *Paradise Lost* and *Pilgrim's Progress,* were followed within a few years by Newton's *Principia.* While Milton and Bunyan moved in the twilight of the older world, Newton and his fellows of the Royal Society were in the sunrise of the age of reason. Since politics were not made by the Royal Society, the political effect was slow. But it was also sure, and the Toleration Act was its first important fruit.

The terms of the act were a compromise between the two worlds. Freedom of worship was extended for the first time to virtually every Protestant. But this was all, at least in theory. The act did not include recusants, and it did not extend to the civil and political rights of dissenters. The Clarendon Code and the Test Act remained on the books for almost a century and a half to come. But their provisions were increasingly honored in the breach, and even the lot of recusants improved as the memory of King James grew fainter. Religious issues gradually sank into bogeys with which conservatives might occasionally terrify the electorate, but which had lost both the grandeur and the ferocity of an earlier day.

Only in Ireland, where religion had become the cloak for other hatreds, did ferocity continue. The Cromwellian settlement had been modified at the Restoration, when the royalism of the Anglo-Irish recusants had been rewarded and an unstable balance of power established between them and the Puritan usurpers. James had upset the balance by encouraging the Catholics, and he soon tried to use them to recover his throne. When he landed in Ireland with a small French army, they rallied to his support. But William soon came to the rescue of the beleaguered Protestants, and on the River Boyne, in the summer of 1690, he met his father-in-law in the one battle of the Bloodless Revolution. James was defeated and fled to France. His hope of a restoration was shattered, and Irish hopes with it.

The suppression of the rising began a black period for Ireland. The House of Commons visited punishment on the whole people, including the Protestants. The laws against recusants were stringently enforced, and the Toleration Act was not extended to the island. Political power remained with the Anglican Irish entrenched in the Dublin Parliament, a small minority of the Protestant minority. The Presbyterians of Ulster had made possible the triumph at the Boyne, but they did not gain even the solace of free worship. To make matters worse, the English Parliament soon undermined Ireland's economy. Her wool trade was beginning to prosper and to compete with English cloth, and was consequently strangled by prohibitive tariffs. Long years of hardship and oppression followed for recusant and Protestant alike, and thousands emigrated. They carried with them, to Europe and America, an enduring hatred of Britain and her works.

The subjugation of Ireland virtually concluded the revolution. But conclusion, as the British had found in 1660, was not final settlement. Much had been accomplished. The prerogative had been subordinated to the will of the oligarchy and the focus of the constitution shifted beyond question to the House of Commons; the local magistrates had defended their autonomy against the encroachment of central power; dissent had achieved a measure of freedom; Ireland had been conquered again. For the next quarter-century, however, these gains were insecure. At almost any moment the whirligig of time might have brought in his revenges.

The principal causes of insecurity were two, the foreign wars and dynastic accident. Except for a five-year truce Britain was fighting Louis XIV continuously from 1688 to 1713, and Louis was the avowed champion first of James, then of his son; a military disaster might have opened the way to a restoration backed by French arms. The Tories were impelled by their whole tradition to deplore the results of the revolution and to dream of a time when the Crown and the Church would regain their own; the time seemed to be approaching because the line enthroned by the revolution was unable to perpetuate itself. William and Mary were childless, and Mary died in 1694. Of the numerous children of her younger sister, Anne, the last died in 1700; the dynasty thereafter consisted of an ageing widower and his middle-aged sister-in-law. These two factors, the wars and the royal family, produced tensions and uncertainties from the coronation of William and Mary to the death of Anne, and the period can best be understood by considering the two in turn.

IV   The Duel with Louis XIV

FOR the first time since the fifteenth century Britain was engaging in a major struggle on the Continent, and on its outcome hinged the

question of whether she would go forward to world power or backward to insularity. By 1688 Louis' moves toward the middle Rhine
had alarmed the German princes and the emperor, and the threat to
the Low Countries had roused the Dutch and stirred the dying energies of Spain. Out of this material William was building an alliance around France, and the adherence of Britain completed his
diplomatic masterpiece. But the strength of Europe arrayed against
Louis had all the weakness of coalition. The allies were short-
sighted and self-centered, while their enemy had a unified command. Their resources, even if combined, were barely a match for
his. He was safe behind impenetrable frontiers, and could strike
where and when he chose against opponents as widely separated by
geography as by their aims. William's diplomatic skill was taxed to
the limit to hold his combination together.

Only sea power could mitigate Louis' advantages by giving the
allies a measure of cohesion and mobility. The British, now that
they were embarked on their first war of coalition, had to learn to
use their fleets to open and maintain water communications around
the enemy's dominant land position. The struggle therefore marked
a new stage in the development of their naval strategy. They learned
by hard experience, and they learned faster than the French because they were more immediately dependent on their navy. Louis'
land campaigns turned his resources and attention from the sea,
and control of European waters passed before long to the British
and Dutch. The latter were progressively subordinated. Holland,
like France, was turned from the ocean by the needs of land warfare, and the decline in her sea power that had set in during the
Anglo-Dutch wars culminated during the Anglo-Dutch alliance.
Thereafter the British navy had only the French for a rival.

The war of the first coalition, known as the League of Augsburg,
ended in 1697. The allies succeeded in stemming the French tide,
and Louis made peace in order to prepare for a greater effort —
nothing less than the acquisition of the Spanish empire. The last of
the Hapsburg kings of Spain was dying childless, and his vast inheritance would pass to whatever heir had the strength to make
good his title. The two major lines with hereditary claims were the
Austrian branch of the Hapsburgs and the House of Bourbon. Each
had force with which to back its lawyers' arguments, but neither
could win its case without upsetting the whole state system of Eu-

rope. If an Austrian Hapsburg inherited the Spanish crowns, the old empire of Charles V would be virtually recreated; if a French Bourbon succeeded instead, a Franco-Spanish combine would stretch from the borders of Holland to the coast of Peru. In either case the balance of power, on the Continent and overseas, would be profoundly altered.

Statesmen were confronted with a kind of problem that was destined to recur throughout the eighteenth century. A state had become too weak to maintain itself; how to dispose of it without upsetting the European applecart? The age of religious wars had given place to the age of anarchy, in which each of the powers was absorbed, behind an ornate screen of legalism, diplomacy, and wars, with the simple and amoral aim of furthering its own position at the cost of its neighbors. In such an age weakness was an invitation to rapacity. The Spaniards could not expect their empire to survive in its traditional form; the only question was whether it would be subordinated to one of their strong neighbors or to several. If it were partitioned among the claimants, change might come peacefully. If any one contender sought the whole, he would be opposed by every state with an interest in the balance of power, and change would come by war.

The initial choice rested with Louis because he alone had the force to defy the rest of Europe. At first he inclined to moderation. He and King William negotiated an agreement for partitioning the inheritance between the Archduke Charles of Hapsburg and Louis' grandson, Philip of Anjou, cadets who seemed safely remote from their own family crowns. But neither Austria nor Spain accepted the agreement. The dying Spanish King, eager to maintain the empire intact, willed the whole of it to Philip with the proviso that in case of refusal the whole should go to Charles. Louis was in a difficult position. He could either accept the bequest and fight for the whole of it, or fight Austria for the share assigned to Philip by the partition treaty. He chose to accept the whole in Philip's name. French armies entered the Spanish Netherlands, and almost simultaneously James II died in exile; Louis, as if to complete the ring of his enemies, acknowledged James's son as King of England and Scotland. He was defying all the powers.

For the British a dynastic union of France and Spain threatened to be catastrophic. French influence was paramount in the Spanish

Netherlands and the great port of Antwerp opened to French commerce; Bourbon power in southern Italy where it could command the Mediterranean; the trade of Spanish America monopolized by France; the Franco-Spanish fleets combined, outnumbering the Royal Navy — these were some of the dangers that stared Britain in the face. Behind them was the fundamental fact that France, if Louis succeeded, would achieve the hegemony of western Europe for untold generations to come. The danger was far from clear to the average Englishman, let alone the average Scot, but it was self-evident to the King.

William was no Britisher; he cared and understood little about the politics of the people who had called him to their throne. In background he was Dutch, but his innate objectivity raised him as far above the short-sighted localism of the burghers as it did above that of Whigs and Tories. The Stadtholder-King was a great European. He battled France throughout his life, not primarily because he saw in her a threat to the profits of Amsterdam and London merchants or to the civil and religious liberties of Protestants or to the sea power of the maritime states, but because French aggression menaced that international polity within which nations could develop. This breadth of view gave William a detachment from the quarrels and bigotries of his British subjects. It led him into political blunders and always kept him from popularity, but it was at the core of his statesmanship. He served Great Britain well because, not although, he was one of her least British sovereigns.

He answered the challenge of the Grand Monarch by forming the Grand Alliance. Its nucleus was the three powers most concerned, Britain, Holland, and Austria. Their geographical location, and that of the Spanish empire in Europe, again meant division of counsel and dispersion of force. The Dutch were intent on ousting the French from the Spanish Netherlands, and on little else. The Hapsburgs naturally applauded this objective because they hoped to be sovereign in the Netherlands, but they were busy defending Austria and grabbing the Spanish possessions in Italy. The British, alone among the allies, had an acute interest in keeping the enemy out of Spain itself, but they lacked the army to do it. In this welter of war aims the prime need was for some effective centripetal force. Although William provided it initially, at the moment when hostilities were opening he abruptly died; the labor of building his last al-

liance had worn him out. The alliance might have died with him if
he had not found a worthy successor to carry it on.

John Churchill, better known as the Duke of Marlborough, had
risen in life by a combination of merit and opportune coat-turning.
He had won favor with King James and then deserted him, then intrigued with him while serving King William; his political morality
was that of his day. But he was indispensable because he had genius. As a diplomat he was William's equal in patience, perseverance,
and acumen, and he had a power to charm men that the King never
possessed. As a soldier he was probably the outstanding figure in
British military annals. The functioning of the coalition required a
great diplomat and a great general, and the two were now fused in
one man. His fame grew until it not only eclipsed William's, but
outshone that of the Sun King himself among the children of
France; they still sing of the day when *"Malbrough s'en va-t-en
guerre."*

The principal theaters of war were the Low Countries, Germany,
Italy, and Spain. Of these, from the British viewpoint, the last was
the most disappointing. The Spanish people showed a preference
for Philip as against the Archduke, and the British discovered — as
Napoleon rediscovered a century later — that thwarting their preference in kings was an expensive undertaking. French armies were
in possession, and the allied attempts to oust them by sea-borne in-
vasions were unsuccessful. These attempts, however, forced the
British fleet to operate for long periods off the Spanish coast, and
its need for bases led to two developments.

In 1703 the British concluded a treaty with Portugal whereby
that small state became an allied beachhead. Britain paid by a commercial agreement that soon had the effect of converting her upper
classes from French claret to port — a change in drinking habits induced by military logic. The same logic, a century later, revived the
Anglo-Portuguese alliance against Napoleon.

For an effective peninsular war Britain needed to control the Mediterranean coast as well as the Atlantic, and Lisbon was too distant
a base for operations inside the straits. In 1704 the British surprised
and captured the Rock of Gibraltar; four years later they seized the
Spanish island of Minorca. These two positions complemented each
other. From Minorca the British could blockade the main French
fleet at Toulon, and from Gibraltar they could detect any large-

scale naval movement into or out of the Mediterranean. The conquests entrenched their power in the inland sea, and opened the quest for naval bases that eventually led them to the Falklands and Singapore.

The conquests went largely unnoticed at the time because the Spanish war was unsuccessful. Sea power alone could not oust the French, and allied land power was absorbed in other theaters. In 1704 Marlborough performed an amazing march from the Netherlands to the Danube and shattered an enemy offensive on the field of Blenheim. Soon afterward the Austrians ousted the French from Italy. The allies then tried for years to invade France from the Low Countries, where Marlborough won a series of famous but fruitless battles; strategically the war became a stalemate. In 1711 the Archduke Charles inherited the Austrian domains, and this dissolved what little unity of counsel remained to the allies. The British and Dutch had not been fighting for nine years to rebuild a huge Hapsburg dynastic empire. They began hasty negotiations with Louis, and in 1713 peace was concluded at Utrecht. In the following year the Emperor was forced to accept its substance.

The Treaty of Utrecht, which established a European equilibrium for the next eighty years, was the first of the great settlements in which Britain played a part. Its basis was the principle of partition, to which the belligerents were forced to return after eleven years of fighting. The bulk of the Spanish empire in Europe went to Charles of Hapsburg, and Spain itself and the overseas possessions went to Philip of Anjou, who was recognized as King Philip V. Thus the balance between Hapsburg and Bourbon was maintained.

The other two principals, the Netherlands and Britain, could not share in the territorial spoils, and they were compensated in other ways. The Dutch acquired the right to extend their defenses against France into what had been the Spanish, and were henceforth the Austrian, Netherlands. The British achieved some of their aims in the terms already mentioned: the Austrian Netherlands and southern Italy could not be dangerous under the weak and distant control of Vienna. For the danger implicit in the Franco-Spanish dynastic tie Britain received specific compensations: from France Nova Scotia, Newfoundland, and the Hudson Bay territory, and from Spain the right — known as the Asiento — to supply slaves to the Spanish-American colonies. The threat of a naval combination by the two

Bourbon kingdoms was mitigated when Spain ceded Gibraltar and
Minorca, for with those bases the Royal Navy might prevent a junc-
tion of the Franco-Spanish squadrons in the Mediterranean with
those in the Atlantic. Thus Britain strengthened her sea power in
Europe, her empire in America. A generation later she was ready to
begin the climactic phase of her struggle with France.

V   The Duel of Tory and Whig

THE REGIME established by the revolution justified itself in the
wars against Louis, and at their close its position would normally
have been secure. But dynastic uncertainty was generating internal
friction within the regime and waking the old feuds of Whig and
Tory. Partisan strife, which had already affected the conduct of the
wars and the negotiation of the Utrecht settlement, was approaching a climax that jeopardized the fruits of the revolution.

James had given the old Tory party a mortal blow. His use of the
prerogative against the church had made devout royalists into split
personalities, and most of them had sacrificed their political to their
ecclesiastical loyalty. A few, including some highly placed churchmen, refused to traffic with revolution and remained true to the
principles the party had had at the time of James's accession; they
were therefore known as Jacobites. Their concept of prerogative
was logical, but they were automatically excluded from power. For
the majority of the party the situation was reversed. They retained
great power, because William owed his throne as much to them as
to the Whigs, but they had no basis in logic. Their best minds working together could not reconstruct the Humpty Dumpty of prerogative, and the concept of Anglicanism on which they had stood for
half a century was cracked apart by toleration. No political philosophy could be built upon such wreckage.

The Tories' attitude, in consequence, was essentially negative.
They devoted themselves to restricting the benefits that dissenters
derived from the Toleration Act. They cooled to the idea of fighting
France and reverted to isolationism. They made life difficult for
William, particularly after Mary's death weakened the aura of legitimacy about the throne. Although they welcomed the accession
of a more genuine Stuart in Anne, she did not give them the power
they craved: Marlborough found them difficult colleagues for carry-

ing on the war, and by degrees he drifted into the Whig camp; the
Queen went with him, largely because her slow, dull spirit was
deeply attached to his wife. For the first eight years of the reign the
Whigs were in the ascendancy.

The dynastic issue was growing more acute. By the Act of Settlement of 1701 the English crown had been fixed upon Anne for her
lifetime and then upon the line of James I's daughter and the Elector Palatine: Sophia, the dowager Electress of Hanover, and her
Protestant descendants. James II and his son, pensioners of Louis,
were out of the question at a moment when Britain was on the verge
of war with France, and the Hanoverian claim was recognized as a
matter of expediency.

The Tories could not accept this solution as definitive. The prospect of a petty German princess on the throne, followed by a succession of German princelings, shocked them even more than the
prospect of Dutch William had shocked their fathers. A true Stuart,
furthermore, was growing to manhood in exile, and as the memory
of James II grew dimmer in their minds the attraction of his son
grew stronger in their hearts. Law was no barrier to such romanticism, for the Act of Settlement could readily be unsettled by another parliament.

The act did not apply to Scotland. Her crown was at the disposition of her own parliament, which was in no mood to accept dictation from Westminster. The Scots had acquiesced in the deposition
of James, and had been rewarded at long last with the recognition
of Presbyterianism as the national faith. But William's government
had won acceptance rather than enthusiasm, and distrust of England was widespread. As long as the Tories fulminated against dissenters, the Kirk remained on guard. The Whigs were equally dangerous to Scottish businessmen, who, ever since the Restoration,
had been turning with avidity to commercial enterprise; trade disputes with England were generating almost as much heat as religion had done in the days of Charles I, and one act after another of
the Westminster Parliament suggested a design to throttle Scottish
prosperity as Irish had been throttled. But the Scots, unlike the
Irish, were far from helpless.

The opening of Anne's reign brought the last crisis in Anglo-Scottish relations. The Scots expected to gain little from a war directed
by English mercantilists, but it gave them the chance to drive a

shrewd bargain; the English had their hands full abroad, and a threat of defiance at home might force them into generosity. In 1704 the Scottish Parliament secured the Protestant succession with one startling proviso: that unless Scotland were assured of complete freedom for her government, religion, and trade, her new sovereign should be different from England's. This declaration of independence, taken at face value, meant that the two countries would draw apart again, reversing the trend of the past century. If the break came during the war, Britain might be reduced to chaos for the benefit of France.

The alternative was to draw together on conditions that satisfied the Scots. Plans for a political union had long been debated, but had made no headway against the stubborn nationalism on both sides of the border; now internationalism was the one road of escape from disruption. The plans were quickly revived, and in 1707 the Act of Union passed both Parliaments. It created a single government for the whole of Great Britain, abolished all internal customs barriers (thereby forming the largest free-trade area in Europe), gave the Scots other economic concessions, and guaranteed them their law and their church. Thus the long process of integration, begun in the sixteenth century, was concluded in the eighteenth. The House of Stuart had brought the two kingdoms closer by assuming both crowns in 1603, and the impending extinction of that house completed the work.

The union was far from popular, for nationalism dies slowly. Scot and Englishman long continued to dislike each other, but both profited from their partnership. The fierce, parochial pride of the Scots was converted, once they received the freedom of the island and the empire, into the pride of building that larger community, and Englishmen found in their new compatriots a shrewdness and tenacity that complemented their own. At the price of national sovereignty the two peoples bought their future greatness.

The Act of Union extended the English dynastic settlement to the new Kingdom of Great Britain. But the prospects of the Hanoverians still depended on the winds of political chance, which within three years began to turn cold. Anne was a Tory at bottom, devoted to the prerogative and the church; she was beguiled only for a time into the company of the Whigs. By 1710 she was tiring of them, and her change of heart weighed heavily on the political scales. The sovereign still had influence in the House of Commons and could determine, within limits, the composition of the ministry. Although the wings of prerogative had been clipped, the bird was far from dead.

Anne alone could scarcely have overthrown the Whigs. Their popularity was waning as the war dragged on. The burden of supporting the allied armies fell particularly on the landowning class; when a Whig government scratched a squire hard enough with taxes, it found a Tory. Another factor also jeopardized Whig power. The rank and file of the clergy were high Anglican and bitter enemies of dissent; they were influential in the countryside, where the pulpit could affect more votes than the pamphlets of Defoe, Addison, and Steele. The principle of toleration that was taking root in Whitehall was still alien to the counties, and the world of Sir Roger de Coverley was quick to respond to the old war-cry of "the church in danger." In 1710 the Whig ministry was dismissed, and in the subsequent election the Tories acquired an overwhelming majority.

The Toryism of 1710, unlike that of 1681, was weak at the core; the sap of ideas had gone out of it. But its immediate tasks were clear, to crush dissent and end the war, and the government quickly tackled them. It plugged a loophole by which the Test Act had been evaded, and it gave the Church of England such a monopoly of education that dissenters might no longer rear their children in their faith. The days of the Clarendon Code seemed to be returning. Simultaneously negotiations were opened with France, and Marlborough was recalled and dismissed. The Queen was then persuaded to create twelve Tory peers, who destroyed the Whig majority in the House of Lords and so broke the last stronghold of the war party. The purpose was to force through the Treaty of Utrecht, but the constitutional effect was even more important: the ministry, backed by the commons and the Crown, forced its will on the Upper House. The method was too drastic to be used often, but as a last resort it was unanswerable. The memory of it sufficed for the future. Two of Anne's successors, one in the early nineteenth century and one in the early twentieth, threatened to pack the lords, and in both cases the threat was enough to paralyze their veto power.

The conclusion of the Treaty of Utrecht, over the seeming corpse of the Whig party, marked the apogee of the Tories. An unpopular war had been ended satisfactorily, if not gloriously, and in the settlement Great Britain emerged as a European power of a stature that would have amazed the Jacobeans. Although her success was less sweeping than the Whigs would have had it, Tory moderation had its advantages. Her gains were commensurate with her new position, but they were not great enough to expose her — as the next great settlement did — to the envy of all Europe.

The signing of the treaty left the government face to face with its insoluble problem. Anne was nearing her end, and at her death who would succeed her — her remote cousin from the wilds of Germany or her papist half-brother from France? The Hanoverian accession would mean, on the plane of theory, the triumph of *de facto* monarchy and therefore of Whig ideas; no myth of divine right hedged Sophia or her son, the Elector George. On the practical plane the House of Hanover was ill disposed toward the ministry, which had given its claims only cursory recognition; in the spring of 1714 the Electress Sophia received such a brusque communication from Whitehall that the old lady supposedly died of the shock. Such treatment in itself, without the whole record of the Tory party, was enough to turn George into a Whig. His accession threatened to extinguish the principles of Toryism and end the careers of the ministers.

Yet what alternative was there? James, the Stuart pretender, was a Roman Catholic; the Tories could not help him to the throne without abandoning their ideal of a church that monopolized power by persecuting both dissenters and recusants. James was also tied to France, and the memory of his father and uncle was still so fresh that no responsible politician could advocate endangering the alignment of British foreign policy and the balance newly established at Utrecht by crowning another Francophile king. The Hanoverian accession, in short, would solidify and perpetuate the revolution in a way that was peculiarly Whig; a restoration of the legitimate Stuart line promised a return to the troubled days before 1688. The Tories hoped for a middle course, a limited and moderate counterrevolution, but they had no middle candidate.

At the end they turned for leadership to Viscount Bolingbroke, whose daring matched his ambition. In the summer of 1714 he set out to fill key civil and military positions with his henchmen, apparently in order to obtain such a hold on power before the Queen died that he would be able to bring in the Elector, willy nilly, as a Tory puppet. This design required time, but he had only five days of undisputed authority. Then the Queen died, and his schemes collapsed about his ears.

The Whigs saw to it that Elector George was proclaimed king and summoned at once from Germany. Even before he landed, the new King replaced the Tory ministers with Whigs, and soon Bolingbroke fled for his life to France. There he took service with the pretender, and helped to plan the Jacobite rising that broke out in 1715. It ignited little more than the Scottish highlands, however, and fizzled out against the apathy of the people at large. The old cause was lost irretrievably, and the Tories who had flirted with it were extinguished as a party.

Church and Crown remained, it is true, but the virtue that the Cavaliers had found in them was gone. The church of Laud and the Tories became riddled with compromise as soon as the Whigs regained control of it and restored its concessions to dissent; its apostolic authority was soon dissipated in a haze of broad-mindedness. Anne's crown sat very differently on George's head. The balm of romance had at long last been washed from the anointed King: this deputy of the Lord was a cold, uncouth man with ugly mistresses; he reigned by the grace of the oligarchs, and the sight of him could not evoke from the most ardent royalist more than a sigh of acceptance.

A prosaic church and crown were a small price to pay for security. The great issues of the preceding age had been largely fought out, and the revolution had been preserved. In the process Great Britain had been unified and modernized. Her system of government was the envy of European liberals, and she was ready for an expansion that would make her, within a century, the world's greatest imperial power. Her heyday was beginning, with the oligarchy for its driving force and the Hanoverians for its hallmark.

VI   The Whig Ascendancy

THE REIGNS of the first two Georges, from 1714 to 1760, were a period of relative domestic calm. Changes there were, of many kinds, but the turmoil of the Stuart era had passed. Religious toleration was established, in practice more broadly than in law, and the repeal of the legislation against dissent was followed by suspension of the penalties imposed by the Clarendon Code. The Church of England came to terms with a materialistic and rational age. The spiritual current in the clergy grew shallower as it grew broader, until holy orders became merely another profession for the gentry.

Wealth accumulated at an increasing rate from trade and manufactures, but men did not decay. The common people were ruled by their betters, and oppressed by them up to a point; beyond that point, however, docility vanished in rioting. Because central and local government was still carried on without effective force, the rulers of the new age were still dependent on consent. Their misuse of power was limited by a knowledge, periodically refreshed by violence, of the people whom they governed, and their triumph over the Crown had not uprooted them from the soil out of which they had grown.

Land remained the basis of good society. Money in itself meant little; money discreetly and patiently used meant admittance to the ruling class. A London merchant, for example, might make a fortune in trade; that alone was unlikely to get him more than a municipal office and perhaps election to Parliament as a member for Middlesex. If he wished to found a dynasty his first step was to buy a country estate, preferably in an area where the titled families had more children than income and were willing to barter the one for the other; he might then arrange suitable marriages for his sons and daughters. He himself, in all likelihood, would never be admitted to county society. But his children would be, by right of their husbands or wives, and his grandchildren by right of birth.

In another way also the merchant class was acquiring new blood from the aristocracy. At a time when families were large and primogeniture was still the rule, few even among the magnates could provide for a brood of children beyond adolescence. An earl with six sons had to plan carefully. The estates would be entailed upon the eldest, who would also inherit the title; his future was secure, although he needed a careful education for his responsibilities. The earl and the countess would probably have at least a bishop and a general among their relatives; in that case the Church and the army would offer good prospects of advancement for the second and third sons. But what of the other three? Family influence could not be overworked. If the earl had no other professional connections, he might place one of the youngsters with his London bankers, ship another to Bengal in the service of the East India Company, and article the last as a clerk with the family solicitors. In such ways the professions and the business world were recruited from the aristocracy.

Land was the basis of political as well as social power. Now that the House of Commons was all important, the system of electing its members was the cornerstone of politics. That system had grown up in the thirteenth century and had never been fundamentally altered. The parliamentary boroughs were still for the most part the towns prominent in the Middle Ages, and the electoral system in each was the product of medieval custom. The disparity in apportionment and in voting methods was fantastic. Many towns that had been thriving in the days of the Plantagenets were now decayed or even turned into sheepfolds, while what had been insignificant villages had blossomed into towns; yet the decayed hamlets and the sheepfolds still sent their representatives, and the new towns did not. In a few boroughs elections were on a basis tantamount to universal manhood suffrage; in others only a score or two of the inhabitants might vote. The system was chaotic and irrational, but it survived because it was the oligarchy's means of maintaining itself.

The core of the system was the decayed, or rotten, borough. In the extreme cases of sheepfold-constituencies, the owner of the land named to Parliament whomever he wished. In less flagrant cases, where there was a handful of electors, they voted with decorous regularity for the candidate proposed by their landlord. Still other towns were for sale at each election: the voters had their price, often fixed by long usage, and any one with the wherewithal could buy a majority. These venal constituencies were openings for the *nouveaux riches* who wished to sit in Parliament, but the demand exceeded the supply; the bulk of the rotten boroughs was held by the landowners generation after generation, and rarely or never came on the open market. The greater the landowner, by and large, the more boroughs he controlled and the more members of the House of Commons were his nominees. They generally voted as he told them to in order to keep their seats, and his word also carried great weight with the independent members from his locality. He was usually a peer of the realm sitting in the Upper House; his younger sons, protégés, and followers sitting in the Lower House were known as his "interest," and their numbers determined his political influence. Government was conducted by a judicious blend of interests.

The blend produced surprisingly stable administration, and one of the reasons was again the rotten borough. The greatest landowner in Britain, and therefore the greatest potential borough-monger, was the Crown itself. Anne, as already mentioned, had used her electoral influence to support ministers of her choosing, but neither of the first two Georges knew or cared enough about the complicated game to play it actively. The royal boroughs passed into the control of the ministry, which used them to strengthen its hold on the House of Commons. Thus the mere possession of office gave the ministerial clique a great advantage over the opposition.

Another reason for administrative stability was the control of honors and patronage. Advancement to or in the peerage, promotion in the Church, in the army and navy, in the civil service — all in practice depended largely upon the favor of the ministers, who exercised favor in return for political support. The maximum length of a session of Parliament was seven years, and in that time the price of most members of the commons could be ascertained. One man might have a son in the Church who clamored for a deanery or bishopric; a second was perhaps a commodore eager to be an admiral, and a third had an impecunious relation whose demands could be stilled by a sinecure in the customs service; a fourth might crave advancement from the peerage of Ireland to that of Great Britain. With such men the ministry could bargain favors against votes, and so build up a phalanx of henchmen.

By now the focus of government was the cabinet. For generations this inner council of ministers had been acquiring more and more executive power. No other solution existed for the constitutional dilemma; the principle that the commons were supreme had little meaning until the executive was responsible in fact to them and only in theory to the sovereign. This change in the status of cabinet members was still incomplete, but it was far advanced.

By 1714 certain practices had become rooted in custom. The members of the cabinet were chosen from leaders of the party that had a majority in the Lower House; they made unanimous recommendations to the sovereign, for which they were collectively accountable, and a dissenting member was expected to resign. The royal power of veto had lapsed because it was no longer needed: the time had gone when the Houses could pass a bill against the wishes of the Crown and cabinet, and the time had not yet come when the cabinet dared to press a bill against the wishes of the Crown. Some elements of the modern system already existed, in other words, but equally important elements were lacking. Anne's advisers bore as little resemblance to the cabinet ministers of today as the rotten borough bore to the present constituency.

The Hanoverian accession increased the cabinet's independence because George I had little interest in domestic affairs. He had taken the crown out of a sense of duty to his House, which was discharged by securing a foreign policy favorable to his German principality. He and his son after him were neither British like Anne nor European like William, but only Hanoverian. "I am sick to death of all this foolish stuff," exclaimed George II in a moment of angry candor, "and wish with all my heart that the devil may take all your bishops, and the devil take your ministers, and the devil take the Parliament, and the devil take the whole island — provided I can get out of it and go to Hanover."

Such an attitude meant that the cabinet was left to manipulate the system and to govern the country with only sporadic interference from the king. This freedom grew into a constitutional habit during the regime of a man who, for a generation, towered over all the other servants of the Crown. Sir Robert Walpole, a cynical, profane, and hard-drinking squire from Norfolk, rose to leadership of the cabinet in 1721 and retained his position, with one momentary lapse, until 1742. He is commonly considered as the first prime minister, not because he was the first to dominate his colleagues (which Clarendon had done) but because he was the first subject to approximate the role of a chief executive.

Cabinet autonomy and the leadership of a prime minister were new elements, but they did not yet constitute responsible government. A cabinet could not long survive the loss of its majority in the Commons; neither could it long withstand the antipathy of the king. The Georges had deputed their power, not abdicated it; Walpole depended on their favor, and he devoted himself to retaining it with the assiduity of a Pompadour. He was actually responsible to both Parliament and the sovereign. As long as the king could make his will effective, he could not be above and dissociated from the functioning of government; he himself was not accountable to Parliament, and no cabinet could be held completely accountable for acts that bore his imprimatur. A condition of responsible government was an irresponsible crown — a sovereign with no more volition than a rubber stamp. Not even the first two Georges, let alone the third, satisfied that condition.

Another prerequisite for the modern system was two coherent parties. Without well-knit opposition, possessed of principles and a program, the majority breaks into factions; cabinets are endlessly reshuffled, and principles give place to the desire for office and its fruits. This was the British situation for the larger part of the eighteenth century. After 1714 any one with serious political ambitions had to call himself a Whig; the Tories shrank to a group that merely decried whatever the government did, and the major opposition was among the Whigs who were out of office and wanted to be in. Intrigue did service for principle; parties remained amorphous, and the constitution with them. It did not begin to set in the modern mold until the issues of a later age again split the political world in two.

So much for the oligarchs and the system by which they governed. They were a worldly lot, whose private morals were little better than their public, and to our eye their sophistication seems tinged with grossness. The crudity revealed by Hogarth underlay the graces that Chesterfield extolled, and *Marriage à la Mode* was the social counterpart of the rotten borough. But these rulers of Britain, gross or graceful, were animated by tremendous energy. It was their salient characteristic. They drove forward with the same unresting determination as the Puritans before them, though toward wholly different goals. Instead of revolutionizing their country at home they revolutionized its position abroad.

Their revolution was a response to forces long at work in British history. Political isolation from Europe, imposed in the fifteenth century by England's defeat in France, had combined in the sixteenth century with the religious isolation of a church divorced from the Continent, and this remoteness had soon been accentuated by the onset of the Puritan Revolution. The counteracting force of commercial and colonial expansion had made little impression on the surface of events. Under the surface it had generated greater and greater pressure, which had appeared in the statecraft of Cromwell and in the cosmopolitanism of Restoration society. But the old aloofness from the European community endured in large measure until the struggle with France that opened in 1688 and ended in 1815. During that struggle Britain emerged from productive but narrow parochialism into the limelight of world history.

VII   The Second Phase of the Duel with France

THE FIRST two decades of the Hanoverian era gave few indications of the developments impending. Walpole was no revolutionary. He wished to let sleeping dogs lie at home and abroad — to keep the peace in order to consolidate the position of the new dynasty and thus of the Whigs. War bred discontent, if only by increasing taxation; it also meant eventual embroilment with France and French support for the Jacobites. As long as the two great powers of the west could be kept from each other's throats, minor wars would burn themselves out without starting a general conflagration. For years, accordingly, Sir Robert cultivated the good will of Versailles, with such success that Britain had her longest interim of peace since the reign of Charles I.

By the 1730's, however, peace was menaced from a number of quarters. The principal threats were colonial, commercial, and European, and the root of them all was Anglo-French rivalry. In North America trouble was implicit in the geography of the settlements. As British colonists pushed westward through the Alleghenies and northward toward the St. Lawrence basin, the long and thinly held line of French posts from Cape Breton Island to the Mississippi was subjected to greater and greater pressure. The French reacted by trying to strengthen their line, and the resultant disputes were soon heard across the Atlantic. The bickerings of colonists were unlikely to generate a conflict in Europe; mercantilist politicians set little store by territory as such, and the wilds of North America were the small change of diplomacy. But the quarrels about them ensured that a major war once begun would engulf the colonies.

British merchants were meeting obstacles to their commercial expansion, particularly in India, the West Indies, and South America. Not even Walpole could be indifferent to these obstacles; trade was still considered a form of national power to be increased at the cost of other nations. In India native authority was collapsing from the center at Delhi outward, just when the East India Company and its French rival were struggling for markets; the two companies were drawn into native politics, and the tension between them mounted. In the West Indies the rise of the lucrative sugar industry was increasing the profits in imperialism, and with them the endemic hostility between the Bourbon states and Britain. In Spanish America, above all, the Utrecht settlement was being strained to the breaking point. The new dynasty in Madrid was tightening its control of trade by reforming the customs service, and British merchants, accustomed to smuggling behind the screen of the Asiento, felt that Spanish law-enforcement was an intolerable grievance. Spanish exports were wholly inadequate to meet the colonial demand, furthermore, and France was acquiring the bulk of the market. Now that the family partnership arranged at Utrecht was yielding cash returns, Britain was growing restive.

By the 1730's the political as well as the commercial aspect of the Utrecht settlement was in danger. The marital good luck of the Hapsburgs, proverbial since the fifteenth century, ran out in the eighteenth: the Spanish branch had already withered with a childless king, and a similar fate hung over the Austrian branch. The Emperor Charles VI had only a daughter, Maria Theresa, and her right to inherit the family domains was doubtful. Doubt was an opportunity for the rapacious powers of Europe; Austria was no more able to settle her own affairs than Spain had been before her. The new, militaristic kingdom of Prussia coveted Silesia, the Hapsburg province on the upper Oder, and France still hungered for the Austrian Netherlands. Another war of partition was impending, in which the Hapsburg state might be extinguished.

Charles worked hard to avoid the danger. He had a touching faith in the sanctity of a scrap of paper, and he peddled around the courts of Europe a treaty that bound each signatory to respect his daughter's inheritance. Most of the major powers signed, usually for a consideration, but Great Britain alone had a keen interest in maintaining the agreement. Although Silesia meant nothing to her, the Netherlands meant much, and the dismemberment of Austria would upset the Utrecht balance to the advantage of France. The worries of Vienna were shared in London.

What ended Walpole's peace, however, was not the Austrian problem but the activities of Spanish customs officers off the South

American coast. British merchants were growing steadily angrier at their exclusion from a rich market, and anger in the countinghouses spread to a nation bored with years of tranquillity. Spain seemed weak enough to be an attractive target; few of the warmongers realized that an attack on her would probably involve France and so lead to another worldwide struggle. The public was in the mood for a cheap and glorious victory, as the American public was in 1898, and only the spark of an incident was needed. It came when a merchant captain by the name of Jenkins returned from South America minus an ear, and claimed that it had been cut off by a Spanish customs officer. Spanish responsibility for the loss of that ear, as for the sinking of the *Maine*, has never been proved, but the ear swept Britain into war.

For a time Walpole rode the wave of feeling. His foreign policy had failed, like Neville Chamberlain's just two hundred years later, but he remained in office to direct a struggle he deplored. It went badly. The navy was unprepared, as usual after a long period of peace, and the Spaniards were less contemptible than the jingoes had supposed. Worse yet, before the war had more than begun the European storm broke. Charles VI died in 1740; immediately the new King of Prussia, Frederick II, marched into Silesia, and in the following spring France, Bavaria, and Spain joined him against Maria Theresa. Walpole negotiated an alliance with her, but the disaster to her fortunes and the unprofitable Spanish war undermined his position. In 1742 he resigned, just when the minor conflict that he had had forced on him was merging with the greater one that he had dreaded.

Great Britain's role in the War of the Austrian Succession was thoroughly undistinguished. On land her armies made no great impression, and at sea she failed to exploit her strength. The fleet had no comprehensive strategy, and the fighting instructions enjoined upon it almost precluded a tactical triumph. Since the late seventeenth century the major maritime states had accepted the idea that a battle was properly fought only when the two fleets sailed in parallel lines, cannonading each other. If they were evenly matched — and engagements rarely occurred unless they were — the cannonade could not be decisive; the guns and gunnery were too inaccurate, and no admiral could press an advantage while maintaining his line. After the one large-scale action of the war, the British commander was court-martialed for deviating from the sacrosanct formation. Such conservatism helps to explain why the navy achieved no conclusive victories at sea.

The land war was equally inconclusive. In America the great French fortress of Louisburg was captured and Canada opened to invasion, but the British government neglected its opportunity for the sake of the European struggle. In 1745 the pretender's son, Charles Edward, landed in Scotland and rallied the Highlanders to the Stuart cause. His invasion of England collapsed for lack of support, and he soon fled into exile again. Meanwhile, however, he had frightened the government into withdrawing the bulk of its troops from the Continent, and the French improved the shining hour by appropriating the Austrian Netherlands. The upshot was that France and Prussia had important gains in Europe, and Britain in Canada, and that neither side could oust the other. In the circumstances further hostilities seemed pointless.

Negotiations led to the Treaty of Aix-la-Chapelle in 1748. Frederick retained Silesia; otherwise virtually everything was restored to its pre-war status. Louisburg was returned to France, the Netherlands to Austria, and the issues behind the War of Jenkins's Ear were passed over in silence. Britain had fought for nine years; she had gained nothing and lost nothing. The settlement seems fantastic by modern standards, but it was intelligible enough at a time when war was a form of business enterprise. If the business ceased to show a profit, actual or potential, reason suggested liquidating it on the best possible terms.

The terms of 1748 satisfied no one except Prussia, and they also ruined no one. For both reasons the treaty was scarcely signed before the signatories were dreaming of new coalitions. The prime mover was Austria. The Hapsburgs did not take kindly to change, particularly at their expense, and the rise of Prussia was disturbing; Frederick had in fact begun the Austro-Prussian struggle for the dominance of Germany that lasted from the invasion of Silesia in 1740 to the Battle of Sadowa in 1866. The government of Maria Theresa was acute enough to sense the challenge and spirited enough to accept it. Vienna had lost the first round, but the second was still to be fought. Prussia had become a great power in one war, and she might be reduced to insignificance in another.

It required a great coalition to crush her. One member was ready to hand, a newcomer to the politics of western Europe: Russia might be lured by the hope of expanding at Prussia's expense, particularly as the Empress Elizabeth detested the Prussian King. But the coalition could not accomplish its aims unless France joined it. Austria therefore abandoned her two-hundred-year-old antagonism and went wooing at Versailles. Her emissaries played on the Pompadour's dislike of Frederick, and dropped hints that French assistance might be recompensed by concessions in the Austrian Netherlands. Such an arrangement would be anathema to Britain. But the Austrians had recently lost Silesia despite their British alliance, and bartering the Royal Navy for the French army seemed a profitable exchange.

Meanwhile the Anglo-French struggle had been informally renewed in America, and Britain found herself dangerously isolated in Europe. When her efforts to revive the Austrian alliance failed, she negotiated a defensive agreement with Prussia. France, convinced that Frederick had turned his coat, then yielded to Austria's suit and joined her against Prussia, while Britain turned from opposing to supporting Frederick. The Diplomatic Revolution was accomplished.

This bewildering shift of alignments was consonant with the two basic rivalries, Austro-Prussian and Anglo-French, about which European diplomacy revolved. The reversal of Austrian policy led Britain to look to Frederick for aid against France, and Britain's move led in turn to the Austro-French accord. The British were primarily concerned with finding an ally in Europe to distract France from the conflict overseas, and this they did. The diplomatic alliances of the period, like so many social alliances in the world of fashion, were *mariages de convenance* contracted in the hope of security or gain.

VIII   Victory Overseas

THE FRENCH design for the new war was based on the lessons of the previous one. The focus of operations would be the Continent, and such forces as could be spared would maintain a defensive against the British overseas. Hanover was assigned the role played before by the Austrian Netherlands: if the French ended in possession of the Electorate, the British would be forced to purchase its return with whatever colonies they might have won. France would

then, with reasonable luck, be left with gains in the Austrian Netherlands.

The British began with no coherent strategy and many blunders.
As early as 1754 the efforts of the French to strengthen their position in the Ohio Valley had touched off fighting in America, and in
the next year Braddock had been defeated and killed in the attempt
to capture Fort Duquesne (Pittsburgh). Nominal peace continued
in Europe, but in the spring of 1756 France struck a staggering
blow by seizing Minorca almost under the eyes of a British relieving
squadron. Three months later Frederick attacked, to anticipate his
enemies, and the Seven Years' War began. For a year British set-
backs continued. In America the French advanced toward Albany;
in India Calcutta was lost; in Europe Frederick was defeated by
the Austrians, a Hanoverian army under a son of George II capitulated at Klosterzeven, and the Electorate was overrun by the French.
Britain again, after more than a century, seemed to be "declining to
contempt beneath the meanest."

The anger of the nation projected an outsider into power. William Pitt was the leading critic of government; the King and his
chief minister, the borough-mongering Duke of Newcastle, strove to
keep him out of office. But Pitt knew that he alone could save the
country, and he knew that the country knew it. Pressure outside
Parliament mounted until the King and the Duke — although they
still controlled a majority of the commons — were forced to capitulate. Pitt took over direction of the war, and Newcastle was de-
moted to his political manager. The eighteenth century provides no
more striking example of the influence of public opinion upon an
oligarchic legislature — the power of "the majority without doors,"
in Bolingbroke's phrase, to force "the majority within doors to
truckle to the minority."

Pitt was a far cry from the Whig magnates. He was incorruptible,
and in an age of rationalism he appealed to the emotions and imagination. The amazing ascendancy he acquired over the House of
Commons was due less to his hold on the public or to his eloquence
— although he was one of the great orators in the history of Parliament — than to his sheer moral stature. He dwarfed the oligarchs
and their henchmen, and they trooped after him. He had the flint of
true leadership, which kindled a fire of enthusiasm even in party
hacks. His arrogance and nervous instability made him a difficult

colleague and were bad auguries for the future, but they had not yet sapped his greatness. He was a poet in action, and the epic on which he was engaged was the British empire.

His imperialism was not that of the mercantilists. Territory interested him more than profits; he dreamed of an expanding power of which trade was only one ingredient, and the Union Jack flying in the wilderness fired his imagination more than the same flag over a sugar plantation. This was a new romanticism. It quickened the blood and gave to the cause of empire a deeper content than the countinghouse had ever given it. Pitt was stirring the emotions of Britain to the service of that cause, and they have remained in its service ever since.

Romanticism, far from weakening Pitt's direction of the war, gave him the vision needed for sound strategy. His absorption with the empire freed him almost automatically from the basic error of the previous war — the division of Britain's energies between Europe and the sea, precluding victory in either sphere. In the Seven Years' War Pitt used military force where it would be most effective, on the sea and in small-scale land operations in distant parts of the globe; scarcely a redcoat appeared on the Continent of Europe except for diversionary raids. Prussia, however, was not neglected. Whether or not Pitt ever said that he would win America in Germany, to a large extent he did so — not with British troops but with British gold. Frederick was heavily subsidized to enable him to buy mercenaries and other military supplies; without the money he could hardly have held his own against a ring of enemies, and even with it he came near disaster. But in the long run he turned out to be Pitt's most profitable investment.

The combination of gold and sea power was the maturing of Britain's grand strategy. From the Glorious Revolution to the Treaty of Aix-la-Chapelle she had tried to fight France equally in Europe and at sea; from the accession of Pitt to the Battle of Waterloo her major military effort was at sea and overseas, and the bulk of Continental fighting was done by her allies. Hence the age-old gibe that she fights to the last Prussian, or Frenchman, or American, or whoever the ally of the moment may be. The gibe had some truth in it while she was waging her land wars as much as possible through the armies of other nations.

This method, which Pitt first demonstrated, derived from the stra-

tegic realities of her position. The British army was not large enough
to play a dominant role in a war in Europe. It could not be made
large enough, if only because of the rooted British opposition to militarism. But a few thousand men who would be brushed aside by
the French in Germany might be supremely effective against them
on the St. Lawrence, provided that a Continental war prevented
France from sending more than a fraction of her force overseas. If
her fleets were blockaded in European waters by the Royal Navy,
the stream of men and supplies to her colonies would be further restricted and the colonists starved of the means for defense. The
British purpose was first to subsidize a land ally or allies to distract
France on the Continent, then to strangle her overseas communications by a blockade in home waters, then to conquer her colonies
with British troops. This was the most effective use of British power,
and effectiveness is the criterion of strategy. In this way Pitt fought
Louis XV and his son fought Napoleon, until Great Britain had appropriated the bulk of the French empire.

Victories began before Pitt had been a year in office. In 1758 Fort
Duquesne and Louisburg were captured, while Frederick held his
own in the Germanies. The fall of Quebec in 1759 was soon followed by the surrender of all French forces in Canada. British naval
supremacy in the Indian Ocean, implemented by successes on land,
ended the French dream of an empire in India. An attempted invasion of the British Isles was stopped by a series of well-timed blows,
climaxed by Hawke's brilliant chase of the enemy through the storm-
wrack of Quiberon Bay; thereafter the remnants of the French fleet
were swept from the seas. The tide of success flooded in, and by the
end of 1760 Britain had to all intents won her war.

But Frederick was far from winning his. He stood at bay against
appalling odds, striking at one enemy after the other until his army
was reduced to a rabble and he was carrying a vial of poison like
the Nazi leaders in 1945. If he had drunk it, the future of Europe
might have been happier. But he held on, and Great Britain was
pledged to support him. Pitt insisted on abiding by the pledge,
partly from a sense of honor and partly from a determination that
this time the old duel with France should be settled once and for
all. His aim was not a negotiated peace on the Utrecht model,
which would respect the niceties of the balance of power, but a settlement that would clear the French forever from the path of British

expansion. This was a modern concept of war, and shocking to some of his colleagues in the cabinet; they feared the incalculable effects upon the state system of Europe. Others thought that his insistence on standing by Prussia was quixotic, now that Britain had gained so much. His position was weakening.

In 1760 the weight of the Crown was thrown against him. George II, who had been converted into his staunch admirer, died and was succeeded by his grandson, George III. The new King was intent on ridding himself of his great minister and bringing the war to an end. Pitt, on the contrary, wished to extend it by attacking Spain, who he knew was about to enter the struggle. The cabinet refused to support him, and he resigned. Three months later Spain declared war, only to lose Manila on one side of the globe and Havana on the other. At the same time the Empress of Russia died and was succeeded by an unbalanced admirer of Frederick, who withdrew the Russian armies. French pressure relaxed as peace negotiations with Britain advanced, and Austria had no stomach to continue the fight alone.

Again, as in the days of Queen Anne, the Whigs who had carried on the war did not make the peace. Newcastle fell soon after Pitt, and King George installed as prime minister his favorite, Lord Bute, backed by a heterogeneous majority often called Tory, though it bore little resemblance to the party of Bolingbroke. Bute's objective was his master's, to end the war quickly; in negotiating with France and Spain he did not insist on every ounce in the pound of flesh to which Britain's victories entitled her, and the resultant peace was far from Carthaginian. In concluding it Bute was largely indifferent to the interests of Frederick, who was left to make what terms he could with Austria in the separate Peace of Hubertusburg. He neither forgot nor forgave Britain's desertion.

Bute's treaty, the Peace of Paris of 1763, had the earmarks of a compromise. In Europe France gained nothing because she had not kept possession of Hanover, and so did not have to be bought out. In America she surrendered Canada and Cape Breton Island to Great Britain. Spain ceded Florida; the Mississippi was recognized as the western British boundary, and Louisiana changed hands from France to Spain. Britain restored the bulk of her other conquests, French and Spanish, although France returned to India on terms that condemned her to military impotence. She retained her fishing

rights off Newfoundland that were valued at a million pounds a
year, the most lucrative part of her North American venture, and
she regained her position in the West Indies. In the eyes of her mercantilists the bargain was far better than they had had reason to
expect.

Yet to French patriots the peace was a bitter blow. Their empire
was virtually at an end, their finances and navy were in ruins; the
proudest monarchy of Europe had been humbled by an oligarchy
of landlords and merchants. The effect on Frenchmen was twofold:
on the one hand, hatred of Britain and a longing for revenge; on
the other, a desire to emulate the methods of a country that could
harness its resources with such spectacular success. Britain became
a subject of serious study. She was the focus of admiration for Anglophile liberals, and at the same time of cold scrutiny by the Anglo-
phobes in power.

One aspect of Britain's strength was obvious. She had succeeded,
to a degree unexampled since the days of Cromwell, by the use of
sea power. France had lost her colonies because she had been unable to get at them through the British blockade; if she were ever
to re-establish her empire, and with it the popularity of the Bourbon
regime, she had to rebuild her fleet in preparation for the day of
revenge. That day might not be distant. Her failure in the war had
the one compensation that it left her with no embittered enemies on
the Continent, whereas Britain had nothing but enemies — Prussia
hopelessly alienated, Austria soured by the British defection, the
minor maritime states antagonized by the high-handedness of the
recent blockade, relations with Russia frigid, Spain dreaming of revenge as fondly as France. Britain for once stood alone, the single
and isolated victor.

Isolation was not the only danger in victory. The ousting of the
French from Canada removed one of the strongest ties holding the
British colonies to the mother country. Colonial independence had
been a thorn in the side of administrators since the days of the Restoration, but it had been mitigated by colonial fear of its consequences. As long as the French were near at hand, threatening the
whole Atlantic seaboard, the redcoats and ships of the line were reluctantly welcomed. Once the French withdrew — as Pitt's opponents had argued as early as 1761 — the stimulus to loyalty was

gone. If Pitt won Canada in Germany, he also helped to lose the thirteen colonies in Canada.

Britain's triumph planted seeds of trouble for her in Europe and America, and the rapidity with which those seeds sprouted was also due indirectly to the same triumph. Peace brought with it a major financial problem. The war, it was estimated, had cost some ninety million pounds, most of which had been borrowed; the national debt had approximately doubled, and the government needed a commensurate increase in revenue to meet its obligations. Instead the treaty brought increased expenses to administer and defend the new territories. Where was the money to come from? Even if the nation could fund the debt, who would bear the increased burden of imperial administration and defense? To attempt to place it on the shoulders of the British taxpayer would be not only unfair but unwise. No cabinet would be likely to survive the attempt, and few politicians in any period welcome the thought of political suicide.

The obvious method was to lay a share of the burden on the colonies, so that they would at least begin to pay for themselves. That course might well mean trouble in America. But any other expedient was sure to mean trouble in Great Britain. The King's advisers knew little about American opinion and a great deal about British; they understandably chose the risk of provoking the one as against the certainty of provoking the other. Their decision to increase colonial revenues, in order to solve a problem created by Britain's victory, precipitated her greatest imperial disaster.

Thus the signature of the Peace of Paris was one of the pivotal moments in British history. The treaty itself was superficially a compromise; actually it recognized Britain's new position as the predominant European power in the world beyond Europe. The oligarchy that had projected her into that position stood triumphant, not only over France but even over the disturbing grandeur of Pitt; his poetry of empire had been largely rewritten in mercantilist prose. The Paris settlement suggested that the future lay open to prosaic competence, which was the genius of the oligarchs.

In fact, however, the problems hanging over Britain required a quite different quality. They could be approached and grappled with prosaically, but they could be solved only by intuition, by a political sixth sense keen enough to feel its way through the unfamiliar. This sense the leaders of the nation lacked. They had common sense where they needed insight, and dogged tenacity where they needed foresight. Their qualities were not a match for the revolutions of the coming decades, which repeatedly threw them onto the defensive and eventually shattered their power.

The first of those revolutions was already preparing. The financial crisis at home, coinciding with the departure of the French from Canada, ensured trouble in the colonies just when Britain's triumph had left her friendless in Europe. As if this crisis were not enough, the domestic power of the oligarchs was simultaneously attacked from a new and unexpected quarter, the throne, and the comfortable house of Whiggism was divided against itself. When the struggle came it was on three fronts, colonial, European, and domestic. From it the ruling class emerged, with its power battered but intact, to confront more devastating struggles. The Peace of Paris, in retrospect, was the apogee of that class and of the empire it built, and also the beginning of the end for both.

Chapter Four

THE DEFENSIVE AGAINST REVOLUTION

1763–1815

I Rationalism and Reform

TWO salient characteristics of the late eighteenth century were rationalism and revolution, and the two seem at first sight disconnected. The work of philosophers and physicists, from Newton to Rousseau, had little apparent bearing on a Boston mob, on the mushrooming of a Lancashire mill town, or on the guillotine in Paris. In fact, however, there was a causal relationship. A widespread human faith in reason is itself a power for revolution, no matter how much the faith may be overlaid and concealed by its destructive results. This was never more fully demonstrated than in the half-century between the Peace of Paris and the Peace of Vienna.

The basic tenet of the rationalist was that the human mind had the means of surmounting all problems, whether intellectual, political, or physical. He believed that man and the universe operated by laws that could eventually be comprehended, and hence that no apparent mystery was too great to be pierced. Human relations might be unhappy, human institutions sadly askew, but these results of stupidity could be rectified by intelligence because man, far from being innately corrupt, was good at heart and therefore perfectible. He was kept from developing his goodness by the fetters of tradition binding him to an unenlightened past, and these fetters could be struck off by the force of reason, of what the philosophers called the enlightenment. Whatever was illogical in man's inheritance — in his creeds, his political institutions, his ways of tilling the soil —

would thereby be eliminated, and he would at last be free to rise to his true stature.

This was the rationalist's solution to an old question, "Which of you by taking thought can add one cubit unto his stature?" Anyone can, was the answer, because thought is the way to perfection. Such utopian optimism was in itself an intellectual revolution. It was squarely at odds with Christian orthodoxy, which had hitherto been the frame of Western culture. The philosophers of the enlightenment did not oppose the Church merely because it was privileged, wealthy, and obscurantist; their point of view was antithetical to that of any theology, Protestant or Catholic. They believed in the capacity of man to lift himself by his own intellectual bootstraps; the Church taught his sinful incapacity. They believed in natural, changeless laws binding creation in an inviolable web of order; the Church taught that the web had been torn at a specific moment, in the reign of Caesar Augustus, by the transcendant miracle of God made man. The two attitudes have not to this day been fully reconciled.

The Protestant Reformation had inaugurated the revolt against traditional authority. But its reformers would have turned in loathing from a rebel against divine authority. Their purpose had been to re-emphasize God's immediate relationship to the individual believer. They had loosed a spirit of inquiry, however, which through the years had gradually fused with the worldliness of the Renaissance spirit, of the capitalist and scientist, to produce a challenging of God's omnipotence. This challenge was a turning point in European civilization. For more than a thousand years the belief in an active and purposeful deity had been at the core of social thinking, however perverted it may have been in social practice. Now the belief and its derivative Christian ethic were assailed by a new creed of man. The new, like the old, rested on faith. But it was faith in reason, not God, and it promised a utopia built with hands.

Rationalism was by its very nature more than an intellectual revolution. Its goal was a millennium as tangible and materialistic as that of communism today, and its followers expected to transform not only ways of thought and belief but the fabric of society. The political and class structure of the eighteenth-century state was a patchwork of archaism, caprice, and illogic; if these absurdities were deleted, the structure itself might collapse. The most obvious case in point was France, where an arbitrary and inelastic regime was exposed to the ruthlessness of the Gallic mind. But every government in western Europe, the British included, was exposed to a greater or less degree to the same kind of ruthlessness.

The force behind such criticism was not exhausted by attacking religious, political, and social tradition. Inevitably rationalists turned their attention to man's relationship with his physical environment. Scientific curiosity had been growing by leaps and bounds since the sixteenth century, and the discoveries of science had been increasingly utilized by kings and capitalists. But the run of mankind had been little affected. Peasants still bred their stock and ploughed their fields as they had in the Middle Ages, and manufacturers had not yet dreamed of the potentialities in power and mechanical tools. Here, in the basic economy of Europe, tradition still reigned supreme. The philosophers gave it little notice, but the spirit that moved Voltaire to fulminate against the Bourbon absolutism moved lesser men to question the ways of raising calves and cabbages and to speculate on the uses of steam. These humble artisans of the enlightenment were merely applying their reason to the humdrum problems of farm and shop, but in the process they were beginning to transform the physical framework of society.

An observer in Great Britain would have seen spectacular signs of this transformation before the century was out, but little sign of a commensurate change in ways of thought or institutions. In religion, where the churches of fashion were weakened by a philosophic anemia, a dynamic revival was at work outside their pale. In political theory the oustanding figure was Edmund Burke, who scorned the single standard of reason and glorified the values of tradition. The constitution evolved during the period, but by force of circumstance and human obstinacy rather than by that of doctrinaire ideas. The age-old British love of the workable, as opposed to the logical, seemed to be proof against the leaven of rationalism.

But under the surface the leaven was at work. Reformers were demanding that the structure of domestic and imperial government should be revised in the light of common sense. Reform at home was virtually impossible; not until the self-interest of the oligarchy had been shaken, first by a revival of royal influence and then by the demands of a new plutocracy, did logic have a hearing. Reform in the empire was another matter. There the unreason of the tradi-

tional system was obvious, the British interests supporting it were
weak, and the financial incentive to change it was pressing. Reform
was therefore attempted. It was based on an analysis that was theoretically sound but that suffered — like so much analytic logic —
from a belittling of imponderables.

In mercantilist theory the British empire existed for the sake of
profit. The colonies were not considered as mere objects of exploitation, but inevitably the emphasis was upon the profit of the mother
country. Because she furnished the preponderant economic and military power and her prosperity enabled the colonies to prosper, her
interests were central and theirs peripheral. The latter should, if
necessary, be sacrificed to the former, and in consequence the colonies could not and should not have a decisive part in determining
over-all economic policy. That was determined for them by the imperial Parliament at Westminster.

So much for theory. In practice the economic subordination of
the colonies was largely mitigated because the statutes designed to
enforce it — the so-called acts of trade — were laxly administered.
Laxity, however shocking it might be to the theorist, was defensible
in dealing with the North American colonies; it had the effect of
giving them an economic freedom commensurate with their political freedom. A government that ignores its own laws is not acting
rationally but may be acting wisely, and this subconscious wisdom
is an imponderable.

For a century and more the American colonies had been nurtured
on political liberty. During that time Great Britain had been distracted from them, first by her own revolutions and then by the duel
with France, and had thus practiced toward them an inadvertent
laissez faire alien to the mercantilist spirit. In this atmosphere the
old seeds of localism, transplanted to America, had thriven as the
green bay tree. The colonists had a large measure of political autonomy sanctioned by law, and of economic autonomy sanctioned
by neglect of the law; one derived from their charters, the other
from a usage so old that it had acquired for them the legality of custom. The two were facets of the same thing, with which the old colonial system was consonant, for all its illogic, and the doctrinaire
logic of mercantilism was not. Economic subordination was no more
compatible with real self-government than it is today. The British
logicians of empire were gradually forced, in consequence, to the

position that the colonists' political rights were as dependent upon the sovereignty of Westminster as were their economic rights.

Logic had behind it the impetus of necessity. The financial crisis arising from the Peace of Paris could not be solved by imperial laissez faire. In the light of that crisis the old colonial system was revealed in its absurdity, as a jumble of regulations and restrictions that were honored in the breach and did not yield the necessary profit. The King's ministers were as anxious to end this anomaly for the sake of revenue as the reformers were for the sake of common sense. "If any of the provinces of the British empire cannot be made to contribute towards the support of the whole empire," wrote Adam Smith, "it is surely time that Great Britain should free herself from the expense of defending those provinces . . . and endeavor to accommodate her future views and designs to the real mediocrity of her circumstances." [1] Ministers shared Smith's premises, but they refused to face his conclusion. Politics is a road of innumerable bridges, and no politician dares cross too many in advance. The politicians in Whitehall were content with deciding that America should in fairness pay for herself, and with elaborating a plan to make her do so; they scarcely considered what they would do if the plan produced resistance. That question had no attractive answer.

The initial plan was sensible. The colonial legislatures could not be asked to increase direct property taxes, which they controlled, because they had already demonstrated that they would neither co-operate to apportion the burden among themselves nor contribute their fair shares individually; if the initiative were left to them, the loyal colonies would pay while the disaffected went scot free, and the sum raised would be grossly inadequate. The alternative, which was the basis of the program adopted, was taxation levied by authority of the British Parliament in the form of imposts on American commerce and business. The acts of trade were to be increased in scope, and the navy was to be used to suppress illicit trade and strengthen the machinery of collection. The resultant revenue, it was hoped, would be sufficient to pay the cost of colonial defense and the salaries of royal officials in America. Thus the empire would be put upon a sound financial basis.

The implementing of this scheme provoked colonial opposition on

---

[1] The conclusion of *The Wealth of Nations.*

many grounds. The smuggling trade, particularly in molasses, had become a vested interest, and the attempt at law-enforcement became a grievance. The colonial oligarchies entrenched in the assemblies were as impatient of outside interference as the English squires had been in the days of Charles I; they particularly resented the idea that each royal governor would thenceforth be free from dependence on his assembly for his salary and therefore for his conduct. The other purpose of taxation, imperial defense, was a minor matter to Americans now that the French had withdrawn from Canada, and the government's concern with it seemed a pretext for extortion. The excitement which these factors aroused was serious enough, but worse was to come.

The financial issue, as often before in British history, raised a far deeper constitutional problem. Many Americans refused to admit that the taxing power rested with the imperial Parliament, and the next step in their logic was to deny that there was an imperial Parliament. "The king," as Benjamin Franklin put it, "and not the king, lords, and commons collectively, is their sovereign." The Crown governed through the local legislatures, in other words, and Parliament had no more jurisdiction outside the mother country than the House of Burgesses had outside Virginia. The taxing power is in the warp of sovereignty itself, and the colonists' dislike of being taxed from Westminster produced a denial of parliamentary sovereignty. The constitutional fat was now in the fire.

Legal equality between the British and colonial legislatures was the logic of the future, from which eventually grew the present concept of dominion status and the British Commonwealth of Nations. But in the reign of George III such logic was premature. If the British had accepted it they would have been precocious indeed, and not necessarily wise. The decentralization that it implied might well have had the result, at a time when dispatches took two months to cross the Atlantic, of pulling the empire apart through its own centrifugal forces. The argument also ran counter to the British view of the constitution, according to which sovereignty was not separable between Crown and Parliament but was vested in the indivisible entity of Crown in Parliament, so that the king could not govern in America independently of Parliament without governing unconstitutionally. For all these reasons the American logic, important as it was to Britain's future, was inadmissible to the British of the time.

The assertion of the colonial claim was particularly dangerous because it coincided with quarrels at home that were weakening the government. That weakness was another imponderable that the reformers of empire left out of account. The new King was developing his attempt at rule by personal influence, and this apparently extraneous experiment was jeopardizing whatever chance of success the imperial experiment might have had. The two, unrelated in their origins, occurred simultaneously within the core of government, and were soon interdependent. The King's effort to rule in England was an indirect but major cause of revolution in New England, and the surrender of Cornwallis at Yorktown forced the surrender of his master to the oligarchs at home. The great colonial revolt is therefore incomprehensible without an understanding of the concomitant civil war in British politics.

II   The Emergence of the King

GEORGE III's experiment, although it was scarcely the fruit of rationalism, was made possible by the irrationality of the existing system. The oligarchs had paid a price for their monopoly of power: the great bulk of citizens had no stake in the system and regarded it — except in moments of national crisis — with a disinterest bordering on apathy. The rural masses had rights guaranteed them by law, but were largely at the mercy of magistrates, landlords, and the gentry of the House of Commons. Office in the church, the armed services, and the national government was as open to venality and influence as to talent. The theory of representation was more highly developed than in any other major state, but Parliament in practice was a fashionable club. The Crown, it seemed, retained power on the tacit condition that the king should not exercise it. Such paradoxes were an invitation to change, and not only to the rationalist; they were equally inviting to the shrewd politician who sat on the throne. He sensed that the Whigs had behind them neither logic nor loyalty.

Their experience had not prepared them to cope with George III. His accession in 1760 came just a hundred years after that of the last man whose greed for domestic power had been matched by his acumen. George's character and opportunity were very different from those of Charles II, but his ambition was fully as disruptive. He seemed at first sight a welcome relief from the first two Hanoverians. He had a charm of manner they had notably lacked, a dignity, for all his short stature, and a keen if limited intelligence; above all he was British to the core, and his energies were focused on British affairs. Those energies were too great for a passive role. He had to assert himself, and an assertive monarch spelled trouble for the Whigs.

George was no absolutist. He was loyal to his idea of the constitution, which was that ministers should serve him in fact as well as theory, by carrying out policies that he initiated. Once he found the right men, he intended to secure them a majority in the House of Commons through adroit manipulation, through borough-mongering and the use of patronage, and to establish by these ignoble means his concept of true monarchical government. When he governed through a subservient cabinet and parliament he hoped that parties would sink into desuetude, and that the nation would shake off its apathy and become united under the throne.

The time was ripe for the design. George was making no new claims for the prerogative, but merely taking back into his own hands the means of influence that his predecessors had tacitly delegated to their ministers; the constitution was still amorphous. George was not destroying the party system, which had disintegrated years before into sterile factionalism; nor was he corrupting Parliament, for the Whigs had already done that. The cabinet was delicately balanced between king and commons, and the venality of the Lower House reflected the general debasement of politics. These conditions were the opportunity for an obstinate and skilful man determined to beat the politicians at their own game.

The intrusion of this unexpected player put the Whigs in an awkward position. They could not admit his interference without abandoning the concept of government that they had been working out since 1714. Yet on legal grounds they could not combat his interference; the tradition of cabinet autonomy had not yet acquired the legality of long custom. In logic they had only one alternative to giving way — a reform drastic enough to remove the foundation of royal influence. If advancement in the church, the military, and the civil service were freed from dependence on favor, and above all if the rotten boroughs were eliminated and the House of Commons made truly representative of the propertied classes, the King would be defeated. So, in all likelihood, would the Whigs. The means whereby they had maintained their ascendancy for generations were now being used against them; if they destroyed the means, would they not also destroy their ascendancy? Their basic choice was between submitting to the King and risking suicide.

Most of them refused to accept either surrender or reform. Instead they struggled to outplay the King at the old, familiar game; but the cards were stacked against them. They became more desperate and more rancorous as royal influence grew, and the American issue became their weapon. They assailed the idea of taxation, now claiming that Parliament lacked the power to tax without consent, now admitting the power but deploring its exercise. While they were inspired to some extent by the old Whig dislike of governmental trespass on the individual, they were also opportunists. The King had not initiated the scheme of imperial reform, but it was being advanced by successive ministries for which he was held in large measure responsible. Inevitably it became linked with his domestic schemes, until opponents of one were opponents of the other. Even in the decade of the 1760's the lines were being drawn for a civil war on two fronts.

During that decade neither George nor his opponents had a secure majority. The result was a rapid succession of compromise ministries; none was amenable enough to please the King or strong enough to survive his displeasure. In such an atmosphere consistent policy was almost out of the question: a minister could not carry out a long-range plan when he had just assumed office and was about to resign it. The imperial problem was therefore handled in the worst possible way, inconsistently, and under that handling it began to grow from an argument into a war.

The blame does not rest solely on George. The opposition had no plan of its own, but its criticisms made up in cogency and eloquence for what they lacked in creativeness. The principal critic was the greatest figure in British politics, William Pitt, by then Lord Chatham; he and his followers harried a succession of cabinets and contributed their share to the fatal oscillation of policy. In the words of Junius, the mysterious satirist of the period, "their declarations gave spirit and argument to the colonies, and while perhaps they meant no more than the ruin of a minister, they in effect divided one half of the empire from the other."

The result was years of wobbling. Coercion gave place to conciliation, conciliation to coercion again, as succeeding cabinets tried to solve the enigma of how to balance the budget and retain office in the face of recalcitrant Americans and critics at home. The questions at issue with the colonies might conceivably have been compromised if they had been handled over a period of time by a single ministry endowed with firmness, foresight, and moderation. This opportunity was lost in the struggle between an ambitious King and an opposition that could not govern and would not let him govern.

In 1770 a measure of stability returned at last. Many Whigs, discouraged by the ministerial chaos, preferred even royal influence to paralysis, and these reluctant royalists joined the self-seekers to form a group known as the King's Friends. At its head was a man after George's heart. Lord North was a gifted parliamentarian and courtier, an aristocrat to his fingertips, and as malleable by temperament as his master was rigid; he believed wholeheartedly in giving the Crown, as he said, the powers that "it is acknowledged to possess by every sound Whig theory." His accession as prime minister signalized the King's victory at home; the remaining task was to bring the colonies into line. To this North turned in a conciliatory spirit, but the time for conciliation was gone. Great Britain had taken a position that the colonists defied, and from which no self-respecting cabinet could withdraw.

The American Revolution, like its two predecessors in British history, resulted from changes initiated by the central government. King George had far less personal responsibility for change than James II or Charles I, but his prestige was as much involved in the collection of North's duty on tea as Charles's had been in the collection of ship money. Involvement was the price of success. Once George became chief executive in fact as well as name, his position depended on the achievements or failures of his servants. By the same token the colonists were forced to abandon their distinction between Crown and Parliament, now that one controlled the other. "They consider you as united with your servants against America," Junius warned the King, "and know how to distinguish the sovereign and a venal parliament on one side, from the real sentiments of the English people on the other."

The real sentiments of the English people were far from clear. The legality of North's program was widely questioned, and the fear of disrupting the empire increased as colonial resistance mounted. But the only means of staving off disaster was to change the government, and by now the King was so firmly entrenched that change would be revolution. A few extremists threatened to go the whole way. But the nation at large, although it had lost faith in the close and corrupt corporation of government, was apathetic rather than rebellious, and regarded the quarrel with America as the King's affair. Official policy, in consequence, was neither restrained by public opinion while war was germinating, nor strongly supported by it when war began.

For several years North tried conciliation. Obnoxious taxes were removed, and even the notorious duties on tea — which lowered its price in America — were intended as a gesture of good will. But the quarrel had gone too deep to be healed by gestures. The jurisdiction of the mother country was not an issue that could be compromised. On one side of it stood the King, determined with all the obstinacy of his nature that his subjects across the Atlantic should accept his constitutional authority, and backed in this determination by a majority of Parliament. On the other side stood a group of intransigent Americans, particularly in Massachusetts, who were by now equally determined to force matters to a head; they were masters of propaganda, political maneuvers, and calculated rioting, and they made the most of every British blunder. Those blunders were frequent, partly because the King's ministers still had only a vague knowledge of American opinion, partly because their instinctive reaction to defiance was the strong line. To North, Samuel Adams and his ilk were demagogues bent on subverting law and reason; to Adams, North and his master were bent on subverting liberty.

These views were irreconcilable, and the men who held them also held the balance between peace and war. North's cheapened tea was dumped into Boston harbor, and the resultant punishment of Massachusetts raised a tumult throughout the colonies. Violence bred coercion, which bred further violence; as the vicious cycle gained momentum, the last chance of settlement vanished. North made a final effort at concession, but by the time the news of it reached America the Battle of Lexington had been fought.

This was the result of the attempt to rationalize the imperial system. The old system had been in many respects irrational, but it had worked in a slipshod fashion. Within its framework the American colonies had grown into the self-consciousness of adolescence, which demanded — and in practice had received — a larger measure of independence than comported with the ties of empire. When Britain attempted to tighten the ties, reasonably but unwisely, the colonies pulled away. The imperial connection was stretched to the breaking point, and the only remaining question was whether force could preserve it where reason had failed.

III   Civil War in the Empire

THE COMPLEX imperial ties — economic interdependence, sentiment, military power — determined the nature of the ensuing struggle. Colonial economy was intimately associated with the British market, and the war upset mercantile interests on both sides of the Atlantic. The tie of sentiment was stronger: in Britain it convinced many men that armed suppression of the colonists was the most ignoble form of civil war, and sapped the will for drastic military measures; in America it created the loyalists, ardent or passive, who were the constant hope and the recurrent disappointment of the British high command for the next six years. Economic and emotional factors made for disunity in both camps and left the brunt of the effort, as in the Puritan Revolution, to be borne by determined minorities.

The military factor seemed to guarantee that the colonies would be speedily brought to heel. They had grown under the protection of British fleets and armies, and initially had little force of their own. They could improvise an army, but not a navy; the lack of sea power should alone have been fatal to the American cause. From beginning to end the war depended on the sea. If Britain had exploited her control of American waters during the three years that she retained it, she might have choked off the rebellion at the ports. Instead she frittered away her opportunity until France intervened and changed the whole character of the struggle. In those first three years Britain's military policy prepared her defeat.

The reasons behind the policy were less military than political and diplomatic. On the political side, the parliamentary opposition now embraced some of the finest minds of the period — Edmund Burke, the philosopher of conciliation; the stormy young liberal, Charles Fox; and behind them the towering figure of Lord Chatham. The Earl was afflicted by gout and arrogance — "lion-sick, sick of proud heart" — but he was still the most respected man in Britain. Although he had no solution to offer, he saw clearly what was at stake. "America, if she falls," he declared, "will fall like the strong man; she will embrace the pillars of the state and pull down the constitution along with her." His followers could not have risen to such metaphor, but they agreed on the idea behind it, that the whole future of British government hinged on the outcome of the rebellion. They were tacit allies of the Americans, ready to exploit a British defeat as a victory for their cause. The government's military planning was circumscribed accordingly; disasters in America, such as those with which the previous war had begun, might have devastating repercussions in Westminster.

On the diplomatic side, Britain was handicapped by her isolation. She had no friend in Europe, and France and Spain were her inveterate enemies; her colonial involvement was their opportunity to join in an assault on her empire. They were loath, it is true, to traffic with rebellion for fear that the virus might spread to their own empires, but that danger was remote. The chance of gain was immediate and grew brighter with time. The longer the Americans held out, the better risk they became. As soon as their cause proved itself viable, it would be a tremendous temptation despite its republican odor.

These two factors, the domestic opposition and the threat from Europe, placed the government in a strategic dilemma at the outset. They pointed to a single conclusion: the rebellion must be settled promptly, to safeguard the King's position at home and preclude foreign intervention. But settled how? On this essential question the two factors suggested conflicting answers. The destruction of the American army would obviously end the war, and hence the foreign menace, in the shortest possible time. Yet it would entail grave domestic problems. Government had set out to raise money in the colonies, and instead had raised the devil of revolt; to provide enough soldiers to put down the devil would be enormously expensive, and success would only add the burden of a subsequent military occupation. Thus winning the war in the field might destroy the King's experiment by way of the budget. For the first two years, while the Bourbon threat still seemed remote, this solution was rejected for another.

The method attempted was a war of blockade. Its purpose was to protect British trade and choke off American until the rebels were forced to a satisfactory settlement. The prime instrument was the fleet, based on the enemy coast first at Boston, then at New York. Naval pressure was gradual, cumulative, and — for the majority of the people affected — inconspicuous; it could therefore lend weight to negotiations, where invasion would only have embittered the struggle. Blockade was also safer than large-scale land operations. The Americans were powerless to get at the ships, and the supporting troops were almost equally secure; they could move faster by sea than their opponents by land. This form of warfare appealed to the ministers. It risked no disasters great enough to unseat them, and laid a relatively light burden on the taxpayer. It was aimed at forcing negotiations, and a negotiated peace was the only solution, short of British withdrawal, that could be lasting.

Blockade, however, is slow in its effects, and the British aggravated this drawback by half measures. At the end of two years they had failed to strangle American commerce; the rebellion was so strong that France was preparing to gamble on it. They had squandered the most precious of military commodities, time, and needed a quick decision at whatever risk. They therefore tried a quite different strategy, designed to force a settlement by land operations. Their aim was to seize a single key area, the line of the Hudson, in order to cut off New England from the central colonies and so end the war. Their logical method would have been twin offensives, one southward from Canada and one up river from New York, to converge like pincers on Albany. But they threw logic to the winds for the sake of extending the naval blockade. While Burgoyne launched the northern attack, the main army at New York sailed off to capture Philadelphia, and thereby sacrificed that command of the Hudson without which Burgoyne was doomed. His contact with Canada had broken behind him before he reached the river, and he could not establish contact with New York. His surrender at Saratoga emphasized the complete dependence of inland operations on logistics.

Saratoga also ended Britain's one real opportunity to win the war. The surrender proved to Versailles that the rebellion was a sound risk. The Americans had survived strangulation by the Royal Navy and had contained and defeated a British invasion; their defensive power was surprisingly great, and their commander had learned how to use it. Washington was no Marlborough in the field, but as a war leader he had many of the great Duke's qualities — the indefatigable patience, the farsightedness, the elasticity, and above all the power to infuse bickering, self-important men with his own singleness of purpose. That purpose was transforming the revolutionary party into the beginnings of a state, and the French government observed the process with detached interest.

The independence of the United States would be indirectly profitable to France as a blow to British power. But direct profit depended on keeping the war going, not bringing it to a close. It was an extremely useful sideshow, which absorbed a larger proportion of British strength than of French. Sound strategy dictated sending just enough force to prevent an American defeat, while France revenged herself on Britain by conquests elsewhere. When these were secured, the time would be ripe for a general settlement. The United States was for France essentially a means of distracting the enemy, as Prussia had been for Pitt or the Netherlands for Elizabeth.

In the spring of 1778 French intervention extended a civil war on the Atlantic seaboard into a world war fought from the Indian Ocean to the Caribbean. From the military viewpoint Britain would have been well advised to end the American war at once. She could scarcely hope to win it until she had vanquished France, which she had never yet done single-handed, and liquidating it would give her the force to defend the rest of the empire. But political considerations outweighed military; even leaders of the opposition bridled at the thought of recognizing the independence of the United States, and the King would not consider it. At the same time he saw the danger in the alternative course. When France intervened and Spain was expected to follow suit, he pointed out that "if we are to be carrying on a land war against the rebels and against those two powers, it must be feeble in all parts and consequently unsuccessful." That is exactly what it was for the next five years.

At the outset Britain abandoned the grand strategy of her previous war with France. Because the navy did not seriously attempt a

European blockade, the French were able to attack overseas whenever and wherever they chose. Once the British knew a French squadron had sailed, the most they could do was dispatch what they hoped was equivalent force to what they hoped was the point of attack. If their hopes were borne out and their force arrived in time, they were safe. But their supine defensive depended on the luck of good intelligence, fast sailing, and competent commanders in the danger spots. Sooner or later their luck would run out.

It served them remarkably well for more than three years. Spain entered the war in 1779 and the Netherlands at the end of 1780, while the Baltic states formed an armed neutrality to curtail Britain's highhandedness toward their trade with her enemies. If the allies had used their strength effectively, the verdict of 1763 would have been modified or even reversed. But they lacked unity and acumen. The Dutch played a negligible part; the Spaniards captured Minorca and engaged in a fruitless three-year siege of Gibraltar, which immobilized their navy in home waters. The brunt of the overseas war consequently fell to France.

The enemy offensive, fortunately for Britain, was as supine as her own defensive. The French had sedulously strengthened their navy since 1763, but they used it with wasteful caution. Instead of concentrating it against a single British position, they squandered it in a series of minor attacks from Ceylon to Rhode Island. It failed to gain the upper hand in any theater except one, North America, where victory was the least profitable to France. There the British blundered irretrievably, and the French and Americans made the blunder final. The independence of the United States and the collapse of King George's experiment at home were assured simultaneously in Virginia.

In the spring of 1780 the British prepared the way by opening an offensive in the Carolinas while they still held New York. They thereby divided their force in two parts when they could not be sure of controlling the water route between the two. The southern field commander, Lord Cornwallis, then defied logistics by breaking contact with his base at Charleston, and fighting his way by a circuitous route northward to Virginia. He reckoned without his hosts. The Franco-American army marched suddenly from the Hudson to the Chesapeake, while the main French battle fleet sailed from the West Indies; only a part of the British West-Indian fleet followed it. When the two squadrons met off the Chesapeake, the British were badly outnumbered; after one of the dullest and most important engagements of modern history they retreated to New York. Cornwallis, already surrounded by land, was now cut off from help by sea. Six weeks later he surrendered, the victim of an intricate and brilliant combined operation. The British thereafter had nothing left in North America to plan for or fight with, and the war in that theater was finished.

Yorktown was more than an isolated disaster or the concluding episode of a campaign. It was the culmination of six and a half years of military improvisation by British ministers and field commanders. They failed to conquer the colonies when the chance was best, during the first three years, largely because they did not marshal the requisite force but relied on negotiations backed by economical and indolent campaigning. They lost the colonies largely because they embarked on an offensive too great for their resources.

These are only partial explanations. Behind the military realities lay the political, which were the true determinants of strategy. If Yorktown was the doom of King George's experiment, the experiment was what led to Yorktown. By 1775 Britain had been divided against herself, and for the next six years this division cut down her available strength and impaired her effective use of what she had; the rancor of domestic politics spread to the camp and the quarterdeck. Generals and admirals made errors aplenty, but their basic handicap was that of the home front, a numbing of the will.

IV   The Repercussions of Defeat

THE news from Virginia was the deathblow to North's administration; the King was at last constrained to let him resign. Rule by influence was virtually ended, and other hands took up the task of repairing the havoc it had wrought. The immediate necessity was peace, and in 1783 negotiations culminated in the Treaty of Versailles. Britain had lost the American war, and had to concede the independence of the United States. But her losses elsewhere had been minor, and so were her concessions to the Bourbon powers. To Spain she ceded Minorca and Florida, but not Gibraltar, and to France only two minor West-Indian islands and a station on the coast of Africa. Except for Minorca these were trifling changes.

Britain had lost heavily in prestige and power, but her traditional enemies had gained nothing commensurate. Of all the belligerents, in fact, the only one that achieved its objectives was the infant United States.

The treaty left that infant in a remarkable situation. The verdict of 1763 was reaffirmed as it related to France and Spain: neither returned to North America in strength. Spain, it is true, held Florida and the vast wilderness of Louisiana, but she did so essentially on sufferance; the sea lanes to her colonies were commanded by the Royal Navy. The United States was even more negligible as a power, for her tiny fleet was abolished and her regular army reduced to eighty men. The only effective force in North America was British.

Britain, as will soon be seen, was learning a new circumspection in the use of force, and her urge for territorial aggrandizement was giving place to the lure of industrial and commercial expansion. She was committed to holding Canada and maintaining naval control of the Atlantic, but no British cabinet seriously planned to reconquer the United States or even to encircle it, as the French had encircled the thirteen colonies. If the republic could accommodate itself to British sea power and resist the temptation to annex Canada, it had the possibility of expansion to the Caribbean and eventually to the Pacific. France and Spain could not bar its way; it was insulated from Europe by the British fleet. For a century the United States was free to grow into a great power without ever possessing, except in her civil war, the army or navy by which every other great power was known. Thus the civilian tradition in British society, developed because of insularity, continued to develop in American society because of insulation.

Great Britain did not provide the insulation from kindness. She acted from necessity and policy — necessity, in that she had to retain control of the western Atlantic for the defense of Canada; policy, in that her distrust of France and Spain predisposed her to favor whatever would curtail their influence in the New World. At bottom her interests complemented those of the United States. Although the tradition of antagonism between the two, derived from the revolution, embittered relations and contributed to periodic crises for another century, it was rooted in emotion more than reason. War was often threatened but materialized only once, and then as much by luck as by design. A basic community of interests, recognized only at rare moments, molded developments on both sides of the Atlantic. It enabled the British to reconcile themselves to the loss of their most advanced colonies, and it enabled the United States to grow to nationhood within the orbit of British power.

The British reconciled themselves because defeat began a transformation in their ideas of imperialism. The mercantilist concept had received a rude shock: the attempt to make the colonies profitable had shattered the empire. Few were as yet ready for Burke's great vision of colonies bound to the mother country by immaterial bonds of affection, kinship, and common experience, "ties which, though light as air, are as strong as links of iron." Equally few were ready for Adam Smith's pessimistic alternative, that Great Britain should slough off unprofitable colonies and "accommodate her views and designs to the real mediocrity of her circumstances." Yet the cash nexus of empire had been assayed by war and found inadequate; a new principle was needed. It did not fully mature for another fifty years, but developments of the 1780's showed signs of a significant departure from the spirit of mercantilism. The change can best be seen in the handling of two imperial problems, one in Ireland and one in India.

King George had made his influence felt as much in Dublin as in London. He had used his control of patronage both to increase his power in Ireland and to reward his British henchmen. The result of this and other factors was to alienate even the Dublin oligarchy, and to stimulate the demand for a legislative independence that would leave the Crown the only link between Ireland and Britain. This demand was similar to that which had been advanced in America, and from the British viewpoint it had the same constitutional drawback: the Crown was inseparable from the Westminster Parliament. But the political setting was wholly different. Ireland was near at hand, and her oligarchs, even if they acquired legal autonomy, could not evade the fact that their power depended upon the British connection.

Events in America enormously stimulated the reform movement in Ireland. After 1776 it came under the leadership of Henry Grattan, a statesman who combined the Irish gift for oratory with an un-Irish gift for moderation. His program included not only legislative independence, but the removal of restrictions on Irish commerce and, most significant of all, on the Catholics. The age-old religious

163

intolerance of Dublin, which had done so much to perpetuate the curse of Cromwell, was being touched by a new spirit. Grattan was seeking to transform a narrow and corrupt legislature into the symbol not of the Anglican or even the Protestant interest, but of Ireland.

This dawning nationalism needed force to be effective, and Britain was compelled to provide it with force. The war with France and Spain raised the old danger of invasion at a moment when the regular army was almost entirely deployed overseas, and the North administration reluctantly allowed the enlistment and arming of an Irish militia. These volunteers put teeth in Grattan's program, and he won two major concessions from Britain. In 1780 the Irish acquired virtual trade equality at home and throughout the empire; in 1782 their Parliament was emancipated from control by the Irish and English privy councils and raised to a position of legal equality with the Westminster Parliament. This step, taken in time of crisis, was a striking contrast to the coming together of England and Scotland in a similar crisis years before. Britain and Ireland moved apart; their legal bond became merely a common sovereign of limited powers. On the surface the settlement presaged the modern concept of dominion status.

Under the surface, however, it meant far less. Patronage was still controlled by the Crown, which therefore had the same sort of influence in Dublin as in Westminster. The Irish Parliament, furthermore, still represented oligarchs who, despite moments of nationalist fervor, had no roots in the nation at large and did not speak for it. They could not be expected to reform themselves by adopting the whole of Grattan's program, for they would never willingly abdicate their power. The emancipation of the Catholic majority, and even of the Ulster Presbyterians, seemed as remote as ever, and without emancipation independence was illusory.

The final weakness in the settlement was that the concessions made by Britain, voluntary as they appeared, had been won by the threat of force. All Grattan's oratory could not conceal this fact, which was part of the tragic pattern of Anglo-Irish relations. The British knew that when their difficulties were serious the Irish would add to them, as in 1598, in 1641, in 1690; the Irish knew that they could wrest concessions from Britain only by force when she was weak.

The auguries for the future were unhappy. But for the moment all was serene. The British had relinquished a fraction of their power with a forbearance and good will they had not shown in their recent stand on the American question. Even if they were making a virtue of necessity, the virtue was novel.

A similar novelty appeared in their attitude toward India. During the two decades after 1763 the Indian problem had for the first time come to the forefront of politics, because the premises which had long underlain British influence in India were crumbling, as they were in America. The one question, like the other, touched the fundamentals of empire, and in the hard light of the American disaster the premises of Indian government were reappraised and altered.

The old premises were those of business more than of government, and they produced a monstrosity. The East India Company, existing essentially for the profit of its shareholders, acquired political influence in spite of its directors. Their hand was forced by their servants on the spot, who were driven deeper and deeper into the maze of native politics by their desire to enrich the company and themselves, and even more by the force of circumstance. The chaos of eighteenth-century India turned foreign traders into politicians willy nilly.

The disintegration of native Indian authority and the disarming of the French produced a power vacuum. The Company was a power. It had behind it stable revenues and an open line of communications with Britain. It had learned in self-defense to employ native mercenaries, trained and officered by Europeans; the glittering hordes of a rajah were no match for this disciplined force of sepoys, and the temptation to use it grew with the growth of native anarchy. At first the Company troops were assigned to protect a well-disposed prince on condition that he pay for them. This technique culminated in Bengal of the 1760's, where a native puppet had the hopeless task of governing the province while collecting its revenues and turning them over to the Company. They were such a rich harvest that the shareholders demanded higher dividends and the government appropriated £400,000 a year. Such inroads deprived the Company of most of its working capital, and Bengal fell into administrative squalor.

This intolerable situation produced the regulating act of 1773, the first direct governmental interference in Company affairs. The directors were required to keep the cabinet informed of their political moves, and administrative changes were imposed on them: a governor-general was created, with authority over the three Company centres in Bengal, Madras, and Bombay, and four men were named to his council and given power to veto his policies. The act was well meant but badly drawn. The complexity of Indian affairs was not yet clearly understood in London, and supervision by an ill-informed government could scarcely transmute the Company's profit motive into a sense of imperial responsibility.

The next eleven years were the crisis of British power in India. Just when the mother country was for the first time facing a hostile Europe, her position in India was threatened by the first great native coalition. Her agents had been sowing the wind by a decade of reckless exploitation and interference, and the seeds grew into a whirlwind as soon as French intriguers promised a fleet and army. The princes of central India, whose disunity had hitherto made possible the Company's position, combined to drive the British into the sea.

If the Company's power was inadequate to meet this threat, the governor-general was superbly adequate. Warren Hastings was as great a proconsul as Britain ever produced. For years he fought a tenacious and daring defensive until he succeeded in splitting the coalition, just before the French arrived to cement it, and in 1784 peace was restored. On the surface the British had neither gained nor lost, but the foundation of their influence had been enormously strengthened. Hastings had won them prestige, that subtle virtue that was more persuasive than armies in the power politics of India.

The close of the war coincided with the passage by Parliament of a new regulating act, which established the main framework of administration for three-quarters of a century. An official board of control, working through the directors, assumed final authority, and the center of Indian government was thus transferred from India House to Whitehall. At the same time the act precluded treaty relations with the native princes, and so continued for a short time the Company's antiquated principle of staying out of politics. The responsibility of power could not be avoided for long by a statute, and the principle did not outlast the century.

Hastings returned home in 1785. Three years later he was impeached. The most prominent liberals in Parliament — Burke, Fox, and Sheridan — saw in him the personification of the ruthlessness and rapacity that had stained the British record in India for the past generation. They hounded him with all the wiles of the prosecutor, and their oratory gave to even the flimsiest charges the sound of thunder from Olympus. After seven years he was acquitted on all counts, and retired to live on a pension from the company he had saved.

In one sense his impeachment was tragedy spiced with vindictiveness, but in a deeper sense it was the sign of a new spirit. Thoughtful Englishmen had long been disturbed by the rumors coming out of India and by the wealth of the returned Company servants who lorded it as "nabobs" at home. The government, instead of limiting the game of exploitation, had joined in it as earnestly as the shareholders, until the scandal lay heavy on the public conscience. The English people, Voltaire remarked, were as jealous of the liberties of others as they were of their own. When they themselves became the oppressors, their sense of guilt demanded a sacrifice. Hastings was the victim, selected unfairly and prosecuted intemperately. He was not accountable for the system; but its iniquity was real, and through him it was attacked.

The impeachment demonstrated a fundamental principle: the Company's governmental functions were delegated to it by the state, to which the Company agents were responsible. This principle implied another: the state itself must be responsible for the people of India; otherwise the irresponsibility of the trader would merely be replaced by that of the bureaucrat. The Crown could justify its intrusion into Indian government, in the last analysis, only on the ground that it was acting for the benefit of the governed. This justification is implicit in the peroration with which Burke closed his indictment of Hastings.

I impeach him in the name of all the commons of Great Britain, whose national character he has dishonored. I impeach him in the name of the people of India, whose laws, rights, and liberties he has subverted, . . . whose country he has laid waste and desolate. I impeach him in the name and by the virtue of those eternal laws of justice which he has violated.

Here was a new ingredient in British imperialism. If the Seven Years' War introduced a romantic emphasis on power, foreign to the mercantilist spirit, the trial of Hastings revealed a more subtle form of romanticism — the idea that power justifies itself in the welfare of subject races. The idea had vast potentialities for the future because it was a blend of reason and emotion. Reason suggested that backward peoples like the Indians could enjoy their laws, rights, and liberties only within a framework of order provided by Britain; emotion added an intoxicating sense that the creation of order was Britain's duty toward the backward. The result, over the years to come, was the distilling of nationalism into an imperialist faith, for which Kipling provided the creed a century after Hastings's acquittal.

> Take up the White Man's burden —
> And reap his old reward:
> The blame of those ye better,
> The hate of those ye guard —
> The cry of hosts ye humor
> (Ah slowly!) toward the light: —
> 'Why brought ye us from bondage,
> Our loved Egyptian night?' [2]

In the decade following the Peace of Versailles the leaven of change was working as much at home as in the empire. New political and economic forces were undermining the foundation of the oligarchy. Their obvious effects were postponed for half a century and more, largely by Britain's involvement in her struggle with the French Revolution, but under the surface the forces were continuously at work to mold the Victorian future.

In politics, the collapse of King George's experiment paved the way for a modern cabinet. George fought tenaciously to keep his power, but he was no longer a match for the opposition. Conservative Whigs had lost their veneration for him, and they joined hands with the reformers to abolish his most flagrant means of controlling the House of Commons. He was so disgusted with his former friends that he then turned to "the boy" of British politics; in December of 1783 William Pitt, Chatham's younger son, assumed the premiership at the age of twenty-four. He held that office, with one brief intermission, until his death in 1806. During those years the British political system began to assume a recognizably modern form.

George, even though his influence was curtailed, had no intention of retiring to a constitutional niche. At the outset Pitt lacked both

---

[2] Rudyard Kipling: "The White Man's Burden" from *The Five Nations.* Copyright 1903, 1931 by Rudyard Kipling, reprinted by permission of Mrs. George Bambridge and Doubleday & Company, Inc.

the prestige and the solid majority needed to force the King into retirement. But he had a great name behind him, a will and pride to match his father's, and an unbelievably precocious skill in handling the House; gradually he strengthened his grip on power. He was no inveterate enemy of prerogative, like Fox, but he was equally far from being a North. He rode his cabinet on a light rein and handled his sovereign with a tactful firmness that gave him no chance to impose his will. George's obstinacy, now aggravated by a recurrent mental disease, was always difficult, and in later years produced one major clash. But in general the King allowed himself to be led slowly out of politics — and so into an unwonted popularity. When he no longer sought to rule he became at last what he had set out to be, the father of his people, and the long war made him the focus of the nation's loyalty. The Crown, in short, was beginning to assume its modern dualism, a character that is intensely personal from the viewpoint of popular emotion and thoroughly impersonal from the viewpoint of government.

The result was true ministerial responsibility, although still in the narrow terms of the period. Pitt was no longer, like his predecessors, accountable in fact to both the sovereign and the House of Commons; the House alone was the center of authority. It was still, however, largely a closed world, immune to popular pressure except at moments of great excitement, and neither Pitt nor the rank and file of the Whigs had any desire to change the situation. They acquiesced in the small reforms needed to exclude direct royal influence, but they opposed any sweeping reform lest it sweep away their own position.

The demand for such reform was appearing in many quarters. The existing system, whether dominated by the Crown or the magnates, was a government isolated from the governed. It had long justified itself to the nation by success, but now the American disaster had shaken its prestige beyond the power of the borough-mongers to repair. Although they took back their power from the King and used it effectively, it was ceasing to be accepted as part of an immutable social order. Radical and even liberal Whigs, jolted by the loss of the colonies and touched by new ideas, were beginning to demand a revision of the system, and the amorphous Whiggism of the previous generation was cohering into two groups, the proponents of a new order and the defenders of the old. The former eventually monopolized the name of Whigs, while the conservatives reverted to the name of Tories. Thus the two parties of the Stuart era, generated by the conflicts over Crown and Church, were regenerated at the moment when both Crown and Church had ceased to be political issues.

This renascence of party was as important for the future of British government as the decline in royal influence, and as gradual. Signs of it appeared in the 1780's, but the subsequent war gave such an overwhelming impetus to conservatism that for years the liberals were an impotent minority. The forces of change, however, were working for them. By the time the oligarchy had weathered the war, it was a house divided against itself; behind the imposing eighteenth-century façade the structure was splitting apart. In 1815 the Tories were still in power, but their days were numbered. The victory they achieved over revolution abroad was the beginning of their end.

V   Economic Revolution

THE UNITY of the oligarchs could scarcely have been shattered by political forces alone. If they had retained that monopoly of wealth from which their political power had derived, few of them could have been argued into improving the governmental machinery, let alone into sharing control of it with outsiders. But by the close of the century the foundation of their wealth was beginning to crack. Some of them were falling on hard times; others, richer than before, were making their money in new ways. Outsiders were rising to fortune almost overnight and clamoring for their share of power. They clamored in vain. The parliamentary system, elastic as it was, could not accommodate the rush of newcomers, and consequently ceased to represent the entire wealth of the country. Oligarchy was no longer synonymous with plutocracy, and excluded plutocrats turned to reform as their battering-ram against the locked doors of Parliament. The Whigs inside eventually became their champions, as they had championed dissent more than a century before, and out of this alliance a new Whiggism was born.

The revival of the two-party system, in summary, was to a large degree the result of economic change. But the result was dwarfed by the cause. Britain was undergoing an economic revolution that transformed agriculture, manufacturing, commerce, social relations, long before it set its mark on Parliament. It eventually remade Britain's character and her position in the world, and then went on to remake the world itself. Even in the 1790's, in its early stages, it was becoming a central theme of British history.

For centuries Great Britain had been amassing the wherewithal for an explosion of material progress. The growth of her commerce, stimulated by the production of wool for export and by the resultant enclosure movement, had been assisted by political accident — the timely decay of Spanish power, the absorption of the Dutch and then of the French into the maelstrom of Continental wars. Britain had capitalized, in the literal sense, on her double blessing of pastures and insularity. The result was that profits, reinvested to create further profits, led at length to a surplus of wealth that sought new fields for investment.

The obvious field was the land of England. Sheepfolds could not be expanded indefinitely, if only because the market for raw wool was finite; but the enclosure movement had broken the shackles of the manorial system and pointed the way to another form of rural capitalism, the exploitation of the arable. The growing population had heightened the demand for food, and the landed interest had the money and power to satisfy the demand. In the eighteenth century an enormous resurgence of enclosure, financed by the oligarchy and legalized by its parliamentary instrument, increased the yield and the profit of farming. Simultaneously the landlords began to improve the methods of husbandry, from turnip-raising to cattle-breeding; the stature of vegetables and animals, if not of man, could be increased by taking thought, and in the process English agriculture was transformed. Its methods had hitherto been medieval; now it became a competitive, scientific, and lucrative form of business.

The agrarian changes were felt throughout the country. For the moment they strengthened the position of the landed interest, and so of the political conservatives, by the flow of wealth from the soil. But other results were more significant. Only a fraction of the new capital could profitably be reinvested in land, and the remainder was a force for expansion elsewhere. Because husbandry required fewer workers than before, those pushed off the land perforce sought other employment. The food supply outstripped the needs of the rural population. Thus agricultural development created three of the prerequisites for the factory system. Without a surplus of capital and manpower, large-scale manufacture would have been impossible; without a surplus of food, the great industrial centers would have starved.

The other chief prerequisite, a demand for English manufactures, had been operative ever since English woolens had become a European staple. But the eighteenth-century wool trade was too inelastic to take full advantage of its opportunities. It had grown under the protection and surveillance of the state, and the price of privilege was conservatism; the trade was slow to gamble on new techniques or conquer new markets even when it began to face serious competition at home. The competitor was cotton. The spectacular rise of cotton manufacturing, which had its ramifications throughout British economy, was both an example and a major cause of the Industrial Revolution.

The British public had acquired a taste for cotton fabrics from the imports of the East India Company. By the early eighteenth century the vogue of "calicoes" (from the Indian port of Calicut) gave birth to a domestic industry, which sprouted despite opposition from the Company and then from the wool interests. Cotton was an urchin among British manufactures — underprivileged, tough, combative, and ingenious in surmounting handicaps. The great head start of the wool trade could be offset only by the most enterprising men experimenting with the newest techniques and implements to give them an edge over their competitors. These men were lone wolves. Their struggles with each other and with the wool magnates brought into being the factory system.

The great obstacle to increasing and cheapening production was lack of equipment. The primitive tools with which the cotton trade had begun were a challenge to reason in a rationalistic age, and the needs and ambitions of the factory-owners gave the inventors their market; if necessity was the mother of invention, profit was the father. Each improvement led to further improvements because the acceleration of one stage in the manufacturing process created the incentive to accelerate, and therefore to mechanize, another. The flying shuttle increased the speed of weaving, for example, to the point where hand-spinning no longer provided sufficient thread, and the result was the spinning jenny and the mule. These machines soon produced thread faster than it could be used, until weaving was speeded again by the introduction of the power loom. Manufacture was by then outstripping the supply of raw material, and that short-age was solved in America by the cotton gin. So the process went, in an intricate web of cause and effect spreading farther and farther from its center.

The immediate effects were on other British industries. As water power, with its seasonal fluctuations, gradually gave place to steam, the need for iron to make machines and coal to run the steam engine transformed the techniques of mining; the vast subterranean wealth of the island began to be exploited. At the same time transportation was being revolutionized, primarily to solve the problem of weight. Coal, iron ore, machinery, and even food and textiles in bulk were too heavy for the mud roads of the period. A partial solution was provided by canals and turnpikes, built with private capital and operated for profit, and by the work of such men as Telford and McAdam in modernizing the king's highway. But these improvements did not fill the need, which grew for another generation until it produced the railroad age.

The effects of industrialization were also felt in Britain's social structure. The dramatic developments there, as in transportation, did not come until after the Napoleonic wars, but even by the 1780's the hallmark of a new order was being stamped upon the north of England. Small villages were mushrooming into factory towns, and whole districts that had been dozing since the Middle Ages were waking to the noise of forges and gears. A vast shift of population was beginning, caused by forces beyond human control. The new machines were cumbersome, expensive, and therefore concentrated; the areas of concentration were determined by economic factors such as the availability of power and raw materials. Because food for the workers was no longer the predominant factor, the center of English agriculture was not the center of the new industry. The food-producing counties, the traditional heart of the nation, were in the south; the foci of manufactures and mining were in the wilds of the north, in the Midlands, and in southern Wales. This change in the whole structure of population created or accentuated grave social problems.

One was a new form of poverty. As the small-scale rural tenants were forced off their land, they became either migrant farm laborers or industrial workers, and in both cases their existence was precarious. Agriculture and industry were in transition. Even their shrewdest capitalists gambled upon an unpredictable future and progressed by a somersault of expansion and retrenchment, during which they took on and laid off hands in bewildering succession. The average hand could not survive for long without work. He had been forced from subsistence farming on the manor into subsistence on wages alone, and he was almost defenseless against unemployment, whether caused by the business cycle or by his own infirmity. In rural England a paternalistic gentry might mitigate his existence, but in a new mill town it was likely to be poor, nasty, brutish, and short. If the mill did not lay him off, working conditions soon incapacitated him through sickness or premature old age. Employers had little time for compassion on themselves or their laborers, and they begrudged any diversion of capital from business to poor relief. The machinery of relief, scarcely changed since the days of Elizabeth, began to break down under the load of pauperism. The result was appalling misery.

Another problem, more immediately disturbing to the oligarchs than the new poverty, was a new form of wealth. The pacemakers of progress were young industries that had grown too fast for the trammels of governmental control, and the men who made their mark were a new breed of capitalist. They were for the most part social parvenus who had forced their way up from the lower classes by a blend of daring, acumen, and ruthlessness, the qualities required for survival in a world of cut-throat competition. Success gave them a contempt for the relatively staid and tidy world of the older manufactures, and for the system of state supervision by which that world was bounded. They clamored for economic freedom — in other words for laissez faire.

The time was ripe for this doctrine. Governmental surveillance had been gradually losing its vitality ever since businessmen had turned against the interference of Charles I. As the Stuart concept of paternalism in the national interest had given place to the oligarchic interests of the Whigs, Parliament had shown an increasing tendency to keep its hands off business, until by the late eighteenth century a large measure of free enterprise was sanctioned by practice. But the new industrialists wanted more than that. They hoped not only to free the manufacturing process from the last remnants of state regulation, but to destroy the elaborate mercantilist system that restricted the marketing of their goods. They particularly opposed the tariff barriers that were an integral part of the system, and their eventual goal was free trade.

A minor episode at the beginning of Pitt's administration fore-shadowed the struggle to come. The Prime Minister, like Walpole before him, was anxious to heal the old quarrel with France, and his method was in effect a reciprocal trade treaty for the lowering of tar-iffs. The leaders of the conservative and long-established industries, nurtured on protection, organized themselves to combat this move toward economic liberalism, and were seconded by intransigent pa-triots who opposed any reconciliation with the Bourbons. The lead-ers of the new industries, on the contrary, considered the treaty a step toward free trade and gave it their vociferous support. They and Pitt carried the day. The signing of the treaty in 1786 was cele-brated by a jingle that breathes, for all its poetic demerits, the spirit of the nineteenth-century free-trader:

> May kingdom 'gainst kingdom no more be at spite;
> For both 'twere much better to trade than to fight;
> And whilst mutual friendship and harmony reign,
> Our buttons we'll barter for pipes of champagne.[3]

Pitt's treaty, like most of his other peacetime policies, was soon lost in the storm of war. But the economic interests that had sup-ported him grew steadily stronger, and as the plutocrats of mill and mine and furnace went on developing their program it gradually turned them into politicians. They could not implement it without far more political influence than they had; their bailiwicks, the new industrial areas, had been insignificant when the system of parlia-mentary representation had taken form in the Middle Ages, and were still grossly under-represented. In the decades to come, therefore, the industrialists turned from their economic aims to the prerequi-site of parliamentary reapportionment, and they eventually became the driving force behind the reform movement.

Great Britain, in summary, was in the grip of revolution. The ef-fects were being felt in society as much as in technology, and even in politics the need for change was widely admitted. The question of the degree and speed of reform was beginning to divide the oli-garchy again into parties. The Tories were circumspect and slow,

---

[3] Quoted by Witt Bowden: "The English Manufacturers and the Commer-cial Treaty of 1786 with France," *American Historical Review*, XXV (Oct., 1919), 25.

willing to move with the times but unwilling to be jostled by them, and for all his liberal measures Pitt was not at heart a reformer; his respect for the past was too great and his political vision too limited. The Whigs were therefore becoming the champions of change, and they had behind them the mounting force of the industrialists' unrest; it might have seemed to an acute observer at the end of the 1780's that they would soon begin to refashion the structure of the country. Appearances were deceptive. Instead of Whig enlightenment, Tory conservatism remained entrenched for another forty years.

VI   War against the French Revolution

THE REASON lay not in Great Britain but on the Continent. From 1789 until 1815 no European country followed a normal process of growth; all were twisted to a greater or less degree by the vast explosion that radiated from Paris. Great Britain was less directly affected than Austria, Prussia, or Spain because she was cushioned by water: the Channel assumed an importance it had not had since 1588 and was not to have again until 1940. But nothing could save her entirely from the concussion, and it warped her natural development. While she increased enormously in economic and military power, she paid a price in social maladjustment and political atrophy. This lopsidedness ensured her survival but necessitated drastic changes in the post-war era.

The opening of the French Revolution aroused few misgivings in England. Patriots congratulated themselves on the apparent disruption of Britain's great enemy, and few were farsighted enough to see that the *ancien régime* had become a strait-jacket on the inherent power of France. Reformers were enormously stimulated by the ideas of the revolution in its early and moderate years, and even conservatives felt, with approving condescension, that the French were at last achieving the advantages so long enjoyed by Englishmen. These views were superficial and therefore transient, for French radicalism was more fundamental than most of its British observers realized.

On its philosophical side the French Revolution was as much a product of applied reason as the revolt of the American colonies or the transformation of Lancashire. French intellectuals had demonstrated the illogic of the Bourbon regime and worked out formulæ for reconstructing it; the revolutionaries grappled confidently with the task of applying the formulæ and creating utopia. Their premise, like that of their American counterparts who had framed the Declaration of Independence, was that government is the means to an end, means that may be abolished and remade in whatever way will best serve the end. This premise was not widely accepted across the Channel even by liberals, and at the close of 1790 it was assailed by Britain's outstanding political philosopher. The assault opened the Anglo-French war of ideas.

Edmund Burke's *Reflections on the Revolution in France* was one of the great political documents of the century. It not merely predicted the development of French liberalism into military dictatorship; far more important, it presented an ideal of conservatism for contrast with the revolutionary ideal – a profession of faith as eloquent as the declarations of the National Assembly, and one that elevated the status quo into a cause worth fighting for. The book was valuable not merely for the moment, nor even for the quarter-century of war ahead; it became the bible of Toryism.

Burke denied that the state is a mere convenience, to be reshaped as reason dictates. For him it is an organic unity, composed of habits, prejudices, past history, as much as of law or logic, and in this living organism the present generation is linked with those that went before and those that come after. If his concept of the state is acceptable, as it was to the vast majority in Britain, operating upon such an organism with the rationalist's knife is constitutional murder.

Burke struck also at the doctrine of natural rights. Every citizen, he admitted, exercises a degree of direct or indirect influence upon the state and is guaranteed certain liberties by it. But he contended that those liberties are an inheritance, enjoyed according to the conditions of the moment and only as the counterpart of duties; and that in the exercise of liberties and the performance of duties the citizen has a moral obligation to "the one great maker, author, and founder of society." This obligation is kept before him by the church, which is the moral force in government and without which government is meaningless. Burke therefore indicted the French revolutionaries as much for their treatment of the church as for their treatment of the monarchy.

His major indictment, however, was of revolution as a method. He insisted on the need of reform in any society, and was fully aware that atrophy means death; "a state without the means of some change is without the means of its conservation." But he also insisted that the reformer must understand the reason behind an abuse before trying to remedy it; the underlying principle may be sound, and the abuse merely a perversion. The radical would sweep away the present mixture of good and bad on the chance that the future will be better. Burke would retain the good in the mixture and gradually and cautiously amend the bad. Guidance in reforming, he contended, is given by the experience of the past, which sets on human institutions the seal of prescriptive value.

This was an intensely national brand of conservatism. Against the universality of French ideas, with their appeal to immediate destruction, Burke set the ideal of slow change and invested it with a majesty of its own; against the abstract rights of man — of all men everywhere — he set the particular liberties of Englishmen. His argument grew from the soil of Magna Carta and the Bill of Rights, from the long tradition of remedying specific grievances in specific ways to accord with the needs of the moment rather than with reason's eternal ultimates. It was this indigenous quality in the *Reflections* that made the book welcome to the oligarchy. The French were preaching worldwide truths in the name of mankind; Burke met them with British truths in the name of John Bull.

He was answered by a number of Francophiles, Tom Paine among them, but the reading public was as much antagonized by their doctrinaire radicalism as it was stirred by Burke's defense of prescriptive values. The common people followed the lead of their betters, and turned with undiscriminating exuberance against the proponents of either revolution or reform. This fact is far more phenomenal than the success of the *Reflections*. From 1790 to 1815 British society was in labor, giving birth to a new proletariat and a new plutocracy, and the former was the sickly twin. Pauperism and misery were rampant among the workers at just the time when the oligarchies of the Continent were dissolving in a ferment of revolution. Why did the ferment not spread across the Channel? Part of the answer lies in the great war, which reinforced the conservatism of the British lower classes with a patriotic hatred of Frenchmen and French ideas. Another and more significant part lies in a spiritual revival that affected the whole character of the proletariat.

More than half a century before, during the prosaic tranquillity of the Walpole era, three remarkable men had gone to war against the spirit of rationalism in religion. All three were ministers of the Church of England — John Wesley, the prophet and organizer of Methodism; his gentler and more conservative brother Charles, the poet of the movement; and George Whitefield, as powerful a revivalist as the English-speaking peoples have ever produced. Those three and their followers went into the highways and byways of the British Isles and America, preaching a new faith to all who cared to hear — and to many who at first did not. Bar-flies, sailors at the docks, mill-hands, colliers, were the "congregations" of the early Methodists. The movement spread like wildfire, and soon Whitefield was addressing crowds of ten and twenty thousand. Within a generation the people at large were being stirred with an enthusiasm unseen since the days of the preaching friars.

Orthodox religion, whether Anglican or dissenting, had made little impression on the bulk of the people. Pastoral care had been largely confined to the world of Sunday church-goers, and even John Wesley felt at the start that saving a soul was almost sinful except in church. Most clergymen were less concerned with salvation than with teaching a reasonable morality, in which the disturbing elements of the gospel were judiciously subordinated. This creed appealed to the minds of the educated, not to the hearts of the illiterate and hungry, and religion was becoming identified with respectability.

The Methodists were spiritual revolutionaries. Their creed, unlike that of the Jacobins, derived from nonrational premises; instead of man's goodness and perfectibility they talked of sin, hell-fire, and a heaven achieved solely through grace. They were often anti-intellectual and even grossly superstitious, and their excesses were almost as shocking to contemporaries as those of the Jacobins; what was hailed by the devout as the workings of grace seemed to the sceptics to be mania. Worse yet, the new evangelists preached a democracy of faith that shocked the established order. They were endeavoring, complained an irate duchess, "to level all ranks and do away with all distinctions. It is monstrous to be told that you have a heart as sinful as the common wretches that crawl the earth." [4]

The Church of England tried to exclude these disturbers of its

---

[4] Quoted by William E. H. Lecky: *The History of England in the Eighteenth Century* (8 vols.; New York; 1888–91), II, 671.

peace. John Wesley, who had begun as a high churchman, was gradually and reluctantly driven to deny apostolic succession and ordain his preachers himself. This was open schism; by the end of the century the Methodists were largely outside the fold, but they had generated a force that transformed the parent church. Their enthusiasm had touched large numbers of the parochial clergy, from whom the so-called evangelical movement spread outward and upward even to the bench of bishops. The effect was to shift the Anglican emphasis from morals to salvation, to set in motion good works ranging from Sunday schools to the abolition of slavery, and to increase the influence of the establishment among the unenfranchised middle class and even — though to a far lesser degree than Methodism — among the mass of the people. Simultaneously the dissenting sects were waked out of their torpor by the bustle of faith around them, and the nonconformist conscience began to stir.

This revival, like other developments of the period, was already determining the character of Victorian Britain. But the immediate effect was to give the nation the spirit it needed to survive the next quarter-century. From the realist's viewpoint evangelicalism was a priceless social asset: it distracted the masses from their miseries in this world by intoxicating them with the world to come, it turned a vast amount of reforming zeal from politics to revival meetings, and it mitigated discontent both by stimulating philanthropy and by emphasizing the brotherhood of all believers. The new faith, though egalitarian, was less revolutionary in its social implications than the duchess feared; for the moment its crude but forceful Protestantism was turned against the Jacobins as Antichrist. While Burke justified the church to the literate as inherited wisdom and religion as the moral core of society, the evangelicals woke in the illiterate a deep religious emotion. These ingredients of philosophy and faith were fused, in the heat of the nation's struggle for survival, into a cause that had the force of crusade.

At the outset the ruling class had little sense of this cause. Pitt himself, like most of the oligarchs, was by nature neither a friend of revolution nor a reactionary; he was a free-thinker, absorbed with the manipulation of power rather than with constitutional principles or the clash of faiths. He was too sensible to fear an insurrection at home and too much a product of the old order to appreciate, as Burke did, the portent of events abroad. For the first three years of the revolution he watched its development without undue alarm, and he hoped until the last minute to avoid a struggle with it.

But war was inherent in the character of the revolution. The very universality of its ideas challenged every other regime in Europe, and the French pressed the challenge. In the spring of 1792 they opened hostilities against Austria and Prussia; soon afterward they imprisoned the King, turned back an allied invasion, and over-ran the Austrian Netherlands, Savoy, and western Germany. As the revolution became European, Great Britain could not long remain aloof. The balance of power was being upset, and the old enemy was again ensconced in the Low Countries, hungrily eyeing the riches of Holland to the north. In Paris the rising tide of radicalism engulfed the King, who was guillotined in January 1793. The British public had had almost a century and a half in which to forget the ex-cesses of revolution, and it was simultaneously outraged by the de-pravity and alarmed by the military gains of the French. In this at-mosphere diplomatic relations deteriorated rapidly, until within a few weeks of the King's execution the French Republic declared war.

Pitt hated war on principle, and both psychologically and mili-tarily he was unprepared for it. As a strategist he lacked the broad vision and intuitive focus on essentials that had made his father great. As an administrator he was handicapped by a decade of peacetime success; he had acquired habits of mind that were detri-mental, and interests that were irrelevant, to the effective conduct of war. His bent was for finance, and his foreign policy had been that of an intelligent financier working within the boundaries of a known international order. When the order crumbled, he continued to be guided by tradition. French aggrandizement was familiar, and he met it with the familiar technique of a coalition. When his first coalition collapsed, he patiently constructed another and then an-other, only to have them destroyed in turn. In his last years he be-came a heroic figure, the personification of British tenacity; but he was never the soul of British power as his father had been.

At the opening of the war that power was at low ebb. The Prime Minister had put government on its feet financially at the cost of the armed services; as late as 1792 he had reduced the size of the army and cut that of the navy almost in half. The methods of recruitment were slipshod and inadequate, and were never greatly improved during his administration. The quality of the high command, civilian and military, was little better in 1793 than it had been in 1775, but it changed markedly under the strain of war; by the close of the century Britain was well served at the admiralty and on the ocean, and she began to bring her full strength to bear when nothing less could have saved her.

At the beginning she frittered away her energies, largely because the government underestimated its task. Pitt went to war as a conservative and made the conventional moves. His aim was to contain the revolution within reasonable bounds rather than to defeat it; he hoped to finish the work in short order and return to the more congenial works of peace. The hope bred in him an almost invincible belief that the French Republic, by its own unsound economy and the pressure of a united Europe, would be brought to its knees without great military effort. He therefore persisted in using financial and strategic makeshifts.

His error was basic. By the end of 1793 the Jacobins had entrenched themselves in power, broken the dissident elements inside France, identified the revolution with the nation, and decreed a *levée en masse*. This first great experiment in conscription produced the nation in arms — mobs who went into battle with an enthusiasm that more than compensated for their lack of discipline, and who could ignore many of the tactical and even strategic limitations of professional warfare. The men could be trusted out of sight of their officers, as Prussians or Austrians could not, and could therefore attack in open order, with the rush of a river in spate, and engulf an enemy drilled in the machine-like maneuvers of the orthodox school; they could also be trusted in hostile territory to forage for themselves without deserting, which gave their armies a mobility that seemed to their opponents like black magic. Political revolution, in short, was revolutionizing the art of war.

The results were soon apparent. By 1797 the wreckage of Pitt's first coalition was scattered across the Continent. Prussia, Sardinia, and Austria had been beaten into submission; France had annexed Belgium and western Germany and turned Holland, northern Italy, and Spain into vassal states. Britain stood alone against a power that had already surpassed the dreams of Louis XIV. She stood solely by virtue of her fleet, and even for it the prospects were dark. Her squadrons had been driven from the Mediterranean in the previous year, without a shot fired, by the forced conversion of Spain to the enemy cause, and during the winter two French expeditions had reached the British Isles, one in Ireland and one in southern Wales. Both had failed, but their appearance had showed how far the Royal Navy was from fulfilling its basic function.

For Britain this year, 1797, was the supreme crisis of the war, almost as desperate as the year after June 1940. The French controlled the Spanish and Dutch fleets in addition to their own, and the crucial question was whether the three could be united in an overpowering armada. Part of the answer came in February, when the main Spanish force left the Mediterranean to join the Atlantic squadrons; it was met and shattered off Cape St. Vincent by an outnumbered British fleet under Sir John Jervis. The victory was enhanced by the brilliant initiative of Jervis's subordinate, Commodore Nelson, and the battle thus brought to the fore the two men who were to do the most in remaking British naval methods. But its strategic value was limited, for the French and Dutch fleets were still to be reckoned with.

The enemy plan was to use those two forces to cover an invasion of Ireland by two armies, one sailing from Brest and one from the Texel. In the spring the way was opened wide by mutinies in the British home fleet. The appalling conditions its sailors had endured for years suddenly produced naval paralysis. The admiralty and the flag officers met the peril with firmness and conciliation, and within two months the mutinies subsided; France lost her one golden chance to win the war. The home fleet put to sea again, and in October it crushed the Dutch in the hard-fought action of Camperdown. The Battle of Britain had been won. The French soon revived their invasion plan, and they nursed it for the next twelve years. But until the summer of 1940 invasion never again became an immediate threat.

Although Britain had rebuilt her defenses, she was as far as ever from winning the war. If the enemy could not reach her, neither could she reach the enemy. The duel between the elephant and the whale had begun, and the whale could only wait until the elephant came down to or into the water. Fortunately the wait was not long. The man who was already overshadowing the government of France had no clear understanding, for all his genius, of how sea power can contain land power. Bonaparte was about to begin his first adventure with the Royal Navy.

The adventure showed his limitations. He realized that Britain could not be invaded, but must be defeated to secure the French position in Europe. He reasoned, as Hitler did in similar circumstances, that Britain's strength depended on her contacts with the East and could best be attacked in the Nile Valley. The seizure of Egypt would paralyze her trade with the Levant and perhaps open the way for a French offensive against India. Bonaparte dreamed of emulating Alexander, and the withdrawal of the Royal Navy from the Mediterranean gave him his chance. In May 1798, accordingly, he sailed from Toulon with a large fleet and army.

His plan rested on faulty assumptions. If Egypt was less important to Britain than he supposed, his expedition might be unmolested but would be no more than a grandiose sideshow. If, on the other hand, Egypt was vital to Britain, he could never secure it: the British could re-enter the Mediterranean at will, and his fleet was in no state to secure the water-borne communications on which his army depended. The French had revolutionized land warfare, but their naval technique remained static. Their ships were qualitatively inferior to the British, their quantitative advantage had been lost off Cape St. Vincent, and their commanders were no match for the new school of Jervis and Nelson. In these circumstances Bonaparte was flirting with disaster.

His departure coincided with a change in Britain's policy. Her prestige in southern Europe was perilously low; to restore it, the government ordered a strong detachment into the Mediterranean. This squadron, under the command of Nelson, found the French fleet gone from Toulon, and after a long pursuit came up with it moored in Aboukir Bay at the mouth of the Nile. Despite approaching darkness Nelson attacked. In the night he fought a battle of virtual annihilation: out of thirteen enemy ships of the line, only two escaped. When the sun rose, Bonaparte's army was cut off from France. He himself escaped a year later, but his men remained until they were captured in 1801. He had had his first lesson in sea power, and Britain had struck the first blow in her counteroffensive.

VII   Crisis in Ireland

THE EGYPTIAN expedition had a further significance. It diverted France from her enemy's true Achilles heel, which for the past two years had been Ireland. If a fraction of the force sent to the Nile had landed instead in Bantry Bay, the results would have been incalculable. For in the late spring of 1798 the Irish were again using Britain's crisis to revenge themselves for their grievances. They were up in arms for the first time since the days of the Boyne.

Irish patriots had come to regard the legislative independence of 1782 as mere empty legalism. Power remained with the oligarchs of the so-called Protestant ascendancy; they maintained their position, to a far greater degree than their fellows in Westminster, by a narrow and corrupt parliamentary system, and reform was their nightmare. At the opening of the war Pitt had endeavored to conciliate the Irish Catholics by enfranchising them, but he had only partially overridden the bitter opposition of Dublin. The upshot had been an unfortunate compromise: the Catholics had acquired the right to vote and to hold most offices but not to sit in Parliament. The Catholic gentry were unimpressed by their new freedom to vote for their enemies, and Pitt's coercion of those enemies into accepting a detested measure showed that London, not Dublin, still held the reins. Ireland was not even self-governed, let alone well governed.

The Protestant ascendancy would not reform itself, and Pitt dared not force it too far for fear of destroying British influence. The Dublin borough-mongers were his only allies, whatever he might think of them, and the alliance was committed by its nature to resisting change. The forces of change were disparate but powerful. The patriots, the Catholics, and the Presbyterians of Ulster agreed in opposing the status quo, though in little else. If Ireland had been left alone, she would presumably have gone the way of Cromwell's England or Robespierre's France: discordant factions would have united to overthrow the existing order, then struggled for power among themselves. But Ireland had never been left alone, and her embryonic revolution was made abortive by forces from outside. One was obviously British. The other, equally devastating, was French.

The impact of the French Revolution was felt particularly by the radical Presbyterians of Ulster, who were ripe for new ideas. A Society of United Irishmen was founded in Belfast to campaign for religious equality and parliamentary reform; soon its objective grew to be an independent republic quit of borough-mongers and British, and communications were opened with France. The movement spread rapidly through the north, but at first it made little impression on the Catholic south, where the peasants were more interested in their economic grievances than in the abstract ideal of independence. In the spring of 1797, however, an event occurred that turned them into revolutionaries. The Dublin government, frightened by the threat of republicanism in Britain's dark hour, ordered the people of Ulster disarmed. Much of the work was entrusted to Protestant volunteers, who interpreted disarmament as license to butcher Catholics, and a great wave of refugees carried word of their doings to the south. This was the fuse to the powder keg. Fortunately for Britain it burned slowly, but by the spring of 1798 the explosion was imminent. Economic ills, bigotry, and fear stirred the peasants to revolt, as much against their landlords and the Irish Protestants as against the British. Once more, as at the time of the Boyne, France was the expected deliverer. But the French were embarking for Egypt.

The actual rebellion was a flash in the pan. The peasant mobs were no match for the Ulster militia, let alone for the regulars who were poured in from England, and the few troops sent by France arrived when all was over. By midsummer Ireland was quiet under a military government. But this was no solution, if only because the British army was urgently needed elsewhere. A re-establishment of the old system was impossible; the Dublin oligarchs had misused it, and Ireland could not be left to their vindictive ineptitude. Pitt turned to the only feasible alternative, a political union of Ireland with Great Britain.

He had the vision to see that the Irish Catholics, far from being penalized for rebellion, would have to be represented by Catholics in the new British Parliament. This was the cardinal virtue of his plan. Under the existing system Catholic emancipation would be politically reckless; it would jeopardize the British connection by destroying the Protestant ascendancy. When combined with union, however, it would be comparatively safe; Catholic votes that would predominate in Dublin would be only a small minority in Westminster. The gift of emancipation, furthermore, would go far toward making the union acceptable in Ireland as an act of equity rather than of force.

Enormous difficulties stood in the way. The Dublin Parliament was legally autonomous and had to approve the union — to vote itself out of existence. The spirit of sacrifice, rare in any legislature, was nonexistent among the borough-mongers, and Pitt was driven to a campaign of bribery that was scandalous even by the standards of the day. Boroughs were bought with money, members with peerages and sinecures, until at last the dirty work was finished: in 1800 the Irish legislature dissolved itself, and in place of this age-old symbol of nationhood Ireland was represented in the parliament of a supposedly united kingdom.

The work was only half done. The keystone of the union, Catholic emancipation, was slipping out of Pitt's hands. The Dublin clique was vehemently opposed to emancipation and had the support of fanatical Protestants in Ulster, of some right-wing British Tories, and — far more important — of the King. George was convinced that he was bound by his coronation oath to maintain Protestantism inviolate, and he refused point-blank to accept the cabinet's measure. This was again the old George, and his flash of self-assertion raised an extremely delicate crisis.

Pitt had the power to defy him. For almost twenty years the principle of ministerial rule had been accepted, and the force of precedent was augmented by the Prime Minister's prestige. He had held office longer than any man since Walpole. He had behind him the cabinet, the majority in the commons, and the bulk of the propertied class. He was the leader of the country's great effort in a great cause. For all these reasons he could have forced the constitutional issue and probably compelled the King to give way.

But to give way how? George, obstinate as ever, might conceivably abdicate; it was more likely that the strain would be too much for his mind, which had failed him before, and that he would relapse into insanity. In either case the onus would be on Pitt, and it was abhorrent to him both as a subject and a politician. The King had grown into the symbol of Britain, and commanded an affection so deep that his disappearance might shake the country's morale; he would be succeeded by his son, as king or as regent, and the accession of a contemptible rake in the dark days of 1801 would be a national disaster. Pitt felt that these dangers outweighed the value of an equitable settlement in Ireland. He had committed himself to the settlement, morally though not categorically, but he refused to force the issue. He promised not to reopen it during the King's lifetime; then he resigned.

This overturn ruined the prospects of the union. The Irish had abandoned their parliamentary emblem of statehood in return for a promise that was not fulfilled. Instead they were governed by an Anglican oligarchy in Westminster, even less responsive to their needs than that in Dublin had been, and the franchise was as meaningless to the Ulster Presbyterian as to the Galway Catholic; it entitled both to choose from among their domestic enemies men to misrepresent them in a foreign parliament. This, in the event, was Pitt's settlement of the Irish problem. His enlightenment was defeated by the tradition of the Test Act and the Clarendon Code, personified in a stubborn and unbalanced old man who in his youth had sworn an archaic coronation oath. After another generation the Irish themselves forced Catholic emancipation, but by then the time had passed when it could be the basis for true union.

VIII   Victory at Sea

PITT'S resignation coincided with the collapse of his second effort to win the war. The Battle of the Nile had waked the hopes of the European powers just when continued French aggression had confirmed their fears. In 1799 Austria had resumed the fight, backed now by Russia, and for the first time Russian armies had emerged into western Europe; they had swept the French from Italy with Austrian help, and then had abruptly disappeared again. Bonaparte had returned from Egypt to make himself First Consul, and had soon redeemed the defeats. Austria, isolated by Russia's defection, was forced to another humiliating peace in February of 1801, the month of Pitt's resignation. The second coalition went the way of the first, and Britain was again left alone against the triumphant revolution.

But her power was far greater than it had been four years earlier. She was acquiring naval supremacy, learning to use her fleets for effective blockade, and making the enemy feel the pinch. The price of blockade, however, as in the Seven Years' War and the War of the American Revolution, was the alienation of the neutral maritime states. The principal sufferers were the Baltic countries, and to them Bonaparte looked for help in breaking the British stranglehold. Denmark, Sweden, and Prussia obliged by reviving the Armed Neutrality of 1780; Russia changed sides and joined them, and her mercurial Emperor Paul even talked of a Franco-Russian expedition against India.

Britain's security was re-established by a combination of force and luck. Nelson attacked the Danish fleet in Copenhagen harbor and neutralized it after a desperate struggle; much of the armament and all of the heart promptly went out of the Armed Neutrality. Almost simultaneously the Emperor Paul was assassinated and succeeded by his son Alexander, who withdrew Russia again into neutrality. The upshot was that neither France nor Britain could reach the other. The elephant and the whale had come to a standstill, and both were winded. Bonaparte needed time to reorganize France without the pressure of blockade, and mature his plans for future conquest; the British were war-weary, anxious to reopen their European markets, and hopeless of re-establishing the balance of power. Addington, the nonentity who succeeded Pitt, saw the chance of a settlement now that Bonaparte was bringing order and almost respectability out of the tumult of revolution. Negotiations were hastily opened, and in the spring of 1802 a treaty of peace was concluded at Amiens.

Britain paid dearly for it. She restored virtually all her overseas conquests from France and the French satellites, and agreed to evacuate Malta and Minorca, two Mediterranean bases that she had seized in 1798; in return she obtained only a few minor promises. France regained her overseas empire without relaxing her hold upon Europe, a defeat for Britain out of all relation to the success of her military defensive. The peace also seemed to be a confession that the cause for which she had fought so consistently was no longer worth the effort.

The cause was the deliverance of Europe from the rule of force. The revolution that had once been pledged to breaking the shackles of the old regimes was degenerating, to the strains of the *Marseillaise,* into an attempt to bind the Continent in the shackles of French power. This nationalizing of the great crusade was beginning to wake resentment in peasants as well as aristocrats of the conquered lands, and Britain was inevitably becoming their champion. Her lone defiance had been the light in a darkening world; now it was extinguished.

She did not extinguish it from fear, but from weariness. The government acted on the perennial misconception that besets gentlemen dealing with a worshiper of force: they imagined that the First Consul wanted peace because to them it was the normal, civilized condition. He imagined, in turn, that they might be gulled or bullied into keeping the peace while he finished enslaving Europe. The two sides misjudged each other as completely as Britain and Germany after Munich.

The Peace of Amiens consequently endured little longer than that of Munich. Bonaparte, now entrenched as First Consul for life and styling himself Napoleon, moved on to new aggressions as rapidly as Hitler. French power was riveted upon northwestern Italy, Holland, Switzerland, and western Germany, and preparations were made to extend it to India, Egypt, the West Indies, and even Louisiana. Napoleon hoped that none of his acts would be flagrant enough to provoke Britain's resistance, and that her passivity would sap her will to resist. "An intelligent victor will, whenever possible, present his demands to the vanquished in installments. He can then be sure that a nation which has become characterless — and such is every one which voluntarily submits — will no longer find any sufficient reason in each of these detailed oppressions to take to arms once more." [5] The words are Hitler's, but the technique was old.

The Corsican adventurer, like the Austrian, miscalculated Britain's will. She refused to carry out the letter of the treaty on the ground that Napoleon was violating its spirit, and prepared to renew the war. When she declared it again in May 1803 the nation was united as never before. The months of truce had cleared the air of false hopes by proving that the consulate was as aggressive as the republic and even more dangerous. The British still had no intention of destroying France as a state, and little interest in undoing her revolution. But they were now determined to fight until doomsday, if need be, to destroy her hegemony of Europe.

Although they had no allies, their own strength was at its apogee.

---

[5] Adolf Hitler: *Mein Kampf* (New York: Reynal & Hitchcock, 1939), p. 968; quoted by permission of Houghton Mifflin Company, proprietors of the basic copyright.

A decade of victories had given the Royal Navy a skill and spirit that no fighting force has ever surpassed, and many of its flag officers would have been famous in their own right if Nelson had not eclipsed them. At the admiralty Jervis, now Lord St. Vincent, had reformed naval administration in two busy years. The cabinet, furthermore, had learned how to use sea power, and Britain lost no time in regaining the stranglehold of blockade.

Napoleon — Emperor Napoleon, as he became in 1804 — realized that all his designs hinged upon breaking that stranglehold. He turned first to the obvious method, invasion, for which he spent two years in marshaling the resources of Europe. He encamped a great army at Boulogne and collected an armada of small boats to transport it across the Straits of Dover. But he had no desire to step into a boat until he was confident of stepping out alive on the shore of Kent; he had to maintain naval control of the straits long enough to cover the passage of his troops, and he did not attempt to crack this hard core of his problem until the spring of 1805.

By then Spain had again been forced into alliance with France. From Brest to Cadiz on the Atlantic coast, from Cartagena to Toulon on the Mediterranean, the Franco-Spanish detachments were held in port by British blockading squadrons. Close blockade was impossible, particularly in the Mediterranean, where Nelson had no suitable base. Napoleon hoped that the Toulon squadron might sneak out of port, shake off pursuit, join forces with the Spanish contingent at Cadiz, and then make for the West Indies; simultaneously the main force at Brest might also escape to the westward. He would then achieve, in the West Indies, his aim of concentrating his divided squadrons, and they would at once return together to seize command of the Channel. He of course expected the British to concentrate in turn, but he hoped to trick them into doing so on the wrong side of the Atlantic. His strategy was a gigantic ruse, to persuade them that he was aiming at the Caribbean instead of at Kent.

His misconception of realities at sea was never so evident. He assumed in the Franco-Spanish navy qualities it did not possess. Seamanship, for one: years of enforced idleness in port had deprived officers and men of the sixth sense they needed on a long and dangerous voyage. Timing, for another: the concentration of widely separated squadrons upon the Caribbean required precise plans precisely executed, and precision could not be guaranteed. Morale, above all else: by now the thought of meeting Nelson had the same numbing effect upon a French admiral that the thought of meeting Napoleon had upon an Austrian general. The Emperor ignored these deficiencies in his own force, and he assumed nonexistent deficiencies in the British. Nelson was no lonely genius among fools; his fellow admirals were supremely competent. To expect them to be eluded and duped by inferior squadrons under demoralized commanders was to expect the impossible. The ghost of Philip II must have looked pityingly after the Spanish fleet as it sailed westward from Cadiz on an April evening in 1805.

The gamble had begun. The French commander-in-chief, Admiral Villeneuve, had escaped from Toulon at the end of March and picked up the Cadiz detachment; he was on his way to the West Indies while Nelson vainly scoured the Mediterranean in search of him. It was soon known in London that the French were loose in the Atlantic; orders went out to strengthen the remnants of the blockade and the defenses of the Channel. Villeneuve reached the West Indies in May, waited for reinforcements that did not appear, and then, just when Nelson arrived in pursuit, doubled back to Spain with the British hot on his heels. When he arrived, his initiative was as exhausted as his fleet; after a half-hearted gesture toward the Channel he fell back on Cadiz. The French, without fighting a major battle, had lost their last great naval campaign.

It had for a postscript one of the outstanding battles of history. Villeneuve, blockaded in Cadiz by a numerically inferior force under Nelson, was being goaded by Napoleon to break out; the Emperor was unused to seeing his strategy go bankrupt. On October 19 Villeneuve put to sea with thirty-three sail of the line and the foreknowledge of defeat; two days later Nelson, with twenty-seven of the line, turned on him off Cape Trafalgar. The Franco-Spanish fleet was in a long crescent struggling northward toward Cadiz when the British bore down on it in two columns. These struck the enemy center and crushed it before the slow-sailing van returned to join the battle and be crushed in turn. Eighteen enemy ships were captured; thirteen battered wrecks escaped into Cadiz. On the *Victory* Nelson was dead, but his work was finished. Napoleon's navy had ceased to exist as a fighting force.

Trafalgar was the culmination of a long process. British sea power, for all its ups and downs, had been gathering strength since the sixteenth century — strength first to turn back the Spanish, then to challenge and overwhelm the Dutch, then to vie with the French. France alone had stood up against that power for more than a century, and the climax of her effort came between 1797 and 1805. During those eight years and a half Nelson and his "band of brothers" harried their enemies from Cape St. Vincent to Camperdown, Copenhagen, and the Nile, and demonstrated at sea — as Napoleon was demonstrating on land — the strategic effect of the single, crushing battle. Trafalgar was the climactic demonstration. From that October day France ceased to be a major sea power, and for almost a hundred years to come no other contender challenged Britain's supremacy.

IX   Victory on Land

THE NEWS of Trafalgar reached London in a dark hour. Pitt had resumed office in the spring of 1804 under pressure of the renewed struggle, and had devoted himself to building a third coalition. He had enlisted Austria and Russia, and Napoleon had broken up the camp at Boulogne to strike with lightning speed for Vienna. On the day of Trafalgar he announced the capture of an Austrian army at Ulm; in November he occupied Vienna; at the beginning of December he shattered the Austro-Russian armies at Austerlitz. Austria was forced out of the war, the Holy Roman Empire was abolished, and Germany was remodeled at the will of the new Charlemagne. Prussia objected too late, and was crushed in a week's campaign. Russia was defeated in the spring of 1807; her emperor met Napoleon on a raft on the river Niemen, where the two concluded the Peace of Tilsit. "What is Europe," said Alexander to his companion, "where is it, if it is not you and I?"

This was a new order with a vengeance. Prussia was eliminated as a major power, Austria was cowed; France was dominant in Germany and had Italy and Holland for dependencies, Spain for helpless vassal. On all the Continent only Russia retained her independence as a power, and at Tilsit Alexander had pledged her not only to join France, but to help in dragooning the Baltic states and Portugal into the grand alliance. Just when Britain had acquired supremacy at sea, she faced a land coalition such as Europe had never seen.

Pitt did not live to witness the end of his hopes. His years on duty had sapped his strength, and the news of Austerlitz shattered it. He died in January 1806, murmuring "my country, how I leave my country!" But he left it strong enough to do without his strength, and that fact was his monument. Throughout the rest of the war, except for a brief coalition under Fox, only little men followed Pitt in office. As they came and went in Downing Street, Britain's vast effort went on with little abatement. Its techniques had become so ingrained that they no longer required one directing hand. "Europe is not saved by any single man," Pitt had pointed out in his last speech. "England has saved herself by her exertions, and will, I trust, save Europe by her example."

By 1807 example was no longer enough, because no Continental state dared emulate it. Britain could defend herself and her friends within the limits of her power, but the only way in which she could carry the war to Napoleon was by extending and tightening her blockade. A military counteroffensive would have to wait on his blundering, for she could no more invade the continent than he could invade the British Isles. Blockade was slow and unspectacular, an instrument of attrition requiring a spider's patience and a spider's time, but it was far from a negligible weapon. Britain had infinite time, as she had not had in the American war a generation earlier; her position now was impregnable.

> Come the three corners of the world in arms,
> And we shall shock them.[6]

She had no further enemies to fear. She could afford to wait, and watch, and spin her web from the Baltic to the Levant.

Napoleon could not wait. He had imposed upon Europe an unprecedented political unification, but he could not consolidate it without an economic framework. The Continent was by no means self-sufficient; its economy had been fed for generations by that of the Americas and Asia, and in recent years increasingly by that of Great Britain. Now the Royal Navy restricted this feeding, and the consequent economic disruption stirred political unrest into an endemic crisis. Napoleon had two alternatives. He might accept the crisis and mitigate its effects as far as possible, trusting to time for the evolution of an adjusted economy; or he might attack the block-

---

[6] Shakespeare: *King John*, V, vii, 116–7.

ade by a counterblockade of Britain. His choice was dictated by his character. Patience had never been his long suit, and his temper was growing more imperious. Now that he had failed to break Britain's hold by naval force, he turned to the force of economic warfare. If his subject peoples could be coerced into living on their own fat and British trade could be excluded from Europe, he reasoned Britain's industry would stop, and unemployment and famine would bring her to her knees. Then the ports would reopen, and the world's commerce would resume under the aegis of Caesar.

His plan had much to be said for it. The bulk of European society was still agrarian, and the pressure of blockade and counterblockade would produce a lowered standard of living, hardship and discontent, rather than large-scale starvation. British economy was far less self-contained. The demands of war had accelerated the tempo of the Industrial Revolution and turned the island into a great workshop. Its food supply, despite agricultural progress, was no longer adequate for its needs. Because imported food had to be paid for with manufactures, Britain was vulnerable as never before to the closing of her major market in Europe. She might or might not survive its loss.

The implications of Napoleon's plan were enormous. It was called the Continental System, and it could be systematic only if it were continental. Europe was not an administrative unit but a congeries of conquered provinces, dependencies, vassal states, plus France and her one powerful, undependable ally. All were pledged to a common policy, but the means to enforce it were another matter; no amount of pressure on a satellite government could provide effective customs administration. Ports were numerous and officials lax, particularly in the two chief peninsulas, the Italian and Iberian, and the only way to exclude British shipping was to police the coast with Frenchmen. Universal blockade, in other words, meant universal empire.

The French had long experimented with embargoes on British goods, and in 1806–7 Napoleon extended them into a European system. He forbade all commerce with the British Isles and ordered the confiscation of any ship that carried British goods into a port under his control. The British retaliated by closing such ports to every ship *not* carrying British goods. Neutral rights were violated by both sides; the United States was the only remaining neutral of any consequence, and she had little economic and less military power. Henceforth her ships might trade solely with Britain and risk capture by French privateers, or they might carry non-British goods to Europe and risk capture by the Royal Navy, or they might carry British goods and risk arrest by French police. The freedom of the seas was in abeyance.

As the pinch of Napoleon's decrees began to be felt in Britain, she struggled for markets. She seized for the duration almost all the overseas colonies of the European states, except in Latin America, and she made abortive attempts on Chile and Argentine. In the North Sea she occupied Heligoland as a way station for smuggling into Germany. In the Mediterranean she used Gibraltar, Malta, Sicily, and the Ionian Isles for the same purpose, and through Turkey her goods trickled into the Danube Valley. These were small leaks in Napoleon's blockade, and they led him to strengthen it. Before he finished, one crucial section broke.

Portugal and Spain were particularly remiss in enforcing the embargo because their governments were weak. Napoleon determined to occupy the peninsula. He began with a raid on Portugal; then he kidnapped the Spanish royal family and replaced it with his brother Joseph, enthroned behind a screen of French bayonets. But he reckoned without the Spaniards. They were as averse to outside dictation as they had been a century before, and they preferred a priest-ridden aristocracy and a despicable sovereign of their own to reforms and efficiency foisted upon them from Paris. The French were confronted with popular risings on every side. The revolution that had battened on nationalism was opposed for the first time, but not for the last, by a people in arms.

The Spaniards alone were no match for a perfected war machine. But they had two allies, geography and Great Britain. The mountain ranges of the peninsula, across which ran the roads from France, were a happy hunting ground for guerrillas acting against the invaders' lines of communication. Britain now had the opportunity she had been seeking for fifteen years, to open a land front in Europe with a fair prospect of maintaining it; the enemy's strength in the field was counterbalanced by his supply problem, and the British had the support of the ubiquitous Spanish irregulars and secure access to any part of the coast. The elephant was at last where the whale could get at him.

In 1809, after a small British expeditionary force had been chased into the sea at Corunna, Napoleon's most famous antagonist landed in Portugal to command another British army. Sir Arthur Wellesley had made a name for himself in India, where his elder brother had been governor-general, and his Indian experience now stood him in good stead. He knew the virtues and limitations of irregular troops, and the power of improvisation he had developed in the Deccan was invaluable among the Iberian hills. He was a cold man, as Marlborough had been, and methodical; he knew the minutiae of his business, but never lost himself in them. Defeat left him unruffled; he could retreat and bide his time, make meticulous calculations, then strike like a rattlesnake. He cast no such spell on men as Nelson had done; his opinion of his troops was low, and they had respect for him rather than enthusiasm. No one except Marlborough in the history of the British army deserved respect more.

In 1809 Napoleon was distracted from Spain by another war with Austria. He crushed her; but the British had a year in which to consolidate their position, and Wellesley used the time to good effect. When the legions poured back across the Pyrenees, he retreated into Portugal and scorched the earth behind him. The French followed him down the peninsula between the Tagus and the sea, where Lisbon beckoned them with the promise of another Corunna. Then they came on the lines of Torres Vedras, fortifications stretching completely across the peninsula. This was Wellesley's work. The French could not take the lines by storm, or starve out the sea-based army behind it; instead they were starving themselves. By the spring of 1811 the wreck of their force straggled back into Spain, leaving more than a third of its men dead in central Portugal. Thereafter the conquerors fought a defensive action, and Wellesley — by then Lord Wellington — pushed them back and back. In the autumn of 1813 he forced the Pyrenees; France was invaded for the first time in twenty years.

During the Peninsular War Britain's blockade was producing tangible effects elsewhere. In 1812 it touched off hostilities with the United States. The American government had been in the impossible position of asserting its neutral rights against both the giant belligerents. Britain was the more obvious transgressor because she ruled the seas, and her chronic shortage of men led her to search American ships for deserters and impress American sailors, at sea or

in British ports, with scant regard for their citizenship. The powers
of search and impressment were vital for manning the Royal Navy,
and they were exercised with a highhandedness that the government refused to curb. The old anti-British feeling in America soon
drowned out the grievances against France, and at the crisis in the
European struggle the United States declared war. Britain could
afford neither troops nor ships for a large-scale effort, and she had
no objective beyond the defense of Canada. For her the War of
1812 was a regrettable but incidental episode, which forced her to
divert a fraction of her strength from the cause she considered to
be that of all free men.

While her position was being weakened by these developments in
North America, it was being strengthened in another way by events
in South America. The chaos in Spain had broken the ties between
the empire and the mother country. The colonists were asserting
their independence, and with the Spanish connection went the mercantilist system; Britain at last had the market she had been seeking
for a hundred years. She needed it desperately. The Continental
System had brought her industrial areas to depression, hunger, and
rioting, and the Latin American trade helped to keep the wheels
turning through the worst years.

Europe by now was approaching the final crisis. The needs of
Continental blockade had led Napoleon to extend his empire to
Italy, Dalmatia, and the northwestern coast of Germany. But the
Tilsit settlement, on which his position still depended, was beginning to crack. The exclusion of colonial produce and British manufactures had been unpopular from the start with Russian nobles and
merchants, and the extension of French power in central Europe
was equally unpopular at the Russian court. In 1810–11 Alexander
withdrew from the Continental System, and Anglo-Russian trade
began to return to normal. Napoleon's blockade could now be turned
from the east, and the British imports could flood into a parched
Europe. Napoleon had to act or see his experiment fail.

A Europe insulated from the outside world had become too small
for two imperial powers, much as it became again in 1941. The
Emperor of All the Russias would not turn back; the Emperor of the
French could not, for success had an irresistible momentum. The
Peace of Tilsit therefore went the way of the Peace of Amiens, as

the Russo-German pact of 1939 went the way of the Munich settlement. In June 1812 Napoleon, with the greatest army Europe had ever seen, struck eastward from the River Niemen.

He found himself in a vast and incalculable world. The scale of operations was as different from that in the West as the scale of the Caucasus is from that of the Tyrol. The farther the Russians retreated, the more fully they utilized their advantage of space. The French pursued recklessly, hoping for the decisive battle that never materialized. They were led into a larger version of the Portuguese campaign: they advanced through a wasted countryside, shadowed by an enemy whom they could not grapple and destroy, until they met an insurmountable barrier. The Russian equivalent of Torres Vedras was the winter, which Napoleon had neglected; in his greatest offensive he had presumed to defy nature. When he recrossed the Niemen in December of 1812, he left behind him half a million men. The *Grande Armée* had vanished.

Almost by spontaneous combustion, Prussia flamed into revolt As the Russians advanced with their new allies, Austria wavered and then joined them. In October 1813 the French were overwhelmed at Leipzig in the Battle of the Nations. After a brilliant but futile defensive on the road to Paris, Napoleon abdicated in April 1814, and went into exile on Elba. But he had not yet accepted defeat. He was still the man who had badgered Villeneuve from his anchorage nine years before. The collapse of the empire plunged France into nostalgia and Europe into chaos; the victorious governments were quarreling with one another, and in this situation he saw his opportunity. In March 1815 he returned, and within three weeks he was master of France. Immediately the four great powers suspended their squabbles and pledged themselves to his destruction.

The impending campaign hinged upon speed. It was vital to attack Napoleon before he could tap the vast resources of French manpower. Attack depended on Great Britain and Prussia; the Austrian armies were far away and the Russian even farther. A small contingent of British troops happened to be in Belgium; Wellington was put in command of it, and the government rushed him every available soldier in Britain. By June he had in the field a polyglot force of over 80,000 — British, Belgian, Dutch, and German — and the

Prussians had massed over 100,000 under General Blücher. If the two armies joined, they would outnumber Napoleon by almost two to one; he was therefore forced onto the offensive.

He struck his enemies before they joined. He himself attacked and defeated Blücher, and decided that he had put him out of the running; he then advanced to support Marshal Ney, who had meanwhile been engaging the British. Wellington retired on the village of Waterloo, where he hoped that the Prussians would join him. There, soon after noon of June 18, Napoleon launched his last assault. Its aim was simple, to crush the British center by sheer weight of numbers, column against line. Some of his marshals knew from their Spanish experience what would come of these tactics. The Emperor mocked them. "You were beaten by Wellington, and so you think he is a great general. But I tell you that Wellington is a bad general, and the English are bad troops; they will be a picnic for us."

The picnic was deadly. For hours the French poured themselves against the Duke's position, while the Prussians moved slowly to his rescue. By late afternoon Napoleon was attacked in flank by Blücher, and still had not broken the British line. But he dared not stop; anything short of victory would undo him. So the attack went on until it spent its force; the French center was then rolled into chaos by the charge of Wellington's last reserves, and the Prussians completed the rout. A mob, not an army, streamed back toward the French frontier. Napoleon had gambled and lost everything; four days later he abdicated for the second time, and in July he set out for St. Helena.

X   The Aftermath

THE LONG ordeal was over. For twenty-three years France had fought to gain and hold the mastery of Europe; she failed only after the Continent had been ploughed into new shapes and sown with new ideas. The ploughing could be largely effaced and the surface of an eighteenth-century world restored, but the seeds had gone too deep to be killed by a superficial restoration. They germinated for years, and then thrust violently upward into a new world.

Great Britain, alone among the powers, had not had ideas forced on her by a conquering army. For her the war had been of a piece with the wars against Louis XIV, and no one yet realized that that long story was over — that France would never again threaten single-handed the equilibrium of Europe. The French cycle had ended, and it was more than half a century before the German cycle began. For the interim Great Britain had secured the ends toward which she had been groping since the Glorious Revolution: her power was world-wide and her security unassailable. Yet in the process of achieving these ends her old regime had been undermined as thoroughly as any on the Continent.

She had paid a high price for survival. Her industrial system was askew, thanks to the uneven demands of war production, and her social structure was dislocated; reconversion to the needs of peace momentarily aggravated her troubles. The result was an intensifying of the demand for reform. The Tories fought it for a time as doggedly as they had fought the war. But the ruling class as a whole had not, like its counterparts across the Channel, acquired a terror of new ideas. Even the Tories began to waver, and before long their policy showed the influence of liberal ideas. They refused to carry them through, however, and within fifteen years of Waterloo Wellington was commanding a desperate political defensive against reform. He lost, and the old oligarchy lost with him. The nation that had followed its leaders so loyally in defying Napoleon's coercion refused to follow them in defying the logic of change.

Chapter Five

REVOLUTION BY CONSENT

1815–1867

I   The Vienna Settlement

WHEN the peacemakers gathered again at Vienna after the interruption of the Waterloo campaign, they had the task of redesigning Europe. Great areas were void on the map: the old frontiers had been gone for a generation in Italy, in Germany, in the Vistula basin, and the Napoleonic frontiers were now erased. Victory had been won primarily by the four great powers; none of them was weak enough to be deprived of its pre-war holdings, and neither was France. Inevitably the Congress of Vienna had to create a new map along the general lines of the old, and so to resurrect a large measure of the eighteenth century in the second decade of the nineteenth. On certain basic assumptions the negotiators were agreed. France, though shorn of her conquests, would remain a major power; Great Britain's direct concerns would be largely overseas; Russia, Austria, and Prussia would gain what they could from the European grab-bag. The last assumption involved the danger of war, for eighteenth-century rivalries woke again in the atmosphere of Vienna. But the ambitions of the rivals were essentially limited, as they had been in the time of Frederick and Maria Theresa. If they could be satisfied peacefully at the expense of minor states, equilibrium would return.

The focus of the old rivalries was in central Europe. There Britain had little stake, and French influence was temporarily in eclipse; Austria, Prussia, and Russia snarled at each other. The principal bone of contention was Poland, which the three had divided among themselves a generation earlier, only to have their work undone by Napoleon. Now they were bent on another partition, and Russia refused to be content with her pre-war share. She had acquired enormous influence in the counsels of Europe, if only because her armies had pursued the French from Moscow to Paris, and she was obviously not going to retire again behind the Niemen; her Polish demands were a symptom of her new position. Austria and Prussia agreed in opposing her, but they agreed on little else. Already they were renewing the duel for the dominance of Germany that Napoleon had interrupted. For these reasons the negotiations threatened to explode.

New factors, however, militated against an explosion. The powers had a common bond in their fear of France: Austria, Prussia, and Russia had learned at first hand the meaning of French aggression, and the lesson remained vivid for another half-century; they were consequently willing to put limits to their greed for the sake of mutual protection. The resultant spirit of compromise was fragile at best, and it might not have been strong enough in itself to bring a peaceful solution. But another factor was working toward the same end: Great Britain was vitally interested in a quick settlement, which was prerequisite to re-establishing her European markets. She was largely aloof from the territorial questions at issue; it mattered little to her who governed the Poles, and the jealousy of Hapsburg and Hohenzollern affected her only if it threatened Hanover. The disposition of the Netherlands touched her more nearly, but here she had her own means of exerting influence. She had seized the bulk of Europe's overseas colonies, most of which she did not wish to retain because she was already glutted with territory; their return, however, depended on her satisfaction with the settlement. Her bargaining position was strong, and her prestige and power were at their zenith. The other three great victors, with whom she was joined in a quadruple alliance, were scrambling for gains that scarcely concerned her, and her eagerness to end the scramble made her work for compromise.

A peaceful settlement was achieved, though by a narrow margin, and it satisfied Britain's desire for stability. The map drawn at Vienna endured in essence for the next fifty years. Russia obtained the lion's share of Poland, while Prussia was compensated with the Rhineland and Westphalia; Austria exchanged the Belgian Netherlands for Italian Venetia, and Belgium was added to the Dutch Netherlands to form a single kingdom of Holland; in northwestern Italy Sardinia was reconstituted and strengthened. Thus the traditional routes by which France had overrun the Continent were blocked against her: a single state now garrisoned the Low Countries, supported by the Prussians in Westphalia and at the mouth of the Moselle valley; Sardinia, backed by the Austrians in Lombardy-Venetia, guarded the passes of the Alps. The peacemakers established a *cordon sanitaire* against the common enemy, and in the process they set the stage for a new Europe.

The settlement was a turning point in the history of the three Continental victors. Russia acquired a salient between Prussia and Austria that advanced her frontiers into the heart of the Continent. Prussia shifted her center of gravity westward, gained what soon became the industrial core of Germany, and became a guardian of the German states against France. Austria sacrificed the Netherlands for a strong position in central Europe: the newly established German Confederation was under her leadership, and in Italy her possession of Lombardy-Venetia made her the one great power among the weak and senile governments of the Restoration. For the next half-century she was a Janus state, looking at once north and south, and her peculiar position made her the hub of European politics.

Most of these changes concerned Great Britain only as they reestablished the balance of power, the traditional framework of her diplomacy. The coastal areas of peculiar importance to her sea power were unaffected except for the Low Countries, which at last were entirely on their own; her role thenceforth was to chaperon them against the advances of Prussia on one side and France on the other. Britain's satisfaction with the settlement was reflected in the return of confiscated colonies; she retained only those that the admiralty coveted for strategic reasons, such as Malta, Mauritius, Ceylon, and the Dutch settlement on the southern tip of Africa. For the last she paid in cash, and so bought her greatest imperial problem of the nineteenth century.

The Vienna settlement dealt with imponderables as well as with territories, for the danger of French ideas was as great as that of French aggression. The seeds of nationalism sowed by the revolution had taken root in central Europe, where the nation-state was unknown, and Austria in particular was committed to destroying them or being destroyed by them. Her empire contained Germans, Poles, Czechs, Magyars, Rumanians, southern Slavs, and Italians; the growth of the nationalist spirit anywhere on her frontiers threatened to break the empire into its constituent parts. From 1815 to 1918 her government fought the threat — first by wars in Italy, then by a war in Germany, then by a war that began in the Balkans and engulfed the world.

The theory of nationalism that the French had sowed had another side. Its emphasis on national solidarity led to an emphasis on national consent as the basis of government. The conquests of the revolution had been justified as liberation, and the French had introduced written constitutions to express the consent of the governed; the European liberals of the Restoration, particularly in Germany and Italy, inherited this French legacy of nationalism and constitutionalism. But they also inherited through France a legacy from Britain. Although some of them were Jacobins, many more derived their ideas from the pre-Jacobin phase of the French Revolution, the phase of a limited monarchy *à l'anglaise,* and were as much Anglophile as Francophile. They wished to see their respective peoples unified under some form of national, parliamentary, and constitutional government, and their thinking was often no more radical than a Whig's of 1688.

Their arch-enemy was the Chancellor of the Austrian Empire, Prince Metternich. He was opposed to constitutionalism as much as to nationalism because he realized that the rulers of the petty German and Italian states, if they were ever forced to give way to liberal pressure, would be taking the first step toward not only their own destruction but that of the Hapsburg Empire. The health of the empire depended on maintaining its eighteenth-century environment. To that aim Metternich devoted himself, and he succeeded in using for his purpose the international system established at the Congress of Vienna. He thereby identified the system with defense of the past, and ensured Britain's eventual secession from it.

II   Great Britain and the Concert of Europe

THE FEAR of France drew Europe together. It made every state, large and small, to some degree aware of its stake in the status quo, to some degree willing to collaborate in preserving public order. This newly found community of interest was epitomized in an old phrase, the concert of Europe, and the powers at Vienna found the means for concerting European policy. They agreed to meet in a future congress whenever the peace of the Continent was threatened, and so they created the congress system. It was short-lived and had many disadvantages. It was rudimentary because it lacked a permanent secretariat and fixed times of meeting; it was dominated by the great powers, first the big four and then, after the admission of France, the big five; its aims were so conservative that it became identified with reaction. Yet in method it was such an advance from the anarchy of the past that it was a foretaste of internationalism.

The system was not designed to be reactionary. Some of its framers expected it to give the monarchs of Europe such a sense of security that they would dare to experiment with constitutional reform. But the sovereigns restored at long last had little taste for experiment; as liberal agitation increased, so did their conservatism and their unpopularity. Did the concert exist to guarantee them against the consequences of their errors by intervening in the name of public order whenever and wherever revolution occurred? On the answer to this crucial question two views developed, so divergent that they vitiated the very idea of concert.

Metternich insisted that revolution anywhere was a threat to the peace of Europe and should be suppressed as soon as it began — or, if possible, before. In 1819 he took action against the liberal movement in Germany; in 1820 a liberal outbreak in Spain had repercussions in Italy, and he convoked a series of congresses in the next two years to consider the problem. By now Russia and Prussia supported him, and France, eager to prove her orthodoxy, offered to suppress the Spanish revolt. But at the Congress of Verona, in the autumn of 1822, the Duke of Wellington dropped a bombshell: Great Britain would have no part in coercing the Spaniards. She was seceding from the concert, in effect, and shattering the unanimity on which it depended.

Her decision had been long maturing. At the outset her foreign secretary, Lord Castlereagh, had been a leading proponent of the system. "The immediate object," he had said in 1815, "is to inspire the states of Europe with a sense that the existing concert is their only perfect security . . . and that their true wisdom is to keep down the petty contentions of ordinary times and to stand together in the support of the established principles of social order." Neither he nor his Tory colleagues, however, believed that the principles of social order had to be supported by a continuous and ubiquitous policing of the Continent. Only a palpable crisis justified intervention. A demonstration by German students, a revolution in Naples or Spain — to call such affairs threats to the general peace savored to the British of hysteria. Their view, so thoroughly at odds with the Austrian that it wrecked the concert, was not the arbitrary opinion of a particular cabinet. It was as much the outgrowth of Britain's position as Metternich's was the outgrowth of Austria's.

Since her emergence as a major European power Britain's concern with Europe had been limited. Before 1793 she had fought in defense of her Continental interests — in the Low Countries, in Gibraltar, in Hanover — and also for her interests overseas; after 1793 she had fought primarily to prevent French dominance of Europe. Now her interests were secure on the Continent and overseas, and no power or group of powers was striving for European hegemony. The traditional reasons for her intervention therefore disappeared, and she reverted to her underlying tradition of aloofness.

She could not share Metternich's fear. Nationalism held no terrors for her at home, now that the whole of the British Isles seemed to be growing into a single people, and in the empire the trend of her policy since 1783 had been away from the Austrian concept of repression. As for liberalism, she had never fought it as such or discovered how it could be perverted by an occupying army, and she did not dread it. The middle-class European liberals were no Dantons or Robespierres; they had due respect for property and its political rights, and a touching admiration for the British system. To aid in suppressing their parliamentary aspirations was out of the question for a cabinet accountable to the mother of parliaments. Even a Tory government, reactionary as it might be in domestic affairs, was committed in foreign policy to opposing its reactionary allies. The commitment derived partly from the nature of British interests, partly from the sympathies of the British public, and it grew more apparent with the years.

By the early 1820's the British position was in sharp contrast to the Austrian. Metternich insisted that public order was indivisible, that no line could be drawn between the internal affairs of a state and the peace of Europe, and that control by the powers could be effective only if exercised everywhere and always. The British insisted that a line could and must be drawn, and that only when the general peace was palpably threatened was internal intervention admissible. In Vienna unlimited surveillance seemed the one hope for peace; in London such surveillance seemed a rule of force as intolerable as the Napoleonic.

The point at issue was fundamental in any international system, whether a concert of Europe or a League of Nations or a United Nations. It is all very well to say, as the British did in the 1820's, that international pressure must be applied only when the peace is threatened. But at precisely what point do the developing forces of aggression within a state come to threaten the community of states? The question is unanswerable, and so was that aspect of the Austrian argument. If international pressure, on the other hand, is applied to block all revolutionary developments within a state on the chance that they will become threatening, the system is a static despotism. These dangers are the horns of the dilemma inherent in an international system, and of the two the British preferred the danger of revolutions to the danger of tyranny.

The risings of 1820 brought the issue to a head. Austria suppressed the Italian rebels, but Italy would not be secure until Spain also was made safe for reaction. Metternich approved the project of a French invasion of Spain, which disturbed the British profoundly because it conjured up the ghost of the eighteenth-century entente between the French and Spanish Bourbons. Latin America was again involved. The Spanish colonies had never fully resumed their broken allegiance and were now asserting their independence. They were an important British market; if the old regime were re-established in Madrid, an attempt would almost surely follow to re-establish it in America, and the commercial gains of this restoration would accrue to France. Largely for that reason Britain dissociated herself at Verona from the French design on Spain, and published the fact that the unanimity of the powers was ended.

In the spring of 1823 France went ahead regardless, and soon crushed the liberal government of Spain. Britain then took a hand. Castlereagh had died and been succeeded in the Foreign Office by George Canning, who had long and openly opposed the idea of the concert. "It will necessarily involve us deeply," he said, "in all the politics of the Continent, whereas our true policy has always been not to interfere except in great emergencies, and then with a commanding force." When Britain interfered in 1823, the fact that she possessed commanding force precluded a great emergency. She notified the French government that she opposed transatlantic intervention, and the whole scheme collapsed. The Royal Navy could not help liberals in Spain, but it could in South America.

Britain's defiance of the concert had another aspect, far more important in the long run than her aid to liberalism. Her economic interest in the independence of the Spanish colonies was equaled by the political interest of the United States; the two countries had for the first time a common objective that produced complementary policies. Joint action proved impossible, and Britain took her stand alone; the United States then took hers in a slightly more advanced position. Canning served notice on France in October 1823. In December President Monroe delivered to Congress the message known since as the Monroe Doctrine.

The President enunciated three principles of American policy. The United States would not interfere in the internal affairs of any European state or of its existing colonies; she would not tolerate European interference in the affairs of any independent state in the western hemisphere; she considered the hemisphere closed henceforth to colonization by European powers. In theory these principles rested upon the sole and sovereign will of the United States, but in practice theory was absurd. The United States had no army or navy with which to make her will sovereign; the idea of her intervening in Europe was only slightly more ridiculous than the idea of her resisting European intervention in the Americas. But her words were not challenged for another forty years because she had behind her the authority of the Royal Navy.

Monroe's message was welcomed by the British public. Some avid imperialists resented its ban on colonization, but the President's timing had precluded official resentment: if the British government repudiated his third principle and accepted the other two, it would imply that it had broken with the concert of Europe in order to be a dog in the colonial manger. Her current interests, furthermore, were in trade rather than conquest, and she tacitly accepted her role as underwriter of the American position. Thomas Jefferson had expected as much when he had heard of Canning's overtures and spoken of marrying Britain's fleet. "By acceding to her proposition we detach her from the bands, bring her mighty weight into the scale of free government, and emancipate a continent at one stroke."

The effect of emancipation was incalculable. The western hemisphere, a focus of European political expansion since the days of the Conquistadores, was suddenly and permanently closed to it. For the next century European powers pressed outward into Africa, the Near East, and the Orient, creating wars and crises from Port Arthur to Fez; during almost the whole of that time the Americas were left to work out their own destiny under the aegis first of British and then of American sea power. In the process the old hostility between Great Britain and the United States gave place to a largely unrecognized partnership.

The American crisis was no more than settled before events were pushing the Tory government toward the support of liberalism in a quite different area. The semicircle of land bordering the eastern Mediterranean, from the Balkans through Asia Minor to Egypt, had been the scene of rivalries between great powers since the wars of Rameses and the Hittites. Britain's strategic interest in the area dated from the formation of her Indian empire, for the Isthmus of Suez was the one portage on her most direct route to the East. If she had not previously had serious rivals, except for Napoleon's incursion, the chief reason had been the existence of the Ottoman Empire. The whole region from the border of Hungary to the edge of the Sudan was at least nominally under the rule of the sultan, whose government was too weak to close Britain's road to the East, too slippery to become the puppet of any power, and yet strong enough to prevent a stronger state from entrenching itself on the Mediterranean coast. For these reasons the maintenance of the Turkish Empire served Britain's interest admirably.

But the decay of the empire, which culminated in the twentieth century, was well under way in the early nineteenth. Russia was pressing against the Turkish frontiers at both ends of the Black Sea, Austria in the Danube valley, and the upheaval of the Napoleonic Wars had begun to release the forces of nationalism among the Balkan peoples. The Serbs had already wrung a large measure of autonomy from the sultan, and in the early 1820's the Greeks also rose in revolt. Serbian developments aroused little interest in London, but Greece was another question. It concerned many segments of the British public, and the government could not remain aloof.

From the strategic standpoint Britain had reason to support the Turk as a defense against Russia. The Greeks looked for Russian help, and the Czar stood to gain by providing it. When Alexander was succeeded by his hard-headed brother Nicholas in 1825, it became apparent that Russia was about to act — to flout Metternich's principles, the British believed, in order to create a satellite on the Aegean and take the Ottoman Empire in flank if and when Russia wished to advance on the Bosporus. The obvious British counter-move was to support the Sultan, but the move was out of the question. The Turkish government, though still known as the Sublime Porte, was an international pariah, and its behavior toward the Greeks shocked Europe. It not only repaid massacres in kind, but hanged the Greek Patriarch of Constantinople and three archbishops in their Easter vestments. The Sultan next turned for help to his vassal, the Pasha of Egypt, whose fleet soon cut off the Greeks from supplies by sea while his army began to exterminate them. Their plight became a European crisis.

In Russia, France, and Britain the Greek cause seized the public imagination. Aristocrats, trained to know the classic world better than their own, saw in the peasants of the Morea the heroes whom Miltiades had led, and in the Pasha the new Darius. Liberals turned from their own frustrations to gathering money, supplies, and volunteers for a people worse oppressed than they were. Romantic poets by the score poured out their passionate sympathy, and the most romantic of them all gave both sympathy and life. Lord Byron dead was worth an army to the Greeks.

The successes of the Egyptians increased public excitement and accelerated intervention. In the summer of 1827 Russia, France, and Britain decided to force a settlement on the Porte by a naval demonstration, which led them inadvertently into sinking the Egyptian fleet in Navarino Bay. The battle saved the Greeks for the moment, but it frightened the British government back into inactivity. Canning was dead, and the Duke of Wellington, who became Prime Minister at the beginning of 1828, was terrified of destroying the Ottoman Empire. Not so the Czar. He went to war with the Porte and won major gains for himself; the most Wellington could achieve was to have the Greek problem submitted to the arbitration of the three powers. The upshot, in 1831-2, was the creation of an independent Greece under the guardianship of France, Russia, and Britain.

The whole affair was scarcely a triumph for British diplomacy. But a major point had been won, in that Greece did not become a Russian satellite. Nicholas had ignored the wishes of Metternich and shown, not for the last time, that the reactionary solidarity of the east-European powers weighed little against Russia's Balkan ambitions. Great Britain and France had contained those ambitions by collaborating with Russia, and so had established a triangular balance of power in the eastern Mediterranean. It was unstable but lasted for another forty years, during which the three powers eyed each other askance; whenever one became unduly aggressive, the other two drew together in opposition. The effect was to serve Britain's underlying interest by preserving what remained of the Ottoman Empire.

The developments of the 1820's, in summary, began the transformation of Britain from a tacit supporter of reaction to a friend of the oppressed and weak. She broke with the Continental powers over Spain; she defied them over South America, and in the pursuit of her own interests assumed the protection of a hemisphere. Her policy toward Greece was more hesitant because it was based on conflicting factors — sympathy with the rebels, fear of Russia, reluctance to undermine the Turkish buffer. Her intervention, nevertheless, helped to flout again the principles of Metternich and to establish another independent state. Her prestige was increasing in the eyes of Europe's liberals. But before she could become their champion she had to liberalize herself at home.

III   The Genesis of Reform

IN British domestic history the years after Waterloo are often known as the Tory Reaction. To reformers the government seemed to have accepted as its guiding principle the Austrian adage, "govern, and change nothing!" The Tories had, in fact, an almost Viennese dread of revolution. They were not at heart reactionaries, but they had to deal with increasing hunger, pauperism, and discontent, and they diagnosed these as symptoms of incipient revolt. The only medicine they knew was repression.

The malady, though less acute than they thought, was real. Its chief causes lay in industrial developments of the war and post-war years. By 1815 British industry was geared to produce more than an impoverished Continent could absorb; the subsequent years of retrenchment brought bankruptcies, unemployment, and a fall in the general wage level. The resultant distress would normally have been mitigated by a fall in food prices with the importation of cheap European grain. But the landed interests passed the corn law of 1815, a tariff on foreign grain for the benefit of the domestic producer, and the law kept food prices high regardless of wages. The sight of the landowners enriching themselves while the poor went without bread did not endear the government to the masses.

The Tory leaders knew little about economics. It was still an adolescent science, largely ignored in their conservative education, and they were ill equipped to deal with economic maladjustments. Instead they struck at the results — at crime through a harsh administration of the penal and game laws, at political agitation through curbing the right of assembly and the freedom of the press. The root of their measures was fear. They had no police force worth the name, and their army was neither large nor reliable enough to protect them against mob violence. Their traditional protection was their own prestige: a squire was obeyed because he expected to be. Now the Tories' fear was driving them to the one course that might make the fear come true. The ruthlessness of worried magistrates, the use of troops against innocuous gatherings, the hiring of informers who fabricated plots with the glibness of Titus Oates — such methods were rapidly depriving the regime of its title to respect. Even intelligent oligarchs were coming to realize that some measure of reform was the only means of self-preservation.

The first sign of a breach between government and governed came in 1820. The death of the aged King, who had been insane for the past decade, brought the Prince Regent to the throne as George IV. The new monarch was a reactionary middle-aged rake, and almost his first act was to demand proceedings for a divorce from his wife. Queen Caroline was a flighty lady of doubtful morals, but her husband's were beyond doubt. The official attempt to prove her an adulteress made her the heroine of the hour. Popular dislike of the ministry fused with dislike of the sovereign, and pressure from "the majority without doors" forced the government to abandon the divorce proceedings. The humiliation shook the throne itself.

Two years later the death of Castlereagh precipitated a reorganization of the cabinet. New men and new policies appeared. The system of hired informers was abolished and the penal code modernized; the navigation acts were amended to encourage colonial trade with foreign powers; the ban on workers' organizations was rescinded. These measures were the entering wedge of reform, and they had the usual effect of splitting the party in power. The split, largely concealed while Canning lived, cracked the surface of Toryism soon after Wellington became Prime Minister. In 1828 the Test and Corporation Acts were repealed as they applied to dissent. Their provisions had long been in abeyance, suspended by annual acts of Parliament, and repeal was primarily a symbol that Whig principles had triumphed. But it had another effect: the emancipation of dissent inevitably accentuated the issue of Catholic emancipation. This question, which Pitt had sidestepped and his successors had not dared to touch, completed the disruption of the Tory party. It thereby burst the dam holding back the flood waters of reform.

The Act of Union had not cured Ireland's political grievances, and her economic problems had grown worse. Because her capital was now London, many of her great landholders no longer came near their Irish estates but left the peasants to the mercies of stewards and farmers. These agents were calloused by their own position. They had to send to the landlords every penny due, and in time of blight and famine they were powerless to temper their demands on the tenantry. In time of abundance, conversely, the tenant was penalized for any attempt to better his holding; improvements increased its value and therefore its rent. At all times he had to pay tithes for the detested Anglican Church in Ireland while supporting his own church by voluntary offerings. Absenteeism, a legal system that encouraged squalor, and the curse of tithes were grievances at the core of the Irish problem, and no change in the political surface could erase them.

Another factor, still largely unrecognized, was even more important. The Irish population was beginning to outgrow the available land. The effect of the increasing shortage of arable was felt particu-

larly among the poorest peasants; they became virtually enslaved to
their landlords by the desperate competition for leases, and lived on
the edge of starvation. Many would have gone over the edge if they
had not had one of the cheapest known foods, the potato, as their
staff of life. But the potato is highly sensitive to blight. The appearance of the potato disease meant famine, and might mean rioting or
even rebellion. The British position in Ireland depended in great
measure upon the activities of a microscopic fungus.

A serious famine struck in 1822, and the hungry were soon ripe for
agitators. The emancipation movement, which had been kept alive
in Dublin since the union, spread rapidly from the middle class to
the masses. The leader of the movement was Daniel O'Connell, a
brilliant orator, organizer, and tactician. Like Grattan fifty years before, O'Connell succeeded in identifying his narrow political objective with the cause of Irish nationalism. The Ulster Presbyterians
naturally held aloof, but Catholics with diverse grievances rallied to
the cause — peasants embittered by tithes and stewards and hunger,
patriots who still resented the union, politicians eager for seats in
Parliament, priests dreaming of new freedom for the Church. Excitement mounted rapidly. It reached a peak in 1828 with the election of O'Connell to a Parliament for which he was ineligible. When
the borough-mongers could not control the electoral machine, the
Protestant ascendancy had indeed descended. The alternative to
emancipation was clearly revolt.

The position of the cabinet was awkward. The Greek crisis was
still threatening, and the domestic situation was even more so.
O'Connell had enough British support so that the outbreak of fighting in Ireland would in all likelihood overturn the government and
bring the Whigs to power, to initiate their parliamentary reforms.
As the Tory leader, Wellington was committed to opposing emancipation, and his lieutenant in the Commons, Sir Robert Peel, had
been stoutly against it. But they were confronted with a choice of
evils, and they decided that surrender to the Irish Catholics was
better than surrender to the Whigs. The bulk of their party, deserted by its chiefs, fought a losing battle against the concession. In
April 1829 Catholics were admitted to Parliament.

Emancipation determined the future development of the Irish
problem. The Protestant minority, it is true, retained a dispropor-
tionate influence, and the social and economic ills that were taproots

of its influence remained throughout the nineteenth century. But the political taproot was cut. For the first time Catholic Ireland had a constitutional focus in the House of Commons, where its grievances could be aired by more civilized means than murder, arson, and revolt. For the next forty years the airing produced few tangible results; it seemed to be no more than wind against the rock of British conservatism, while in Ireland the old cycle of violence and repression went on. During those years, however, the Catholic leaders acquired a political training in the school of frustration at Westminster. Their hope was essentially the same, generation after generation — peaceful independence through repeal of the union. The hope was blocked on one side by British intransigence and threatened on the other by Irish revolutionaries; generation after generation it failed. But out of failure and bloodshed it developed into a cause that could not be ignored. The Irish Catholic members in the Commons cohered into a party, which grew in importance as Home Rule grew into the dominant issue of British politics. These were the seeds of the future, hidden in Catholic emancipation.

The immediate effects were disruptive in a different way. To the orthodox Tory, Wellington and Peel had betrayed the principles of the party — as indeed they had. On its ecclesiastical side Toryism had rested upon the Clarendon Code and the Test Act; now the Anglicans shared political power with dissenters and Catholics. On its constitutional side Toryism had rested on the assumption that the time-tested fabric of the state was inviolable; now the need of change in Ireland had been recognized, and the logic of resisting change at home was undermined. The Tory philosophy that had prevailed in Britain for almost half a century was going bankrupt.

Wellington refused to see the implications of what he had done or to admit that further change might be necessary. But his party was dissolving around him. The left wing was breaking away toward the Whig camp, and the right wing suspected even the Duke of a secret sympathy with reform. Only his prestige and the favor of a reactionary king kept the Prime Minister in office. Then suddenly, in June 1830, George IV rendered his people the service of dying. He was succeeded by his brother William, a bluff and simple man with mildly liberal views. The accession of the new King automatically dissolved Parliament and necessitated a general election.

In July came a revolution in France. The Bourbon regime, grown reactionary, was overthrown with surprising ease and superseded by a limited, moderate, and liberal monarchy; the change was engineered and carefully controlled by the middle class, and the new sovereign, Louis-Philippe, was himself respectably bourgeois. His moderation was soon put to the test by a revolt in Belgium, which split that country away from Holland and threatened to make it an appendage of revolutionary France. The new French regime yielded to pressure from Britain, however, and eventually joined with her in defying Metternich and supervising the creation of an independent Belgium. Such level-headedness in Paris was a far cry from the Jacobin attitude of 1792–3, and the contrast was noted across the Channel.

These developments were an object lesson for the British electorate in the years 1830–2. If a violent revolution could be dammed into liberal channels and made to behave, what became of the Tory argument that peaceful reform would open the floodgates of anarchy? The argument and the party were repudiated. King William's first parliament had been in session only a few weeks when Wellington resigned, and a half-century of Tory rule was ended. The new Whig ministry, under the premiership of Earl Grey, promptly began the drafting of an act "to amend the representation of the people of England and Wales." Britain was in the first throes of revolution by consent.

IV   Liberalism and the Reform Bill

WHILE Toryism had been decaying, the Whigs had been gradually — in many cases reluctantly — acquiring a liberal creed. Its principles derived from the Whig tradition of the seventeenth century as modified by the political and economic revolutions of the eighteenth, by the religious fervor of the evangelicals, and by the rationalist spirit. The product was classical liberalism, one of the cardinal factors in the development of nineteenth-century thought. The liberal program was both concrete and utopian, and for decades after 1830 it progressed from triumph to triumph. Its success seemed to be irrefutable proof of its validity. By the 1850's Great Britain was so liberal and so prosperous that only heretics dared question the causal relationship between her principles and her position. Her-

etics there were, on the right and on the left. But the majority accepted the tenets of classical liberalism, which became the faith of
Victorian Britain.

Complacency was short-lived. The faith contained paradoxical
seeds of change that sprouted in a changing economy. A new Toryism arose to challenge the orthodox position. Europe refused to be
converted and grew more militantly pagan, until the fire and iron of
the Bismarck era forced the British to reappraise their values. Under
the prodding of necessity liberal leaders began their slow movement
toward the left — from Earl Grey to Gladstone, from Gladstone to
Lloyd George — until eventually the remnant of the party was swallowed in modern British socialism. Along the way segments became
detached, joined the Tories, and passed on their heritage to modern
conservatism. The reactionary of today has much in common with
the pre-Victorian Whig, and the moderate Tory, whether American
or British, often speaks in Gladstonian terms. The metamorphosis of
classical liberalism, in short, is a central phenomenon in the evolution of modern political ideas.

The Whigs who triumphed with Grey were far from the modern
liberal. They were no more democratic than Wellington, for their
whole tradition was oligarchic; they had resisted Jacobinism as
stoutly as the Tories, and still denied as hotly that the franchise was
one of the rights of man. For them it was a privilege inherently connected with property; as for the unpropertied masses, the Whig felt
with Charles I that "their having a share in the government . . . is
nothing appertaining to them." This attitude seems illiberal today,
when the idea of universal suffrage is accepted in theory and curtailed only in practice, but a century ago it seemed self-evident.
The masses were illiterate and nearly destitute; enfranchising them
would open the way for any demagogue who promised to transfer
the wealth of the country from rich to poor by use of the taxing
power. The bulk of the reformers accepted the principle of minority
rule. They wished to confine political power to those who had a
stake in the existing order, and to extend the franchise only as the
number of property-owners increased.

Where the Whigs differed from the Tories was in the criterion of
property. Because the landed interest had traditionally been the
core of the oligarchy and land the basis of taxation, the conservative
insisted that the only constitutional guarantee of stability was a

franchise giving predominance to landholders. The Whigs, on the contrary, insisted that all forms of property should be given equal weight — that every one of sufficient substance, regardless of what he lived on or where he lived, should have an equal voice. This could be achieved only by reform of two sorts. The disparate electoral systems in the boroughs, where representatives were chosen in one case by a landlord, in another by a close corporation, in a third by virtually universal manhood suffrage, would have to be replaced by uniform property qualifications for the vote. The rotten boroughs would have to be abolished and new constituencies created in the new centers of wealth and population. Thus the Whig program had two parts, a standardization of voting requirements and wholesale reapportionment. Both were to the interests of the industrialists, whose wealth was rarely in land and whose strength was in poorly represented areas. Both were anathema to the landed interest, whose power depended upon the inequalities of suffrage and apportionment.

If the Whigs could not appeal to the people as champions of democracy, they could and did appeal as champions of popular liberties. The Tories had carried their emphasis on strong government so far that the nation identified it with repressive government. The Whig tradition, on the other hand, stressed the rights of the subject, and the tradition had now matured into a theory of government, according to which the primary function of the state is to guarantee to each citizen the greatest degree of liberty compatible with that of his fellows. On the positive side, the state maintains order and ensures due process of law; on the negative side it eliminates all artificial restrictions, statutory and otherwise, that benefit a particular group or interest at the cost of the general welfare. Laissez faire — leave society alone, and it will regulate itself by the competition of the individuals who compose it; if each is as free as possible to follow his own interest, the result will be the greatest possible good for all. Here was the core of the liberal creed.

Laissez faire derived from many sources. One was the distrust of government that the Whigs inherited from seventeenth-century Puritanism; they regarded government as a necessary evil even when they controlled it themselves, and the more it governed the worse it was. Another source was the rationalistic optimism of the eighteenth century: only a faith in man's inherent goodness justifies the doctrine that the self-interest of each is enlightened enough to make the sum of interests social good, not social evil. These two sources were largely intangible, but a third was concrete and peculiar to the period. Laissez faire satisfied the specific self-interest of the industrialists. As they translated the phrase, it meant hands off business, and their economic doctrine was the logical extension of this idea.

They were as rugged individualists in the economic sphere as the Puritans had been in the spiritual, and they had the same impatience of state interference. If government left them alone, they could run their mine or mill or shop on any terms the market would bear — terms of wages and hours, of housing, of working conditions, of the labor of women and children. Their desire for free trade in the labor market was dignified as a natural right of the individual, the right to freedom of contract. This dogma of economic liberalism asserted that a workman should be free to sell his labor on whatever conditions he chose to accept, and that his freedom should not be curtailed by the state or any other extraneous agency. A factory act to limit hours and a trade union designed for collective bargaining were equally infringements of free contract. As the liberal opposed them in theory, so the industrialist opposed them in his own interests. Because a laborer who was free to contract was free from the means of raising his wage by collective bargaining, the new principle worked itself out on the books of industry in pounds, shillings, and pence.

Economic liberalism had sweeping implications for foreign and imperial policy. The liberal believed that government should not only be limited but cheap; his ideal was a small, trained bureaucracy functioning within a narrowly circumscribed sphere. He was the inveterate enemy of militarism, with its vast and costly establishment, and of war as the greatest extravagance and the greatest unreason in which a nation can indulge. He was convinced that wars grew from economic rivalries, expressed in tariffs, and he looked forward to a day when free trade would usher in the utopia of peace. For all these reasons he deplored armaments and advocated a foreign policy of logic and negotiation, not of force.

His attitude toward the empire derived from the same premises. Britain's colonies yielded her a dubious profit, which he expected to see evaporate with the advent of free trade, and involved her in the perennial danger of war. Colonial status, furthermore, meant to him a subordinate kind of citizenship that violated his ideal of self-government. For economic and political reasons, therefore, he wished to extend colonial autonomy as fast as possible.

Much of his liberal program was still embryonic when the Whigs came to power in the autumn of 1830. The one fully developed issue was parliamentary reform. Earl Grey had a majority in the Lower House, but in the lords the Tory old guard was still firmly entrenched. It had lost ground steadily since Castlereagh's death, and now it was driven back to the innermost citadel of the constitution. The lords' power of veto could be circumvented only if the King chose to create enough new peers, and William, although he favored reform, was strongly opposed to such drastic coercion. Here, then, was the pattern of revolution: an obdurate minority with the determination and the legal right to block the majority will.

Even the narrow electorate had deserted the Tories. When Grey dissolved Parliament in 1831 to seek a specific mandate, the voters triumphantly vindicated the Whig slogan of "the bill, the whole bill, and nothing but the bill." The lords threw out the bill. The common people — whom it did not enfranchise, but who sensed that change was to their interest — responded with serious riots. The crisis came to a head in the spring of 1832, when the King refused to create the necessary peers and the ministry resigned. Wellington desperately tried to govern but could not. He resigned in favor of Grey, who at last obtained the King's agreement to coerce the lords; to save the Crown from being humiliated and the aristocracy from being swamped, the Duke withdrew his opposition. The titled diehards stayed away from the Upper House, and the measure became law.

The effect on the old order did not seem catastrophic. The bill eliminated the worst of the rotten boroughs, increased the representation of the industrial areas, and created a roughly uniform qualification for voting in town and country; in substance the result was to enfranchise the middle class — shopkeepers, industrialists, merchants, well-to-do farmers. The electorate was more than tripled, and the basis of the oligarchy was proportionately broadened. But it remained an oligarchy. The new bourgeois elements of strength in the nation had battered against the door of an aristocratic parliament; the aristocrats had held the door until the whole house threatened to fall on them, and then had opened to let in their opponents.

Thereupon both sides joined to lock the door against the mass of the people.

The Tories had prevented revolution by giving way, and had kept their party intact. For the next fourteen years they struggled to preserve the share of power left them, while the Whigs struggled to complete their victory by enacting their liberal program. The Tories lost, essentially because they no longer had a tenable position. Its two traditional fortresses had been sapped, the Crown and the House of Lords, and even reactionaries realized that the majority in the Commons was henceforth sovereign. Far more important, the principle of change had been admitted. The constitution, set in its mold since the Glorious Revolution, was now shaken into fluidity again, and the only question was how fast it would be altered in the future.

V   The Fruits of Liberalism

IN the years immediately after 1832 reform was at full flood. Problems at home and throughout the empire, some of them going back for generations, were raised for discussion and settlement in the new House of Commons. The East India Company was deprived of its last remaining commercial privileges and reduced to an agency of government. Slavery, which had been forbidden as a traffic in 1807, was abolished as an institution, and colonial slaveholders were compensated to the tune of £20,000,000. At home the boroughs were modernized; the close and corrupt corporations gave place to elected councils, and municipal administration soon became a model of enlightenment. A hesitant first move was made in financing elementary education. Child labor in textile mills was curtailed by an act liberal in its mechanism (a centralized, bureaucratic staff of inspectors) but a departure in spirit from liberal orthodoxy. Parliament was unwilling to sacrifice children to the principle of laissez faire.

Almost simultaneously liberalism was triumphing in another social field. The Poor Law Amendment Act of 1834 was reform long overdue. The Elizabethan system of poor relief had broken down under the pressure of industrialization and the long years of war, and since the turn of the century pauperism had become the most pressing social problem before the country. The authorities had attempted to solve it by doling out public money to bring wages up to the subsistence level, but the principal results had been to undermine the self-respect of the workers, to free the employers from the necessity of paying a living wage, and to impose a crushing burden on the taxpayers. The new poverty created by the Industrial Revolution, like the new wealth, required a sweeping reform, which was begun by the act of 1834.

The system there established was intended to decrease pauperism by forcing the able-bodied poor to choose between employment and what was virtually prison. The dole was largely eliminated; the parishes were grouped into districts, each with a workhouse, and the inmates of the houses were set to labor on a near-starvation diet. An elected board of guardians in each district was supervised by a poor-law commission in London. The commissioners used to the full their authority under the act; they, rather than Parliament, gave form to the new system. Here was the liberal's ideal instrument, a centralized, efficient bureaucracy with power adequate for its task. The needful social surgery was performed with a minimum of confusion and expense. The able-bodied poor soon found that almost any form of employment was preferable to the workhouse; the manufacturers were thereby assured of abundant cheap labor, and the cost of relief to the taxpayer was cut in half.

But efficiency was purchased at a price. English country life received a jolt from which it never recovered. Previously the major concern of the parish and the justices of the peace had been with poor relief; the Elizabethan principle that each parish should look after its own had grown into the fabric of the community, and was accepted by every one from squire to pauper. This parochial self-sufficiency had its evil side in the waste and corruption of amateur administration. It also had its good side in the sense of responsibility inculcated in the rural gentry. That sense was the root of the gentleman's power. Now it was withering in every parish in England, and the time was coming when

> the last sad squires ride slowly towards the sea,
> And a new people takes the land: and still it is not we.[1]

The poor law accentuated the distinction between this new people and the proletariat, for the workhouses made the poor man con-

---

[1] G. K. Chesterton: "The Secret People." Reprinted by permission of Dodd, Mead & Company from *The Collected Poems of G. K. Chesterton,* copyright, 1932, by Dodd, Mead & Company.

scious, as never before, that his betters had deserted him. Previously he had received a slipshod charity; whatever he had paid for it in self-respect, he at least had not felt a pariah. Now his poverty was tantamount to crime, and was dealt with in a flint-like prison where life was designedly reduced to the edge of starvation. Hatred of the workhouses and of the oligarchy responsible for them was widespread among English laborers; the shadow of what they called the Bastilles fell on them all. They had played their part in agitating and rioting for the Reform Bill; politically it had brought them nothing, and socially it had brought them the bitter fruit of the poor law. Small wonder that they felt betrayed.

Their "bitter discontent grown fierce and mad," as Carlyle called it, gradually took form as chartism. This was a movement unique in British history. It was entirely proletarian, and it was revolutionary. Not since the days of Cromwell had the common people so troubled the waters of government, and the Levellers had been a ripple by comparison with the chartists. In 1836–7 agitation began simultaneously in different parts of England, and soon crystallized in the "people's charter" from which it took its name. The six points of the charter were all political, and all radical: universal manhood suffrage, vote by secret ballot, equal electoral districts, annual parliaments, the abolition of property qualifications for members of the House of Commons, and the payment of members. These demands foreshadowed the democratic state. They were premature, for middle-class liberalism had not yet begun to spend its force. But their appearance was more than an augury of the future. They focused attention on Carlyle's two nations, the rich and the poor, and proved that the liberals had not begun to answer his "condition of England question." They set men to thinking in new ways, shook the complacent theorists of laissez faire, and prepared the ground for a new liberalism and a new conservatism.

The movement itself had no chance of success. The chartist leaders were divided between advocates of legal agitation and of violence, and both methods were hopeless from the start. The oligarchy was not open to peaceful persuasion; its members, regardless of party or social standing, were a solid phalanx against this threat from without. Force was equally impossible; even if the chartists had been agreed on its use, they lacked the necessary coherence and discipline. Successful revolution is not made by the unprivileged

alone; they must find allies, if not leaders, within the privileged order itself. So the popularism of the Puritan Revolution developed
as a result, not a cause, of the aristocratic and middle-class revolt
against prerogative, and was suppressed because it ran counter to
the interests of Cromwell's new oligarchs. So also with the revolution that began at the death of George IV. Its impetus came from
an alliance of unprivileged industrialists and privileged Whigs; the
triumph of the alliance touched off the popularism of the chartists,
and they failed, like the Levellers, because their aims were anathema to the oligarchy. Only later, when the oligarchs split into
factions and some of them sought support from demos, did the
points of the people's charter begin to find their way onto the statute book.

Chartist agitation reached its climax in the beginning of a new
reign. In 1837 William IV died and was succeeded by his eighteen-
year-old niece, Victoria. On her depended the future of the monarchy. The recent sequence of a senile and insane king, then a dis-
solute and reactionary king, then a genial but undignified king had
tarnished the crown until it meant little to the nation. Victoria had
to refurbish it, and she did. Her youth and her lonely position in the
limelight appealed to the chivalry of a romantic age; her rigid standards of conduct, her patience under stress, even her insistence on
what she conceived to be her rights were middle-class virtues as
intelligible in her as in any housewife; her dignity, above all, added
respect to affection and understanding. She was far from a great
woman, but she was superbly fitted for her job.

She needed all her qualities during the first decade of the reign,
for it was a period of perennial crises. By 1839 the outbreak of a
chartist revolution seemed to be imminent. The government acted
with phenomenal good sense; it did almost nothing to repress verbal
agitation, yet massed enough military force to discourage violence.
A few riots, one minor insurrection, and the emergency passed. It
never recurred with the same intensity. The workers were losing
faith in the chartists, and a wholly different form of propaganda was
turning their energies into a new movement.

That movement was directed against the corn law. Demands for
the political rights of the masses gave place to demands for the economic rights of all consumers, and this transformation, effected
largely by middle-class liberals, had a profound effect on the work-

ingman. It shifted his interest from the abstraction of the vote to the concrete reality of a loaf of bread, and the struggle to cheapen his daily bread gave him experience in the ways of campaigning. The chartists had brought him only frustration; this campaign, as it swelled to its triumphant climax, showed him that he had a real, if indirect, political weight. The "condition of England" question was entering a new phase.

The effect of the campaign on the upper classes was much more immediate than on the workers. The crisis of 1832 had shaken the principle of minority rule but left it intact, and victors and vanquished had soon agreed that the reform bill was a final settlement; they remained primarily oligarchs and only secondarily Whigs and Tories. In the 1840's their agreement melted in the heat of another argument and another crisis. The Whigs took their cause to the nation, and organized such support in the people at large as would have scandalized Lord Grey. They won, but at a price. They could never erase the memory of their party's appeal to the unenfranchised, and before long the remnants of the Tories were persuaded to make their own appeal. Thus the Whig triumph split the oligarchy again, this time beyond repair, and so made possible the later rise of a democratic liberalism and a democratic conservatism.

The attack on the corn law had been impending for a generation. As soon as the industrialists had won power in the House of Commons, they had begun to work toward their economic objectives. The chief one was free trade, and the keystone of the whole protectionist system was the corn law; by it the system would stand or fall. The assumptions on which the law rested were under attack from the theoretical economists, whose arguments could for once be translated into popular terms. The landed interest that defended the law was a formidable but relatively isolated group, which drew its strength from grain and would weaken if grain prices fell. Hence the assault on the corn law served not only the economic purpose of securing free trade, but also the political purpose of upsetting the balance struck in 1832 and completing the triumph of industrial liberalism.

The cause of repeal, like that of reform a generation earlier, was not initiated by the Whigs. The party was converted by a group of liberals operating outside regular political channels, appealing to almost every segment of the population, and controlling as effective a propaganda machine as the world had yet encountered. In 1838 a group of Lancashire manufacturers founded the Anti-Corn-Law League. The moving spirits were Richard Cobden and John Bright, the two outstanding prophets of mid-century liberalism. They opposed governmental intervention of almost any sort, at home or abroad, and preached against the ultimate social sin of war their new gospel of internationalism founded on free trade. The whole gospel was implicit in the campaign against the corn law, and they brought to bear upon that narrow issue the force of their reasoning and their passionate moral conviction. The league they inspired grew by leaps and bounds. In the eight years between its founding and its triumph it remade public thinking on economic matters, captured the Whig party, and eventually shattered the Tories.

The League, true to the rationalism of the liberal creed, rested its case upon logic. The gist of its argument was that the corn law benefited a small minority at the expense of the nation at large. Britain was no longer self-sufficient in her food supply, and the pretense that she could be — which was the Tory justification for the tariff — was disproved by the high price of domestic grain. Her prosperity now depended more on industry than agriculture, and the corn law impeded industrial expansion. By limiting the natural exchange of foreign grain for British goods, the law forced the grain-growing countries into an unnatural and competitive industrialization. By keeping domestic food prices high, and with them wages and production costs, it impeded the sale of British goods abroad. It was a tribute, in short, levied upon the new economy by the vested interest of the old.

This general line of argument was adapted to particular groups. The agricultural laborers were assured that a fall in the price of bread would more than compensate them for any decline in their wages; the farmers were told that repeal would lower their rents; the industrial workers were fired with the prospect of cheap bread, a luxury transformed into a staple, and the manufacturers were fired with the prospect of a drastic wage cut. The campaign was carried to every part of the island by every known technique — vast sums in subscriptions, investigators paid to exploit the evils of protection, endless mass meetings, campaign buttons, pamphlets by the millions. This was political agitation of a sort never seen before. It took no account of social status or occupation, of the gulf between the voters and the unenfranchised; it appealed to everyone except the landlord, in varying terms but on one specific issue, and it accordingly tapped the most disparate sources of unrest.

The agitation for repeal was blocked by a Tory majority in Parliament. The Whigs had shared the fate of most reform administrations: the more liberal measures they had passed, the smaller their following had become. Sir Robert Peel, the new Tory leader, had rebuilt his party and brought it to power in 1841 with a substantial majority. He had labored long and with considerable success to educate it in the acceptance of change; in time he might even have weaned it away from protection, as he was being weaned. His experience in office suggested that tariff reduction increased revenue by increasing consumption. He was able to learn from experience and even, unlike most politicians, from the arguments of his opponents. Once he was convinced, he had the moral stature to follow his conviction at the cost of his career and his party. Such a man was not the one to lead a last-ditch defense of the corn law.

Peel's political tragedy arose from the pressure of time. The tariff might have been reduced by cautious stages to the vanishing point, but matters came to a head too fast. In September 1845 it became known that the Irish potato crop was diseased, and during the autumn the news grew steadily worse. The English grain crop had failed as well, and at least half the Irish peasants would soon have to be fed on grain; the alternative was famine beyond all imagining. The Anti-Corn-Law League made full use of its opportunity, and public excitement grew explosive. Peel realized that the corn law, if once suspended, could never be reimposed, but he could not persuade the cabinet to recommend repeal. The bulk of the Tories clung to their old beliefs that the price of grain was the gauge of their prosperity and power, and that the country's traditional institutions were rooted in the land and would collapse if the roots were tampered with. Against their obstinacy Peel was helpless. He refused to lead them in what he considered their battle for reaction, and they refused to follow him in what they considered betrayal.

He resigned. The Whig leader, Lord John Russell, had at last come out for repeal, but he could not form a ministry. The Tories still controlled the House, and the emergency was too acute for a general election. Peel returned to office. Only he could force repeal on such a parliament, and he was determined to do it at the cost of splitting his party. A group of his personal followers, the Peelites of future years, followed him into alliance with the Whigs, and in May 1846 this odd majority pushed the bill through the commons. In the lords the Duke of Wellington once more helped a cause he detested; "it is a damned mess," was his comment, "but I must look to the peace of the country and the Queen." His great prestige, backed by the memory of 1832, induced the peers to pass repeal. That same night Peel lost his ephemeral majority in the Lower House; he had stolen the Whigs' thunder and betrayed the protectionist Tories, and they combined against him. He resigned for the last time, his work completed and his career destroyed.

Repeal also destroyed the old Tory party. Its liberal wing broke off and eventually coalesced with the Whigs, who for the next twenty years were in the ascendant. This was the first but not the last major party schism: the Liberals split in 1886 and the Conservatives in 1906, and in all three cases their opponents acquired a long tenure of office. But the Tory debacle of 1846 was even more than a schism. The Reform Bill had sucked the marrow from the party's principles, as the Glorious Revolution had from the principles of an earlier Toryism. The years after reform were a breathing spell for the rank and file. They gathered themselves for the last battle against the advancing liberals, but their campaign had been lost before the battle was fought. Their program was at bottom the defense of a status quo that had become indefensible, and the outcome was the eclipse of Toryism.

The Irish emergency that had occasioned repeal was not cured by it. The food shortage of 1846 developed into a catastrophic famine. During the next five years almost a million Irish died; another million emigrated, and bore with them the conviction that the blame for the famine rested squarely on the British. Unrest in Ireland came to a head in 1848, but the government was more successful in coercion than in feeding. Rebellion was put down, and the depopulated island sank into such torpor that it ceased temporarily to be a major problem.

In Britain the crisis of 1846 began the apogee of liberalism. The new doctrine had largely won over the Whigs by 1830, and now brought the most progressive of the Tories into the Whig fold; even the name of the newly reinforced party was changing from Whig to Liberal. Its economic ideas were triumphant. The end of the corn law ended the protective system: duties intended to regulate the flow of trade were promptly removed and the navigation acts repealed, and by 1850 Britain was the world's one great exemplar of free trade.

VI Liberalism and the Empire

ECONOMIC liberalism was exposed to the test of experience, and the result was enormously gratifying to the faithful. British industry boomed, and British agriculture — to the discomfiture of the Jeremiahs — throve almost equally. This prosperity convinced the liberal that the rest of the world would be led by self-interest to emulate Britain. The maze of tariff walls would then disintegrate, goods would flow freely everywhere, and utopia would be at hand. Under the light of reason and the warmth of profit international friction would melt away

Till the war drum throbbed no longer and the battle flags were furled
In the parliament of man, the federation of the world.[2]

This was the liberal's hope. Ingenuous as it looks a century later, in 1850 it seemed for good reason to be in process of realization. Progress was not a theory, but a demonstrated fact. Science and invention were rapidly bettering man's lot, industrialism was bringing him a prosperity without perceptible limit, and in this vast amelioration the British were taking the lead. God, as Milton had pointed out two hundred years before, had a way of revealing Himself first to Englishmen, and God was now working through the machine.

This conviction was not blasphemous. Victorian liberalism had in it a strong religious element, from which it derived much of its crusading zeal. The evangelical's emphasis on good works had made a deeper impression on society than his emphasis on sin, partly because works were more comprehensible to the hard-working, individualistic middle class, partly because works could be assimilated — as the concept of sin could not — with the rationalist's idea that man is good and is progressing toward utopia. This assimilation produced the liberal's faith that the New Jerusalem could be built by unfettering private enterprise and private philanthropy, by eliminating grievances between nations, classes, and individuals, by expanding legal and economic freedom. The central article of faith,

---

2 Tennyson: "Locksley Hall," 1842.

free trade, was central less because it was economically sound than because it promised peace on earth. In the decade of the 1850's protectionists, militarists, imperialists seemed to be retreating before the light and leaving the future to the sons of light. "The liberal," it was written, "deviseth liberal things; and by liberal things shall he stand." [3]

The optimism of this faith was to a great extent the unconscious reflection of Britain's position in the world. She was still in the high noon of the *Pax Britannica*. The foundations of her peace were less permanent than they seemed, but as yet they were imposing. In the spheres of activity to which she largely confined herself she still had no serious rival. In the economic sphere her industry was in a position of pre-eminence verging on monopoly, her merchant marine was larger and busier than ever, and Lombard Street was the financial center of the globe; much of the world's wealth was in her hands, and with it power. In the political sphere the states of Europe were in an equilibrium that permitted her to devote most of her attention to her interests overseas. In the military sphere her development was taking the course indicated by the political situation: because she seemed unlikely to intervene in a major Continental war her army was stagnating in the best Anglo-Saxon tradition, while her navy maintained the post-Trafalgar standard of superiority to any two fleets that might combine against it. This naval force, so overwhelming that it rarely had to be used, was the framework of power within which the colonies developed toward the modern dominions.

The liberals accepted the framework, little as it accorded with their pacific principles, and worked within it to refashion imperial ties. During the first three decades of Victoria's reign Britain's colonial policy underwent a transformation as drastic as that of her domestic constitution. A new concept of self-government took form in institutions, statutes, and ways of thought, and out of it grew the British Commonwealth of the twentieth century. This vast political experiment was largely the outgrowth of early-Victorian liberalism, and was one of its major bequests to posterity.

The character of the experiment was also determined by certain external factors in the Victorian era. One was the lull in European expansion. The great age of mercantile imperialism had ended with

---

[3] Isaiah, 32. 8.

the eighteenth century; the Napoleonic Wars had proved to the maritime states of the Continent that their colonial riches were precarious while Britain ruled the seas, and the post-war era brought those states so many internal problems that they had little energy to spare for their external possessions. The great age of industrial imperialism, on the other hand, did not begin until after the wars of national unification in the 1860's. In the half-century between Waterloo and Sadowa the future British dominions grew in the laboratory of self-government, with little interference from outside powers.

Their growth was accelerated by a second factor, emigration from the mother country. In Britain industrialization and improvements in public health contributed to such a sharp rise of population that there were not enough jobs to go around, and in Ireland there were neither enough tenements nor enough potatoes. The most enterprising, by tens of thousands every year, gambled on opportunity across the sea. They helped to push back the wilderness in Canada, to settle the coasts of Australia and New Zealand, and to begin the transformation of the small colony at the Cape of Good Hope into the Union of South Africa. But their arrival was not an unmixed blessing, for everywhere they upset the colonial status quo. The French Canadians grew fearful that they would be swamped by Anglo-Saxons; the penal colonies in Australia suddenly became an anachronism; the settlement of New Zealand brought trouble with the fierce natives, the Maoris; the British in South Africa were soon at loggerheads with the Dutch. These difficulties were the price of sudden growth, and they concerned the home government as much as the colonists.

A third factor in imperial development was the Victorian's zeal for religion. Evangelicalism was not channeled entirely into the evangel of free trade; it also produced a missionary movement that touched the remotest corners of the empire. The abolition of the slave trade and then of slaveholding had been due in great part to the missionaries' influence at home, but their influence did not stop there. Whenever one of them brought a group of natives into the Christian fold, he became their defender against exploitation by the whites. His defense was backed by a powerful organization in Britain, for the missionary societies exerted political pressure through the pulpit and the press and, more directly, through a group of evangelical bureaucrats in the Colonial Office. If the settlers in New

Zealand trespassed upon the land of the Maoris, or the Dutch of Cape Colony attacked the Kaffirs, the result was likely to be clamor from the missionaries, questions in Parliament, and action by the home government to protect the natives. Such action would run counter, in all probability, to the wishes of the white settlers. Thus the missionary spirit, on the frontiers of empire and in the mother country, tended to curtail colonial autonomy in the name of native rights.

The missionaries were not the only group working in this direction. Another school of thought advocated restraint for economic rather than religious reasons. These scientific reformers, as they considered themselves, argued that the home government should control such undeveloped colonial lands as were suitable for farming, and allot them to carefully chosen settlers; in this way the tide of emigration, channeled from London, would increase population and prosperity overseas until the colonies were strong enough to take from the British taxpayer the burden of their own defense. The reformers influenced government, although they never persuaded it to adopt their program in its entirety, and they also formed chartered colonizing companies to put their theories into practice. Australian immigration grew with such speed, thanks largely to their efforts, that what had been predominantly penal settlements in 1830 became viable, self-governing colonies by 1850. In New Zealand progress was equally phenomenal, although there the Crown retained an element of control for the protection of the Maoris. Both these nascent dominions throve on the work of the reformers, and soon outgrew the need of it.

A third group carried the political and economic premises of liberalism to their logical conclusion and rejected the whole idea of empire. This school developed a strong argument in terms of Britain's welfare. The traditional justification of imperialism as profitable to the mother country had disappeared along with the mercantilist system. In an era of free trade Britain's colonies brought her little economic gain that they would not bring as independent states, and they imposed upon her a heavy burden of defense. By the 1850's her military establishment was costing almost £4,000,000 a year; her forces were dispersed over the globe, and she faced the ever-present danger of being dragged into war by the blunder of a colonial government or the greed of a foreign power. Because the liberal hated war, militarism, and strong government and hoped for the advent of universal peace, it was natural for him to become an anti-imperialist.

Like his intellectual ancestor, the eighteenth-century rationalist, he ignored a number of imponderables. Chief among them was the character of colonial nationalism. The colonists were intensely proud of their autonomy, but few of them wished to carry it to the point of independence. They were beset with dangers — the Maoris for the New Zealanders, the Kaffirs and Zulus for the South Africans, the United States for the Canadians — and the long arm of British power was comfortable in time of crisis. Self-interest as well as sentiment held them within the empire, and they had no intention of being pushed out of it. Their attitude, even more than the support they received in Great Britain, prevented the breakup of the empire. But the anti-imperialists did contribute to the extension of self-government; their dislike of empire, consequently, was instrumental in building a kind of empire of which they never dreamed.

The chief focus of liberal experimentation during this period was Canada. There the problem of autonomy was not complicated by backward natives as in South Africa and New Zealand, or by penal settlements as in Australia. The Canadians had troubles of their own. The constitutional relations between the elected provincial legislatures and the executives responsible to the Crown were initially almost unworkable; the British immigrants were at odds with the French; annexation by the United States was a constant threat. The situation grew steadily worse until the beginning of Victoria's reign. Thereafter the roots of trouble were gradually eliminated by the loyalty and level-headedness of the Canadians and the vision and forbearance of the home government, until thirty years later Canada was setting the pace of imperial development.

The crisis came in 1837. The friction that had been growing for years at last erupted in rebellions in Upper and Lower Canada, the modern Ontario and Quebec. Both were suppressed without great difficulty, but they thrust the whole Canadian problem on the attention of the home government. One of its most radical members, the Earl of Durham, was sent to investigate conditions, and in 1839 he published his *Report on the Affairs of British North America*. This great document enunciated the principles on which the subsequent development of the dominions has been based. Durham's central theme was the necessity for putting the government of Canada into the hands of the Canadians. He advocated an executive responsible to the local legislature on all matters of domestic concern, and to the Crown only on matters demonstrably touching the welfare of the empire at large. This proposal was drastic indeed. It meant turning over almost complete control of their own affairs to provinces lately in rebellion.

The British government had the courage to make the experiment. In 1840 Upper and Lower Canada were joined, and in 1847 Lord Elgin was made Governor of the newly united colony; he and the Colonial Secretary, Lord Grey, proceeded to implement the *Report* in constitutional practice. Elgin withdrew into a neutrality as complete as that of the Queen at home and refused, under extreme provocation, to intervene in domestic affairs. The real executive became the cabinet responsible to the colonial parliament, and over the years the jurisdiction of this government steadily increased. By the 1860's the Canadians' fear of economic and political subordination to the United States stimulated a movement to combine the eastern maritime provinces with Canada proper; the main step was taken in 1867, and soon thereafter the whole of British North America except Newfoundland was included in the Dominion of Canada. This vast federal state, spanning the continent, was the first born in the British Commonwealth of Nations. It was created primarily by the Canadians themselves. But credit is also due to a succession of British statesmen, from Durham to Gladstone, who had the courage of their liberalism.

In South Africa the efforts of much the same statesmen were leading, through one difficulty after another, down the long road to war. The bulk of the white population was descended from the original Dutch settlers, and a gulf of time separated these Boers from the British administrators in Capetown and London. Since the seventeenth century the Boers had been a self-contained and almost unchanging cultural island, cut off from Europe by distance and the autocratic rule of the Dutch East India Company; they would have been far more comprehensible to Cromwell or William III than they were to the bureaucracy of the Colonial Office. They were a nomadic people who required thousands of acres for each family; they lived much as the patriarchs of Israel, and their Calvinism was close to the faith of Israel. They also had the frontiersman's independence and his dislike of the tax-collector. The Dutch authorities had not had an easy time with them, and the British were soon in hot water.

The two peoples might have learned to collaborate, as the British and French were learning in Canada, if they had had the colony to themselves. But together they were a tiny white minority in a land thick with blacks, and the Negro question accentuated the divergence between Englishman and Boer. To the Colonial Office and the missionary the natives were children to be converted and protected against exploitation. To the Boer they were to be either tamed into serving him or driven before him off the land. His iron hand with servants scandalized the missionaries and evoked intervention from Downing Street, to which his answer was escape into the wild veldt.

There he was soon involved in more serious difficulties. The requirements of his flocks impelled him to possess large areas for himself and his sons; he felt crowded if he could see a neighbor's chimney-smoke across the veldt. This land hunger inevitably spelled trouble; it meant that a single Boer family required a space that might support a whole native tribe. The farther the Boers expanded, the more hostility they roused in the tribesmen and the greater the danger to all of white South Africa. When a crisis came, the Boers were glad of British troops; when it passed, they reasserted their right to do as they pleased. They were consequently an administrative problem that surpassed the wisdom of government.

Trouble first came to a head when slavery was abolished throughout the empire. The Boers felt that they were inadequately compensated, and were bitter over the loss of their property and the dislocation of their labor supply. Their grievances were fanned to white heat when the Colonial Secretary warned them, from the safe distance of London, that the natives were victims of "systematic injustice" and must be left unmolested. The most energetic Boers thereupon took to the wilderness. They preferred its freedom and dangers to living under a government that stole their slaves and coddled their enemies.

The Great Trek of 1836–7 burst the old frontiers of Cape Colony to the northeast. The Boers spread across the basins of the Orange and Vaal Rivers — the future Orange Free State and Transvaal — and then crossed the mountains eastward to the coast of Natal, breaking the natives' power as they went. The British government was puzzled and alarmed. In its eyes the Boers were British citizens, but they were encircling Cape Colony with independent states that had access to the sea and might make contact with outside powers, and they were stirring the natives to fury. After much hesitation Britain annexed Natal and extended her sovereignty to the Vaal. Soon afterward she changed her tune, partly because the Boers were incensed and partly because the European situation was threatening; in 1852–4 she recognized the virtual independence of the two Boer republics, the Orange Free State and the Transvaal. The problem then entered a new phase.

Between 1815 and 1854 the shortcomings of British policy were only in part the result of inherent difficulties. They were also the result of contradictions between two different schools of liberal thought. Missionary influence was exerted to protect the natives, by treaty terms if possible and by outright annexation if necessary. The anti-imperialists were categorically opposed to annexation, and were inclined to leave the Boers and blacks to fight out their quarrels. This conflict of opinion in Britain produced vacillation in South Africa, and vacillation produced a profound distrust among the Boers. The grant of autonomy did not wipe out their bitter memories, or make them more tactful in dealing with the natives, or establish once and for all that they had ceased to be British citizens.

For the next decade and more the Boers, in their self-contained republics, retired from contact with the world of the nineteenth century. But to the south of them the pressures of that world were mounting, and the veldt — although no one yet knew it — concealed enough riches to draw adventurers from the corners of the earth. It was only a question of time before Boer seclusion would be shattered, Boer fury aroused, and South Africa plunged into crisis. This was the cost of the liberals' failure to solve the problem. Perhaps they could never have solved it, given their principles and the nature of the Boer. In any case they did not solve it, when reason and forbearance were in the ascendant. In later years, when the cult of force had revived, the problem grew and was solved by other means.

In the empire as a whole, seen from the perspective of another century, liberal policy in this period was as impressive as colonial development. In 1832 the major colonies were mere toeholds on the edge of great land masses, toeholds won by a commercial people intent on doing business across the seas; the colonists were few and often divided among themselves, and the vast resources of the hinterlands were untouched. By 1867 the coastal settlements had expanded inland, thanks primarily to the railroad, and their populations had multiplied as fantastically as their areas; already they were embryonic nations. This phenomenon created such tensions as had lost the United States to Britain; if imperial policy had again been in the hands of a North and a George III, the empire would doubtless have split again. Instead the liberals applied, wherever they could and as far as they dared, their panacea of freedom. They tempered its application to local conditions and to the arguments of missionaries and scientific reformers, but on the whole they used it with singular courage. Although many of them expected, and some would have welcomed, the secession of the colonies, their policy had a different outcome. It helped to fashion a family of nations united by the bonds that Burke had glimpsed — "the close affection that grows from common names, from kindred blood, from similar privileges and equal protection. These are ties which, though light as air, are as strong as links of iron."

VII   Threats to Liberalism

THE LIBERAL'S outlook on the empire was enlightened and tolerant, and above all progressive; the concept of progress was at the core of Victorian thinking. Change was assumed to be the means toward a better day, and change in the empire was only one example. The world seemed orderly, for all the speed of its advance. Natural laws were more complex than they had been for the eighteenth century, and natural rights had broadened into economic principles. But nature was still inherently law-abiding, man inherently rational, and his reason was progressively subjugating nature. In this dazzling conquest the British saw themselves as the vanguard, and they assumed with some justice, if little logic, that their enlightenment and strength would keep them permanently in the van.

But by the 1850's shadows were already falling across the line of march, and on the horizon were flickerings that were not the serene sunshine of reason. Progress, in Europe as a whole, was turning out to be advance toward a world quite unlike that in which liberal orthodoxy had begun, and even less like utopia. Orthodox principles were still strong, but their ascendancy was coming into question. New forces at work on the Continent were beginning to evoke an unwonted and even illiberal militance in British policy. At the same time the liberal creed was being challenged at home by the rise of a dynamic conservatism. These two trends, one in foreign affairs and one in political theory, foreshadowed drastic changes to come.

The Whig triumph in 1846 did not mean the beginning of an isolationist era. Even liberal politicians were aware that eternal vigilance was the price of the *Pax Britannica*. Among them was Viscount Palmerston, the outstanding spokesman of Britain's rights and prestige. He had begun as a Canningite Tory and never became a typical Liberal. His métier was foreign affairs, and in the 1830's and 1840's he seemed to be Britain's permanent foreign secretary. His haughty tone and forceful acts had made him notorious in the chancelleries of Europe. "As the Roman in the days of old held himself free from indignity when he could say *civis Romanus sum*," Palmerston declared in 1850, "so also a British subject, in whatever land he may be, shall feel confident that the watchful eye and the strong arm of England will protect him against injustice and wrong." Here was the imperial spirit rejoicing in its power. But it was power, to Palmerston's mind, used not merely for British subjects but for the weak and oppressed wherever they might be; the universality of his concern with injustice was as marked as the vehemence of his concern with Britain's position, and both were enormously popular. His arrogance and sense of drama appealed to a public grown bored with the logical, conciliatory tone of more orthodox liberals.

By 1850 the Europe with which he had to deal was no longer the familiar one of Metternich. In 1848 a wave of revolutions had momentarily drowned the old order in central Europe. The Hapsburg Empire had been torn into its national segments, and German and Italian liberals had seized their opportunity. Their attempts to unify their nations had failed, however, and by 1850 the forces of reaction had patched together the former frame of things; German and Italian patriots were forced thereafter to look to other means of unification — the means of Machiavelli, of duplicity and force. But if liberalism had spent itself, so had conservatism; Austria and Prussia were temporarily weakened by the after effects of revolution. The balance of power was altered, and France and Russia acquired freer play for their ambitions.

France was entering her last period of predominance in western Europe. The pedestrian regime of Louis-Philippe had given place to that of Louis Napoleon, the Emperor's nephew, who by 1852 was established as Napoleon III. This return of caesarism aroused suspicion in the powers, but they did not move. Great Britain, even if she had been in a position to protest alone, had little incentive to do so.

Her interests did not seriously conflict with those of the new French regime. She had fought the first Napoleon partly to defend her empire, partly to break his grip on Europe. The new Napoleon was intent on winning her friendship, and confined his overseas ambitions to areas where she had little stake. On the Continent he showed no sign of regaining his uncle's conquests, although his attempt to maintain French influence in central Europe involved him more and more deeply in the problems of German and Italian unification. These problems loomed larger in the Tuileries than in Downing Street. Britain's strategic interest in Italy was secure whatever happened, for not even a united Italian kingdom would dare, in the predictable future, to challenge the mistress of the Mediterranean. Britain's strategic interest in Germany had previously been premised on her tie with Hanover and her need of an ally against France. Now Hanover, which descended in the male electoral line, had been lost since the accession of Victoria, and France was no longer the great menace. At the beginning of the nineteenth century Britain had still needed German help against France; at the beginning of the twentieth she needed French help against Germany. In the interval between she could afford detachment from the affairs of western Europe.

The affairs of eastern Europe and Asia, however, were of growing concern to her. There her rivalry with Russia was becoming a major diplomatic factor. British trade was expanding, from the Levant to the China coast, and Russia was simultaneously expanding across the land mass of Eurasia; as the points of contact between the two empires increased, so did the friction. Russia occupied the interior position, and she could back her policy with the threat of enormous manpower. Only in India did Britain possess a comparable force; elsewhere she was dependent upon sea power, which in itself was no match for the Russian armies. She therefore had to have an ally, actual or potential, and her capacity to find one determined her effectiveness in every major crisis.

By 1852 Russian penetration toward the Persian Gulf and the

Himalayas was coming uncomfortably close to the borders of India, and Russian pressure on the Turk was even more disturbing. The three-sided balance of power in the eastern Mediterranean was becoming unbalanced. It had functioned for twenty years because neither France, Russia, nor Britain had been willing to push her designs to the point of war with the other two. Now Russia, freed from the likelihood of Austrian intervention on her flank, was turning her eyes again toward the straits. Simultaneously the French Emperor was scheming to upset the status quo for his own ends. This conflict of ambitions drew Britain into war for the first time since Waterloo.

Napoleon was eager for an entente with Britain, and at the same time he was seeking a cause to unify the discordant domestic elements — liberal, chauvinist, Catholic — on which his new empire depended. He saw in the tangled affairs of the Sultan the chance to achieve both ends. In 1850 he secured from the Porte the recognition of French influence over Roman Catholic monks in the Holy Land. Czar Nicholas, incensed, countered with the far more sweeping demand that Russia be recognized as protector of all the Sultan's Orthodox Christian subjects. This claim undermined Turkish independence, and London was no more disposed than Paris to countenance it. Even if the Turk were as sick a man as Nicholas said, Russia could scarcely be allowed to monopolize the inheritance and then arrange for the demise. The Czar's army invaded the Rumanian principalities, a sphere of particular Russian interest within the Ottoman Empire. The Anglo-French fleet was then ordered to the Dardanelles, and the crisis came to a boil.

The British cabinet was seriously split. On one side were the orthodox liberals, trusting to negotiation and opposing any provocative acts. On the other were the proponents of the strong line, chief among them Palmerston; he was convinced that Russia must be halted, by war if necessary, and that the best chance of peace lay in making Britain's position clear. This conflict of views vitiated policy. The chance that Britain would stand aside led the Czar to press his demands; the chance that she would intervene led the Sultan to resist. None of the principals desired war. But the Czar had been maneuvered into a position from which he could not retire without humiliation; the Sultan knew the impossibility of opposing Russia single-handed, and he now had the likelihood of strong allies; Napoleon saw the prospect, if worst came to worst, of winning prestige while the British bore the brunt of the fighting; Palmerston preferred war to retreat. In these circumstances war came.

In the autumn of 1853 the Turks declared war, and in the following spring France and Britain joined them. The logical target was the Russian Black Sea fleet, on which depended the enemy's drive toward the straits; the war therefore resolved itself into an attack on the Crimean naval base at Sevastopol. The great fortress was besieged for a year, one of the grimmest in British military annals. The organization of supply was appalling, the medical service worse; even the work of Florence Nightingale and her fellow nurses was only a small light in the gloom. For the first time war correspondents reported conditions to the British public, and the resultant outcry forced reform; Palmerston became Prime Minister and modernized that departmental dinosaur, the War Office. Simultaneously Czar Nicholas died, and soon afterward the fall of Sevastopol and its fleet paved the way for settlement. Napoleon III invited a European congress to meet in Paris, and in the spring of 1856 the treaty of peace was signed.

Its principal points were two. The sick man of Europe was resuscitated: Russia renounced any exclusive interest in the Rumanian principalities, which became autonomous; the integrity of the Ottoman state was guaranteed by the powers, and they bound themselves not to intervene in its internal affairs. The Black Sea was neutralized: Russia promised not to rebuild the fleet she had lost, and she and the Turks agreed to maintain no arsenals on the coast. These were the terms the allies had bought with thousands of lives and millions of pounds, and the settlement was precarious from the start.

The alliance by which it had been done was already dissolving. Napoleon had posed as the champion of liberalism against autocracy, of the Roman Church against the Greek; he had won his war and brought Europe to him in congress assembled. His restless ambition veered from the Near East to Italy, and soon he was preparing for a quarrel with Austria by conciliating Russia. The British were disillusioned: the man was like a drop of mercury, bright, quick, and unpredictable; by working with him they had learned to distrust him for the rest of his career. That distrust had profound effects. It helped to prevent joint action by France and Britain in America during the long crisis of the Civil War, and it was of incalculable benefit to Prussia in the unification of Germany. It reversed the Anglo-French rapprochement that had existed, despite occasional quarrels, ever since 1830, and of which the Crimean War was both the climax and conclusion.

The British could scarcely have relied on France, in any case, to guarantee the Peace of Paris. Such interests as she had in the Near East were traditionally focused in Egypt, where they were almost as unwelcome to the British as those of the Czar in Constantinople. A more logical British partner would have been Austria, whose territorial concern with the Balkans complemented Britain's naval concern with the straits. But Austria's strength was increasingly absorbed in the attempt to hold her own in Germany and Italy, and she was no more to be counted upon than France to keep the Russians in line. Great Britain alone was committed to maintaining at least the substance of the treaty terms. The integrity of the Sultan's dominions, once she had spilled her blood for it, became a cardinal tenet of her policy, and the Crimean War consequently opened a struggle with Russia that has since been twice suspended but is not yet resolved.

The struggle involved more than the Ottoman Empire. Russian pressure in the Middle East, which had been mounting for years, helped to produce a crisis in India. For a generation the East India Company had been alarmed by the spread of Russian influence through Persia and Afghanistan, and had responded by a rapid extension of its own authority westward and northwestward to forestall a Russian attack. One native state after another had been annexed or reduced to dependence, until the Company governed from the Bay of Bengal to the Khyber Pass. This extension and the attendant reforms upset the conservatism of native ways and interests. Simultaneously the means of dealing with discontent were gravely impaired: the sepoy army was overworked and spread thin across the new conquest just when the core of British troops was depleted by withdrawals to Europe, and tales of British blunders and defeats in the Crimea began to erode the prestige on which white rule was founded.

The result was the explosion of the Sepoy Mutiny, which during the summer and autumn of 1857 jeopardized the existence of the

Company's dominion. Only in a few provinces did the mutiny approximate a national movement; elsewhere it was the uprising of a privileged military caste against its masters. The courage of British officers and bureaucrats was equal to the emergency that their shortsightedness had helped to produce; many of the sepoys remained loyal, and the ruling princes were either passive spectators or active allies of the British. By the end of the year the worst danger was over, and the rising slowly petered out in guerrilla warfare.

British India had been shaken to its foundations. The immediate effect was the extinction of the Company: in 1858 the Crown assumed sole authority, and a new era began. Under the aloof paternalism of the viceroys public works were begun, financed by British investors and guaranteed on the security of the Indian revenues; India soon became one of the most lucrative markets in the world for British capital. But her rulers had had their sense of security shattered, and they tended to draw apart into an administrative Olympus. At the same time the sprawling subcontinent was pulled together by roads, telegraphs, and, above all, railroads. The spread of education created an Indian intelligentsia familiar with Western thought and speaking English as its lingua franca, and the growing civil service included a small percentage of natives. The new era was the seed-time of Indian nationalism.

In summary, then, certain aspects of British policy in the 1850's showed an illiberal toughening. Expansion in India led to mutiny; mutiny led to firmer, more paternalistic government. Russian pressure upon the Turk evoked counterpressure from London, and the resultant war left Britain with a commitment to support one of the most despicable governments in Europe. All this scarcely seemed to the liberal like the road to utopia. And it was not the only trend that troubled him. Some of his basic assumptions about domestic as well as foreign affairs were coming under attack. The Tories, who had seemed to be intellectually defunct, were showing a vigor unknown since the days of Burke. They were challenging the dominant, complacent creed of liberalism, and they were soon to find support among heretics within the Liberal Party. Orthodoxy was being pushed onto the defensive.

VIII   The New Toryism

SINCE the death of Pitt the Tory Party had been on the defensive. By denying the need for Catholic emancipation and parliamentary reform it had lost the liberal followers of Canning; by identifying itself with the landed interest against the new forces of industrialism it had lost the Peelites. The upshot after 1846 was a body of men whose spirit was demoralized and whose thought was fossilized. Fashioning a modern party out of such ingredients was a herculean task.

The brunt of the work fell on one leader, Benjamin Disraeli, who devoted forty years to it. He worked out his own conception of Toryism while he was rising to influence within the party, between his first election to Parliament in 1837 and the Peelite schism of 1846; then he gradually educated the party leadership in his ideas; lastly, in 1867, he assumed the leadership himself, and in the next decade brought the revivified party into office with a substantial majority. By then the new Toryism was so firmly established that it still survives.

No outline of Disraeli's career can give an inkling of its difficulties. At the start they seemed insuperable. In 1837 he was a young Jewish novelist and political pamphleteer, with a taste for fantastic clothes, sitting in the House of Commons among men who judged an aspirant by his wealth, birth, and connections. Disraeli did not belong, and he was never gladly accepted by the members of his party. They distrusted him for substantially the same reason that their counterparts of the 1930's distrusted Churchill — "too brilliant to be sound." But they could not keep him down for long because he had something to say. After 1846 the rest of them did not; their rump party had no mission except to deplore. A conservative out of power is often capable of enlightenment; his hunger for office leads him to accept new ideas, and on this hunger Disraeli played. If the Tories continued to resist all change, he argued, the Whigs would acquire "a monopoly of power, under the specious title of a monopoly of reform." After some twenty-five years his point sank in.

The wellspring of his political ideas was his romanticism. He believed that the search for profits had produced a society in which comfort was mistaken for culture, and that this society was doomed.

The materialism of the early Victorian era, mirrored in the program of the liberals, was breeding discontent in the lower classes and frustration in the upper, because materialism starved an age that was, he insisted, one of "craving credulity." He set himself to feed ordinary men with extraordinary ideas. The ideas were never wholly clear; he loved to juggle with thought as with language. But after the countinghouse atmosphere of liberalism they had the freshness of a sea wind.

The romanticism of Disraeli's outlook developed especially in the field of imperial and foreign policy. Here he learned much from Palmerston, and transmitted it to his party. The Liberals, on the other hand, never fully outgrew their embarrassment at Palmerston's saber-rattling; many of them remained sufficiently orthodox to expect the eventual secession of the colonies, to oppose the extension of empire as unjust and extravagant, and to deplore a belligerent foreign policy. They were inherently isolationists, eager to be quit of outside distractions in order to concentrate on domestic progress, and their attitude was anathema to Disraeli. It derived primarily from the mores of business, for which he had no use. It envisaged the dissolution of empire; he dreamed of a paternalistic state ruling the far corners of the globe for the good of the natives and the glory of the Crown. It minimized the danger in foreign developments, whereas he insisted that imperial greatness depended upon keeping the fingers of government continuously and firmly on the pulse of world affairs.

He was too cautious to develop the economic implications of his views. Just as the liberal attitude was inherently connected with free trade, so his was with protection. If the centrifugal trend within the empire were ever to be reversed, the obvious means would be the re-creation of an overall tariff system for integrating colonial and British economy. But Disraeli was trying to educate his party to the need for progress, not for reaction, and he recognized that free trade had become the core of the nation's economic faith. He only hinted at the possibility of an imperial tariff system, and then let the matter drop. A generation later his hint developed, with the developing logic of imperialism, into a movement that split his party and threatened its existence.

In the 1860's imperialism and foreign policy were only one focus of national interest. The other was the rising demand for a democratic franchise. On this issue Disraeli also had strong views, and they conflicted with the established tenets of his party. If he had followed in the footsteps of Wellington and Peel and opposed extending the franchise, the Tories might well have been extinguished. Instead he persuaded them to take the initiative in reform. The underlying reason why he succeeded was that their sojourn in the political wilderness had starved their allegiance to the system that had exiled them, until they were in the same position as the Whigs of the 1820's — conservatives opposed to conserving the status quo. This was Disraeli's opportunity to convert them, but his purpose was more than mere opportunism. He had long intended to lay the foundation of the new Tory Party upon a democratic electorate.

He shared Burke's belief that the masses lacked the wisdom and ability to govern themselves. Yet from the beginning of his career he believed that they must eventually receive the vote and that the Tories could and should give it to them. The explanation of this apparent paradox is that he never considered the franchise as the determinant of political power, and never shared the conviction, widespread among both radicals and conservatives of his day, that universal suffrage would be equivalent to dictatorship by the proletariat. He was willing to enfranchise the masses for the very reason that they would never, he felt, exercise a power commensurate with their numbers.

He insisted that the Reform Bill had destroyed the old principle of British government, that of representation without election. Before 1832, he argued, the people had been represented through the constitutional trinity of Church, lords, and commons — the peasantry by the great landowning peers, the legal fraternity by the judiciary lords, the mercantile interest by members of the House of Commons, and so on. After 1832 the Church was shorn of its privileges, the peers were coerced into impotence, and the House of Commons became omnipotent. Because the House was elective but did not represent the nation, the old principle of representation without election had been replaced by the absurdity of election without representation. The people suffered by the change. The old aristocratic minority had monopolized political rights on condition of guarding what he called the civil rights of the nation — the rights of all to a modicum of social and economic security. The larger minority of the middle class, which received political rights from the Reform Bill without any condition, began legislating in its own interest and leaving administration largely to hired bureaucrats. Popular discontent was directed against this bureaucracy and its employers, not against the idea of a governing class *per se*. The remedy was to extend the franchise until the House of Commons represented the whole nation. The masses would then need a leadership they could not provide for themselves; they would look for it not to the middle class, their natural enemies, but to the gentry and aristocracy, their natural friends. "The wider the popular suffrage, the more powerful would be the natural aristocracy." The dominance of the middle class would be ended by an alliance of the top and the bottom.

This would not mean rule by the top, which Disraeli looked on as the outmoded aristocratic principle. Rule by the bottom he feared, and rule by the middle he detested. Then what was left? His answer was that no one class should rule; each should have a voice, but neither its training nor its wealth nor its numbers justified predominance. The following sentences, from the Tory platform of reform in 1867, are crucial in the development of the party: "It is contrary to the constitution of this realm to give to any one class or interest a predominating power over the rest of the community." "What we desire to do is . . . to prevent a preponderance of any class, and to give a representation to the nation."

Against this background of balanced representation the Tory function, as Disraeli conceived it, was to provide a leadership that was both paternalistic and responsible at the polls. Its objective was the broadening of civil rights. These he considered more important to the people than their political rights — an idea more familiar today than to his contemporaries, and the key to his social program. Because he did not believe that the masses were able to improve themselves unaided, or that poverty resulted from individual incompetence, he felt that a measure of security must be provided by the state. Under its aegis concessions might be made to certain groups of the people, such as trade unions, in order to build a counterweight to the industrial bourgeoisie and maintain the balance of classes. But the essential paternalism of the program would function through a governing class. "The proper leaders of the people are the gentlemen of England. If they are not the leaders of the people, I do not see why there should be gentlemen."

If gentlemanly leadership was to be responsible, every citizen had to participate, if only as a critic, in the common endeavor of government. Disraeli made such participation a matter of principle, which underneath its romantic trappings was the principle of Burke that political rights have duties for their counterpart. The awareness of duty, for Disraeli as for Burke, is closely associated with the Church. The government protects the Church and controls its property; it in turn makes governors and governed conscious of their duty to the state. Unless both have this consciousness, administration is a mere system of police; "if government is not divine it is nothing." Here is the perennial Tory argument for the establishment.

Another element in Disraeli's concept of the state was the Crown. For him it was far more than a stage prop. From the moment of accession, he insisted, the monarch is in touch with the ablest statesmen, informed on the thorniest issues, and in a position to acquire political wisdom for the service of future ministries. The sovereign's advisory role, in consequence, is constitutionally quite as important as the symbolic role.

Disraeli's ideas were in essence what came to be known after his death as Tory democracy. This concept adapted conservatism to the late-Victorian world, and the same concept, further adapted, is still at the core of conservative thought. It is worth attention not merely because it has affected the development of a great party for the past ninety years. It is a brand of democracy as alien to the modern socialist's brand as to the Victorian liberal's, and it constitutes an interesting critique of both.

On the economic side Tory democracy is the antithesis of laissez-faire liberalism, the hands-off-business school of thought. The teachings of this school have the effect of subordinating the power of government to the power of wealth, whether in the hands of "economic royalists" or of Whig oligarchs. The Tory democrat not only desires to increase the security of the laboring classes but also is willing to increase their power, on condition that they are competently led, that power is not used selfishly, and that it is not great enough to upset the balance of classes. If these conditions are fulfilled, he is far less hostile to an energetic labor movement than the old-guard liberal.

On the social side, Tory democracy is a denial of what Disraeli called "that pernicious doctrine of modern times, the natural equality of man." The Tory believes in an elite composed of those with the ability to lead. This is the governing class, which in conservative practice is commonly identified with the upper class; in conservative theory, however, its members should be recruited from all levels, and the careers that by tradition have been largely reserved for privilege — the church, civil service, and armed forces — should be opened to talent from every class. But whether the membership of the elite is determined by talent or by the old school tie, whether it is responsible to a narrow or broad electorate, its function is to govern.

On the political side, Tory democracy is opposed to the simple notion that all questions can be settled by counting noses. This notion ignores the rights of the minority and leads to government by and for the lower classes because they are the most numerous; the result may be Marxism but is not democracy. Restraint on the power of the majority is widely accepted by both liberal and Tory as part of the democratic process. The liberal would achieve restraint primarily by emphasizing the rights of individuals and minorities as against the state. The Tory would achieve it partly by leadership, partly through the working of indirect representation. He denies, as Disraeli did, that men can be represented only through periodic elections; therefore he stresses the role of the House of Lords, the Church, the monarchy, all of them unelected representatives of some group or aspect of the nation. For the same reason he distrusts the House of Commons. He is less likely than the liberal to associate freedom with the legislature and tyranny with the executive, and is far more ready to countenance strong and independent executive action.

Modern Toryism is thus founded on certain principles. One is the paternalism of an elite, as opposed to the materialism of plutocrats and bureaucrats. Another is the concept of the state consecrated by the Church and buttressed by the duties owed to it by all citizens. A third is emphasis on the balance of power between groups and classes, on indirect representation, and on the executive. These principles were no discovery of Disraeli. He drew them from the long tradition of his party and restated them in terms of his period. The period was one of rapid change, in Europe from the age of Metternich to that of Bismarck, overseas from the quiet of the *Pax Britannica* to the cutthroat scramble of the powers for colonial empires, at home from oligarchy to democracy. In this collapse of the early-Victorian world the Tories might well have disappeared, as the first Tory party disappeared with the collapse of the Stuart world, for the conservative is always likely to sacrifice the claims of the future to those of the past. Disraeli's achievement was to formulate a program, incomplete and in many respects transient, that was nevertheless both radical and founded on the tradition of the party. He thus brought Toryism to life again and gave it the vitality to survive in a new world.

IX   The Beginning of Democracy

BY the early 1860's signs of that world were appearing on every hand. On the Continent the cult of force was gaining ground, and Britain's influence was waning. Her diplomacy was effective in assisting the unification of Italy, but thereafter she met a number of unwonted snubs. Although Palmerston was again Prime Minister, his power to bully seemed to have deserted him. When a Polish insurrection led him to lecture the Czar on the blessings of liberty, he was politely told to mind his own business — and did so. The government had no more than swallowed this slice of humble pie before it cut itself another. Austria and Prussia attacked the Danes and beat them, while Britain looked on in vocal but helpless indignation. When Bismarck was asked what he would do if the British landed an expeditionary force, he answered that he would send the police to arrest it. To this the *Pax Britannica* had sunk.

The external event that had the deepest effect upon British opinion during this period was undoubtedly the American Civil War. A number of factors created sympathy for the South among the ruling class — the aristocrat's picture of the Southern gentleman, the liberal's emphasis on minority rights, the imperialist's fear of a strong United States, the industrialist's dependence on Southern cotton. But the common people of Britain were largely on the other side; to them the struggle, particularly after the Emancipation Proclamation, was between popular rights and slaveholders' entrenched privilege. The focus of Northern support was Lancashire; the workers were reduced to unemployment and misery by the Union blockade and the resultant cotton famine, but they steadfastly supported the Union cause. Their endurance and firmness impressed the country and contributed to the rise of a democratic movement.

The triumph of the North in 1865 was followed within six months by the death of the Prime Minister. The great prop of oligarchy was gone. Throughout his half-century on the political stage Palmerston had remained the champion of freedom abroad, but he had grown steadily more averse to change at home; his domestic policy was that of an earlier liberalism, which his longevity and prestige maintained beyond its normal term. His death meant the beginning of a new era. The question was not whether the system of 1832 would be altered, but when, how, and by whom.

The prime ministership came briefly to another Liberal veteran, Lord Russell, who was willing to concede a pallid measure of reform. But the real leadership of the party was in stronger hands. William Ewart Gladstone had begun his parliamentary career as a Tory in 1832, had seceded with the Peelites after 1846, and for the past seven years had been Palmerston's Chancellor of the Exchequer. He was already approaching sixty; but his major political career was only beginning, and it was to last for thirty years. His long background had bred into him certain orthodox liberal tenets, particularly in regard to economics and foreign affairs, but in his domestic creed he, like Disraeli, was far more radical than most of his contemporaries. As Disraeli transformed the negative Toryism of Castlereagh and Wellington into a positive program, so his great opponent transformed the heritage of the Liberal Party into a body of principles so dynamic that it continued to evolve during the decades of his leadership, and after his retirement transformed the party again.

Gladstonianism was thus a halfway point between the liberalism of 1832 and that of 1906. But it was itself a moving point. Gladstone had a phenomenal vitality of mind, and his ideas changed at an age when most men are clinging more and more tenaciously to the status quo. For that very reason his liberalism cannot be precisely defined. Disraeli had essentially the same creed when he retired in 1880 as he had had in the 1840's. Gladstone developed his under the spur of experience — the demand now for a broader franchise, now for social reform, now for a solution of the Irish problem. Most of these developments are part of a later era; here only the first is relevant. When Gladstone advocated drastic electoral change in the crisis of 1866–7, he set his party on a new and unmapped path.

Russell's administration introduced a mild reform bill. When it was mildly amended, the Prime Minister insisted on resigning and retiring from public life. His disappearance left Gladstone to command a divided party. On the one hand was the old guard, opposed to any breach in the oligarchic principle. On the other was a group of radicals led by John Bright, the orator of the Anti-Corn-Law League who had grown into the champion of the democratic movement. Between him and the right-wing Liberals no compromise was possible; Gladstone had to throw his support to one or the other, and he chose the radicals. The choice was fateful. It aligned the moderate bulk of the party with the progressives in a vague commitment to the democratic principle, and future events soon made the commitment more sweeping than the moderates had intended. The Liberal Party, like the Tory, was slipping the anchor of tradition.

Once Russell resigned, the dissension among his followers precluded another Liberal ministry. The Tories came into office, though scarcely into power; their titular head and Prime Minister was Lord Derby, and Disraeli was their leader in the House of Commons. The cabinet was at once embroiled in the issue of reform. A number of its members were still as much averse to the idea as the old-guard Liberals, but Disraeli saw the chance to lure his party into boldness.

After much hasty argument, and two resignations, the cabinet introduced a cautious and slightly absurd reform bill. Amendments by the opposition were welcomed, on the ostensible ground that no measure could be passed unless it were bipartisan. Gladstone, Bright, and their followers soon amended the original proposals out of all recognition; the bill became far more drastic than anything previously submitted by either party, and conservatives on both sides of the House joined in opposition. Disraeli accepted the amendments with serenity, while his followers grew increasingly restive. But they followed, and the Gladstonian Liberals were committed to supporting a measure they had helped to shape. In August 1867 the second Reform Bill became law. Lord Derby called it "a leap in the dark," and Carlyle moaned that it was "shooting Niagara." It more than doubled the electorate, and in urban districts gave the vote to every male householder. If this was not yet universal manhood suffrage, it was a tremendous advance toward the goal.

The advance was not made by either party, but by a conjunction

of the progressive elements in both. Disraeli's tactical skill had beguiled the Tory rank and file, in the excitement of debate, into en-
dorsing his principles. On the other side of the house Gladstone now
towered above all other Liberals; he had shaken himself free from
the shadow of Palmerston, and broken with the prophets of doom
who saw in reform "a perpetual whirl of change, alteration, innovation, and revolution." [4] When the clamor of argument died away, a
new Toryism and a new Liberalism were taking form, and two
strong men faced each other.

The reform movement that precipitated this remoulding of parties was itself a symptom of deeper change. The Industrial Revolution had created a powerful middle class, which had forced its way
into control of the oligarchy. But after 1846 its control was undermined by the revolution that had created it. As industrialization
spread, the workers were steadily increasing in numbers, importance, and political awareness; by the 1860's they were a real if inchoate force, and the very fact that they were unorganized made
their enfranchisement seem reasonable. The days of oligarchy were
not yet over. It was years before the gentlemen of England, whether
Liberal or Tory, lost their control of the House of Commons, and
years more before they began to lose their hold on the Church, the
armed forces, the civil service. But the oligarchic base for an oligarchic government crumbled in 1867, when the ruling class became
responsible for its rule to a majority of the male citizens. That responsibility, in the new age that was opening, came to pervade every aspect of politics.

---

[4] Robert Lowe, quoted by Sir John A. R. Marriott: *England since Waterloo*
(third edition, New York and London, 1919), p. 354.

Chapter Six

THE VICTORIAN TWILIGHT

1867–1906

I Major Themes

THE LAST three decades of the nineteenth century were a period when change became more and more bewildering. What the Victorians had accepted as the stately march of progress soon lost its stateliness and quickened from a walk to a trot to a runaway gallop; the route grew less familiar, the destination more obscure, until the old self-confident optimism was shaken loose and lost by the wayside. The Victorians came to realize that they were alone in a hostile world. Their mood changed for a time to defiance, but the sense of insecurity persisted. At the beginning of the twentieth century they began to look for friends, and their search led them toward a world war.

The development of external policy, foreign and imperial, was only one among the major themes of the period. In the earlier decades it vied with two others: the domestic force of democracy unleashed by the second Reform Bill, and the inexorable problem of Ireland. In the 1870's the external and domestic themes alternated as the focus of politics. In the 1880's the Irish problem rose to a climax that dominated everything else. But the question of Britain's imperial security was inseparable from it, as always, and the chance of satisfying the Irish was sacrificed to security; for the rest of the century the Irish and domestic themes were subordinated to a crescendo of imperialism. Then the force of democratic reform reappeared, imperialism changed character, and by 1906 a new age was beginning.

The sequence and interplay of these three themes give significance to what would otherwise be a meaningless succession of ministries. After 1867 the Liberals and Conservatives, like the Whigs
and Tories after 1832, alternated in office, until in 1886 a large element seceded from the Liberal Party as the Peelites had seceded
from the Tories forty years before. The Conservatives returned to
power and soon coalesced with the dissident Liberals, and this coalition reigned supreme until Victoria's death. Then it disintegrated in
the face of a rising Liberal opposition, which triumphed overwhelmingly in 1906. The period thus falls into two main phases. Before the
schism of 1886 the two parties alternated; after 1886 the Conservatives were predominant for twenty years and then collapsed. Why?
The explanation of this odd surface pattern lies in the attitude of
Liberals and Conservatives toward the issues that successively held
the public attention. Each party had its peculiar outlook and emphases, and neither was equipped to handle domestic, Irish, and external policy to the lasting satisfaction of the voters.

Until the last years of the century the Liberal Party was dominated by the personality and ideas of Gladstone. In the field of domestic reform Gladstonianism was a far cry from the ideas of Cobden; the old faith in laissez faire was giving place to the faith that
progress could be legislated. In the field of foreign and imperial policy, on the other hand, the Liberals were traditionalists, so deeply
absorbed with internal affairs that they were slow to believe in outside dangers. They had been bred in the rationalistic optimism that
Britain's security had engendered in the mid-Victorian world, and
they clung to it despite the new factors that were undermining the
Pax Britannica. They believed that diplomacy could and should be
conducted by logic and mutual compromise rather than the threat of
force, and they considered the extension of empire as an illiberal
and immoral distraction from the battle against entrenched privilege at home.

The Conservative attitude was wholly different. Privilege played
an integral part in Disraeli's scheme of things, and his successors accentuated his caution in tampering with it. Conservative domestic
policy was more restful than exciting, and after periods of drastic
Liberal housecleanings the voters inclined toward restfulness at
home. In foreign affairs, for contrast, the Conservatives offered ample excitement. Their tradition went back to the eighteenth century,

when Britain's position had been relatively insecure, and they did not share the Liberal's optimism about the *Pax Britannica*; they were consequently predisposed toward imperialism and its corollary, a strong foreign policy. During Disraeli's premiership his diplomacy, whatever else may be said of it, did not lack vigor or imagination, and through him the Palmerstonian technique became grafted onto the party. This Conservative emphasis on the strong line, and the Liberal aversion to it, go far to explain the transition from a period of party balance to one of Conservative dominance. For by 1886 the pressure of domestic reform was less than that of outside forces, and the voters preferred the power politics of the Conservatives to the detached rationalism of the Liberals.

Between 1867 and 1886 three major ministries, two of Gladstone's and one of Disraeli's, covered the transition from mid-Victorian calm to late-Victorian storm. The character of the period cannot be sensed from a chronological survey, for the focus shifted bewilderingly from Westminster to the Bosporus, to Dublin, to the Nile; a better approach is to survey the main themes struggling for dominance. Although they were interwoven and essentially related, in retrospect they appear as separate topics, and topics that are of unequal importance. Domestic reform was the logical outgrowth of what had already been done, and much of it was later redone in the terms of a new age. The Irish problem, by destroying Gladstone's party, paved the way for the rise of a new Liberalism in the twentieth century. External affairs were perhaps the most significant of all, for Britain's growing aggressiveness was not only the precursor of her coming imperialist debauch but the symptom of a fundamental change that has affected her policy and history from that day to this.

II Domestic Reform

THE YEARS after the second Reform Bill, like those after the first, saw intensive remodeling. The aim was no longer to rationalize an oligarchic society but to make ready for a democratic. Although leadership remained with the oligarchs, their time was running out. They felt the need of preparing the masses to exercise power, and under pressure of a widening public opinion they reassessed many accepted institutions and traditions. For this purpose Gladstone was ideally equipped. He was unafraid of change, even in his own thinking, and he could view the needs of the moment with an objectivity untouched by Tory nostalgia for the past.

When he first became Prime Minister in 1868, one of the major needs for reform was in education. Britain conformed in this respect to a virtually universal pattern: an oligarchy fashions a school system primarily to educate oligarchs, and a major extension of the franchise requires a commensurate change in the schools if the new voters are not to be illiterate prey for bosses and demagogues. This lesson in democracy, taught eighty years before in the French Revolution, the British now had occasion to learn. "It will be absolutely necessary," one of Gladstone's colleagues had pointed out in 1867, "that you should prevail on our future masters to learn their letters." [1]

The immediate problem was the elementary schools. Less than half the children of England received any formal teaching, and much of it was grossly inadequate; there was no national system even of governmental supervision. The evil was glaring, but specific remedy was difficult. Granted that the state should supervise and, where necessary, subsidize elementary education, what were the limits of its interference? Much of the best teaching was being done by the Anglican clergy, and the Church was up in arms at the suggestion that religious instruction should be undenominational or omitted entirely. Many Liberals were equally incensed at the suggestion that attendance should be compulsory; parents of a working-class family, they argued, had the right to decide whether their child should be learning or earning because the decision affected the family's income. Laissez faire was a tenacious doctrine.

The Education Act of 1870 was a compromise, but it opened the way to future progress. It divided the country into school districts, gave the government supervision of existing schools, and empowered it to create new ones as needed under elective local boards; the questions of religious instruction and attendance were left largely to these boards. Within a decade all districts were provided with boards, and school attendance was made compulsory; soon afterward the state assumed the entire financial burden. Gladstone's original measure led rapidly to an effective national system, and Britain's new masters began to be literate.

---

[1] Robert Lowe in Hansard: *Parliamentary Debates*, CLXXXVIII, 1549. The quotation is edited and improved by Marriott: *England since Waterloo*, p. 397.

The reforming appetite of the Cabinet grew with eating. In 1873 the labyrinth of the central law courts was reconstructed to eliminate the overlapping jurisdictions, the procedural oddities, the competing staffs of judges and officials, by which the legal profession had bewildered and impoverished its clients. Gladstone's reform, as completed by Disraeli, produced a single court with many articulated parts and a comprehensible procedure, and above it a committee of law lords acting on appeal for the House of Lords, the nation's highest tribunal. What had been one of the most archaic judicial systems in the western world became, within a few years, one of the most efficient.

Another simultaneous reform was the recognition of the rights of British labor. Since 1825 the trade unions had had a dubious legal status: they were not criminal, but they were outside the purview of the law; their funds were unprotected against misuse by their own officers, and they could scarcely carry out a legal and effective strike. Their numbers and activity increased, nevertheless, and by the 1860's they were wealthy national organizations. Their leaders realized that they needed political influence to change the law, and they agitated for the second Reform Bill; its passage projected the question of the unions' status into the forefront of politics. By the 1870's they were strong enough to have the long-accepted doctrine of free contract modified in their favor.

By two acts, one of Gladstone's and one of Disraeli's, the unions acquired a privileged position. Thenceforth they might organize a strike by all means short of intimidation and violence; freedom of contract was converted, for them alone, into freedom to concert the collective violation of the workers' contracts with their employer. Unions were also financially privileged: their funds were protected against their own officers and presumably (although on this point the statutes were silent) against suits for damages done by their members. These were substantial gains. The Liberals had done much, the Conservatives more, to adjust the law to the new self-consciousness and power of organized labor, and the demand for further adjustment did not grow pressing until a quarter-century later.

The cataract of reforms in Gladstone's first administration became a slower stream after Disraeli succeeded him in 1874. The Conservatives continued and in many respects sharpened the changes begun by their predecessors in the fields of education, the judiciary, and labor relations, and accelerated state intervention in other fields; Disraeli showed that the new Toryism, on its domestic side, was not a barren program. But his major achievement was far too subtle for the statute book. He was able to implement his concept of monarchy, and in six years he did more than any man in Victoria's reign to raise the prestige of the Crown.

After the death of her adored husband, Prince Albert, the Queen had retired more and more from the public eye. She had felt that her strength was insufficient for both business and ceremonial, and had sacrificed the second to the first. By the early 1870's the people were losing patience; the barometer of her popularity was dangerously low, and talk of republicanism was in the air. Gladstone was alarmed, and remonstrated with the Queen to little effect. She was as obstinate as her grandfather; remonstrance could not move her.

Disraeli used finesse. He remarked that he treated her as a woman, where Gladstone never learned that she was more than a department of government. But his witticism is misleading: he exalted her as a department while he flattered her as a woman. He had preached the importance of the sovereign's advisory role. He now consulted the Queen assiduously and deferred when possible to her prejudices; she rewarded him with a confidence and affection she had not given to any prime minister in a generation. Delicately but firmly he led her back to the center of the stage, to the spotlight and the cheering, and in 1876 he had her proclaimed Empress of India. She found her return agreeable, and it was unquestionably popular. The transition from oligarchy to democracy at home and from quiet to perennial crisis abroad was bewildering to the nation, which craved a symbol of continuity. Disraeli sensed the craving, and Victoria satisfied it. The more the lonely old woman threw herself into her role, the stronger her throne became. Her character and longevity, and the conditions of the times, were the important factors in this process, but it was helped at a critical moment by Disraeli's courtliness.

In 1880 Gladstone returned to office, to the Queen's regret, and Disraeli died before his wit could play upon the troubles of the Liberals. For they were soon engulfed in troubles from South Africa to Ireland, and as a consequence their domestic policy was far less vigorous than it had been a decade before. Their only legislation of outstanding importance was a further extension of the franchise, accomplished by two acts in 1884–5. The first gave the vote to virtually every male householder, rural as well as urban, and the second divided the nation for the first time into equal electoral districts. These measures, known collectively as the third Reform Bill, aroused no such controversy as that of 1867, let alone of 1832, for they were an inevitable development. The second Reform Bill had recognized the principle of household suffrage in urban areas, which at the time had contained the most mature elements of the laboring population. By 1884 new conditions, particularly the increase of adequate schooling, had broken down the distinction between industrial and agricultural workers to the point where the principle of 1867 was applicable to the nation at large. Application, by a change in franchise and reapportionment, established at last a truly democratic electorate.

The bill was the last major legislation that Gladstone put on the statute book. He continued for another decade to dominate the Liberal Party, and became again Prime Minister, but the great period of his career was ending. The reason was not in him, although he was now in his seventies; his incredible energy and mental powers seemed impervious to age. Part of the reason was in Europe, where a growing chill in the diplomatic climate numbed the statecraft of the Grand Old Man and lost him the confidence of worried voters. But the primary reason was in Ireland. In his early years as Prime Minister the Irish problem, more than any other, had forced him to modify and modernize his liberalism. As the problem developed, so did his absorption with it and his ideas about it, until he committed himself to a solution so drastic that for the better part of a generation it destroyed the hopes of his party and of Ireland.

III The Irish Question

THE CALM of exhaustion that had fallen over the Irish in the 1850's began to be dissipated on the eve of the second Reform Bill. The effect of the famine years was wearing off, and the emigrants who had fled to the United States were agitating Ireland's cause. Many of these men were veterans of the American Civil War, which had given them a training in violence; the reckless among them welcomed a chance to fight for Irish freedom from the base of the

United States. They were the material of the Fenian Brotherhood, a secret organization with members in Britain, Ireland, and the United States, but largely directed and almost wholly financed from America. Its purpose was to force Great Britain to grant Irish independence, and its method was any form of outrage that might be effective.

The United States was a promising center for Fenian activity. During the Civil War Northern opinion had been exasperated by the widespread sympathy for the Confederate cause among the British ruling class, and infuriated by specific actions of the British government. When the Union triumph left the United States, for the moment, one of the strongest military powers in the world, American imperialist ambitions and anti-British rancor were an explosive combination. The best hope of the Fenians was to precipitate an Anglo-American war, and in 1866 they tried to touch it off by attacking Canada. The United States government failed to prevent the attack, but did nothing to support it; American public opinion did not catch fire, and the "invasion" petered out ignominiously.

The Fenians then transferred their attention to England. They opened a new phase of propaganda by a series of outrages in England that brought the Irish question again to the fore. Gladstone, in particular, concluded that only a broad and enlightened settlement could kill Fenianism at its roots; in 1868 he began to struggle with the problem, and he continued for the thirty years left him. Uprooting the Irish upas tree became the dominant interest of his life. But the roots were too deep for him. He only cut off branches, and from their stumps the poison went on flowing.

His first attack was ecclesiastical. In 1869 the Anglican Church in Ireland was disestablished and disendowed, and the island was at last freed from the incubus fastened upon it in the sixteenth century. But disestablishment was by now little more than a gesture. The basic question, as Gladstone realized, was the land. Famine and depopulation had broken the traditional web between landlords and tenants; the peasants were exposed, as in the days of Cromwell, to the ruthlessness of absentee landlords, and the tenant rights sanctioned by Irish custom were unknown to British law. Free trade in land was as much to the benefit of the capitalist as free trade in labor, but the cost in Ireland was hatred and perennial murder.

Gladstone grappled confidently with the task of humanizing the law. The Irish Land Act of 1870 was intended to discourage evictions, to compensate the tenant for improvements he had made, and to facilitate his purchasing the land — to curtail, in short, the owner's freedom to do as he pleased with his own. The act was a significant departure in principle from the old liberal insistence on the rights of property, but as a remedy for Ireland it was inadequate because it set no rent ceilings and gave no protection to tenants in arrears. The Irish lost what little faith they had had that the agrarian problem could be cured by legislation. Fenianism offered no solution, and they turned their attention more and more to another cure.

By the end of Gladstone's first ministry the Home Rule movement was under way. Its leaders, unlike the Fenians, were moderate in their objective and legal in their methods. They desired for Ireland substantially what Canada already had, a Parliament and responsible executive controlling only internal affairs; they were convinced that this end might be achieved without violence. Their chances seemed slight, with both Gladstone and Disraeli opposed to them, but events soon played into their hands. In 1878 an agricultural depression struck Ireland, and grew worse with time. Because the steamship and the newly developed American railroads now brought to the British markets an abundance of cheap grain, Irish arable land could no longer be cultivated at a profit and was increasingly converted to pasture. This meant, as in sixteenth-century England, wholesale evictions and unrest. A Land League was organized to resist evictions. Offending agents and landlords were ostracized, among them the Captain Boycott who gave his name to the practice. Beasts and men were murdered, and for such crimes an Irish jury would almost never convict. The government had either to solve the problem itself or accept the Home Rulers' solution.

At the start of his second ministry Gladstone advanced along the familiar lines of conciliation and coercion. On the one hand he attempted a more drastic remedy for tenants' grievances: the Land Act of 1881 made the tenant and landlord virtually co-owners, created land courts to fix a fair rent, and forbade evictions as long as that rent was paid; later legislation attempted to liquidate arrears. On the other hand the Irish executive was given broader powers to deal with crime and conspiracy, and the Land League was suppressed and its leaders imprisoned. Neither side of this policy succeeded. Agrarian conditions largely vitiated the operation of the land courts, and violence continued to spread.

The logic of Home Rule, although it was still unpalatable to the British public, appealed increasingly to men of good will as the Liberal policy proved unworkable. Unless the struggle between repression and revolt were to go on endlessly, why not turn over to the Irish the onus of settling their difficulties? Home Rule was a more moderate aim than the extremists' goal of independence, and for Britain it was certainly the lesser evil. Behind the Home Rulers in the House of Commons stood the revolutionaries in Ireland, ready to seize the lead if moderation failed.

The Home Rule movement, like the demand for Catholic emancipation a half-century before, was the political crystallization of a discontent generated primarily by economic forces. It was also dominated by one man, comparable in power with O'Connell. Charles Stewart Parnell was English on his father's side, a landlord and a Protestant; but from his American mother he had inherited a hatred of all things British. He had an inflexible will and a mind of ice; Home Rule was his passion, and he was contemptuous of whatever man or institution stood in his way. He opposed violence as a blunder more than as a crime; his scruples were no nicer than those of the Fenians, but he believed that British public opinion could be more affected by legitimate — if ruthless — parliamentary sabotage than by bombings and bullets. Before long the accidents of politics raised him to a key position in the House of Commons, from which he had a chance to paralyze the very functioning of the state.

In 1880 he assumed the leadership of the Home Rule group in the House, and soon reduced it to an obedience that a drill sergeant might have envied. He then embarked on his campaign. Its strategy was simple: to make the parliamentary system ridiculous and unworkable, so that the British would be glad to be rid of the Irish in order to have government again. His opportunity lay in the character of the House. For all its change of personnel, it still retained much of its eighteenth-century tone. The press of business had not yet greatly curtailed free debate; the atmosphere was leisured and gentlemanly, and the members got through their work by virtue more of tacit agreement than of the complicated rules. Parnell was no party to the agreement, and he knew the rules. The Irish used every courtesy accorded debaters, every chance of amendment and point of order, and all the techniques of filibuster to obstruct the essential task of legislating. They did not confine themselves to bills dealing with Ireland. Their purpose was to bring the machinery to a standstill, and for a time they almost succeeded.

The House was losing its old role in government. The enlargement of the franchise was making electoral campaigns and the daily press more important than Westminster as the forum for national debates, and the tightening of party organization inside and outside Parliament was beginning to shift the center of power from the floor of the House to party headquarters. Parnell's tactics accelerated the process by forcing the Liberals to limit debate and curtail irrelevant motions, and so to adopt the Disraelian principle of strengthening the executive's control of the legislature. The Conservatives later continued the process, until little was left of the robust independence that the House had so long maintained in the face of kings and cabinets.

Parnell's position was being strengthened by another factor. Gladstone's failure to solve the Irish problem cost him considerable support, and his foreign policy cost him more. The Conservatives gained what he lost, until the balance was so delicate that neither party could hold office without a measure of support from Parnell. In 1885 a general election, under the terms of the third Reform Bill, gave Gladstone a slim majority and increased the strength of the Home Rulers. They could now paralyze government by throwing their votes to the Conservatives.

The crisis was at hand. The Conservatives, now under the guidance of the Marquis of Salisbury, refused to collaborate with the Liberals in solving the problem. Salisbury could not form a stable ministry himself, even with Irish support, because the coalition would be almost exactly balanced by the Liberals. Gladstone, on the other hand, could not govern in the face of such a coalition; he had to have Irish support. He thereupon abandoned his hope of reaching a settlement independently of Parnell, and declared for Home Rule.

His decision may have sprung partly from opportunism, partly from conviction that the Queen's government must continue on any possible terms. But it was more than that. For years he had tried whatever alternative path promised a solution for Ireland; each had led him deeper into the morass. His ideas did not grow stiff with age but could always be remolded by new evidence, and to his rational mind the evidence that Parnell's answer was the right one eventually outweighed all the tactics of the Home Rulers, the criminality of the terrorists, and the passions aroused in the British public. The evidence was partly the existing situation, partly the trials and errors of British policy in the previous two decades. Gladstone became convinced, and his conviction, like Peel's before him, was stronger than considerations of self or party. In 1886, at the age of seventy-seven, he began the greatest battle of his career.

The proposal to repeal the Act of Union split the Liberal Party, as forty years earlier the proposal to repeal the corn laws had split the Tories. The adhesion of Parnell was more than counterbalanced by the secession of some of Gladstone's most influential colleagues, and after bitter debate the first Home Rule Bill was rejected in the Commons. The Prime Minister appealed to the country in the second general election within nine months. He was overwhelmingly defeated, and resigned. Although he carried on the fight for another eight years, he fought against hopeless odds. The backbone of his party was broken, and even his magic was powerless to mend it.

The break was not really caused by the issue of how Ireland should be governed, any more than the Tory break in 1846 had been caused by the issue of a grain tariff. Home Rule raised basic questions, which explain the acrimony of the struggle for the next forty years. One was a question of principle. Gladstone proposed a unitary solution for the problem of a divided Ireland, and the solution was anathema to Ulster. For two centuries, with momentary exceptions, the instinct of the northern Irish had led them to oppose any move in that direction. Their social and economic ties with Britain were closer than those of the rest of the island, but the crux of the matter was political: their liberties were better secured by a parliament at Westminster than they could be by one at Dublin, particularly after the Catholic gentry and peasantry of the south had been enfranchised. Gladstone, according to his opponents, advocated the illiberal coercion of a minority, and of one that had remained loyal and law-abiding while the southern Irish were proving, by terrorism and sabotage, their unfitness for self-government. This view prevailed in Britain.

It did not prevail merely because of its logic. Home Rule also brought into question the security of the home islands, and for this reason it conflicted with the rising force of British nationalism. The Act of Union was a known quantity; the dangers of continuing it were measurable while those of ending it were not. It had begun as a war measure at the time when Ireland might have become the base for an enemy invasion; a crisis like that of 1800 might recur, and the Irish were adept at utilizing crises. Previous concessions to them had only played into their hands. To repeat the experiment when they were seething with unrest, and the European skies were darkening, seemed to the British nationalist an invitation to disaster. Sooner or later, he felt, Home Rule would diminish Britain's power to guard her overseas lifelines, perhaps even to defend herself at home. He was not basically concerned with the rights and wrongs of the Irish question. For him it did not depend, as it did for Gladstone, on political morality; it was determined by the old argument, *salus populi suprema lex.*

Gladstone had been reared in an era when liberalism had been pacific because it could afford to be. The strategic determinants of Britain's security were largely outside his consciousness; he thought in terms of common sense and fairness, and instinctively shunned the amoralities of power. As a result he had begun to estrange the nationalists within his own party by what they considered his spineless foreign policy, and his conversion to Home Rule turned them into open rebels.

The most interesting Liberal malcontents were the radicals, led by Joseph Chamberlain. This stormy petrel had entered politics as a reforming mayor of Birmingham, and by 1880 he had risen to cabinet rank. His advanced social views and his intense and forceful nationalism made him restive in the Liberal camp. In the general election of 1885 he advanced a startling program, including disestablishment of the Church and differential taxation of the rich; Gladstone could not accept it, and the Irish question completed the breach between them. Chamberlain resigned to fight the Home Rule Bill and was instrumental in defeating it. Thereafter he and his followers wandered into the political no man's land.

Many right-wing Liberals also refused to follow the Prime Minister. They were steeped in the Whig tradition, with its memories of the Boyne; for all its stress on toleration Whiggism was identified with the Protestant cause, and a self-governing, Catholic Ireland was more than these conservatives could swallow. They seceded in company with the radicals, whose domestic program shocked them, and the strange assortment of rebels took the label of Liberal Unionists. They were Liberal only in origin, and they gradually abandoned the adjective. As Unionists their destination was clear. They could no more resist the pull of the Conservatives than the Peelites, as free-traders, had been able to resist that of the Liberals. By 1895 they completed their alliance with the Tories. Chamberlain held office in Salisbury's cabinet while his followers joined hands with radical Tories, the heirs of Disraeli, in the cause of democratic reform. They could not move the old guard; it remained in power, and after 1902 the sterility of its domestic program brought the coalition to disaster.

Gladstone's party followed a different road. He himself retained for a time his extraordinary hold on the voters, but his political vitality was narrowed to the one issue of Home Rule. When the electorate tired of this issue in the 1890's, the Liberals and their Irish allies went into the wilderness together. There Liberalism transformed itself and gained strength for a triumphant return in 1906. It returned as it had gone, committed to the Irish, and the commitment eventually brought civil war before it was redeemed.

The Irish crisis of 1886 thus precipitated a complete realignment in British politics. The balance of parties that had endured for twenty years was upset for another twenty. The Conservatives, with their emphasis on imperialism, were joined by the most nationalistic of the Liberals, and the allies guided the country through a phase of belligerent expansion. Gladstonianism was destroyed within a decade, but the Liberal Party survived to raise the Irish question again in the twentieth century. These were the consequences implicit in Gladstone's defeat.

IV   The New Europe

AFTER 1868 the fluctuating judgment of the electorate was increasingly affected by issues of foreign and imperial policy. These issues played a relatively minor part in Gladstone's first and greatest ministry. They dominated the scene during Disraeli's term and helped to defeat him in 1880. Thereafter they harassed Gladstone, drove him in one case far from his principles, and contributed almost as much as Home Rule to the disruption of his party. In the 1890's they became the central theme of British history.

As early as the 1860's Europe was in the throes of a vast readjustment of power. It was analogous to that produced by the rise of France two centuries before, and it had equally powerful repercussions on Britain's diplomacy and political ideas. At the same time her military and industrial position was being weakened and her empire exposed to the pressure of European expansion overseas. Some of these forces of change seemed remote and irrelevant, but in fact they were undermining the bases of the *Pax Britannica* and endangering the edifice of British power. The Victorians' golden age was drawing to a close, and this fact conditioned the statecraft of Gladstone and Disraeli.

After 1815 the problem of Britain's security had appeared to be solved. Her diplomats had been backed by such force that they had been able to defend her interests by threatening rather than fighting, and the public had assumed that her interests were permanently safe. The Crimean War had jolted the assumption, and soon came changes that began to invalidate it.

The most obvious change was political: the extinction of Metternich's world in the decade after 1861. First the Kingdom of Italy was created; then Prussia, under the guidance of Bismarck, defeated Austria and France in turn, and in 1871 fashioned the German states into an empire under her dominance. Simultaneously the unifying force of nationalism was at work in other continents. The American Civil War prepared the way for the phenomenal rise of the United States as a world power, and the Japanese revolution of 1867–8 did the same for Japan. The old order in Europe was gone, and thenceforth the new order was increasingly affected by the weight of outside states.

The indirect effects of German unification, and to a lesser extent of Italian, altered the framework of Britain's Continental diplomacy. Previously both Austria and France had been too much absorbed with their interests in central Europe, where Britain had no vital concern, to give consistent and undivided attention to areas where she had. By 1871 this absorption was gone. Austria, excluded from Italy and Germany, had reconstituted herself as the Dual Monarchy of Austria-Hungary, and the emergence of Hungary implied that the Hapsburg Empire was looking for its future toward the Balkans. As its interest there increased, so did the prospect of friction with Russia. During the Franco-Prussian War the Czar had denounced the Treaty of Paris and begun to remilitarize the Black Sea. He was obviously considering another move in the Near East, where Austria was now replacing France in the old triangular balance of power. Of the three participants, Britain alone had static interests; both Austria and Russia wished to expand. If Germany held aloof, Britain might be able to maintain an uneasy equilibrium by her old methods. But if Germany aligned herself with Austria or with Russia, those methods would no longer serve. Britain would then, sooner or later, have to revise her whole traditional policy in the eastern Mediterranean.

France, like Austria, was set on a new path by German unification. The dream of re-establishing her hegemony in Europe had led France to the most humiliating defeat of her history. She never forgot or forgave the German annexation of Alsace and part of Lorraine, and the very existence of the German Empire reduced her to a subordinate position in Europe. She accepted what she could not redress, but she was impelled to recover her lost pride by gains elsewhere. As Austria turned to the Balkans, she turned to Africa. From her foothold in Algeria she began to expand to the south and southeast toward the Sudan and the Belgian Congo. Here was the heart of her empire; its outworks stretched through Indo-China into the islands of the Pacific. Out of defeat she fashioned for herself, within a quarter-century, an imperial position second only to Britain's.

This renascence was of increasing concern to the British Foreign Office. Britain had never lost her distrust of France, and in the late nineteenth century, as in the eighteenth, distrust was heated by friction overseas. French designs in the Far East stimulated British expansion and precipitated crises, but the crux of rivalry was the Nile valley; there the two powers struggled for influence, first in Egypt and then in the Sudan, until they were on the verge of war. As France turned overseas, she reverted for a time to her former role of Britain's implacable enemy.

The German Empire itself, for all its indirect influence on Britain's position, did not begin to be focal in her diplomacy for the better part of a generation. Bismarck's aim was peace, so that the empire might cohere and develop its strength; for the two decades of his chancellorship he maintained a *Pax Germanica*, while Germany's population and industry expanded at a phenomenal rate, and she became the most powerful and influential state on the Continent. Not until after 1890, when Bismarck retired, did the world-wide expansion of her power make itself acutely felt in London.

If the new Germany had at first an indirect impact on British diplomacy, her impact on British political thinking was at once more subtle and more immediate. From the liberal viewpoint the German Empire was a disturbingly successful heresy. The way in which unification had taken place and the kind of nationalism it bred were as alien and alarming to the mid-Victorian mind as the result was impressive. Unification had come not from the people but from the amoral statecraft of Bismarck and the force of the Prussian army. German nationalism bore the Prussian imprint, and Prussianism was essentially illiberal. It stressed the individual's duties to the state rather than his rights and liberties. The state was organized power; its supreme instrument was the army, through which its able-bodied male citizens served it as their master.

When this cold Prussian creed became the vehicle for the desires of the German people, it acquired a new force and direction. For centuries the Germans had had no souls to call their own. Their weak governments had been playthings of the powers, their territory open to attack, and they had learned the uses of force by being its victims. As the last great people to achieve a nation-state they needed to establish their self-respect by compelling others to respect them. They had less faith in the liberal creed, with its emphasis on rights and its dream of an international reign of law, than in German destiny and German power to achieve it. The worship of the state regimented the cultural and political differences that sprang from their localism, and gave focus to the inchoate, mystical fervors of the patriot. For him the nation tended to become identical with the state, the state with the government, until he believed that the cardinal function of citizens was to obey — to serve the collective will as the one overriding imperative. *Deutschland über alles.*

This virulent form of nationalism was not a German invention. It derived in great part from the cult of force that tinged many aspects of the period, such as the Napoleonic revival in France, the battle hymns of the American Civil War, and John Bull's enthusiasm for Palmerston. The cult also appeared in forms unconnected with nationalism. The Marxian socialists were preaching the inevitability, for economic reasons, of a revolution in which the masses would sweep everything before them. The followers of Darwin were proclaiming the law of the jungle, of survival through brute strength guided by intelligence, and so were purporting to give the sanction of science to the idea that force, in an amoral world, was the major criterion of fitness. The spirit of Machiavelli was suddenly appearing in many guises, in the arguments of patriots, of Marxian determinists, of the popularizers of evolution. It was challenging the eighteenth-century values out of which liberalism had grown, and the liberal faith was being forced onto the defensive.

The new nationalism, because of its profound emotional appeal, was the most powerful force in this warfare of ideas. It drove the liberal back, through his outworks of qualifying logic and compromise, to the final defenses of his Christianity and his rationalism. As a Christian he could not admit that his supreme duty was to obey the state, or he would render his soul unto Caesar and violate the first commandment both of Moses and of Christ. As a rationalist he could not admit the divinity of the nation-state, with its priesthood of bureaucrats and generals and its sacrament of war, or he would violate his faith in reason. For the new religion was in essence irrational. It implied that the nation was an entity with transcendant virtue, which its human components served by obeying rather than by thinking for themselves. It taught that progress was not toward an international utopia but toward the apotheosis of national power, and that the only natural law was the jungle law; it admitted no optimism beyond the hope of collective survival, and no logic but force. This was a creed as alien to eighteenth-century philosophy as to the Sermon on the Mount.

British liberals were slow to take alarm. The nationalism of John Bull was for the most part in the bones, where it seemed proof against the new virus. To a generation bred in the Whig tradition the state was an object of distrust more than of worship, and the concept of organized power made little sense: Britain's economic power could not be organized in an era of free trade, and the exercise of her sea power was rarely conspicuous enough to impinge on the public consciousness. German ideas seemed to be as irrelevant as they were strange.

In fact, however, those ideas in domestic dress were soon shaking the Victorians' complacency. Many British intellectuals, from Car-

lyle to Bosanquet, were fascinated by German thought and disseminated it in one form or another. The way was opened for their
teaching by other forces working far below the level of philosophy,
forces that were altering the framework of Europe and contributing
to a rising sense of insecurity in Britain. The more insecure the Victorians felt, the more they turned to integrating and increasing their
own strength, and the more they were impressed by the German
techniques for organizing power and by the philosophy behind the
techniques. The result was that orthodox liberalism was rejected,
and the Liberal Party collapsed. Britain, once she caught the nationalist virus, began a breakneck race for empire.

Of the forces that opened her to contagion, three are particularly
significant. The first was military: the changing nature of armies and
of warfare were reducing Britain's capacity to intervene in Europe,
and with it her diplomatic weight. The second was economic: Britain was ceasing to be the one great workshop of the world, and was
being forced to relearn the hard ways of competition. The third was
political: most of the great powers were setting out to partition the
globe, and Britain could not remain idle without seeing her imperial
position go the way of her industrial. These three factors are worth
examination, for they helped to convert the tolerant, progressive nation of Gladstone's first ministry into the most successful exponent
of *Machtpolitik* in the world of the 1890's.

In military development Germany forced the pace. Prussia had
compensated for a small population by organizing the *levée en
masse* of the French Revolution into a permanent peace-time system
for conscripting the manpower of the state; the German Empire
adopted the system. France followed suit after her defeat, and soon
almost all European countries had some form of universal military
service. The Prussians had also shown that the mass army could deliver quick and crushing blows: the Austro-Prussian War had been
decided within three weeks, the Franco-Prussian within seven. This
was blitzkrieg, and the prospect of its repetition forced every Continental power to be continuously prepared to put into the field its
maximum strength in the minimum time. Europe was beginning one
of the longest periods of peace in its history, but it was a peace of
precariously balanced forces and nervous men.

Although Britain was not directly influenced by these developments, indirectly her position was weakened. Her small professional

force became a drop in the great bucket of European manpower, and the accelerated speed of war suggested that the drop might fall too late to have any effect. Far more important, the navy might not have time to make its pressure felt; no exercise of sea power could have saved Austria in 1866 or France in 1870. Britain, in short, could no longer improvise her intervention on the Continent. Either she would plan it far in advance, which presupposed an ally, or she would become a helpless spectator. The first alternative was contrary to her whole isolationist tradition. But the second meant abandoning her even more basic tradition of intervening to protect such key areas as the Low Countries or to oppose a power seeking the mastery of Europe. Sooner or later she would have to choose between her isolation and her security.

Meanwhile the spread of the new nationalism, in conjunction with industrialism, was changing the economic order. Britain no longer monopolized the Industrial Revolution; her capital, exported in search of a market, had helped to finance foreign manufactures, and their rivalry was being felt. Her gospel of free trade, on the other hand, had not been successfully exported. It was incompatible with the concept of the state as organized power; it was anathema to foreign industrialists, who wished to capture their own markets; its essential internationalism, above all, ran counter to the new spirit of national self-sufficiency. Here again the lead in Europe was taken by Germany, whose tariff walls rose with the rise of her manufactures. The other new giant of industry, the United States, was equally committed to protection, and the rest of the industrial world followed suit. The dominions raised tariffs even against the mother country, and Britain was left to practice her principles virtually alone.

The practice grew increasingly difficult. The British industrial plant was the oldest in the world; it represented an enormous investment, which its directors were understandably slow to sacrifice for experiments with new tools and techniques. The individualistic tradition was still strong, and manufacturers were almost as much averse to the dominance of a trust or cartel as to the interference of the state. Their hold on outside markets was weakening, however, with the rise of tariffs and competition, and even their domestic market was no longer secure. By the 1880's some of them began to agitate for what they called fair trade, a return to limited protection as a means of retaliating against foreign governments and defending the British market. Though this movement made little headway at the time, its appearance in business circles was a sign that Cobdenite liberalism was no longer above question. In the world at large mercantilism was reviving in the upsurge of national loyalties, and the British were not economically strong enough to ignore the revival as a mere error of the unenlightened.

Another form of mercantilism was also loose in the world. In the last quarter of the nineteenth century all the great states and many smaller ones developed a lust for territory. Africa was the principal scene of activity. But European empires expanded simultaneously in Asia, Japan fought China for a foothold on the Asiatic mainland, and the United States acquired desirable remnants of the Spanish dominions. By 1900 almost every part of the globe that was available and in any way attractive had been seized by some colonizing power.

This worldwide upheaval had many causes. The new industrial states awoke to the advantages of colonies as sources of raw materials and as protected markets for capital and manufactures. The scientific techniques that made large-scale industry possible — advances in public health, communication, engineering — also eliminated the obstacles of geography and climate that had hitherto kept the white man from occupying large areas of the earth. Nationalists were fired with the prospect of the fatherland's enhancing its prestige and invigorating its soul by conquests overseas. Strategists wished to seize territories for defense or as bases for attack. These and other factors produced an intensive race for empire such as the world had never seen.

The Victorians had grown up during the long lull in European expansion, when theirs had been the only global empire. They were accustomed to localized and transient conflicts of interest, with Russia here, with France there; suddenly they found themselves at odds with most of the powers of Europe most of the time. For a decade and more the public failed to realize what was going on, partly because its attention was focused on Ireland and partly because it cherished the stubborn liberal hope that the world was moving toward international order. By the 1880's that hope had waned so much that Gladstone, its last great exemplar, aroused grave misgivings by his foreign policy. In the 1890's the British finally decided to leave the Irish problem hanging fire and plunge into the colonial scramble in Africa. Thereafter they never regained the aloofness that had been their pride since 1815.

The high noon of British supremacy had passed. In the political sphere it had depended on the balance of power established at Vienna, a balance of five great states with limited objectives; now Austria and France were turning to new paths, and behind them, too close for comfort, was the dynamic and incalculable German Empire. In the sphere of ideas Britain had been the cynosure of progressives throughout the world; now her constitutional and economic principles were being widely discarded for the worship of the nation-state. In the military and industrial spheres she was still powerful, but it was the power of a muscular middle age. In the imperial sphere she was exposed to relentless competition for the first time since the days of Chatham. These forces of change gradually remolded her foreign policy. It grew harder, more aggressive, as her self-assurance declined. After 1886 she began a militant expansion, and her principal motive was fear.

V   The Renascence of Imperialism

THE HARDENING of mood set in long before. Its progress was reflected in the three successive ministries of the years 1868–86, and can be seen from a glance at the external problems and policies of each. The contrast, in this respect, between the opening of Gladstone's first term and the close of his second is a measure of the transition in public attitude.

Between 1868 and 1874 Gladstone had his one opportunity to handle foreign and imperial affairs by the principles on which he had been bred. No great crises or insoluble conflicts of interest appeared, and the government could afford to follow the liberal tradition. When the Franco-Prussian War jeopardized the independence of Belgium, Britain safeguarded her protégé by guarantees from both belligerents. When Russia menaced Afghanistan, she in turn was stopped by diplomacy; her repudiation of the Treaty of Paris had to be either fought or accepted, and it was accepted at an international conference. Negotiations, in short, replaced Palmerstonian bluster.

The most fruitful negotiation was with the United States. The years immediately after the Civil War were the lowest point in Anglo-American relations since 1814. Northern rancor against Britain, heated by the Fenians, fused with a new imperialist spirit in the desire for American annexation of Canada. A dispute was needed for pretext, and the most pressing dispute was over the *Alabama* claims. The Confederate commerce-raider *Alabama* had been built in a British yard and allowed to escape by the negligence of British officials; the United States claimed compensation for the damage she had done, and one form of compensation unofficially suggested was the withdrawal of Britain from the western hemisphere. London at first was haughty, Washington pugnacious, and tempers on both sides grew dangerously short.

When Gladstone fell heir to the wrangle, he applied his panacea of negotiation. In the face of enormous difficulties, legal and psychological, the discussions continued until in 1871 they produced an agreement for international arbitration of all the major questions at issue between the two powers. As a result Britain was assessed for the *Alabama* claims more than three million pounds. Gladstone was hotly denounced at home for betraying the national interests, but in fact he had served them well. The money spent was a bargain for Britain: on the eve of her intense rivalry with the states of Europe for empire in Asia and Africa she bought security for her empire in America. She also began the process of reconciliation with the United States that soon became a fixed principle of her diplomacy. After 1871 the two nations ceased to have crises, except for minor disputes over Venezuela at the turn of the century, and began to advance slowly but surely toward the tacit alliance of the present day.

Gladstone handled the empire as liberally as the *Alabama* claims, and with as little concern for national prestige. He refused to extend Britain's territorial commitments, despite pressure for annexations in Africa and the Pacific. He did all in his power, conversely, to encourage colonial self-government, and in one case forced responsibility on colonists who dreaded it. In the midst of a Maori war in New Zealand he began to withdraw the British garrison. The New Zealanders felt that they were being betrayed and forced toward independence; their alarm was echoed in the other nascent dominions, and at home Gladstone's action was arraigned as a first step in the breakup of the empire. Reaction quickly set in. For decades the assumption had been widespread in Britain that the colonies would soon go their ways; the New Zealand affair suggested that they had no such intention, and even Liberals recoiled from forcing them. Anti-imperialism began to wane, and the British welcomed all evidences of colonial loyalty. Their increasing anxiety about their own position in the world reawoke their interest in their dominions.

The spokesman of the new attitude was Disraeli. After the second Reform Bill he became the champion of imperialism against what he portrayed as the supineness of the Liberals, and his victory at the polls in 1874 changed the tone of British policy. He intervened in Egypt and South Africa, but in both areas his policy can best be considered in connection with Gladstone's later amendment of it. The focus of Disraeli's attention, and the main theme of his ministry, was the defense of the empire against Russia. Here his maneuvers brought Britain to the thin edge of war, and then achieved a diplomatic triumph as spectacular as it was ephemeral.

The revived Russian interest in the straits, shown by the repudiation of the Treaty of Paris, came just when the opening of the Suez Canal had made the Mediterranean into one of Britain's main arteries of empire. The Turkish barrier across the straits had become proportionately more valuable to her, and Disraeli was determined to defend it. In 1875 a Balkan uprising against the Turks provoked them to atrocities that nauseated Europe. Gladstone demanded that they be expelled from the Continent, and his view was gaining ground with the British public when Russia intervened alone. Her armies advanced to the gates of Constantinople, where in the spring of 1878 she dictated the Treaty of San Stefano. By it the Sultan recognized the complete or virtual independence of Serbia, Montenegro, Rumania, and Bulgaria, and a large measure of autonomy for Bosnia and Herzegovina. He signed away most of his empire in Europe; the Balkan question was apparently settled by Russian fiat.

This Disraeli refused to accept, ostensibly because the Treaty of Paris precluded a unilateral settlement and actually because he feared that the states recognized at San Stefano would give Russia access to the straits. The wisdom of his position was questionable. He ignored the possibility that the Balkan peoples — who had no desire to be freed from the Sultan in order to become puppets of the Czar — would constitute as effective buffers against Russia as the decrepit Ottoman Empire. The morality of his position was also questionable, because he sought to regain for the Turks the provinces they had ravaged. But he wore the blinders of Russophobia, and so did the bulk of the British public. The fleet moved to Constantinople; the reserves were called out; Indian troops were ordered to Malta. The pattern of 1854 was repeating itself.

At the last moment Russia gave way. Her reason was the danger not only from Britain but also from Austria-Hungary. The Hapsburg government had no more desire than the British to see the Balkans dominated by Russia, and it feared that the spirit of Slavic nationalism evoked by San Stefano would have repercussions within its own empire. If the Dual Monarchy elected to play the part that France had played in the Crimean War, the Russian armies in the Balkans might be caught between the Austrians on the Carpathians and the British in the Black Sea. The Czar consented to submit the terms of San Stefano to the consideration of a congress, and Bismarck invited the powers to meet at the new capital of Europe.

The Congress of Berlin was the one great gathering of the concert of Europe as Europe had been redefined by the wars of unification. But the concert was by now more myth than reality; a conflict, not a community, of interests had produced the congress. Most of its business had been settled by prior negotiations between the powers, and the resultant Treaty of Berlin rode roughshod over the wishes of the Balkan peoples. Serbia, Montenegro, and Rumania retained their independence, but none realized the hopes nourished by San Stefano; part of Bulgaria remained autonomous, part was returned to the Turk. Russia acquired territory at the eastern and western ends of the Black Sea. Austria-Hungary gained the right to occupy and administer Bosnia and Herzegovina. Britain received from the Porte a similar right to the island of Cyprus, in return for a guarantee to defend Asia Minor against any future Russian attack. This was the settlement that Disraeli, on his return from Berlin, proudly proclaimed to be "peace with honor."

It was a turning point in European history. The Balkan problem might have been settled on the lines laid down at San Stefano; it could not be settled on those laid down at Berlin. All the Balkan peoples were dissatisfied, and ready to better their lot by fighting each other or the Turk, by peddling their allegiance at Vienna or St. Petersburg, as the hope of gain might dictate. In addition a change in German policy, growing out of the crisis of 1878, began gradually to develop into an Austro-German drive toward the Balkans and Near East, the *Drang nach Osten* of later years. In 1914 the forces loosed by this drive brought on a general war.

The momentous shift from neutrality to alignment with Austria was forced on Bismarck by the nature of his diplomatic problem. In order to prevent France from finding an ally for her war of revenge he had established close relations with both Russia and Austria-Hungary. But in 1878 they were pulling apart, and he could not stay with both. He chose Austria. In 1879 he concluded with her a defensive alliance that grew steadily more important over the next thirty-five years until it drew the allies into war. Russia was rebuffed and isolated. Although in the 1880's she came to terms for a time with the Austro-German combine, the solidarity of the three powers had been shattered by the Balkan question.

For the moment the congress had achieved the peace of which Disraeli boasted. If the peace was fragile, on the surface it was a triumph for British diplomacy. Disraeli basked in the limelight of victory, and even Bismarck applauded. "The old Jew," was his comment, "there's a man for you!" This praise from St. Hubert was well merited. Disraeli was the peer of the Iron Chancellor in subtle, ruthless patriotism, and peace with honor was his masterpiece.

Gladstone denied that it was honorable. For him the claims of national interest and strategic security were subordinate to those of morality and justice, a view that seemed quixotic even to leaders of his own party. But Disraeli's policy angered him, and his anger was still a power in the land. He set out to rouse the British conscience. At the start of this Midlothian campaign he had against him a large majority of Parliament and public and an almost unanimous press; within two years he talked the government out of office. Disraeli helped him by embarking on dangerous adventures in South Africa and Afghanistan, which brought home to the voter the price of the strong line. But the essential reason why the campaign succeeded was the voter's moral sense. The amorality of power politics had not yet bled white the ideals of liberalism. When they were thundered from Sinai by the last great liberal, they were still strong enough to change national policy.

If Gladstone's victory showed the strength of liberalism at the polls, his conduct in office showed its weakness in the world of the 1880's. To denounce Disraeli's strong line as dishonorable and dangerous was one thing; to find an alternative line that would be neither provocative nor pusillanimous was quite another. Gladstone retreated from Afghanistan, for example, only to see the Russians begin to move in, and he was forced to stop them by almost the Disraelian technique. But it was in Africa that he met his thorniest problems, one in the Nile valley and one in the Transvaal. He inherited both from Disraeli, and he failed to settled either. On the Nile he was led against his will to an expansion of British influence and commitments such as Disraeli had never dreamed of. In the Transvaal, on the contrary, he practiced liberal principles, and for all their abstract justice they unquestionably made the problem worse.

The opening of the Suez Canal defined Britain's long-standing concern with the eastern Mediterranean. Thereafter her general purpose of safeguarding her naval power acquired a territorial focus: she strove to prevent any other strong state from dominating, by land or sea, the Isthmus of Suez. By an analogous process, at the opening of the twentieth century, the strategic interests of the United States became focused upon the Isthmus of Panama. If American imperialism in the Caribbean was less conspicuous than British imperialism in the Mediterranean, part of the reason was that Britain, unlike the United States, was working within reach of several major powers. The Bosporus and Dardanelles were one road to Suez, Asia Minor another, and after the crisis of 1878 Britain hoped that she had barred them both. A far more direct road was through Egypt. This nominal fief of the Ottoman Empire was in fact a weak but independent Arab state. If its khedive kept himself free from foreign domination, no matter how bad his rule, Britain could remain aloof. If he came under foreign influence, or opened the way for it by bringing his government to anarchy, Britain would have to take the lead in intervention in order to protect Suez.

In the 1870's Egypt was falling into confusion. The khedive of the period, Ismail, had grandiose ideas of spending money and a child's notion of where it came from. He borrowed recklessly from European financiers, and then borrowed more to pay the interest on the loans. The effect was twofold. Egyptian bonds, marketed by the great banking houses of Europe, created a widespread financial interest in the solvency of Ismail's government. At the same time that government was headed toward bankruptcy and chaos, and the political implications were obvious in Downing Street.

They were equally obvious on the Quai d'Orsay. Ever since the days of the Directory France had had a particular interest in Egypt, and her rising imperialism quickened it. A French company had built the canal, French capital had partially financed it, and French influence at Cairo was strong. If intervention proved necessary, French patriots were insistent that Britain should not act alone.

Events moved rapidly. In 1875 Ismail sold to the British government his holding of almost half the shares in the Suez Canal Company. In the following year his finances were subjected to the authority of an international commission, in which Britain and France were soon predominant. When he intrigued against this dual control, the Sultan was induced to depose him in favor of his son. The Egyptians themselves then took a hand. Their nationalism was aroused by Turkish and European interference, and the new economics fell with particular weight on the army. A revolutionary movement began to develop under a Colonel Arabi. The dual control, created to prevent anarchy, was instead precipitating it.

This was the situation when Gladstone took office. His policy over the next five years is the classic illustration of how empire may be acquired by inadvertence. He wished to limit Britain's responsibilities, and he greatly extended them; the cry of "Egypt for the Egyptians!" roused his sympathies, and he proceeded to occupy Egypt. If he had not done so, the Egyptians would have misgoverned themselves into chaos while the British bondholders howled for his blood; if the French had then moved in, his cabinet could not have survived the storm. With all his high moral sense he was in the clutch of circumstance, and it led him down an extraordinary path.

Early in 1882 the one hope of avoiding unilateral action disappeared, when a political upset in France brought to power a cabinet as averse to acting as Gladstone would have liked to be. Some action was imperative: Arabi, now the real ruler, was bringing Egypt to a state where the lives of all Europeans were in jeopardy. An Anglo-French naval demonstration off Alexandria only stimulated rioting and massacre, and the French squadron withdrew. The British thereupon landed troops — to re-establish the Khedive's authority, as Gladstone proclaimed to Europe, and then depart. The idea was naïve. Arabi's army was promptly destroyed in battle, and with it the only native force on which the Khedive might rest his authority. The British could not then depart without confounding the confusion that had brought them.

They remained. In the next quarter-century they revolutionized the administration, economy, and social condition of the country, along the lines of benevolent despotism already laid down in India. Yet Britain never acquired legal suzerainty from the Porte or formal governing power from the Khedive, and half the revenues remained under international control. The anomalies of her position constantly embarrassed her and invited the intrigue of other states. France was unreconciled, and did all in her power to increase the difficulties; Bismarck bartered his consent to Egyptian reforms for concessions to Germany elsewhere. But the British had caught the tiger's tail; they could not let go if they would until the Egyptians were educated to govern themselves and were secure from outside danger. Political education was at best a long task, and security involved the further problem of the Sudan.

This vast southern hinterland was an Egyptian dependency, which Ismail had endeavored to bring under effective control. His agent had been a devout and single-minded Scot, Charles Gordon, whose genius was as much the saint's as the soldier's, and who commanded phenomenal respect from the Sudanese. Gordon trusted to his star more than to orders, and as Ismail's governor he had had a free hand. When he left in 1879, Egyptian garrisons were scattered throughout the country, and it was acquiring a semblance of order. But at his departure his work collapsed. The tribesmen rebelled under a leader who called himself the Mahdi, or Messiah, and the Egyptian garrisons were soon threatened with annihilation.

Gladstone moved reluctantly. He was determined not to extend and prolong Britain's hold on Egypt by occupying the Sudan; his liberal principles could stand no more rough handling. But he recognized responsibility for the imperiled garrisons, and he was persuaded that Gordon was the man to evacuate them. In 1884 Gordon returned to Khartum, the Sudanese capital, and there the Mahdi's forces quickly surrounded him. Although the Queen and the public clamored for a rescue, Gladstone's attention was absorbed by Ireland, and months were wasted before the relief expedition got under way. When at last it fought its way to Khartum, in January 1885, Gordon and his men had been exterminated two days before.

Retreat was ordered, and the Sudan was turned over to the depredations of the Mahdi.

So ended one of the sorriest chapters in British imperialism. Its effect at home was to increase the bitterness against Gladstone within and without his party, and so to contribute to the Liberal debacle. Its effect on the Egyptian problem was more fundamental. Only an artificial frontier divides Egypt from the Sudan, and the Egyptian army was demoralized. While the Sudan remained in anarchy, spawning fanatical tribesmen, Egypt could be protected against their incursions only by British forces. Gladstone had called a halt at an illogical point: as Suez was insecure without Egypt, so Egypt was insecure without the upper Nile. Until the British repeated the march to Khartum and avenged Gordon, they had to remain in Egypt.

By 1886 Britain had improved her strategic position in the Near East at the cost of diplomatic isolation. Disraeli's intervention in the Balkans had ensured Russian hostility, and Gladstone's intervention on the Nile had ensured French. For France felt that she had been cheated out of Egypt, and she looked to the Sudan for recompense as soon as the Egyptians and British had abandoned it. She pushed her empire eastward across the Sahara toward the White Nile; if she could reach the river, she might turn the flank of the British position and even make it untenable. Sooner or later this ambition was bound to precipitate an Anglo-French crisis on the upper Nile.

Meanwhile another crisis was preparing in South Africa. There again Disraeli took the first step, by abruptly ending the policy of laissez faire toward the Boers that had prevailed since the 1850's. His primary reason was the native problem, and in particular the Zulus. This formidable tribe, living between Natal and the Boer republics, was organized into a rudimentary army, and the scattered white settlers were no match for it; if the Boers stirred up the hornet's nest in Zululand, Natal and even Cape Colony would feel the consequences. The solution that appealed to London was to federate the Boer states with the British colonies, so as to make possible a joint policy and joint defense, and the first step was to overcome the prickly independence of the Transvaal Boers.

The time seemed ripe. The Transvaal government existed only in name; its treasury was empty, its citizens did as they pleased, and those of them who looked ahead feared the Zulus more than they disliked the British. London sent an investigator, who reported what he wished to find and Disraeli wished to hear. In 1877 the Transvaal was annexed, with the promise of future self-government. The British were promptly involved in a Zulu war, and they were roughly handled before they won it. Their prestige was at a low ebb, and the Boers were watching with interest. Annexation had not been popular in the Transvaal; those who had approved of it were quick to change their minds once the Zulu menace was removed.

Gladstone inherited a difficult situation, which he had aggravated during his campaign by denouncing annexation as iniquitous. The Boers concluded that he would undo it, but he gave them nothing beyond vague promises; once in office he was too busy, as often happens, to remedy all the evils he had attacked before election. The hotheads in the Transvaal thereupon revolted, declared a republic, and prepared to invade Natal. The mouse, with complete self-confidence, was attacking the lion.

Gladstone immediately opened negotiations. He carried them on during the fighting, even when the British were sensationally defeated at Majuba Hill; he hated war, and he refused to admit that the Boers had weakened the justice of their cause by winning a battle. The upshot was that they acquired independence as the South African Republic, which was given all the attributes of sovereignty except control of its external relations. This action of the British government was either the acme of enlightened liberalism or abject surrender, depending on the point of view. In South Africa both races accepted it as surrender. Hopes of federation were blasted, and Boer nationalism was rekindled; the Orange Free State, which had taken no part in the rising, thenceforth followed increasingly the lead of its northern neighbor. The Boers, furthermore, took the little war to mean that Britain would capitulate before a show of force.

Thus Gladstone, with the highest motives, helped to lay the powder-train for the coming explosion. He distrusted coercion like Cromwell before him, and his policy in the Transvaal might be summed up by "that you have by force, I look upon it as nothing." But situations arise where the avoidance of force may be more disastrous than its use. Abandonment of the Sudan and retreat in the

Transvaal are examples in point. One left the Sudanese to a decade of horror under the scourge of the Mahdi and his successor, and opened the way for the most serious Anglo-French crisis since 1815. The other encouraged the Boers to believe that they could, if necessary, defy the strength of the British Empire. The belief was natural, but dangerous for them and for Britain.

By 1886 the principles of the older liberalism, in summary, were no more valid for external policy than for internal. Gladstone modified them far more throughly in dealing with domestic and Irish problems than in dealing with the outside world, and his diplomacy grew progressively less successful. During his first ministry no major crises arose. Then came the Tory interlude, with trouble in the Balkans and the beginnings of trouble in Africa. In his second ministry these African problems plagued him, and his failure to solve them cannot be fully explained by his mounting absorption with Ireland. The world of the 1880's was alien to him. Its stock of good will seemed to be exhausted; he confronted the hostility of Russia and France, the scheming of Bismarck, a cauldron of intrigue at Cairo, pugnacity in the Transvaal. He was not made to be a power politician, and power was the ascendant value.

The value was recognized by Tories and many Liberals. The Palmerstonian concept of the strong line, which Disraeli had adapted to a new age, was gaining ground despite the temporary reverse of a Midlothian campaign. Largely because of Gladstone's towering prestige, the concept did not capture the Liberals while they held together. When their imperialist members seceded to the Tories and the resultant coalition came to power, the spirit of Disraeli came with it. The Liberal schism, therefore, was as much a turning point in foreign as in domestic policy. After 1886 Britain shook off her complacence. She remained isolated but grew increasingly defiant, until by the turn of the century she discovered that the strong line is the shortest distance from tranquillity to crisis.

VI   Conquest in Africa

IN the decade after 1886 the alliance of Liberal and Tory imperialists was cemented by the Irish question. In 1892, after Parnell's death, Gladstone returned to office with a bare and flimsy majority for Home Rule. The old man was indomitable. With all his former energy and skill he pushed a second Home Rule Bill through the commons; when it was thrown out by the lords, he wished to appeal to the country again. But his colleagues dissuaded him; the country was tiring of Ireland and would almost surely not give him a mandate to coerce the Upper House. In 1894 he retired for the last time, and four years later he died. His party and the cause on which he had staked it seemed to have died before him. He had glimpsed the Promised Land only to have his hope betrayed; the success that actually lay ahead was not for the Moses of Victorian politics. "Thou shalt see the land before thee; but thou shalt not go thither unto the land."

After the second Home Rule Bill the Liberal Unionists despaired of reconciliation with the Liberals and closed ranks with the Tories. The election of 1895 gave this Conservative coalition an overwhelming majority over the Liberals and Irish combined. The voters had put a quietus on Home Rule for fifteen years to come, and had endorsed an imperialism that flouted Gladstone's principles. The African problems that had plagued him were outbidding Ireland for the attention of the new government, which met them with a firmness reflecting the popular mood. Now that the European powers were scrambling for influence and territory in the Dark Continent, the British were determined to hold their own. They could do so only by tightening their authority and advancing their frontiers wherever competition threatened. This stimulating and dangerous game, which might at any time explode into war, the government played to thunderous public applause.

The partition of Africa had begun in the early 1880's. Before long the acquisitive fever had spread to Germany, in spite of Bismarck's reluctance, and by 1895 the Germans had colonies in east and southwest Africa; the latter, in particular, was too close to the Boer republics for Britain's comfort. Far to the north the French were pushing across the Sahara toward the upper Nile. In both the Sudan and the Transvaal Gladstone had left unfinished business, and the intrusion of foreign powers was now making it more pressing: unless Britain settled it quickly, it might be settled for her.

The first problem the Conservatives tackled was the Sudan, where a number of factors spurred them on. French ambitions were crystallizing in an exploratory expedition from the Congo area toward the Nile. The Mahdi's successor had decimated the Sudanese population in a reign of terror. Egyptian finances had been so strengthened that they could now bear the costs of reconquest, and the Khedive's army had been molded into an effective force by its British commander, Sir Herbert Kitchener. The public at home was in a mood to revenge Gordon by finishing his work. For all these reasons Kitchener was ordered into the Sudan. In two years he broke the tribesmen's resistance and extended Anglo-Egyptian authority southward to Khartum. He had no more than gained the capital in 1898 when he heard that the French had reached the White Nile far to the south, at the village of Fashoda. This move threatened the whole strategic purpose of his advance. He was ordered to Fashoda, and annexed the whole area, while the French remained as witness to their prior claim. The crisis was transferred to London and Paris.

France was willing to withdraw from Fashoda only at a price. Her purpose was to force the simultaneous negotiation of all the outstanding differences between the two empires, and in particular to raise again the dormant Egyptian question; she would then be in a position to trade her claims on the Nile for substantial concessions elsewhere. Britain, on the contrary, intended to meet each difference separately, with a minimum of concession, and at all costs to keep Egypt out of the discussion. She was in a fighting rather than a bargaining mood.

Throughout the autumn of 1898 the tension mounted, and for a time war seemed inevitable. But the French were in the throes of a domestic scandal, their African armies were in danger of being cut off from France by the Royal Navy, and the Sudan, now that it had failed to force Britain to terms, was not sufficiently important to them to justify a war. For all these reasons the French government gave way. It recalled the expedition, and in the spring of 1899 it acknowledged British control of the entire area. This was unconditional surrender.

Britain was supremely lucky in the timing. Six months later the simmering kettle in South Africa boiled over at last, and the Boers started to drive the British into the sea. If this attack had coincided with the Fashoda crisis, instead of following it, Britain could scarcely have defied the French in the north while defending herself against the Boers in the south. As it was she secured the Nile in the nick of time by sheer intransigence, and then provoked the Boers by the same intransigence. They had deeper grievances than the

French, less understanding of the government with which they dealt, and far less military imagination; they would capitulate to force only after testing it.

The struggle that broke out in 1899 had been brewing more and more patently since 1886. During those years the whole situation in South Africa was changing. Cape Colony, Natal, and the Boer re-

heir centuries of isolation into
caught in the rush of modern
s began to be exploited. The
part, were ready to move with
l their willingness to utilize in-
he exploiters of their mineral
their political and cultural is-
the outsiders whom they ad-
olonists and capitalists of Brit-
British government. The veldt
empt to keep it so was in one
ant struggle for freedom.
anged the situation after 1886
d the inroads of modern capi-
he north, was a potential base
and so toward the Transvaal;
Cape Colony, and was sepa-
st only by the wilds of Bechu-
ing among the Boers was wel-
eat Britain and strengthened
influence had a double effect. It
tinacy, and it gave the British
n.

he Transvaal, like the jinni re-
vas discovered on the Witwa-
richest gold field known, and
over the world; the little Boer
cade from three thousand to a
l economy were turned upside
ned to govern themselves now
population of outsiders, or Uitlanders, who threat-
ened to outnumber them. This task alone might have baffled more sophisticated politicians, but it was not alone. The Uitlanders were

only the advance guard of a new world knocking at the gate, and the politics of Johannesburg were inseparable from those of Capetown and London.

The government of the South African Republic was headed by a man who personified Boer conservatism. Paul Kruger came straight out of the seventeenth century; his Calvinism, rooted in the Old Testament, equipped him for leadership in the last community of Puritans. Great Britain he detested. As a boy he had joined in the Great Trek, and as a man he had played a leading part in the revolt of 1880–1; he hoped eventually to make all South Africa Dutch. When he was elected president of the infant republic in 1883, the hope was visionary. But the opening of the Rand changed the whole prospect.

Kruger disliked the Uitlanders on many grounds. They were preponderantly British, and they threatened to be the means of reasserting British influence. Before long they were sure to demand the suffrage, which he could not give them without undermining his own authority. They represented modernity at its worst, and were corrupting the manners and morals of the young generation of Boers; Johannesburg was defined as "Monte Carlo superimposed upon Sodom and Gommorrah."[2] But Kruger did not discourage their immigration, for they had one cardinal virtue: they paid taxes. For the first time in Boer history the government had sufficient funds to be effective; much as the President feared the newcomers, he was anxious to gather and husband their golden eggs. Gold was the means by which he intended to maintain his political supremacy and increase his military power against the day of reckoning.

The result for the Uitlanders was taxation without representation. They financed the state, and received almost nothing from it except an increasingly dictatorial administration; they had few political rights even in the towns they had created. The flotsam and jetsam of the mining camps, transients who came only to make a quick fortune and leave again, were poor material for citizenship. But as the years passed and conditions became stabilized, a growing proportion of the immigrants settled into respectability, and their demand for representation became more persuasive. Kruger gave only one answer: he had not asked them to come and did not ask them to

---

[2] Quoted by Elie Halévy: *A History of the English People: Epilogue* [1895–1915] (2 vols., London, 1929–34), I, 75, note 1.

stay; while they were in his country, they must conform to his laws. He was adamant because he felt no need to conciliate. He was crushing dissent among the Boers and accumulating a store of arms and ammunition; Dutch and German experts were beginning to develop the resources of the country. He would soon be ready to ride roughshod over the Uitlanders and achieve complete independence.

At this point his policy ran head on into that of Cecil Rhodes. As the Boer personified the old world in South Africa, the Englishman personified the new. Rhodes had made an enormous fortune in the diamond fields of Kimberley and augmented it from the gold of the Rand; he was the organizing and directing genius of the South Africa Company, which was chartered by the British government to exploit and colonize the vast tract between the Transvaal and German East Africa; he was a successful politician, and since 1890 the Prime Minister of Cape Colony. His many projects were means to a single end. Imperialism was his religion, and in its service he amassed power. His methods were often unclean, for he had no more scruples than Machiavelli; but his vision of empire had a spaciousness that commands respect. He thought in vast distances, and dreamed of Britain's dominating the whole length of Africa from Capetown to Cairo; his sense of the map, like Chatham's, had an epic quality. But he did not think in vast stretches of time. He was obsessed by the brevity of all life, particularly his own, and by the need to fulfill his mission quickly. Kruger had in him the patience of the centuries; Rhodes was driven by the unforgiving minute.

The only sure starting point for an advance toward the Nile was a federated South Africa. The opposition of the Boer republics still blocked federation, and Kruger's dream of Dutch expansion was squarely at odds with Rhodes's dream for Britain. The Englishman resolved to surround the Boers, turn them in on themselves, and so force them to choose between federation and stagnation. In the decade before 1895 he had made phenomenal progress. Bechuanaland had become a British protectorate, to keep the Germans from linking hands with the Boers; the South Africa Company had pushed to the northward, and in 1895 the whole area from Lake Tanganyika to the Limpopo was brought under British control and christened Rhodesia. The Boers were hemmed in on the west and north, and on the east they had lost all hope of a seaport. In the same year a railroad from Delagoa Bay in Portuguese East Africa reached Kruger's capital at Pretoria; although this was a tenuous link with the outside world, it strengthened the President's means of resistance. The pressure of encirclement made him not more amenable, but less. He refused economic co-operation with British Africa, and his attitude toward the Uitlanders stiffened. He was antagonizing both the management of the great mining companies and their employees. The Rand was ready to explode.

Rhodes did not want a spontaneous explosion, with its unpredictable timing and results; he was used to controlling events. When he found that some of the Uitlanders were plotting a rebellion, he prepared to aid them with a force of Company troops under the command of his friend and agent, Dr. Jameson. At the end of 1895 Jameson tired of waiting and invaded the Transvaal, where he was promptly captured by the Boers. Years of planning, of encirclement and pressure, had culminated in a fiasco.

It ended the era of Rhodes. He resigned as Prime Minister and went into retirement. The Jameson Raid destroyed his scheme for forcing the republics into co-operation, and it reawoke the old antipathies. The large Boer population of Cape Colony grew restive at the threat to their compatriots, and many began to think seriously about Kruger's dream of Dutch ascendancy. He had been criticized even by the Transvaal Boers, but the raid rallied them behind him. The Orange Free State also fell into line, and Kruger stood out as the leader of his whole scattered people against British aggression.

He seized his opportunity to increase the purchases of arms and ammunition. Public opinion in Europe was shocked by the raid, and the German Kaiser congratulated the republic on handling the crisis "without appealing to the help of friendly powers." This thinly veiled hint infuriated the British, and encouraged the belief at Pretoria that the time had come to establish the Dutch claim to South Africa in the teeth of the British Empire. Rhodes had had his day; now Kruger had his.

But he was dealing with an opponent even more dangerous than Rhodes. The Colonial Secretary, Joseph Chamberlain, was also an avid imperialist, and in African policy his influence in the cabinet outweighed that of the aging and cautious Salisbury. The Uitlanders were taken more and more openly under the wing of the British government. Negotiations dragged on while the Boers completed their armaments and the British completed their quarrel with

France. When the latter was settled in the spring of 1899, Chamberlain demanded of Kruger that the Uitlanders should be enfranchised after a five-year residence. The idea was reasonable, but the demand was illegal: Gladstone had recognized the sovereignty of the republic in internal affairs. Kruger accepted the demand, however, on condition that Britain should recognize the sovereignty of his government for the future. Whether he intended to use that recognition to nullify the Uitlander's franchise is beside the point; for the moment his position was unassailable in equity and law. The British government ignored both. It raised its terms and insisted on unconditional acceptance. Kruger thereupon withdrew his proposals, and attacked.

Fortunately Gladstone was in his grave. Never in his day had British statesmen flouted so openly his concept of morality, to the applause of a public crazed by the goddess jingo. Britain had a strong moral case for her concern with the Uitlanders. They were largely British subjects, with grievances for which the Boers were to blame; redress was improbable except through outside pressure. But Chamberlain's way of exerting pressure was so high-handed that it ruined his case. The Boers came before the bar of world opinion as gallant and innocent men defending their freedom, and Britain's standing sank to the lowest point in her modern history.

Her moral weakness accentuated the danger of her diplomatic position. By 1899 the three greatest powers in Europe were her enemies. Russia remembered the Congress of Berlin; France had just been humiliated at Fashoda; Germany was stubbing her toes on the British Empire in Africa and the Far East, and was the professed friend of the Boers. Britain's isolation exposed her to the possibility of joint intervention, backed by widespread popular sympathy for the Boers. The attempt to form a coalition eventually failed, partly because the Royal Navy was still a barrier to effective action and partly because the memory of Alsace-Lorraine was even stronger in Paris than the memory of Fashoda. But Britain's escape left her profoundly conscious of her isolation.

At the outset it seemed as if the Boers needed no help to expel the British. The Conservative government had precipitated the war without preparing for it; the garrisons of Cape Colony and Natal were pitifully weak, and the Boers turned out to be superb soldiers. Their offensive bogged down, however, while their wholesale annexation of invaded British territory proclaimed their own imperialism. Britain was appalled at her defeats, and lost her light-hearted jingoism. But she had only begun to fight. Troops poured in from the mother country and the dominions as well. The Boers had challenged the community of British peoples, and for the first time the response came from all over the world; thousands of volunteers from Canada, Australia, and New Zealand put the quietus on the old belief that the empire was dissolving.

When the British counteroffensive began, its issue was never in doubt. By the autumn of 1900 the Boers' field armies were dispersed and their principal cities occupied, Kruger was in exile, and the republics were annexed. The struggle seemed over, but in fact its worst phase was beginning. The Boers, like the British in their own dark hours, lacked the imagination to know that they were beaten. For a year and a half they waged a gallant, brilliant, and essentially hopeless guerrilla war against the occupation forces. Although the British increased their army to 200,000 men, its helplessness made it the laughingstock of Europe until Kitchener became commander in chief. He attacked the problem with methodical efficiency. Railroads were guarded by blockhouses, nearby farm buildings destroyed and the inhabitants put into concentration camps, and the guerrillas driven across the veldt like game and herded against barbed-wire entanglements. Meanwhile fever was taking heavy toll among the troops and in the concentration camps; the deaths of thousands of women and children prisoners raised a storm in the House of Commons. This was a new kind of war, shorn of glamour, and it completed the disillusionment of the British public.

In the spring of 1902 the government opened negotiations with the remaining Boer leaders, and both sides negotiated in a new spirit. Each had learned to respect the other, and respect bred the beginnings of confidence. This paradoxical result of battle appeared in the ensuing settlement. By the Treaty of Vereeniging the republics were annexed to the empire with the promise of future self-government; they retained their language in schools and courts, the Boer fighters kept even their weapons, and Great Britain — the victor — paid three million pounds in reparations. Those terms, after two and a half years of war, showed a remarkable breadth of view. They could not end the conflict of nationalities, but they did open a new era. The extinction of the republics took most of the meaning out of the political divisions that had so long cursed South Africa; the Boers of the veldt emerged from their isolation to become part of the larger Dutch community, and the Uitlanders of Johannesburg were thrown together with the British of Capetown and Durban. The foundation was prepared for a unitary state, in which the two peoples could continue their struggle at the polls and in Parliament instead of by diplomacy and commandos.

Vereeniging marked a turning point for Britain as well as for South Africa. The 1890's, in spite of the Aubrey Beardsleys and the Oscar Wildes, was a period of savage new gods. The worship of force and of the militaristic state was in the ascendant; admiration for Germany was widespread, and men as prominent as Chamberlain talked of a future when the "Teutonic race" — British, German, and American — would rule the world by strength for the world's good. British policy reflected these ideas. It was solicitous toward the German Empire and the United States, but other countries were handled with a roughness that achieved more and more success through the Fashoda crisis. The nation applauded so immoderately that it seemed, as Kipling warned, to be "drunk with sight of power." The culmination was the Boer War, which promised to be both glorious and cheap. It was neither. It turned into a kind of warfare that not only shocked Britain's conscience but demanded hard effort from her and her dominions. Shock and effort are sobering, and by 1902 the imperialism of the previous decade had lost its reckless ebullience.

The change in public mood coincided with changes on the stage of public life. In 1901 Victoria died, and her already ageing son succeeded her as Edward VII. In her last years the Queen had played less and less of a role in politics; but few of her subjects remembered when she had not been on the throne, and her death left a void that Edward could scarcely fill. In 1902 her most prominent servant, the Marquis of Salisbury, retired from the premiership that he had held with one intermission since 1886. He was the last aristocrat of the old school, akin to Wellington in his opposition to headlong change at home or abroad; beside him Disraeli seemed like a radical. Shrewd, cynical, and aloof, Salisbury was always on the side of caution and moderation, whether in wooing the Unionists or in grabbing the waste lands of Africa. He did not succeed in mastering the forces personified by Chamberlain, but he curbed them enough to maintain a surface of concord within the cabinet and party. It was fitting that this conservative of Conservatives should retire at a moment when the Victorian world was beyond conserving.

VII   Forces of Reform

THE ENDING of the Boer War unloosed a clamor for domestic change such as had not been heard for thirty years. By 1906 Britain was once more on the verge of a revolution by consent; at the same time she was revolutionizing her foreign policy to conform to her new position in the world. These two upheavals were interrelated in their causes although disparate in their effects. Between them they refashioned the Victorian framework into that of modern Britain.

The demand for social change was in large measure the effect of foreign economic competition, which by 1900 was becoming serious. In industry Britain was far behind the United States and Germany in the production of iron and steel, and behind the United States in the output of coal. In agriculture the amount of land under cultivation had fallen by more than a quarter in thirty years, and the number of agrarian laborers had decreased proportionately; British farmers, it seemed, were drowning in a flood of imported American wheat. In commerce the great North Sea ports of the Continent were handling, for the first time in centuries, a greater volume of foreign trade than English ports. The heyday of Britain's economy was passing just when her experiment with democracy was beginning.

The most notable effect was on the labor movement. The trade unions had hitherto drawn their strength from the aristocracy of skilled labor, and their principal efforts had been devoted to collective bargaining; the masses of unskilled labor had been left, for the most part, to a few earnest missionaries of Marx. The doctrinaire violence of the Marxist creed was in the spirit of the revolutionary chartists, and for that very reason it failed to win mass support. The British workingman, like his compatriots, had too much sense of humor to be led to the barricades by logicians. The Marxist missionaries did succeed, however, in regimenting segments of the forgotten proletariat for dramatic and successful strikes, which so impressed the young generation of labor leaders that they began to organize the less skilled trades. The oligarchy of trade unionism was broadening its base.

Another brand of socialism was at work among the intelligentsia. The members of the Fabian Society rejected the dogmatic romanticism of Marx for the slow, prosaic workings of public opinion. They hoped eventually to see the industrial process brought under the direct control of a government responsible to the mass of the people; until that time came their function was propaganda, to spread the idea that the socialist state was inevitable — was, indeed, already in being — and to support any measure that promised to bring it toward maturity. They were professed opportunists without party allegiance, but their bias was more toward the new conservatism than the old liberalism. They tended to exalt government as the medium of reform, and were deeply impressed by Bismarck's uncompleted program of state socialism. For all their Germanic worship of the state, however, their program was thoroughly British, and it enlisted some of the finest minds in the country, from the Webbs to Bernard Shaw. It had no creed or eschatology, and because it was amorphous it permeated — a favorite Fabian verb — the thought of intelligent labor leaders and politicians of both parties.

The labor movement was tending for other reasons toward a Fabian emphasis upon the state. Although the unions were increasing in membership, the newly organized workers were too poor for effective strikes and hence for effective bargaining. But they had numerical importance at the polls, and they stood to gain by state interference; their leaders were consequently forced to be in some measure socialists.

Another factor which heightened their interest in the state was an offensive waged against them by the industrialists. By the 1890's the employers, caught between the rising pressure of labor and of foreign competition, combined in large numbers to battle unionism not only by lock-outs but also through the courts. In 1901 the House of Lords, in its role of supreme court, handed down two decisions that were a catastrophe for labor; one apparently outlawed the boycotting of a recalcitrant employer, and the other made a union liable for civil damages committed by its members during a strike. Within a month the lords had wiped out the reading of labor law that had prevailed for twenty years. The defeat accelerated the conversion of

the labor leaders into politicians, for they could not appeal successfully to the legislature until they acquired greater political weight.

They had already begun to make their presence felt in the commons. As early as 1892 the left wing of the labor movement had organized its members in the House, and at the turn of the century
the central representative body, the Trade Union Congress, authorized the creation of an independent parliamentary group that soon
became known as the Labour Party. Its aims were implicitly social-
istic, and its technique was Fabian: it would ally with neither major party but would support whichever one might, at the moment,
"be engaged in promoting legislation in the direct interest of labor."
The arrival of this political infant, of dubious parentage and unpredictable strength, came at a critical moment.

The Conservative Party was at loggerheads on an issue that
closely concerned labor. Salisbury's retirement had left the center
of the stage to Chamberlain, who was the hope of many socialists.
He was still the radical of his earlier years, and his imperialism
sprang in part from his fascination with the democratic dominions,
in part from his emphasis on the state as power. Here was the man
who could win labor's support, if any one could, for a dynamic program of Tory democracy. Just when the opportunity was brightest,
however, he chose to advance a program that alienated the rank
and file of the working classes.

In 1903 he resigned from the cabinet to campaign for protection.
Britain's position in the world, he was convinced, was now so precarious that she could no longer afford the luxury of free trade. She
existed as a power primarily because of her empire, and could compensate for her weakening political ties with the dominions only by
strengthening her economic ties through a system of preferential
tariffs, to pump the blood of trade through imperial arteries; such a
system was obviously impossible unless she herself abandoned free
trade. The logic of imperialism, in short, led him to attack the economic gospel accepted by both parties for half a century. Although
his program of domestic tariffs was largely borrowed from the fair-
traders of twenty years before, his motive was different. Where they
had been concerned with protecting the economic strength of Britain, he was concerned with the whole empire. At home he advocated
sweeping social reform, financed by the taxation of imports, but he
envisaged a Britain that would be only the hub of a vast community,

more than three hundred million people, bound together by ties of self-interest and standing defiantly against the rest of the world.

His program implied enormous changes, and enormous obstacles stood in his way. The dominions were jealous of their tariff autonomy because they were beginning to compete with each other and with Britain, and several of them — Canada in particular — were busy forming commercial ties with outside states; Chamberlain's proposal would disrupt their economy. Opposition in Britain, however, was the immediate obstacle. Protection would increase prices and diminish foreign trade; when its protagonists argued that these sacrifices would buy Britain her security as part of the larger imperial community, their argument fell on a number of deaf ears. Manufacturers refused to accept it for fear of the effect on wages, markets, and profits. Trade-union leaders dared not accept it, even if their socialism inclined them toward the principle of a state-controlled economy, because the bulk of their followers refused to vote for dearer food no matter what promises of social reforms might be offered with it. After sixty years the ghost of the Anti-Corn Law League was abroad, and cheap bread was again the shibboleth of politics.

The wheel of Chamberlain's fortune had come full circle. In 1886 he had helped to ruin the Liberal Party in what he considered the cause of imperial security. Now, in the same cause under a different guise, he was ruining the Conservative Party. Some of the radical imperialists followed him as imperialists; others, as radicals, refused to tax the food of the poor and deserted to the Liberals, among them a young scion of the House of Marlborough named Winston Churchill. Most of the aristocratic Tories had always distrusted Chamberlain, the parvenu from Birmingham, and they now washed their hands of him. The coalition forged by Home Rule was disintegrating.

At the same time Chamberlain's program was uniting the Liberal Party, which had long been torn by dissension. The right wing, faithful to Gladstone, was still opposed to adventures abroad or at home; many moderates, on the contrary, were ardent imperialists, and the left wing was adumbrating a program of domestic reform that stole the thunder both from Chamberlain and the socialists. But one thing all Liberals had in common: the ingrained tradition of free trade. The attack upon it brought them together, and as disgruntled Unionists began to join them the prospect of a sweeping victory dawned.

Such a victory was impossible, even in defense of free trade, unless the party shook off the Gladstonian albatross. Britain was in two simultaneous crises, in her domestic growth and her world position, and the Liberals had to convince the electorate of their ability to handle both; they needed a daring domestic program to win the independent labor vote, and a strong imperial policy to win the confidence of a nation that was still, though sobered, far from humbled. In the grip of necessity the right wing gave way. The party adopted a domestic platform of virtual state socialism, and in external affairs it accepted the new principles on which the Conservative government had been acting since the close of the Boer War. By 1906 a Liberal triumph at the polls meant drastic change at home, but abroad it meant diplomatic continuity.

Continuity was badly needed. From 1902 on, the Conservative government was abandoning the nation's time-honored aloofness toward other powers. A few months before Vereeniging Britain broke her unwritten law against a peacetime standing alliance by concluding a defensive treaty with Japan. In 1904 she came to terms with France, and so ended the antagonism that had overshadowed her statecraft for a generation. In 1905–6 she went a step farther, and gave France active support. These events revealed a shift in her foreign policy commensurate with her changed position in the world, and the Liberals' acceptance of the shift precluded a return to isolation.

VIII   The Diplomatic Revolution

THE DIPLOMATIC revolution that began in 1902 can be understood only in the context of European diplomacy during the previous decade. In the years after Bismark's retirement in 1890, a new spirit animated the German government, and a new alignment took form on the Continent. Britain at first paid little attention to developments that seemed remote from her, but all too soon she discovered her mistake. French and Russian policy made her position difficult, and German policy made it untenable.

The crux of developments was in Berlin. Germany had come to the parting of the ways, and the path she took would inevitably determine — though not, perhaps, as she expected — the path Great

Britain would take. The chief question before the government of the new Kaiser, William II, was how to handle the principles of statecraft that Bismarck had bequeathed to it. One principle was the retention of good relations with Russia. A second was the maintenance of the status quo in central Europe by the Austro-German accord, to which Italy had been added to form the Triple Alliance. A third was moderation in dealing with Great Britain, a middle course that utilized her isolation to wring concessions from her but avoided provoking a final breach. A great deal depended on how Bismarck's successors handled these three elements of his legacy.

The first was soon jettisoned for the second. Germany sided more and more overtly with Austria in the Balkans, and the *Drang nach Osten* crystallized in the project of a railroad from Berlin to Bagdad. Russia, thus cold-shouldered, quickly took alarm and moved toward the other friendless power of the Continent, France. After 1893 Europe was divided between the Dual Alliance of France and Russia and the Triple Alliance of Germany, Austria-Hungary, and Italy. Britain alone remained in isolation. Although she now called it splendid in order to make it palatable, nothing could make it safe. The powers were impinging on her interests as they expanded overseas; she might handle one alone, but combinations were another matter.

In the closing years of the century the Dual Alliance was directed primarily against her. France had little immediate concern with Russia's Balkan worries, or Russia with French designs in Africa, but both powers shared an active Anglophobia. It forced Britain into considerable dependence on the Triple Alliance, which Berlin was convinced she would have to join on Germany's terms. When Salisbury's government refused to take this step and to underwrite, in effect, German hegemony of the Continent, Berlin abandoned moderation for a more and more patently anti-British policy, designed to further German interests while coercing Britain into line. In South Africa came the threat of joint intervention under German aegis. In the Near East a British effort to influence the Porte was brusquely frustrated by a conjunction of Germany, Russia, and France. In the Far East the same three powers, intent on partitioning China among themselves into spheres of influence, paid little more heed to British interests than to the rising ambition of Japan. By collaborating with the Dual Alliance Germany was feathering her nest and making the value of her good will painfully obvious in London.

Another development in Germany was even more painful: she was building a navy. As long as she had none her growing empire existed on sufferance; its insecurity galled her and limited the pressure she could put on Britain. The case for naval expansion had already been made by an American naval officer, whose argument had been aimed at his own country but found its first mark in Germany. Captain Mahan's *The Influence of Sea Power upon History, 1660–1783* had for its theme the triumph of British over French imperialism, and its thesis was that Britain had achieved the prerequisite of empire, control of the seas, by defeating and blockading the Bourbon navies; the core of sea power is the battle fleet, according to Mahan, and victory comes to the side that seeks decisive battle. This was the German concept of land war applied to the ocean, and it inevitably appealed to minds bred on the theory of Clausewitz and the practice of Von Moltke. The Kaiser was deeply impressed, and distributed copies of the book to the officers of his infant fleet. "Before everything else," he wrote, "I must provide myself with a navy. In twenty years' time, when the navy will be ready, I shall speak a very different language." [3]

The naval program was launched in 1898, when the Fashoda crisis was underlining the importance of sea power in diplomacy and the American victory over Spain was projecting a new and unwelcome complication into Germany's Far Eastern designs. Then came the Boer War, which brought home to Germany the need of a great fleet much as the Seven Years' War had brought it home to Bourbon France; in 1900 the Reichstag, on a wave of frustrated Anglophobia, doubled the speed of naval construction. The British Admiralty realized that for the first time in a century it had to face a determined and methodical challenge.

The challenge seemed as hopeless as David's to Goliath. But the Germans, like David, had technical and psychological advantages. Because they were beginning from almost nothing, they could incorporate the newest developments in their ships; Britain had millions invested in the existing fleet, and solicitude for the taxpayer combined with professional conservatism to retard modernization.

---

[3] Quoted by Elie Halévy: *A History of the English People: Epilogue*, I, 112.

The Germans were building with one primary aim, to gain control of the North Sea, and could subordinate everything in a ship to its fighting capacity in home waters; British ships might have to fight off Singapore or the Falklands, and coal bunkers were as important as armor. The Germans consequently had reason to hope that their fleet would be superior in power, if not in numbers, to the part of the Royal Navy that could be concentrated against it.

Concentration was the crux of Britain's problem. Her strategic position had hitherto been rooted in geography: her control of European waters had prevented Continental fleets from combining against her or escaping into the Atlantic to attack her empire, and no extra-European power had had a navy; she had therefore been supreme everywhere. But by 1900 the old geography was out of date. The United States and Japan were emerging as sea powers — weak still, to be sure, but strategically important because even a weak fleet, operating in its own home waters, might be a match for a strong one operating at extreme range. These infant navies threatened Britain's hegemony in the western Atlantic, the Caribbean, and the Pacific, and her problem was how to meet the threat while concentrating against Germany at home.

The problem was insoluble in naval terms. No cabinet would have dared propose a building program sufficient to keep Britain supreme in all parts of the world at once; the cost would have been astronomical. Even keeping a safe lead over Germany, it soon appeared, would strain the patience of the taxpayer. It would also require concentrating all available ships in home waters, and so weakening the squadrons on foreign stations. "Far called, our navies melt away."

To this strategic retreat Britain's diplomacy adapted itself as best it could. In 1901 she abandoned her treaty right to participate with the United States in building the Panama Canal, and thereby recognized the preponderant American interest in that crucial area. In 1902 she concluded her alliance with Japan, which bound the signatories to join forces if either were involved in a war in the Far East against two powers: in plainer language Britain would hold the ring by diplomatic means if Japan fought Russia, and Japanese sea power in return would buttress Britain's position in China. The Foreign Office was beginning to prepare the way for a naval concentration in the North Sea.

The Boer War revealed a depth of antagonism in Germany that shocked the British public, and the cabinet virtually abandoned hope of an accord. Russia was acutely hostile because of the Anglo-Japanese alliance, and France was still smoldering after Fashoda. Britain was no longer minded to face the three corners of the world in arms, but where could she look for help? The answer was suggested by a number of factors, and all of them pointed to Paris. King Edward knew and liked France, and had a real if intangible influence on foreign policy. The French were still interested in bargaining, despite their bitterness, and the focus of their African ambitions had shifted to Morocco. The British were also willing to bargain over Morocco, as they had not been over the Sudan. They were intent on keeping any major power away from the Moroccan coast opposite Gibraltar; the rest of the country mattered little to them. They at last agreed to discuss simultaneously all the sources of Anglo-French friction, and even to talk about the Nile Valley. Their earlier intransigence was gone, and they hoped to exchange an Egyptian *quid* for a Moroccan *quo*.

The diplomatic horse-trade that resulted was global in scope. It touched on French privileges in the Newfoundland fisheries, frontiers in Nigeria, spheres of influence in Siam, customs rights in Madagascar. The crux of discussion was North Africa. Here France finally renounced her interest in Egypt; Britain in return agreed to the establishment of French hegemony in all Morocco except the northern coast, which was assigned to the innocuous Spaniards. The final agreement, reached in April 1904, gave birth to the Entente Cordiale.

The entente was in no sense an alliance. It was based on the settlement of intricate and far-ranging differences, not on mutual commitments. The two governments, it is true, promised to support each other diplomatically in carrying out their agreement, but who knew what such support might mean? Not Whitehall or the Quai d'Orsay, for the diplomacy of each would be guided by events more than words. Not, above all, the Wilhelmstrasse. Any measure of understanding between Britain and France was unwelcome to Germany because it decreased Britain's dependence on the Triple Alliance. But was the entente a real understanding, or only a fragile truce that would break under pressure? The German government resolved to find out. In the spring of 1905 the Kaiser landed at Tangier and proclaimed himself the defender of Moroccan independence.

The moment was shrewdly chosen. For more than a year Russia, France's ally, had been at war with Japan in the Far East, and was losing so disastrously that revolution threatened at home; she suspected that the French, furthermore, were deserting her for the British, and she was no more willing than able to act in the west. This was the German opportunity to humiliate France, break the backbone of the Dual Alliance, and prove to Britain that she was ill advised in her choice of friends. The ostensible German argument was like Disraeli's after San Stefano: the Moroccan question had been regulated a quarter-century earlier by an international conference, and it should now be settled in congress and not by two powers alone. To this demand Britain and France grudgingly acquiesced, and at the beginning of 1906 the congress met at Algeciras.

If its meeting was a German victory, its outcome was a German defeat. Morocco, except for the north coast, was virtually recognized as a French sphere of influence. This result was due in large measure to Britain's consistent support of France. As soon as Anglo-French difficulties were settled, while Anglo-German difficulties remained, Britain acquired a self-interested preference for France as against Germany. The preference applied with particular force to Morocco, one of the last places where Britain wished to see a strong naval power entrench itself. Hence the Moroccan crisis, designed in Berlin to destroy the entente, began to tighten it. Germany was left with nothing but a Pyrrhic victory. Britain, on the other hand, took the first step toward a new Continental policy, which has endured until the present day.

These spectacular developments were the recognition, in diplomatic terms, that the Victorian world was giving place to another. The disintegration of the Conservative Party and the swelling demand for reform were parts of the same transition. It had set in a generation earlier: by the 1880's the spread of industrialism throughout the world was undermining British primacy, stimulating imperialist rivalries on the one hand and competitive manufactures on the other, and by the turn of the century Victorian ideas of security were as antiquated as the Victorian social and economic structure. After

1902 the government that had gloried in splendid isolation began the flight from it. The reasons undercut partisan politics, and radicals later continued what conservatives had started.

The parallel domestic crisis brought no such agreement. Chamberlain and his followers advanced the panacea of protection. The Tories parted company with them and reverted to the perennial role of defending a dead status quo. The Liberals remained as conservative as the Tories on the tariff issue, and became full-fledged radicals in social policy. Their program swept the polls in the "parliamentary revolution" of 1906, which was followed by eight years of revolution by statute. During those years the nation was absorbed with its internal quarrels, while in foreign policy the Liberals were leading it unwittingly but inexorably toward war. By the time the storm broke in 1914 the Britain of the *Pax Britannica* was like the peace itself, only a memory.

Chapter Seven

GEORGIAN BRITAIN

1906–1932

I The Socialist Experiment

THE NEW Liberalism had eight busy years before war engulfed it. The same three themes of the earlier period — reform, Ireland, and foreign affairs — continued throughout the Liberal ascendancy. First radical social legislation produced financial difficulties, which led in turn to the greatest constitutional upheaval since 1832. Next, before the dust had settled, Ireland was in a crisis that threatened civil war. Then the crisis was postponed, but not resolved, by the advent of a greater war. Meanwhile Britain's diplomacy had developed largely in the background; after 1906 its principles were rarely a partisan issue, and their implications, discussed behind closed doors in Whitehall, were not apparent to the public at large until August 1914.

The general election of 1906 was an unprecedented landslide: the Liberal Party acquired a large majority in the commons, and could usually rely as well on the support of the Irish and Labour members. In domestic policy the party leaders rode roughshod over the Conservative opposition, until they had legislated a startling social program and reshaped the constitution. By the time they tackled the Irish problem they had dissipated their majority, and partisan rancor had become dangerously acute.

The first spate of reform legislation, in the years 1906–9, was impressive in scope. Parliament reformed itself by providing salaries for members of the House of Commons, which thereby ceased to be a rich man's club; it freed the trade unions from liability for strike damages and permitted them to use their funds in politics. It regulated hours and conditions of labor, universalized the principle of workmen's compensation, established a national network of labor exchanges, grappled with slum clearance and state care of children, and inaugurated old-age pensions as a first installment of social security; simultaneously it interfered with the system of land tenure in order to encourage peasant proprietorship. This cataract of change, unloosed by the party once dedicated to laissez faire, had two immediate effects. It created conflict between the Houses of Parliament, and it placed a heavy burden on the Exchequer.

The House of Lords, like the Supreme Court in the United States, tends to acquire the political color of a party long in power, and to change slowly after a change of administration. In 1906 the peerage was a motley assortment, ranging from the old landed families to plutocrats recently ennobled for contributing to Conservative party funds. But most of the peers agreed in opposing increased state activities and the concomitant increase in taxation. The Upper House was consequently the instrument of the Conservatives.

The situation was analogous to that produced thirty years later in the United States by the attitude of the Supreme Court. The Liberal government, like the New Deal, struggled against an unelective body that it could not control. The lords were circumspect; they knew from the experience of 1832 that on a major issue they could not defy the will of the commons backed by the electorate. But their legislative veto was far from defunct, and they were in the habit of pruning bills to their taste. They had often halted Gladstone on minor points, and had climaxed their recalcitrance by throwing out his second Home Rule Bill amid widespread applause. Now they were applying the same tactics to the new liberalism, amending and delaying until they had the chance of a real blow, and their obstruction was angering an impatient cabinet.

The financial problem was as disturbing as the constitutional. Almost every change in the statute book required an increased bureaucracy to supervise it, and measures such as old-age pensions were a direct drain on the Treasury; further drains came from the attempt to pay off the costs of the Boer War and from increased naval construction. A developing struggle for priority brought out the divergence inherent in any government that faces, Janus-like, inward and outward simultaneously: domestic reformers insisted on spending the bulk of available funds for social welfare, while the protagonists of a strong foreign policy insisted on spending the bulk for armaments. The two groups could not collaborate smoothly unless the revenues were greatly increased.

The same problem had afflicted the Conservative administration. Tariffs had been Chamberlain's solution, and with them he might have redeemed his promise of reform; without them the Conservative government had largely ignored reform for a strong line overseas. The Liberals, committed to free trade, reform, and armaments, had no alternative to heavy direct taxation. Their budgets soon indicated that they were going to kill two birds with one stone — to cover rising expenses and to redistribute the wealth of the country. The brunt of taxation fell on unearned income and accumulated fortunes, to make the rich pay for ameliorating the lot of the poor. The House of Lords was the house of the rich, and its opposition to the Liberal program was sharpened by fear.

In 1908 the most formidable of the left-wing Liberals became Chancellor of the Exchequer. David Lloyd George was a dynamic Welshman with a mind as acute as any in Europe, and the tide of reform carried him into the position where his acuteness was most dangerous to privilege. In 1909 he introduced a revolutionary budget. It further increased the taxes on great wealth, and was designed to break up the large estates that were still the hallmark of the landed interest. As if to goad the peers still further, the substance of several reforms they had already rejected was included in the bill embodying the budget. This was far more than partisan politics. It was class warfare against the aristocracy and its House, waged by a government confident of its popular mandate. The peers had helped to precipitate the battle, and they accepted it. When the bill came before them, they mustered the courage of desperation and threw it out.

Courage was required because they were on shaky ground. They had long lost their right to initiate or amend a money bill, and for almost half a century had not vetoed one; a veto would paralyze administration. Even the hardiest peers were not ready to defy a cabinet supported by the voters. The Conservatives did claim, however, that they were entitled to force the cabinet to make sure of its support. The purpose of a second chamber was to be a brake on an overhasty House of Commons, they argued, and to prevent major changes of policy upon which the electorate had not been consulted; if the Liberals chose to disguise a social revolution as a finance bill, the Upper House was justified in reasserting its veto power as the only way to force the government to dissolve and seek a specific mandate from the voters.

The government took up the challenge, and was returned early in 1910 with the slimmest of majorities. Liberals and Conservatives were now so evenly balanced that the Labour and Irish members were of key importance. Both groups sided with the Liberals, one because of what had been done and was promised for labor, the other because the lords were still adamant against Home Rule. With this reduced and ill-assorted following the cabinet advanced confidently to the attack. As a result of the election the lords accepted the budget, but they had now precipitated the constitutional issue. A bill was brought in to curb their veto power. They rejected it. For the second time within a year the Liberals appealed to a sorely confused electorate, and they were returned with the same meager majority as before. This time the Upper House refused to give way.

Meanwhile King Edward had died. His son, George V, took the crown at a moment of boiling crisis. The Conservatives insisted that the nation had not pronounced decisively. The Liberals insisted that it had. Their position was strong because they and their allies could carry on the government, whereas their opponents could not. The new King consented to create the necessary number of peers to pass the bill — some four hundred, who would have swamped the aristocracy with titled Liberal nobodies. Before this threat, at once social and constitutional, the lords capitulated. In 1911 the Parliament Bill became law: the Upper House lost all control over whatever was certified by the speaker of the House of Commons as a money bill, and retained only a two-year suspensive veto over other legislation. The flood of reform could no longer be effectively dammed.

Lloyd George used the opportunity to push through a far-reaching scheme of social insurance. Old-age pensions were supplemented by health insurance for all wage-earners, and the attempt was begun on a small scale to insure against unemployment. Such state socialism, largely financed by taxation of the rich, aroused bitter controversy. But it was nothing to the storm raised by the next step. In the spring of 1912 the government introduced the third Home Rule Bill.

For six years the Liberals had almost ignored their old commitment to Ireland. They had wished to enact their domestic program before tackling the issue that had once before destroyed their party, and the House of Lords would never have accepted Home Rule. Until 1910 the Irish had been in no position to prod the cabinet, but thereafter they and the Labour Party held the balance of power. The Parliament Bill could scarcely have passed the Commons without their support. The Home Rule Bill was their reward, and the curbing of the lords' veto seemed to remove the last obstacle.

The Conservatives were frantic with alarm and frustration. They had been defeated on every major issue, and their constitutional fortress had been sacked; they felt that the nation was being destroyed by its own government. They were equally disturbed by the danger from without. Europe was already under the shadow of a war from which Britain had little chance of holding aloof, and the project of Irish autonomy struck them as bordering on lunacy or treason. They fought it as the last hope of unseating the government before it subverted both social order and national security.

But what could they do? The lords' veto was a broken reed, and the Liberals had the votes to force through Home Rule within two years; legal resistance was hopeless. But an illegal method soon appeared: Ulster prepared to fight. By the spring of 1914 a hundred thousand volunteers were enrolled, a provisional government was being organized, and officers in the British regular army — among them the chief of staff — were making it clear that they would not serve against the Ulstermen. The Conservatives fanned the flame. They asserted that the cabinet was violating the spirit of the constitution by legislating Home Rule without consulting the voters, and a group of prominent men declared publicly that they would hold themselves free, if the bill was passed, to take "any action that may be effective to prevent it being put into operation." This was close to treason, and it meant that the impending civil war would not be confined to Ireland. Ulster was ready to rebel, British Conservatives were ready to support rebellion, and the army was not ready to suppress it.

Feverish negotiations got nowhere, for neither side could compromise. The Ulster leaders had sown the wind and were caught in the whirlwind; they dared not moderate their demands lest their followers desert them. The Home Rule leaders in the south knew that they must triumph or give place to the extremists. The cabinet was too deeply committed to turn back half way, particularly when the cause of Ulster was linked with embattled privilege at home. The Conservatives were determined to use the Irish issue to win public opinion and avert the disaster they foresaw. The cleavage in the British political world was deeper even than in 1886, for this time it involved fundamentals of both domestic and foreign policy.

In 1914 the third Home Rule Bill was finally pushed through, just when the European crisis was becoming desperate. Irish affairs were once more, as in the days of the Directory, a factor in diplomatic calculations, and in Berlin the hope grew that Britain's troubles would immobilize her. How could a government faced by a civil war dare to gamble on a foreign one? The question was reasonable, but it ignored the extraordinary blend of stolidity and romanticism in the British character. By September 1914 the public had forgotten the Irish for the Belgians, the Home Rule Bill was suspended for the duration of the war, and Conservatives were at one with Liberals. Underneath the vociferous passions of the previous eight years was a core of unity.

II The Road to War

BRITAIN'S intervention in Europe in 1914 was the outgrowth of the uncompleted diplomatic revolution that the Liberals inherited from the Conservatives. By 1906 the Entente Cordiale was evolving, thanks to the Moroccan crisis, from a negative settlement of differences into positive collaboration. But France had to walk warily for fear of alienating her one ally, Russia, who was still at loggerheads with Britain. If the entente was to become truly cordial and the policy that it represented was to be fully developed, Britain had to come to terms with Russia.

The Liberal government was more open to this idea than its predecessor had been. The Gladstonian tradition, unlike the Disraelian, was largely free of Russophobia, and diplomacy by negotiation had been Gladstone's forte. The Conservatives had borrowed a leaf from his book in concluding the entente, and the Liberals were anxious to go further. The pacifists among them dreaded all crises, and the imperialists wished to safeguard the empire against the rising German menace. To both groups an accord with Russia was attractive.

The Russian government also was interested. It had recently experienced a disastrous defeat by Japan, followed by an abortive revolution at home, and the Czar's ministers were convinced that the Romanoff regime could be bolstered only by success abroad. Their interest turned away from Manchuria and Afghanistan back to the Balkans; there they confronted the Austro-German drive, which began to bulk larger in their calculations than the old rivalry with Britain. In these circumstances Anglo-Russian negotiations were opened, and in 1907 they bore fruit in an agreement whereby the two powers defined their respective rights and spheres of influence in Thibet, Afghanistan, and Persia. On the surface this was a minor accord, but it had major implications.

The cardinal question it raised was about the Ottoman Empire. After more than eighty years of a Turkish policy that precluded real agreement with Russia, Britain suddenly came to terms with her. The terms made no mention of the Porte, but their crucial test was there. Did they mean that the *Drang nach Osten* was forcing Britain to abandon her traditional role as watchdog of the straits? If so, the cause for which she had fought in 1854 and been ready to fight in 1878, and the virtual protectorate she had assumed over Asia Minor, would all go by the board; the Turks would be alienated and might be driven into dependence on Germany; Russia's Balkan ambitions would be encouraged at a time when they were already threatening the peace of Europe. These were some of the potentialities in Anglo-Russian collaboration.

Britain had to risk them. She was even less minded to commit herself to Russia than to France, but Russian designs no longer governed her diplomacy. German pressure — in Africa, Constantinople, the North Sea — was becoming the focus of her calculations. Older and deeper than her interest in the straits was her interest in preventing a single power from obtaining the hegemony of Europe. To this central concern her Foreign Office, when pressed, sacrificed some of its firmly established concepts. The Germany of William II was looming over the Continent like the France of Louis XIV, and with a similar effect. Britain was drawing toward France and Russia, as she had drawn toward the Netherlands long before, because her lesser enmities were overshadowed by a greater one.

The Anglo-Russian agreement extended the Entente Cordiale into the Triple Entente. In 1907, as in 1904, no one knew what the new phrase meant, and uncertainty again contributed to a crisis. In 1908 the Young Turk revolution disrupted the Ottoman state, and Austria-Hungary seized the opportunity to annex the provinces of Bosnia and Herzegovina, which she had administered since 1878. Russia demanded, in return, the right of passage for her warships through the Dardanelles. Britain made it plain that she would not be drawn into the quarrel; she protested both Austria's action and Russia's demand. Berlin, on the other hand, supported Vienna wholeheartedly, and Russia had to capitulate without compensation.

This Balkan crisis, like that of thirty years before, brought Europe to the brink of war, but it did not produce even a temporary settlement. Instead it touched off the powder-train that led to the explosion of 1914. Austria violated the Treaty of Berlin and flouted what was left of the public law of Europe. Germany, in supporting her, showed that what she considered her encirclement by the Triple Entente only increased her belligerence. But the effect in the Balkans was the most important. There a situation was developing, thanks in great part to the annexation of Bosnia, that soon defied settlement by peaceful means.

Both Russian and Austro-German imperialism operated largely through influence in the Balkan capitals. The small states were not puppets, but each looked in some measure to the support of Vienna or St. Petersburg. Austria's particular protégé was Bulgaria; Russia's was Serbia. For years the Serbs had dreamed of including Bosnia-Herzegovina in a great kingdom of the southern Slavs, ruled from Belgrade; once the provinces were incorporated into the Hapsburg Empire, their liberation and consequently the destruction of the empire itself became the goal of Serbian nationalists. To the Austrian government that goal appeared steadily more dangerous as Russia's concern for Serbia increased, and in high circles at Vienna the idea gained ground that the preservation of the empire depended on crushing Serb agitation once and for all.

The attitude of Russia was equally dangerous. As she turned toward the West, she began to consider herself the protector of all the Slavic peoples; this sense of her mission was the one active, popular principle of an otherwise inert autocracy. The Serbs were the test of her intentions. If she abandoned them, she would abandon the Balkans and the old dream of controlling the straits; the Czar's ministers feared that such a retreat would tear the last shred of prestige from the dynasty. They were playing for high stakes. After they lost once in the Bosnian crisis, they dared not lose again. Both the Romanoff and Hapsburg governments, in short, were growing desperate because each was convinced that the alternative to a Balkan triumph was disintegration at home.

The attitude of Britain was far from clear. The entente had certainly not won her support for Russia in the Balkans as it had for France in Morocco; even the Liberals had adhered to tradition in refusing to countenance the opening of the straits. But the bases of tradition were crumbling. The Young Turks came increasingly under the influence of Berlin, until from the point of view of London their empire was less a barrier against the Russians than a highway for the Germans. If Russian influence were now eliminated from the Balkans, the *Drang nach Osten* might penetrate to Suez and the Persian Gulf. This was a fantastic reversal, to which Britain could not fully accommodate her diplomacy — in part because her Russophobe traditions were too strong, but primarily because her central purpose was to prevent the Balkan problem from precipitating a general war. She consequently dared not let Russia feel confident of her support, and at the same time dared not alienate her too far. As yet the Anglo-Russian entente was scarcely cordial.

The annexation of Bosnia generated further crises. Italy, not to be outdone in looting the Sultan's possessions, invaded Tripoli. While the Ottoman Empire was thus engaged in Africa, the Balkan states joined forces to partition its holdings in Europe. They won their war, then fought each other over the spoils. The upshot was that Bulgaria and the Ottoman Empire, the two centers of Austro-German influence, were eclipsed in defeat, and that Serbia, Russia's protégé, almost doubled her territory. The *Drang nach Osten* received a serious reverse; the elated Serbs turned to their designs on Bosnia, and the Austrian government grew intensely alarmed. The Balkans were a magazine with enough explosives to blow the Continent apart.

Britain might remain noncommittal, but she was within range and could not escape an explosion. She was becoming more and more firmly tied to France, Russia's ally. Germany seemed determined to complete this Anglo-French rapprochement: she was pursuing the naval race despite British efforts to curb it by agreement, and was widening the Kiel Canal to accommodate her latest battleships; at the same time she was hastening to increase her army, and was still pressing her designs upon Morocco. She thereby alarmed both Britain and France, and their common fears pulled them closer.

The German plan of campaign, if war came, was known in general outline. It was as disturbing to the British Foreign Office as to the French general staff, because it involved the invasion of Belgium. The reason was not one of politics but of military geography. The formation of the Dual Alliance had confronted German strategists with the problem of war on two fronts, and their solution was to destroy the French armies before the slow power of Russia could be mobilized on the east. The need for a quick victory over France precluded attacking her hilly and fortified eastern frontier, and dictated an invasion of the northeastern lowlands by way of Belgium. The design for this movement, sketched in 1905 by the German chief of staff, Count Schlieffen, provided for a concentration on the German right wing, which would swing into northeastern France like an opening door with its hinge at Metz, and push the French armies before it southward and southeastward until they were crushed against their own border fortresses. The crux of the plan was the attack through Belgium. In 1839 Prussia had been one of the powers that had guaranteed Belgian independence and neutrality, and Germany had inherited the obligation. Now, under the plea of strategic necessity, she was preparing to violate it.

Britain's concern was more than traditional. Although she was the particular guarantor of Belgium, she had not always been ready to honor her commitment. In 1914 she was, because it touched her fundamental interests. If she opposed the expansion of German sea power in Morocco, she had infinitely more reason to oppose it on the Channel coast. The defense of Belgium, furthermore, was the defense of France, and a French defeat would leave the islanders alone against a triumphant and pugnacious Germany. By coming to terms with one side and not with the other Britain had involved herself. The fact that the involvement was largely unintended and even more largely unrecognized deepened the anomaly of her position.

The Liberals were determined to do all in their power to avoid war, from which Britain had little to gain and much to lose. She had no Balkan protégé to lure her on, no Serbia to crush in self-defense, no Alsace-Lorraine to reconquer, no ring of hostile powers denying her a place in the sun. Her principal motive for fighting was the defense of what she had, and war, particularly for a government in the thick of domestic reforms, would be an unmitigated calamity. Britain had two possible ways of avoiding it: to commit herself publicly and explicitly to the Dual Alliance; or to retain her freedom of action until the crisis arrived. Both courses were dangerous.

A formal commitment might deter Germany and Austria from provoking a crisis. Again, it might not. The Germans already felt themselves blocked in Africa by British sea power, in America by the willingness of the United States to fight for the Monroe Doctrine, in Asia by the Anglo-Japanese alliance; the Balkans and Near East were the only outlet left them, and they might react violently to a fresh proof of what they called encirclement. The French and Russians, for their part, might be encouraged to greater belligerence by a British guarantee. Public and Parliament at home, intent on domestic issues, could scarcely be educated to such a complete reversal of the isolationist tradition without a propaganda campaign, which would defeat its object by heating the international atmosphere. For all these reasons the government dared not formalize the Triple Entente.

Retaining complete freedom of action would increase Britain's chances of mediating a crisis, but it also involved great risks for her. One was diplomatic: uncertainty about her position might hearten both sides to gamble on a war, as it had the Sultan and the Czar in 1853. Another and greater risk was military: because British intervention could not be improvised after the outbreak of war, it had to be concerted in advance with the French and, if possible, with the Belgians in order to stop the expected German avalanche. Advance military preparations were obviously inconsistent with a noncommittal foreign policy. Diplomatic factors were pulling the cabinet in one direction, strategic factors in the other.

The result was an extraordinary division of policy. While the Foreign Office maintained Britain's freedom of action, the Admiralty and War Office took steps that effectively bound her to France. Anglo-French staff conversations had begun at the time of the first

Moroccan crisis. When they revealed that the British army was unprepared to act on the Continent, it was reorganized into a small
but supremely efficient expeditionary force ready to be transported
across the Channel; the French naturally made plans to receive it
and deploy it with their armies. Meanwhile the French and British
Admiralties reached an agreement in 1912, whereby the French
moved the bulk of their fleet to the Mediterranean and the British
denuded their squadrons there for a further concentration in home
waters. Thenceforth the fate of France, if war came, depended in
large measure on Britain. If the Royal Navy did not guard the
French Channel coast, it would be open to a German attack from
the sea; if the British army did not promptly take its assigned position, the French would have to revise their defensive at the last
minute and with inferior numbers. Yet Britain had no formal
commitment.

The scale of the military preparations was unknown to the public. Some steps had been revealed, such as the naval agreement, but
their implications were almost universally ignored in the excitement of the domestic crisis. When the storm clouds suddenly gathered over Europe, the leaders of the cabinet were in a quandary.
They had not taken into their confidence all their official colleagues,
let alone the House of Commons, and they had certainly used a freer
hand in dealing with France than comported with a strict interpretation of responsible government. They could not give a categorical
warning to Germany, or assurance to France, without first securing
the support of Parliament — at the cost of revelations that would
have been highly embarrassing and inexpedient to make. Only the
Germans could resolve the dilemma. If their invasion of Belgium
aroused British public opinion, the cabinet would have the backing
it needed and could move in time on the preconcerted lines. If not,
the prospect was too dark to contemplate.

At the end of June 1914 the British heard that the heir apparent
to the Hapsburg Empire had been assassinated in Sarajevo, the Bosnian capital. The news seemed trivial by comparison with that from
Ireland, but the European powder-train was burning in the magazine. The Austrian authorities learned that the murder had been assisted, if not planned, in Serbia, and they suspected complicity in the
Belgrade government. This was the opportunity for which they had
long been waiting, and in dealing with it they seemed likely to have

a free hand. The crime shocked the Kaiser into promising full support; Russia was gripped by serious strikes, the President and Premier of France were at sea returning from a visit to St. Petersburg,
and Britain was menaced by civil war. On July 23 the Austrian government delivered a two-day ultimatum to Belgrade. Its acceptance
would have eliminated Serbian independence.

This sudden assault on the peace took the chancelleries of Europe
by surprise. They woke to fevered activity. The British Foreign Secretary, Sir Edward Grey, took the lead in pleading for time and mediation. Austria refused to wait, although Germany was by now endeavoring to restrain her. On the 25th Serbia, under pressure from
the Triple Entente, accepted most of the ultimatum and offered to
refer the rest to arbitration. But her soft answer failed to turn away
wrath. On the 28th she received the Austrian declaration of war.

Not even the Austrians desired a general war. They hoped that
the Austro-German combine would again immobilize Russia as it
had done in 1908. But they were ready to take any risk in order to
destroy the Serbian threat to their empire. Germany, once she had
endorsed their gamble, surrendered the initiative to them; she could
not control them and dared not repudiate them if Russia moved.
Russia, in turn, dared not face the humiliation of being excluded
from the Balkans, for the autocracy might not survive the shock. In
response to the Austrian declaration against Serbia the Czar, after
agonizing indecision and under intense pressure from the military,
ordered general mobilization. The die was cast.

The inexorable military machine now superseded the improvisa-
tions of diplomacy. Warfare had reached the point where a short
head start in mobilization might be decisive, and no power could
wait on diplomats after its opponent had begun to mobilize. The
German ability to concentrate faster than the Russians made possible the Schlieffen Plan; if Russia meant war, the German general
staff begrudged every hour wasted on negotiation. Berlin consequently resumed the initiative. On August 1 Germany declared war
on Russia, and the next day demanded of Belgium free passage for
the German armies; it was refused. On the 3rd she declared war on
France.

The British public was bewildered. But in the maelstrom of developments one fact was clear: King Albert of the Belgians had
called upon King George for help in resisting the Germans, who

were already pouring across the Belgian frontier. The British people neither knew nor cared about the strategic imperative behind the Schlieffen Plan. They were shocked at the assault on an unoffending state that Germany was pledged to defend, and their political mood veered. Conservatives closed ranks with Liberals, Ulsterites, and even Home Rulers. Several members of the cabinet resigned rather than approve the ultimatum to Berlin — which was sent on August 4 and expired unanswered at midnight — but the government had behind it a solidly united nation. The bitterest partisan strife in modern British history was transmuted into singleness of will.

The causes of this transmutation went back for years. When Germany had begun to achieve hegemony in Europe, her concepts of power had been temporarily emulated in Britain. But by the turn of the century their appeal had faded. Thereafter the public had grown increasingly alarmed as German militarism had taken to the sea, increasingly angry as German bullying had troubled the peace with crisis after crisis, and the attack on Belgium brought this popular feeling into focus. It scoured away factionalism for a time, somewhat as the feeling against James and Louis XIV had scoured away the blood feuds of Whigs and Tories. The British rallied to what they considered the old cause of resisting aggression, and their mood was all the more fervent for the rancor it superseded.

> Honour has come back, as a king, to earth,
> And paid his subjects with a royal wage;
> And Nobleness walks in our ways again;
> And we have come into our heritage.[1]

III   From Blitzkrieg to Deadlock

IN this exalted mood Britain embarked on the struggle for which the government had been preparing her. She assumed, like her allies and her enemies, that the war would be bitter but brief, and for such a war she was more nearly ready than ever before in her history. The Royal Navy, thanks to the efforts of the Foreign Office, had been able to mass almost nine-tenths of its strength in home waters. Its base had been shifted from the Channel to the Firth of

---

[1] Rupert Brooke: "The Dead," I. Reprinted by permission of Dodd, Mead & Company, Inc., from *The Collected Poems of Rupert Brooke*, copyright, 1915, by Dodd, Mead & Company.

Forth and the Orkneys to command the North Sea, and the First Lord of the Admiralty, Winston Churchill, had made sure that the Grand Fleet was ready. Under its cover the regular army was transported to France quickly and without loss, and took its prepared position on the left of the French. The allies moved into Belgium to meet the German assault.

There rude surprises awaited them. They were not given the time for which they had hoped because the Belgian border fortresses crumbled. The Germans had half a million more men than expected, and their advance was irresistible. The Belgian army was brushed aside. The British were torn loose from their hold on the coast and swept southward to the defense of Paris. The French line swung down, hinging west of Metz, until it was level with Paris in the basin of the River Marne. But its commander, General Joffre, stood imperturbable; he massed his reserves and waited his chance. The Germans began to outrun their communications, and their headquarters in Luxembourg lost touch with the unrolling battle; troops were detached to bolster the eastern front, where the Russians, although still unready, were advancing with reckless gallantry. When Joffre launched his counterattack, the Germans were halted. They retired and entrenched themselves, and the allies could not budge them. Each side then tried to outflank the other, but succeeded only in prolonging the front northward until it reached the sea in the westernmost corner of Belgium. There the Germans tried to break through the British army to the Channel ports of Calais and Boulogne. When the drive collapsed in the spring of 1915, the front became stabilized in a line of trenches from the North Sea to the Swiss frontier. Blitzkrieg had failed.

Its failure blasted the plans of both sides. The Prussian victories of 1866 and 1870 had blinded Europe's strategists to the suggestive deadlock of the American Civil War, and the subsequent improvement of weapons and communications had convinced them that a quick military decision was inevitable. Kitchener, now Secretary for War, was almost alone in his belief that the struggle might last for three years; the public at large, and even his own department, were sure that his idea was fantastic. It had to be. How could Europe, in the conditions of the twentieth century, endure such a protracted ordeal? The answer — that it could not, and remain the Europe men knew — was as repellent to the soldier as to the civilian, and was instinctively rejected. But the halting of the Germans at the Marne and the subsequent stabilization of the line ended the warfare of maneuver, the soldiers' only method of forcing a quick decision. On the Eastern Front also, in spite of staggering Russian defeats at the outset, the line was stabilized by the close of the year. A wholly different kind of war was beginning. No one had expected it or prepared for it. No one had a way to win it quickly. No one understood how to wage it except by squandering blood.

The essence of trench warfare was the superiority of defense over attack. The defenders had enormous fire power, thanks to the improvement in rifles and artillery and, above all, to the machine gun; they had barbed wire to preclude surprise; they had dugouts from which only an extravagant barrage would move them, and more dugouts to which to retire. Their position could not be turned, for neither the Eastern nor the Western Front had vulnerable flanks. Frontal assault was the sole way to decide the war by military means, and the available means were insufficient.

The generals of both sides refused to admit the insufficiency. They had been trained on the doctrine of the offensive, and offensives they would have. When one failed, they improved their techniques for the next, always hoping and planning for the breakthrough that never came. The cost in matériel and in human life rose to astronomical proportions; still the experiments went on. But battle was no longer the decisive factor. Europe was locked in gigantic siege operations, in which victory would come by the attrition of manpower, industrial resources, food supplies, and morale, rather than by generalship.

In Britain the demand for manpower had revolutionary effects. When the government had committed the regular army to the Western Front, it had embarked on a policy from which there was no turning back. By the spring of 1915 the regulars, as a fighting force, had ceased to exist.

> These, in the day when heaven was falling,
>   The hour when earth's foundation fled,
> Followed their mercenary calling
>   And took their wages and are dead.[2]

---

[2] A. E. Housman: "Epitaph on an Army of Mercenaries." From *Last Poems* by A. E. Housman. Copyright, 1922, by Henry Holt and Company, Inc.

The nation had to replace the initial force of a hundred thousand with armies of a million and more. For such a staggering total voluntary recruitment was inadequate and unwise, but it was maintained for a year and a half. In that time the energetic and adventurous in all walks of life, from the mine and factory to the country house, went into uniform and left the home front to look after itself. Much of the cream of Britain's manhood was skimmed off and poured into the French and Flemish earth.

Early in 1916 the government at last succeeded in introducing effective conscription. This step was a turning point in Britain's history. For the first time she was compelled to use all her resources, not only financial and industrial and naval power, but manpower as well. Although the dominions gave her impressive support, it was of secondary importance; 65% of the imperial armies came from Great Britain, and 80% of the casualties were hers — roughly two and a half million out of a population of less than fifty million. Since the days of Chatham her traditional strategy had served her well, but it no longer served. She had entered the struggle essentially because she did not dare to stand alone; by the same token she dared not permit her Continental allies to be overwhelmed, as they had been time after time in the wars against Napoleon, and she therefore had to participate to the full in the greatest land war yet known. Conscription was her badge of commitment.

The leaders of the government did not accept meekly the need for pouring more and more blood into the Western Front. They were handicapped, like any democratic administration in wartime, by the enhanced reputation of the military; civilians rarely dare to override the admirals and generals, who are experts with a great hold on public confidence. Two cabinet members, nevertheless, had the courage and imagination to interfere in the conduct of the war, and both played major roles. One was Winston Churchill, the other Lloyd George.

Churchill was a born strategist. By the end of 1914 he realized that the situation in the West was a stalemate, and that it would take hundreds of thousands of casualties to drive home the truth to the generals. He saw two possible solutions, either to by-pass the Western Front by attacking elsewhere or to find new tactical methods for breaking the stalemate. His restless mind explored both paths. The first led him into a disaster, the second to a development that changed the character of warfare.

The need for a diversion from the Western Front arose in the autumn of 1914, when the Ottoman Empire allied itself with Germany and Austria. The principal reason for this step was the Russo-British rapprochement, which convinced the Young Turks that their only hope lay in a German victory. The principal effect was to isolate the Western allies from Russia. Their only remaining contact with her armies was by sea, either around Scandinavia or across the Pacific and the Transsiberian Railroad. Russia's industrial resources could not begin to meet her requirements, and she was soon desperately short of supplies. Unless Britain and France broke through to her, she could not keep up the fight for long.

This was the problem Churchill attacked. He found a bold solution, that the navy should fight its way through the straits to Constantinople, knock the Turks out of the war, open a Balkan flank, and link the Eastern with the Western Front. He overrode the opposition of his First Sea Lord and gained the consent of the cabinet for the gamble. Britain, after a century of guarding the straits against Russia, was now trying to open them for her.

The expedition was appallingly mismanaged. Early in 1915 a Franco-British naval force was driven back from the Dardanelles with heavy losses. An army, predominantly of Australians and New Zealanders, was then sent to open the straits by seizing the peninsula of Gallipoli. The troops met a blistering reception. Throughout the summer and autumn they clung to their beachheads, and in the winter they were evacuated. Meanwhile the Serbs had been overwhelmed, and the central powers reigned supreme in the Balkans. The attempt to turn their position had failed disastrously.

The failure cost Churchill his position at the Admiralty. Before he resigned, however, he initiated one of the major experiments of the war. He believed that the deadlock in the west could be broken not by sending men, as he put it, "to chew barbed wire," but by a vehicle that would carry them through it and protect them from the machine gun. The vehicle was the tank. When the War Office was sceptical of its possibilities, he nourished experimentation with Admiralty funds. The process of development was slow, and the enlightenment of the military mind was slower. Not until the autumn of 1917 did tanks achieve the breakthrough for which they were designed, and then the opportunity was wasted because it had not been foreseen. Exploitation of the new weapon demanded mass production, a different system of tactics, and re-education of the high command, requirements that had not been fully met by the time the fighting ended. Yet the tank was the one great tactical innovation of the war, because it restored the possibility of surprise and maneuver. The Germans grasped this possibility, and in the next twenty years they built a new kind of warfare upon it. Churchill in 1940 had cause to regret the weapon he had fathered in 1915.

His resignation, under the cloud of the Dardanelles disaster, left Lloyd George as the most forceful figure in the cabinet. The fiery Welshman was less disposed to direct interference with the military, but he was beginning to realize how much they underestimated the magnitude of their problem. In the spring of 1915 he became Minister of Munitions and set himself to remedy the desperate shortage of supplies, particularly of shells, that faced the army in France. His task was staggering. British industry was wholly unprepared for the demands upon it; the French were of little immediate help because the bulk of their manufacturing plant, most of their coal, and practically all their iron mines were in German hands; the munitions output of the United States grew slowly. Lloyd George performed prodigies, however, and he was assisted by a tightening of governmental control over labor and management such as even socialists had not thought possible. By 1916 he had weathered the worst of the crisis.

He was then involved in a political crisis. Soon after the beginning of the war the Conservatives had forced their way into the government, but the coalition cabinet was unwieldy. Control of the war effort devolved upon a small committee in which Lloyd George was the real force, and at the end of 1916 he became Prime Minister. The executive was immediately reorganized. The committee became a cabinet of five, with whom final decisions rested; most department heads were relegated to subordinate rank as ministers. Under this centralized authority, animated by the ferocious energy of the Premier, the nation was regimented as never before and responded with a will.

The most important aspect of the stalemate on land, from the British viewpoint, was that it brought sea power into its own. Until late in the war Britain's advantage of mobility was little used, except for the Gallipoli fiasco; the French and British generals were interested only in the Western Front, and Lloyd George could not overrule them. But in other ways sea power was crucial from the beginning. It helped to induce Italy, with her vulnerable coasts and dependence on water-borne imports, to desert the Triple Alliance and join the Western powers, whose hold on the Mediterranean then became incontestable. Japan insisted on honoring her alliance, in order to further her own Far Eastern interests, and she helped to sweep German warships from the Pacific. The oceans of the world were highways for the allies.

Britain's naval effort was focused on the Channel and the North Sea, where she established her blockade of the Central Powers. Blockade was a stronger weapon than when she had last used it against Napoleon, thanks to the development of steam power and wireless, but its application was retarded for a time by the insistence of the United States on her right to trade with neutrals. Through the ports of Scandinavia and the Netherlands, Germany received quantities of American goods, and the flow was not entirely shut off until the United States entered the war. Yet Britain checked it more and more as she became more confident of American sympathy for her cause, and the Central Powers were gradually thrown back upon their own dwindling reserves.

The effect was to drive Germany to a counterattack that completed the alienation of the United States. The great advantage of the submarine was that it could by-pass superior sea power to establish a blockade of its own, by which Germany hoped to circumvent the deadlock on land and do what Napoleon had failed to do, starve Britain into surrender. The great disadvantage of the submarine was not its illegality — for the British were just as cavalier about international law — but the character of its illegality. The U-boat was so vulnerable to surface attack that its effectiveness depended on sinking ships without warning or succor, whereas a British destroyer could herd a merchantman into port for the formalities of confiscation. The two procedures might be equally illegal, but in the eyes of the world the difference between them was that between murder and decorous robbery.

Early in 1916 the German U-boat campaign reached major proportions. It took its toll in American property and lives, and evoked stronger protests from Washington than Britain had ever received.

The climax came in April with a virtual American ultimatum, to which Germany responded with a conditional promise to safeguard noncombatants; for some months her campaign slackened. The reason was a change not of heart but of strategy. She was at last ready to use her battle fleet, and needed her submarines to support it.

She had paid a heavy price for her dreadnaughts. They had diverted money, men, and effort from the army, and they had been the greatest single factor in alienating Britain. The High Seas Fleet was far stronger than necessary to control the Baltic, and its only justification was to live up to its name — to bid for control of the North Sea. But for a year and a half it had played hide-and-seek with the British, and the few surface engagements had been at most drawn battles. In the spring of 1916 came a change of policy, produced by the stalemate on land and the growing pressure of blockade, the deterioration of civilian morale, the American protests at the U-boat campaign, and the promotion of a fighting admiral, Scheer, to command of the fleet. Scheer did not intend to engage the whole British fleet. He hoped to lure it out from its bases into ambuscades of submarines, and use his surface force to overwhelm a detachment before the remainder could arrive in support. If he succeeded, he might eliminate the British superiority in numbers — a ratio of roughly eight to five — and fight thereafter on equal terms.

At the end of May 1916 the entire High Seas Fleet ventured from port. It encountered the British advance guard under Admiral Beatty off the peninsula of Jutland; when Beatty was lured into contact with the main German line, Scheer was on the verge of the triumph he had planned. Suddenly, steaming to the rescue out of the mist, came the whole force of the British Grand Fleet under Admiral Jellicoe. The battle that ensued was unique both in scale and confusion. The contestants were shrouded first in fog, then in darkness, and their actions have since been shrouded in controversy. But certain facts are clear. Although the Germans were heavily outnumbered, Jellicoe refused to press his advantage in the face of the destroyer attacks with which they covered their retirement; the effectiveness of the torpedo was still unknown, and he dared not risk his battleships. The Germans fought brilliantly, and escaped in the night. Their ships proved almost unsinkable, their losses were only a fraction of those they inflicted, and with reason they claimed the victory. But they never repeated their experiment.

Jellicoe was the only man, as Churchill pointed out, who could have lost the war in an afternoon. He could have lost it, however, only by the most profligate squandering of his strength, which instead he hoarded like a miser. In doing so he helped to prolong the war. If Blake or Nelson had been in his place, British losses would have been appalling; but the German fleet, in all probability, would not have returned to port. In that case the British would have been able to mine Germany's coastal waters, attack her submarines almost at harbor mouth, enter the Baltic to cut off her trade with Sweden and, above all, to carry supplies to Russia and so postpone or perhaps avert the impending debacle in the East. "A victory," as Jervis had remarked before the Battle of Cape St. Vincent, "is very essential to England at this hour." But at Jutland victory slipped through her fingers.

The results were far-reaching for all the powers, including the United States. The battle convinced the German government that Britain's naval superiority could not be overcome in time to affect the issue. Germany was being slowly strangled by the blockade, and her only chance to break it was to concentrate her whole naval effort on submarines. The result would undoubtedly be war with the United States, it was argued on the Wilhelmstrasse, but what had Germany to lose? American bankers were floating the loans to finance allied purchases of the munitions that American factories were supplying. The German High Command calculated, quite accurately, that American armies could not be a significant factor in Europe for at least a year; within that time Germany would in any case have to win or lose. These arguments prevailed with the imperial government. In February 1917 it declared unrestricted submarine warfare on practically all ships in European waters, neutral or belligerent. President Wilson immediately severed diplomatic relations, and by April the United States was at war.

The American action has subsequently been explained in a number of ways. It has been laid, for example, to the superiority of allied over German propaganda, and alternatively to the growing American economic interest in allied victory. The first explanation deals in symptoms rather than causes. Allied propaganda was more effective because the allied position was more comprehensible to the American public. The German infatuation with power grew under the stress of war into a cry for world dominion or destruction, *Welt-*

macht oder Niedergang, and this developed frenzy was as shocking to the United States of the New Freedom as its earlier phase had been to Gladstonian Britain. No subtlety of German propaganda, furthermore, could disguise the fact that the Kaiser's armies had invaded the West, or that his submarines were actively murdering noncombatants, allied and neutral, while Britain was merely waiting for an enemy populace to starve. German ideas and conduct, in short, gave power to allied propaganda.

The economic explanation is less superficial but equally inadequate. American industrialists and bankers unquestionably had a stake in allied victory, for the British and French governments were their best customers. The stake was not acquired by choice, however; it was the product of British sea power. The control of the Atlantic by the Royal Navy kept the American markets open to one set of belligerents and closed to the other. The United States, in consequence, developed an economic interest in the cause of the allies.

Yet this was not her basic interest. The factors that created it created also a military involvement; the German submarine offensive was a threat not merely to her prosperity but to her security. She had grown, like the dominions, within the framework of the *Pax Britannica,* and had been able to afford isolation because the Royal Navy had been her buffer against European powers. At the opening of this century the British concentration on the North Sea had preforce stimulated American naval development: by 1914 the United States fleet had become superior to all others except the British, and the building program of 1916 envisaged equality with Britain. One major reason for this sudden expansion was the situation in Europe, where the submarine offensive threatened to destroy Great Britain. British sea power was a known and predictable force, which even in the imperialist orgy of the 1890's had not seriously threatened the United States. German sea power was another matter. If it became dominant in European waters, the United States would be confronted by a triumphant nation whose ill will she had richly earned by her aid to the allies, and whose ambition for *Weltmacht* was all too clear. By 1917 American security depended on Britain's survival, much as Britain's security by 1914 had depended on the survival of France.

President Wilson virtually ignored this factor of self-interest. His initial emphasis on international law and the freedom of the seas developed into a crusade to save the moral order; in this great enterprise the American people joined with an enthusiasm both genuine and temporary. The sight of a moral goal can be intoxicating, like the sight of power, but the reaction is likely to be painful. When the war was won and the world remained dangerous for democracy, most Americans denied the validity of the crusade and sought explanations for it. They seized on the myth of Machiavellian intriguers, munitions-makers and financiers; they largely ignored the economic realities and wholly ignored the strategic. Not until it was drawn into the second World War did the nation begin to suspect the nature of the forces that had drawn it into the first.

IV   Victory and Versailles

THE ENTRANCE of the United States in the spring of 1917 came when catastrophe was brewing in the East. Russia had suffered the greatest losses of all the combatants; she was starved for supplies, and the British showed no sign of breaking a road to her. Under the strain her social and political structure crumbled. In March the Czar abdicated. The provisional government attempted to continue the war while the country disintegrated in revolution and the Germans advanced. In November the communists seized power. They were pledged to peace at any price, and they paid their price in the Treaty of Brest-Litovsk; the Central Powers partitioned European Russia from the Baltic provinces to the Ukraine — an indication of what German victory would mean to the West.

Before the effects of Russia's collapse became apparent, her allies had fought and won their battle with the submarine. During most of 1917 the U-boat was the crucial problem of the war. Germany had prepared her campaign thoroughly, and its effects were devastating. Losses mounted to their peak in April, when Britain had only a six weeks' reserve of grain; roughly a quarter of the ships leaving her ports never returned. She was on the brink of destruction. Lloyd George for once overruled the professionals, and forced a reluctant Admiralty to adopt the convoy system. Simultaneously the United States threw in her resources: she sent destroyers to Europe, and began the intensive construction of merchantmen; her shipyards did as much to win the war as all her armies a year later. Convoys, new construction, and improved methods for detecting and attacking the

U-boats brought down the rate of loss, and by the spring of 1918 Germany's great gamble had patently failed.

Only one more chance remained to her. She was slowly but surely starving for raw materials and foodstuffs. The leaks in the blockade were plugged now that the American government had forgotten its solicitude about freedom of the seas, and the European maritime neutrals were rationed to pre-war quotas of imports; the territories that Germany had gained at Brest-Litovsk were too badly devastated to be of immediate use in feeding her. But her triumph in the East freed her armies, for the first time since the Marne, to concentrate against the West. Time was pressing. Her submarines could no longer hope to impede the flow of troops setting in across the Atlantic, and she had to strike before the Americans reached France in decisive force.

In the spring of 1918 the blow fell. The British were driven to the gates of Amiens, the French once more to the Marne, and the allied line was stretched to the breaking point. But it held, thanks in part to the Americans, who for the first time were heavily engaged. The gravity of the crisis frightened the allies into agreeing, after three and a half years, on a single commander in chief, and by summer Marshal Foch was ready to launch his counterattack. He had expended his French and British reserves in stemming the German tide, but he now had almost a million Americans and an ample supply of tanks. As he struck now here, now there, the enemy gave ground. German morale at the front and at home was disintegrating fast.

Simultaneously allied offensives exploded on other fronts. The Italians swept the Austrians back toward the Brenner Pass, while in the Balkans a Franco-British force advanced against the other flank of the Hapsburg Empire; British troops operating from Egypt overran Palestine with Arab assistance, and an Anglo-Indian army moved northward through Mesopotamia. The Central Powers were at the end of their tether, without supplies or hope. In October the Turks surrendered, and the Dual Monarchy disintegrated in nationalist revolutions. By November the German army and navy were mutinous; the Kaiser fled to Holland, and a provisional republican government signed an armistice with the allies. The Hohenzollern and Hapsburg regimes had gone the way of the Romanoff, through defeat to revolution.

The armistice terms, designed for the immediate military security of the West, bore the hallmarks of the British Admiralty and the French general staff. Germany surrendered almost the whole of her fleet, and its last voyage was to Scapa Flow, the British base in the Orkneys; such an unparalleled triumph seemed to banish Britain's anxieties of the past twenty years. The German armies abandoned all their conquests and withdrew from the entire left bank of the Rhine and from three bridgeheads on the right bank; allied occupation forces moved in. Germany remained helpless as long as the victors continued their watch on the Rhine, and her helplessness was security for France.

The ensuing peace congress, like the Congress of Vienna, produced bitter wrangling among the powers. Each of the three major victors had entered the war for reasons of its own, and each brought to the Paris Conference its own peculiar point of view. The United States had not fought for material gains or, consciously, in self-defense, but because she had been outraged by German ruthlessness. She had not endured an ordeal like Verdun or seen the shadow of starvation thrown by the U-boat, and she knew little about the impact of these experiences upon her allies. She was willing to assist in rebuilding a new and better Europe, but she lacked the concern and understanding to involve herself deeply in the task. France, on the contrary, had borne the brunt of the war in the West, and it had bled her white; defense against the Germans was a central thread of her history, as it was not of British or American, and she was determined to exploit her one great chance to safeguard herself. Britain's position was halfway between the other two. She and the dominions, unlike the United States, had a territorial objective: to acquire as much as possible of the German colonial empire. But toward Europe her attitude was similar to the American. She had entered the war essentially to protect the Continent against German hegemony and herself against a naval threat; the flight of the Kaiser, the collapse of his armies, and particularly the surrender of his fleet had left her almost carefree about the future. She and the United States had achieved their fundamental aims before the peace conference met. France had not.

The British and American delegations had common premises, and on many issues they saw eye to eye. President Wilson had awaked the idealism of a war-weary Europe, and when he reached

Paris his reputation probably stood higher than that of any man in modern history. His diplomacy had been gravely impaired, however, by the defeat of his party in the congressional elections of 1918; no one knew whether the American people would endorse or repudiate his work at Paris. Lloyd George's position was both stronger and less detached. At the close of hostilities he had fought and won a general election. On issues of immediate concern to the voters, such as German colonies and reparations, he fulfilled the election promise "to squeeze the orange till the pips squeak," but on territorial issues in Europe he held out for moderation. He realized that Britain's interests demanded, as in 1815, quick economic recovery on the Continent in order to re-establish markets, and he was as firmly opposed as Wilson to creating what he called new Alsace-Lorraines — areas lost but never forgotten by the vanquished. He therefore worked for a settlement that would leave Germany, in particular, economically and politically viable.

This British attitude, largely shared by the Americans, seemed quixotic to the French. They were more obsessed than their allies with the German menace, and approached it with the realism not of the economist or statesman but of the strategist. From their viewpoint the arguments for a convalescent Germany, and against arousing the German will to revenge, were as nothing beside the need for French military security. They were thinking in the language of terrain, of army corps, of industrial potentials for war, a language that history had not taught the Anglo-Saxon powers. Disagreement among the victors was implicit in their backgrounds, and no peace conference could reconcile it.

The settlement begun at the conference table took longer to work out than the war had taken to fight. Not until 1925 was the peacemaking substantially complete. It was far more than the Peace of Paris, the name often given to the Treaty of Versailles with Germany and the concomitant treaties with other vanquished states. Some major issues, particularly in eastern Europe, were scarcely touched at Paris; others could not be settled there because the ambitions of the victors clashed; still others were settled only to be modified by the resistance of the vanquished. But the settlement as a whole was more important for the future than its chronological development. Three of its aspects were of particular concern to Britain: the terms imposed upon the vanquished, the great experiment in international organization written into the treaties, and the resolution of the Anglo-American disagreements generated by the war.

The principle of self-determination underlying the territorial settlement was not created out of whole Wilsonian cloth. The right of peoples to governments of their own choosing had been implicit in nineteenth-century nationalism, and had been dramatically asserted in many parts of Europe before the Paris Conference met. The Treaty of Brest-Litovsk had detached the Baltic states from Russia; the Hapsburg Empire had broken into its national segments; the allies had pledged themselves to a reconstituted Poland, on which the Poles were already hard at work. The peacemakers had to deal with a map that had come alive and was reforming itself; they could determine its details, but not its broad outlines. Their efforts were focused on drawing frontiers to accord with national divisions, and they succeeded so well that only a tiny percentage of Europe's population remained under alien rule. The principle guiding them was old, but its application was so thorough as to be revolutionary.

The resultant map had one salient feature, a band of new or drastically altered states stretching from the Arctic to the Aegean. Out of the wreck of the czarist empire came Finland, Latvia, Esthonia, and Lithuania. Out of what had been Russian, German, and Austrian territory emerged the vast bulk of Poland with an outlet to the Baltic, the so-called Corridor, which cut off East Prussia from the rest of Germany. Bohemia became the core of a new republic, Czechoslovakia. The tiny states of Austria and Hungary kept alive the names of the Dual Monarchy, while the remaining Hapsburg territories went to Rumania and to the new kingdom of Jugoslavia. Nationalism was not the unifying force that it had appeared to be a half-century earlier. It had disrupted the old empires into a congeries of smaller states, and the "Balkanization" of Europe had now spread from the Danube to the Baltic.

The price was instability. The substitution of untried governments for old loyalties or habits of obedience produced tensions in all the new states, and their nationalism often resulted in tariff walls that dammed the traditional channels of trade and impeded economic recovery. From the viewpoint of power these states were almost a vacuum. They had little military strength even in combination, and they were beyond reach of effective assistance from the West. They were safe only as long as the settlement was maintained inviolate. Once a predatory power arose on either side of them, they were its predestined victims.

This structural weakness of the peace was accentuated by another factor. Three major states were determined to revise the settlement when the chance arose. The first and least of the three was Italy. She had entered the war after deliberate bargaining, and came to the peace table to raise her terms and secure dominance of the Adriatic. When her hope was blocked, many Italians felt that the fruits of victory had been filched from them because they lacked the strength to assert themselves. They began to long for a leader who would make Italy into the great power she patently was not.

A far more important revisionist state was Russia. Her former allies were embittered by her wartime desertion and alarmed by communism; they interfered in the civil wars against her regime, and treated her as an international pariah. She was excluded from Europe more thoroughly than at any time since the eighteenth century; the cordon of new states, many of them created wholly or in part out of her former territory, now sealed her off from the West. The communists accepted the losses partly from weakness, partly from a revulsion against imperialism and a hope that immediate world revolution would make all frontiers meaningless. But as the hope faded with time, the settlement took on the aspect of another Brest-Litovsk. The force of Russian patriotism was fused with communist aversion to the states upholding the settlement, and the fusion generated that distrust of the West that is today one of the greatest threats to world security.

The most obvious revisionist power was Germany. In the West she was forbidden to fortify or maintain troops in the Rhineland, and was obligated to support the allied armies of occupation for years to come; she ceded Alsace-Lorraine to France and sustained minor losses elsewhere. In the East she had the greatest blow to her pride: the surrender of Danzig and the Polish Corridor cut her off from East Prussia, the province as dear to German patriots as Virginia to American. Overseas she lost everything — in China and the north Pacific primarily to Japan, elsewhere to Great Britain and the dominions as mandatories under the League of Nations. Her fleet and army were reduced to police forces. She admitted her guilt for the war, and agreed to pay an indeterminate sum in reparations.

Turned in on herself, disarmed, mortgaged, she seemed to have lost her capacity for troubling the peace.

The European aspect of the settlement, harsh as it was, represented a defeat for France. She had striven for a Carthaginian peace — in the West for the complete separation of the Rhineland from Germany, in the East for a gigantic Poland as a buffer against both Germany and Russia. Britain and the United States, however, had insisted that some hope must be left to Germany, lest she be driven in desperation to embrace communism. They had offered France, if she would abate her demands, a guarantee to defend her frontiers against attack, and the French had given way grudgingly. They complained that Lloyd George was being statesmanlike at their expense.

The gibe had considerable truth. On issues of equivalent concern to him he showed little sense of moderation. In the division of colonial spoils he secured the lion's share for Britain, and in the treaty he obtained naval provisions that seemed to safeguard her future security; the surrendered German fleet had by now been scuttled and was at the bottom of Scapa Flow. On the question of reparations, above all, his moral position was weak. In the armistice Germany had agreed to pay for all damage done to allied civilians; a reasonable interpretation of the agreement would have left France and Belgium with the major claims, Britain with little, and the dominions with less. The British public, however, was determined to make Germany pay the cost of the war. Although Lloyd George knew it could not be done without disrupting British as well as German economy, he refused to be statesmanlike at the expense of his career. Instead he took the lead in inflating the bill to whatever sum the Germans might conceivably pay. The treaty wisely left the amount to a reparations commission. But the Weimar Republic was saddled with a huge initial installment, and was forced, in addition, to turn over most of its existing merchant marine and to pledge future construction. The French thereafter were unimpressed when the British pot called their kettle black.

Britain was also much concerned with the settlement of the Near and Middle East. There the collapse of Russia and Germany had at least temporarily eliminated the old dangers, and the disintegration of the Ottoman Empire permitted Britain to feather her own nest. The Turks' Arabian dependencies had already broken away, but only one, Hejaz, was allowed even nominal freedom. France acquired the mandate of Syria, Britain the mandates of Mesopotamia (Iraq), Transjordania, and Palestine; Greece, the British protégé, annexed Turkish territories in Europe and Asia Minor. From the Aegean to the Persian Gulf, Britain's influence was predominant.

It was soon impaired by the rise of Turkish and Arab nationalism. The Turks went to war with the Greeks, expelled them from Asia Minor, and regained control of the straits; Britain was in no mood to fight, and was forced to acquiesce. In Egypt and Iraq she was faced with independence movements that gradually weakened her control. In Palestine she had complicated her problem by the Balfour Declaration of 1917, which had promised a Jewish "national home" in the Holy Land while simultaneously guaranteeing the rights of the Arab population. The promise was a contradiction in terms, and it sowed the seeds of trouble with both Jews and Arabs for the next thirty years.

Britain had thrown her imperial mantle over a number of hornets' nests. The stings were painful, but they would be dangerous only if one or both of her former rivals, Germany and Russia, began to meddle again in the affairs of the Near and Middle East. In the 1920's that possibility seemed remote, and her position proportionately secure.

In Europe also the settlement seemed to have brought her security. Dangers of war were less imminent than they had been in 1815, if only because none of the major belligerents retained the will and the means to fight. Italy was discontented with her lot but too weak to do more than ruffle the surface of the peace; Germany was exhausted and disarmed, Russia in anarchy. France emerged for the last time as the chief force on the Continent. She and her satellites among the new states were intent on maintaining a status quo of which they were the beneficiaries, and for the time being they were more than a match for any aggressor. A balance of power had returned, and the British felt that they could once more afford to withdraw from active intervention in Europe. This feeling colored their whole attitude toward the new international order that grew out of the Paris Conference.

V London, Geneva, and Washington

THE COVENANT of the League of Nations, incorporated in the peace treaties, became an integral part of the settlement. After 1815 the congress system had soon broken down, but the treaties had endured for generations. After 1919, on the contrary, the system and the treaties stood and fell together. The great achievements of the League were in the first decade, when the treaties were still binding, and its decline in the second decade was the obverse of Hitler's success in abrogating the Versailles terms.

The battle over the League reflected the same divergence of aims as the battle over the Rhineland. The French wished to achieve security by an international commitment to intervene wherever and whenever the peace was threatened. They hoped to make of the League a superstate with an international army and general staff, and to transfer from the members to the central authority the power to take action. This proposal ran counter to the tradition of the English-speaking peoples. They had been bred with a distrust of any government wielding military force, and with a belief in voluntary collaboration and compromise rather than in rigid commitments and coercion. These factors out of their past determined the kind of League they proposed — an organization dependent for its functioning upon its members' sense of common interest and unable to act without their virtual unanimity, little more than a forum for focusing public opinion and concerting joint policy. Nothing more would have been acceptable in Britain and the dominions, let alone in the United States. "If the nations of the future are in the main selfish, grasping, and warlike," in the words of the official British commentary on the covenant, "no instrument or machinery will restrain them. It is only possible to establish an organization which may make peaceful co-operation easy and hence customary, and to trust in the influence of custom to mould public opinion."

The question at issue was an old one. The French regarded the League as Metternich had regarded the concert of Europe: where he had feared a resurgence of French power, they feared a resurgence of German; they were as determined to prevent the one as he the other, and to use for the purpose a coercive international system. To the British and Americans a League so designed and used was unthinkable. They had the memory of 1823 to guide them, and the conviction that a military instrument for repressing aggression would repress progress as well.

To the French the Anglo-American scheme was inadequate in its structure and quixotic in its premise. They fought it at Paris, but on point after point they were forced to give way. The League defined in the treaty was a far cry from the instrument of security for which they had hoped. Members were precluded from going to war, it is true, until an elaborate machinery of mediation had been tried and found wanting; any state that violated this obligation risked boycott and whatever military sanctions the League Council might recommend and the national governments be willing to provide. But such sanctions were not guarantees in the French sense. They depended upon the will of sovereign states, and they were meaningless if the will were lacking.

If the commitments of the covenant were too little for France, they were too much for the United States. The American isolationist tradition was younger than the British, but deeper, as the Atlantic is deeper than the Channel, and it seemed to be founded on geographic and strategic immutables. The United States had gone into the war on a wave of emotion. Emotion was a volatile substitute for insight, and evaporated quickly when Wilson was forced at Paris to compromise with his proclaimed principles. The defects of the peace and of a League that would tie the United States to surveillance of the peace were denounced by the Republicans with mounting rancor. Their triumph in the election of 1920 began the American repudiation of the treaty and the covenant.

The effect was shattering. The League was based upon Anglo-American concepts unfamiliar to much of Continental Europe; they had been embodied in the covenant primarily at Wilson's insistence, and his defeat at home weakened the standing of his ideas abroad. The machinery for maintaining peace, furthermore, was designed for the motive force of agreement among the major states; the small ones could and did contribute enormously to the work of the League, but the great ones determined, by their unanimity or lack of it, the crucial question of whether the machinery would work to halt aggression. The withdrawal of the United States destroyed all chance of unanimity. It also widened the disagreement between Britain and France, the two principal powers that remained committed to the settlement.

The American action was felt at once throughout the British dominions. Their isolationism had much the same roots as that of the United States, and it gained strength from her example. At a time when Britain was absorbed with her relationship to them, their attitude affected hers. For her own part, also, she was averse to deep involvement in Europe. The war had left her nearer exhaustion than ever before, and the emerging balance of power on the Continent seemed to offer her the chance to recuperate quietly at home. The upshot was that she did not assume the leadership that the United States had relinquished, but began to withdraw into her old aloofness.

France felt the foundations of her security crumbling. The Anglo-American guarantee to defend her frontiers was repudiated by the United States, and Britain's commitment also lapsed. France had sacrificed her ambitions in the Rhineland only to be left with a kind of League in which she had no trust, and the great wartime coalition that had saved her was dissolving. Italy was weak and disgruntled, the United States a self-righteous anchorite, even Britain aloof. France had only herself to rely upon, and she acted accordingly. For a time she occupied the Ruhr, ostensibly to collect reparations; she negotiated alliances successively with Belgium, Poland, Czechoslovakia, Jugoslavia, and Rumania; she began enormous fortifications on her eastern frontier. In her quest for security she was reverting to her pre-war techniques.

The reversion antagonized the British. They stigmatized her invasion of the Ruhr as sheer Prussianism, and they had little sympathy with her attempt to encircle Germany by alliances. The idea of keeping the Weimar Republic permanently bankrupt and impotent outraged their commercial interest, their belief in fair play, and their sense of political stability. Britain was intent on recovery, France on security, and this difference in viewpoint separated the two when everything depended on their close collaboration. During the first and crucial decade no firm foundation for peace was laid.

A foundation was attempted. By 1925 Germany had recovered sufficiently to treat with France as an equal but not enough to rouse acute French fears, and the Weimar Republic had reconciled itself to accepting its western frontier. Out of this situation came the Locarno treaties, by which Germany, France, Belgium, Italy, and Britain guaranteed the Versailles settlement as it applied to the Rhineland and the Franco-German border, and promised military action to prevent revision by force. Britain refused to be involved with Germany's eastern frontiers, but in the West she formally committed herself to war if the status quo were attacked. Eleven years later her commitment proved to be a scrap of paper.

Outside Europe Britain was left by the war with two outstanding problems in foreign relations, and both had to do with the United States. The first was financial. American loans had been a major factor in financing the war; Britain had been the chief borrower, and she in turn had lent to her allies. After Versailles the debtor states hoped to obtain from German reparations the wherewithal for payment. When reparations yielded only a fraction of the sums expected, Britain was caught; her Continental debtors could not reimburse her, yet the United States insisted on being reimbursed by her. The burden fell on the British taxpayers, who felt that the Shakespearean plot was being reversed: after they had paid for the war with their blood, "Uncle Shylock" was requiring the pound of flesh. Anglo-American relations were embittered for a decade and more, until in 1932 debts and reparations alike were forgotten in the worldwide economic crisis.

Britain's other problem with the United States was naval. By the end of the war the American building program of 1916 was bearing fruit. The primary cause of the program was the altered American position in the Pacific: the war had shown that the effective operational range of a fleet was steadily decreasing, and the security of outlying American possessions was decreasing with it. Manila was much closer to Japan than to Pearl Harbor; the Japanese had also outflanked the Philippines by seizing the German holdings in the Carolines and Marianas and retaining them under the euphemism of mandates. In the shadow of these developments American naval authorities pressed for further expansion.

The British were uneasy. The United States had just fled like a frightened bull from the European china shop, but she was now building a great fleet. Why? She had none of the traditional incentives, such as a huge merchant marine, a worldwide empire, or a position exposed like the British to overseas attack. The situation in the Far East looked far less menacing from London than from Washington; the Anglo-Japanese alliance was still in force, and to the British the yellow peril seemed like the yellow convenience. American naval expansion, even when considered in context, was difficult for them to understand. Yet they had either to accept it passively or to embark on a naval race for which they were psychologically and financially unprepared.

The United States, fortunately for them, had no desire to race, and Japan realized the limitations of her resources. The result was the Washington Conference of 1921–2, which produced agreements limiting naval construction and establishing ratios of strength. These treaties were the one great attempt at disarmament in the inter-war years. They were also the formal end of Britain's naval predominance, for she recognized the parity of the United States. At the same time she abandoned her alliance with Japan. It had lost its original character of defense, against first Russia and then Germany; the dominions, particularly Canada, objected to it as being counter to American interests and an encouragement to Japanese expansion. Its end opened the way for a new era of Anglo-American collaboration in the Far East.

The Washington treaties, at the same time, opposed grave obstacles to such collaboration. The agreed ratio, which gave Japan a navy three-fifths as strong in capital ships as the American or British, made her the dominant power in her own home waters. The United States increased the difficulty of defending American Pacific interests by agreeing to halt fortification of the Philippines, Guam, and the Aleutians. These steps were in keeping with the American isolationist mood, yet they involved the country more than ever in the affairs of the outside world. The defense of the status quo in the Far East depended thenceforth upon Anglo-American sea power, which together had an exiguous margin of safety over Japan. If a crisis in Europe ever again forced Britain to concentrate her strength at home, the United States Pacific Fleet might be left with an impossible defensive task. Any development in Europe that imperiled the British Isles, in consequence, would imperil the Philippines as well. The Washington naval treaties strengthened this interrelationship. By conceding to Japan primacy in the western Pacific they contributed to the Anglo-American retreat from Asia twenty years later.

VI   The British Commonwealth

IN the period 1918–32 two other developments growing out of the war concerned Britain even more immediately than the international settlement. One was a readjustment of imperial relations that culminated in the legal entity and logical anomaly known as the British Commonwealth of Nations. The other was the evolution of a new political and social order in Great Britain herself. These two developments were part of a single process whereby the British peoples, at home and overseas, sought to adapt themselves to the conditions of an altered world.

The birth of the Commonwealth can best be understood by a backward glance into the nineteenth century. The years between 1867 and 1914 were the formative period during which the dominions expanded rapidly. But the process was not marked, except in South Africa, by sensational events. Canada steadily gained cohesion, as wheat brought immigration to the prairie provinces and the Canadian Pacific Railway tied them to the coasts. In Australia the states grew together around the periphery of a central desert, and in 1900 they were federated in a single commonwealth. Remote New Zealand embarked on a program of state socialism, which attracted worldwide attention and provided an object lesson for pre-war British Liberals. In South Africa the same Liberals had the courage to give the defeated Boers responsible government, and then in 1910 to permit the four colonies to join in a unitary state. Union did not end the old troubles, for the Boers themselves were divided between the nationalists, who remained true to the spirit of Kruger, and the moderates, who advocated reconciliation of the white races, a large measure of collaboration within the empire, and a less primitive native policy. The struggle between these two groups, one entrenched among the back-veldt farmers and the other in fluctuating alliance with the British minority, did much to keep the Union the most isolated and self-absorbed of all the dominions.

The first World War began a period of rapid growth in the dominions' self-consciousness and sense of interdependence. The war proved what the Boer War had suggested, that they were ready to support the mother country to the limit of their capacities. They provided money, ships, and men; the Canadians distinguished themselves in France, the Australians and New Zealanders at Gallipoli, while the South Africans — after suppressing a brief nationalist rebellion — attended to the nearby German colonies. The experiences of the war modified dominion loyalty in two ways: Britain's traditional condescension toward "colonials" galled men and governments who felt that they were fighting her battles for her, and their own military exploits heightened their sense of nationalism. Although the war pulled the empire together in common effort, it also increased the centrifugal forces within it. The dominions had entered the struggle by declaration of the British government; they emerged from it determined to make peace for themselves and stand thenceforth on their own constitutional feet. They signed the treaties and were admitted to the League as sovereign states, and several acquired mandates; they soon were accorded, or appropriated, greater and greater diplomatic freedom. Britain could only acquiesce. They had reached their majority, and the family structure had to be revised accordingly.

During this period the two chief foster children of British imperialism, India and Ireland, were also growing toward independence. In India the climax of benevolent despotism had come at the turn of the century, and had stimulated a rapid increase in nationalism. No amount of benevolence could reconcile the intelligent Hindu or Moslem to alien rule. The outbreak of war, however, aroused a wave of loyalty, and India's assistance soon won recognition from Britain. In 1917 came the promise of eventual dominion status; two years later a new constitution accorded considerable powers of self-government, and India received independent representation in the League. But the British consistently refused to grant responsible central government. Their reasons were more than mere traditionalism. The cultural and economic disparities between different parts of the great subcontinent, the position of the native princes, and above all the bitter antipathy between religious groups, especially the Hindus and Moslems, made responsible government look like a euphemism for anarchy. Although progress was made even by the standards of militant nationalists, they considered it woefully slow. Their own dissensions and the conditions of India retarded it as much as the British dislike for constitutional gambling. Only a cataclysm could speed the tempo of change, and the cataclysm was still twenty years away.

To Ireland, on the contrary, the war brought a climatic crisis and a solution that has endured in essence until the present day. The outbreak of hostilities in Europe postponed hostilities in Ireland only for a time. Home Rule was enacted, but its immediate suspension ensured the renewal of agitation. Extremists soon began to supersede the Home Rulers, as they had been threatening to do since the days of Parnell. They called themselves Sinn Fein, "Ourselves Alone," and argued that Ireland must seize her opportunity to win complete independence while British power was mired in France. In 1916, with feeble assistance from Germany and from fellow-extremists in the United States, they attempted a rebellion. The British suppressed it and executed many of its leaders, who acquired as martyrs far more influence than they had had when alive. The attempt to introduce conscription into Ireland won further support for the Sinn Feiners; by the end of the war they were strong enough to convene an assembly at Dublin and proclaim an Irish republic. Its president was a Spanish-American-Irish veteran of the rebellion, Eamon de Valera.

The third Home Rule Bill was by now as dead as its predecessors. It was too much for Ulster and too little for the rest of Ireland. Parliament, in desperation, passed a fourth bill, which for the first time separated the north from the south. Each was to have representation at Westminster and a parliament for internal affairs. Ulster accepted this solution and is still governed by it. Southern Ireland rejected it, both because it fell short of independence and because it partitioned the island. A year of ugly civil war ensued, the war that had threatened in 1914. But the mood of the British public had changed; Conservatives and Liberals were no longer at daggers drawn, and the nation craved peace. Lloyd George opened negotiations with the Sinn Fein government, and in 1921 concluded a treaty that established the Irish Free State as fully autonomous; Britain withdrew from all but a few naval bases. This concession was inadequate for de Valera and other extremists, who spurned all connection with the empire, but by 1923 the government of the Free State succeeded in establishing its authority. Southern Ireland took her place as a fifth dominion, with entire control of her own affairs and only a nominal allegiance to the British Crown.

For more than three hundred years the bond between Britain and Ireland had galled the tempers of both. The British had tried a number of experiments to make endurable a tie they dared not break, but they had been defeated by a nemesis out of the past. Elizabethan ruthlessness and ineptitude, Jacobean plantation, Cromwellian conquest, Whig exploitation — the background of brutality and blunder had generated failure. The Irish had provided no solution. Their inability to agree among themselves or to discipline their violence had precluded effective resistance; even in Britain's most critical moments their weakness was greater than hers. She finally broke the bond, not during the war when she was hard pressed, but in its aftermath of weariness and fancied security, and her terms were probably as generous as the situation allowed. Partition was a bitter pill for Irish patriots. But Ulster was given the option, which she refused, of joining the new dominion, and the possibility remains open. The Irish problem entered a new phase, in which the onus of finding a solution for the entire island rests with the Irish themselves.

The recognition of the Free State as a dominion in 1923 came at a time when the whole question of dominion status was under review. In 1926 the principle was expressed at an imperial conference that the dominions and the mother country were equal juridically, "in no way subordinate one to another in any aspect of their domestic or external affairs." In 1931 the principle was legalized and fully defined in the Statute of Westminster, which is the constitution of the British Commonwealth of Nations. After a century and a half the vision of Burke came to reality in a way that would have startled that wise Irishman only slightly more than Durham or Elgin.

The Commonwealth is a kind of league new to history. It is a collection of sovereign states with no legal ties between them except a common monarch (who is monarch by virtue of being powerless), no institutional means of concerting policy except the conference and the telephone, no obligation on any member except to give notice to the others of actions affecting their interests, no bonds of unity except those of sentiment and mutual respect. The Commonwealth functions only as its members recognize their community of interests and ideals; it is the essence of voluntary collaboration, an experiment less in international organization than in international relations. Although it rests upon much the same basic premises as the League of Nations, its structure is infinitely more amorphous. Before 1914 few men could have conceived of empire in such terms.

The conception was forced upon post-war Britain, and only in part by dominion pressure. She was tired. The war had skimmed the cream of her manpower, disrupted her economy and markets, forced her to liquidate much of her foreign investment, and saddled her with an astronomical public debt. During the struggle Japanese and American industry had thrived, and even in India native manufactures were competing with British. By the 1920's Britain's economic sinews were no longer strong enough to hold the empire together. Her imperial position was further weakened by her withdrawal from all but a foothold in Ireland, and even more by the ending of her naval predominance; she now had to trust, as a sardonic observer put it, to "faith, hope, and parity." These changes largely dissipated her imperialism of the previous generation. She began to adjust herself subconsciously to a recession of power, and the Statute of Westminster was a symptom of adjustment.

VII Domestic Change

THE PRESSURE of a multitude of problems was simultaneously forcing Britain toward a new order of society at home. The core of these problems was economic, and continued to be for a decade. British markets did not recover sufficiently to compensate for the ending of war production; by 1929 the volume of shipbuilding and of coal, iron, and textile exports — the old marrow of the national economy — was markedly below that of 1913. The basic cause was not the war. Britain depended on foreign consumers; the spread of industrialization throughout the world and the effect of improved techniques in increasing the worker's productivity were cutting down the foreign demand for her goods. Her halcyon days had ended. By the early 1920's depression was endemic in the old industrial centers, and particularly in the mining areas of Wales and northeastern England. The unemployment figures, rising steadily and ominously, represented the central problem that faced successive ministries, and against which none prevailed.

In 1922 the wartime coalition dissolved. Lloyd George's handling of the Irish question, in particular, cost him the support of the Conservatives. They ousted him, and for two years they tried to remedy the nation's economic ills. Without a blush they followed the lines laid down by the pre-war Liberals in unemployment insurance and differential taxation of the rich; they attempted to encourage the type of state-controlled emigration that the scientific reformers had advocated; they advanced an unsuccessful program of tariff reform. In 1924, after the brief interlude of a Liberal-Labour coalition, they carried the polls again. This time their victory was at the cost of the Liberals, who almost disappeared as a party.

The extinction of Liberalism had long been preparing. In 1906 the party had represented the force of a thoroughly British radicalism, evangelical in its goal and empirical in its means, with a determination unhampered by the niceties of logic. At that time the Labour Party had still been in swaddling clothes, and the Liberals had been the only immediate hope for the left. In their eight years of power before the war they had educated Britain to the potentialities of state control; their main achievement, aside from curbing the House of Lords, had been to suggest what might be done with the taxing power, pensions, insurance, as means of social welfare. The party suckled on laissez faire had become the champion of strong government, while the Conservatives had rejected Disraeli's principles in order to champion laissez faire.

The war destroyed the Liberals' monopoly of new ideas. During the years of coalition their leaders dared not endanger national unity by pushing social reforms, and many of them — especially Lloyd George — soaked up caution by osmosis from their Conservative colleagues. Labour, on the other hand, matured rapidly under the stress of crisis, and the party began to recruit to its ranks many impatient Liberals. The Conservatives also matured. They were forced to acquiesce, and in some instances to lead, in a tightening of governmental controls over the nation's life, and they ceased to be Whigs in disguise and returned to their Disraelian tradition. The result, by the 1920's, was the evolution of two coherent and contrasting parties, Conservative and Labour.

Both discarded laissez faire for a large measure of state control, but there they parted company. The Conservatives wished to retain as far as possible the traditional system of private enterprise; they admitted that government must supervise and, if necessary, subsidize industry, but they opposed direct control. The Labourites, on the contrary, advocated a gradual expansion of the state into every aspect of Britain's economy, and the nationalization of key industries. The Conservatives were willing to use the taxing power to break up great accumulations of wealth and put idle capital to use, but they looked to tariffs as well as to direct taxation for financing the social services rendered by the government. Labour spoke of a capital levy, and opposed tariffs in general and particularly any tariff on foodstuffs. The pull of these opposing programs gradually broke the Liberal Party in two. Most of its less radical members were absorbed by the Conservatives; its left wing, which had steadily advocated greater socialization, gravitated inevitably toward Labour. Liberalism, the fighting faith of a decade before, was now a compromise deserted by all but Lloyd George and a handful of his followers.

Thus the 1920's, like the 1880's and the 1840's, witnessed the schism of a great party. This time each wing, instead of only one, had another party to absorb it, and schism meant virtual extinction. In the short run the Conservatives were the principal gainers. They acquired men of caliber and ideas, notable among them Winston Churchill, and strengthened their hold on the electorate; in time of deepening crisis the voters trusted more and more to the veteran party, and for the next twenty years, with one brief exception, it played the major role in government. The Conservatives probably gained less in the long run, however, than their opponents. Labour had always been in danger of becoming what its name implies, the party of a single class. As long as socialists in other classes, the heirs of the Fabians, looked to Liberalism for the realization of their hopes, Labour remained too much under trade-union influence to have a broad appeal for the public at large. Once it acquired the left-wing Liberals, however, it began to grow toward its present stature, a socialist party with a national program and a national base, as open to an Attlee or a Cripps as to a Bevin or a Bevan. Its growth was delayed by hard times and dissensions within the ranks, but led eventually to the triumph of 1945.

In the 1920's such triumph seemed remote. When the sickness of the coal industry became acute in 1926, the trade unions tried to show their power and force a restoration of wage cuts by means of a general strike. The nation rallied behind the Conservative government; serious violence was averted partly by the British sense of order and partly, as in the days of the chartists, by a display of military force. The strike collapsed, and the unions subsequently modified their tone. They largely calmed the fears of the country, and the Labour program, trimmed of its most controversial plans, seemed more attractive than the seven-year Conservative record of failure to deal with the depression. In 1929 Labour had the misfortune to win the election, just when the depression was becoming worldwide and irresistible.

By the spring of 1931 British unemployment was more than double that of 1929, and relief payments put a heavy strain on the Treasury. The United States was no longer the great lending market; American creditors were calling their loans. Even the Bank of England was short of gold. The Labour Prime Minister, Ramsay MacDonald, advocated drastic economies in relief and in the social services as the only chance to stave off bankruptcy. The majority of the cabinet denounced this course as a betrayal of the socialist cause, and the division of counsel forced MacDonald to resign. But he was persuaded, partly by the personal intervention of the King, that the situation was too dangerous for constitutional etiquette, and could be met only by the wartime method of a coalition. He resumed office at the head of the so-called National Government, which ostensibly represented all three parties. This administration, in one form or another, ruled the country for the next fourteen years.

The coalition at once went to the people, on a platform of protection and retrenchment, and was triumphantly returned. The Conservatives acquired a majority of the House; the bulk of Labour, which had refused to follow MacDonald, now formed the opposition. The situation had an element of fantasy: a prime minister repudiated by his own party led a government dominated by his late opponents. The cabinet, nevertheless, acted energetically, and its first care was to protect the domestic market from foreign competition. It had already devalued the pound in international exchange by abandoning the gold standard, and had thereby discouraged imports; by 1932 it established a comprehensive system of tariffs for the first time since the 1840's. Even the bedrock of the old liberalism had now crumbled and been swept away in the tide of depression.

The most immediate effect was in the Commonwealth. The imperial economic consolidation that Chamberlain had vainly urged, MacDonald could now attempt, and in 1932 a conference was summoned at Ottawa to discuss ways and means. The outcome was an intricate system of agreements for preferential tariffs, embracing India and the Crown colonies as well as the Commonwealth. The system actually raised Britain's tariffs on foreign goods without decreasing commensurately dominion tariffs on her goods — scarcely the way back to her Victorian prosperity. She was no longer the magnet for the Commonwealth. Canadian trade with the United States, and Australian with Japan, subsequently grew faster than that of either dominion with the mother country. The Ottawa experiment revealed the self-assertiveness of the dominions, the changed economic position of Great Britain, and the allure of her competitors.

The period between the first World War and 1932, in summary, was one of epochal changes in Britain's domestic and imperial position. They brought home to her the fact that the days of her predominance were gone. The Liberal Party, for all its metamorphosis, died soon after the era of free enterprise in which liberalism had matured, and the passing of that era was equally manifest in the curve of unemployment, the abandonment of gold, and the flight from free trade. The Washington naval treaties, although their full significance was not recognized until later, revealed a striking recession in British sea power. Within the Commonwealth Britain admitted a declining role by recognizing the Irish Free State and the diplomatic independence of the dominions, and the terms she made at Ottawa underlined the admission. She was beating a strategic retreat on many fronts.

The post-war years had thus been for her a period of self-absorbed adjustment to straitened circumstances. By 1932 the worst of the adjustment was over, but it had left its mark. She was turned in on herself, her confidence weakened by the mood of retreat, just when a wholly different problem was arising. After 1932 the focus of her destiny shifted once more to Europe, and the shift demanded a commensurate shift in her outlook. Before she had time to achieve it, she was on the brink of destruction.

Chapter Eight

SLEEP AND WAKING

1932–1945

I   The Background of Foreign Policy

IN the seven years between the Ottawa Conference and the invasion of Poland foreign affairs were again the crux of British history. But the public long remained indifferent to them, and condoned a policy of fumbling that a pre-war government could scarcely have survived. This indifference was less complete than that of the dominions in the same period, let alone that of the United States; it was phenomenal, nevertheless, in a nation so close to the cauldron of Europe, and it challenges explanation. Events were driving the British out of their isolation toward their greatest crisis, but certain factors were delaying their awareness of events. The factors were of two sorts. The first was domestic: the problems of economic and social transition that distracted public attention. The second was foreign: the novel characteristics of the danger, which made it difficult for the public to apprehend. The sum of these factors does not account for Britain's policy, but it does go far toward making it understandable.

The nadir of the depression was passed in 1932. From a staggering total of almost three million the unemployment figures steadily decreased, and within three years prosperity was again in sight. But it was prosperity differently based. While the manufacture of highly specialized consumer goods was blossoming in the south under the shadow of protection, mining and heavy industry were still in the doldrums; what had been some of the world's busiest districts, in Wales and the north, were now "special areas" filled with idle factories and populated by unemployables. The nation was faced by a shift of labor, like that of the eighteenth century in reverse, and the resultant problems of poor relief once more weighed heavily on government and taxpayers.

The nation was also undergoing social readjustment. Until 1914 the old oligarchy, for all the swelling of its ranks and the curtailment of its power, had retained a privileged position; land and the country house had still been the hallmarks of a ruling class. But for the landed interest, in particular, the taxation of the war and post-war years had been calamitous. By the 1930's surtaxes and death duties were absorbing the wealth upon which country estates depended, and many of them were sold to *nouveaux riches,* or turned into schools, or donated to the National Trust as monuments of a vanishing past. In business and even in government the sons of the gentry were competing on almost equal terms with the graduates of board schools and provincial universities. Land was losing its political character; it was no longer a hallmark but merely an unprofitable form of investment.

The upper ranks of society had always been rooted in the land. Now that their roots were withering, they were profoundly uneasy. At the same time they had what may prove to have been their last opportunity to lead the country, for the disintegration of Labour soon gave them control of the National Government. They led with ebbing self-confidence, afraid of communism at home, of the strong line abroad, of anything that might accelerate their own decline. Their residual courage scarcely appeared until 1940, when class interest gave place to national survival.

The Conservative leaders had another characteristic. They were not only anxious but elderly. With the single exception of Anthony Eden, who resigned early in 1938, the makers of British policy were too old to have seen active service in the war. The slaughter on the Western Front had left a gap in the sequence of rising leaders; men who might now have been invigorating public life had been dead for twenty years. In their stead were ageing, worried politicians, who looked behind them and around them but rarely dared to look ahead.

The state of politics during the period gave little stimulus to foresight. The Labour Party adhered to the doctrinaire, pacific internationalism of the socialist creed. Its leaders trusted to the League as if it were God, and had no thought of keeping the nation's powder dry; as late as the spring of 1939 they fought the return of conscription. But they had little effect on policy-making. The bulk of the party was in opposition, and the segment that had followed MacDonald exercised less and less influence in the cabinet. In 1935 MacDonald resigned the prime ministership to Stanley Baldwin, the Conservative leader; thereafter the National Government was Conservative in all but name. Its foreign policy, far from being in the Tory tradition, was essentially Gladstonian, based neither on the League at one extreme nor on national power at the other, but on negotiation and good will. For four disastrous years the Conservatives persevered in this policy, while Disraeli turned over in his grave.

Their perseverance was facilitated by the parliamentary situation. Labour was too badly rent by its own quarrels, growing out of the schism of 1931, to be an effective opposition; most of its members, moreover, shared the cabinet's basic misunderstanding of realities in Europe. The most powerful critics were not Labourites but dissident Conservatives hobbled by party allegiance. Thus in the crucial area of foreign affairs the opposition lost its traditional role: it could not criticize the substance of policy, let alone offer an alternative, and it had no hope of turning out the government; the Prime Minister consequently had all too free a hand. Baldwin's successor, Neville Chamberlain, used his freedom to the full. When in the spring of 1939 he at last admitted to the nation that his policy had failed, and reversed it almost overnight, he still retained office. In a period of normal parliamentary balance the admission of so gigantic a failure would have unseated the government and brought the opposition into office. But in 1939 there was no opposition worth the name, and it was sorely needed.

If the state of politics prevented criticism from coming into focus, specific domestic issues also distracted attention from the doings of the Foreign Office. During Baldwin's ministry the issue was a sudden constitutional crisis. At the beginning of 1936 the death of George V brought to the throne a man who was not passive enough for kingship; Edward VIII had the political interests without the subtlety of his grandfather, Edward VII. A political king in the 1930's needed to be infinitely subtle; the significance of the monarch as the legal and symbolic nexus of the Commonwealth was rapidly increasing, and a legal symbol is difficult if it comes to life. Edward's first step as sovereign was to claim sovereignty over his private life. His insistence on marrying a divorcee roused against him the latent power of the bishops and the nonconformist conscience, and the cabinet demanded, in effect, that he either admit himself the tool of government or abdicate. He chose to sacrifice his position to his individuality. When he was succeeded by his brother, as George VI, the long process of protecting the crown from the personality of its wearer reached its final stage. But the events leading to the abdication had coincided with a crisis abroad, and the excitement aroused by King Edward had helped to mask appalling blunders in British diplomacy.

In these years Ireland was also a distraction. In 1932 de Valera had been voted to power in the Free State. He broke the remaining ties with Britain and created an independent republic, Eire, which retained the Crown only in external affairs as a symbol of co-operation with the Commonwealth; he thereby carried the freedom legalized in the Statute of Westminster to the point of virtual secession, which in 1949 became complete secession. De Valera's government was soon involved in a tariff war with Britain, which was resolved in 1938; as part of the settlement Britain agreed to evacuate the three Irish bases reserved to her by the treaty of 1921. This withdrawal was bitterly opposed by Churchill. He represented the imperialism that for fifty years had fought concessions to the Irish as dangers to Britain's security, and his argument was cogent. The bases were invaluable for sea and air patrol in the event of war, and their loss greatly curtailed the patrolling range. (Britain and the United States soon paid the price in lives.) But Churchill stood alone. Britain was retreating before Eire as she had retreated elsewhere, in the illusion that retreat was the road to peace.

These domestic factors underlying her myopia were not the sole cause of it. Before 1914 her government had reconciled a far graver domestic situation with a foreign policy that was certainly not myopic; in the 1930's, it seems clear, her difficulty was only in part her self-absorption. In equal part it was her inability to see the foreign crisis for what it was. Its dangers were too unfamiliar to be grasped either by the government or the nation. They were easier to minimize than comprehend, and they were largely dismissed for more palpable concerns.

The British hoped that the world refashioned at Paris was in fact made safe for democracy, and the decade of the 1920's had given them ground for hope. The Anglo-Saxon concept of the state as the guarantor of individual rights even against itself seemed to be widely accepted. But history is not exportable. The English-speaking peoples had hammered out their rights on the anvil of experience, and the idea of rights against the state had little meaning for peoples who had not had similar experience. They might adopt a democratic system in emulation of Britain or the United States, but it had no tap root. It sickened in some countries, such as Italy and Germany, when the regime had to bear the onus of an unpopular peace settlement, and it died during the depression. The underpaid and the unemployed lost interest in being free if freedom meant destitution, and patriots longed for strong government to advance the national interest. Both turned from democracy to the preachers of new faiths.

The immediately dangerous faith was national. In the powers that troubled the peace of the 1930's — Japan, Italy, Germany — the collectivism of the nation-state was more deeply rooted than democratic individualism or the communist collectivism of class, and the worship of the state had been strengthened by the wartime emphasis upon its central sacrament, the submersion of the individual in the group. This secular religion provided the dictators with the wherewithal for their fanatical crusades. But the British, like the Americans, instinctively minimized a fanaticism that repudiated all their postulates; they assumed that it was not too alien to be amenable to reason, to the logic of moderation, to a sense of honor. The assumption was an unwise but understandable mistake.

The other great collectivist religion was equally alien. Communism was in theory far more international than the liberal creed, and the faith that the workers of the world would unite to bring in their own utopia appealed increasingly to Continental radicals as their democracies withered in the depression. These rationalists of the left now looked to Russia, as their predecessors had once looked to France, for the lead in universal revolution. The Soviet government, however, was no longer dazzled by the hope of an immediate millennium. Instead it was working to strengthen Russia as the nucleus for a still-distant world upheaval, and therefore to enlist Russian nationalism, paradoxically, in the service of an international faith. The

Kremlin assumed that the capitalist democracies wished to destroy Russia in self-defense, and that she was therefore as much at war with them as with the dictatorships; any duplicity was justified, in consequence, if it benefited her or the communist cause. Such an attitude was no more comprehensible in London than that of Hitler or Mussolini.

Even during the depression communism made little headway in Britain. Although the social climate was changing, class distinctions were still as much in the fibre of the British workingman as of the aristocrat; the missionaries of Lenin, like the missionaries of Marx before them, could not remold the British sense of humor and of compromise, even among the unemployed, into the stuff of revolution. But they did succeed in alarming the upper classes. The communist bogey assumed much the same role for the Conservatives that the Jacobin bogey had once played for earlier Tories. The effect, as Conservatives came to dominate the government, was to make still fainter the chance of Anglo-Russian collaboration.

On that chance hinged the peace of Europe, for only a revival of the Triple Entente could possibly create the force to contain German expansion. In 1935 France and Russia reverted to the precedent of forty years before and concluded a defensive alliance. It had little vitality, but it disturbed Great Britain. Her distrust of Russia had endured for a century, her experiment in co-operation for only the decade after 1907, and she now had more than the fear of communism to dissuade her from repeating the experiment. A revived Triple Entente might not only encourage communist activities throughout the Continent but precipitate a German attack; it would certainly expose the French satellites in eastern Europe to Russian occupation in the event of war, and so push them out of the Nazi frying pan into the Soviet fire. These reasons in sum were not conclusive. But they were strong enough so that Britain refused until too late to look to Moscow for help.

Many Britons looked instead to Geneva. In the mid-1930's popular faith in the League and in collective security was widespread. But it rested on a misapprehension. The preponderant moral, economic, and military force behind the defenders of the status quo assured security only if they had the will to use it collectively. But the peace-loving states loved their own particular parts of the peace rather than peace as a whole, and they could not agree in advance that violation of any part was violation of the whole. If they had, the League might have acquired a rigidity to which Britain, among others, was unalterably opposed. Instead the League remained flaccid: the disparity of its members' interests kept them from agreeing, when the question arose, that any one part of the settlement was crucial, and fragment after fragment the peace went by default. The aggressors synchronized their blows, striking now here, now there, without ever setting in full motion the machinery of sanctions. Aggression was in fact more collective than security, and the League as a means of preventing war was a reed shaken with the wind.

After Hitler came to power in 1933, the wind mounted rapidly. Nazism was more than a challenge to "the dictate of Versailles." The Nazis began where the extremists of the Second Reich had broken off in defeat, with the ambition for *Weltmacht oder Niedergang,* and the destruction of the Versailles settlement was only the prelude to another bid for world power. The opportunity was greater than ever before. On the diplomatic side it grew from the division between Russia and the West, which permitted Hitler to advance by carefully planned steps, each integrated with all the others, none provocative enough to bring on a major conflict before he was ready. On the military side the opportunity grew, paradoxically, from Germany's previous defeat: her army and air force had to be built from almost nothing and were unencumbered by obsolete equipment and obsolete thinking, whereas the French and British high commands were saddled with the material and ideas of 1918. For these reasons the second German bid for *Weltmacht* was even more dangerous than the first.

The British, however, found it much more difficult to grasp. They had never understood the character of German nationalism, and the collective Nazi psychosis seemed unbelievable. They had long been eager for German recovery; when it came, with phenomenal speed, they were slow to realize what it meant. Hitler had no immediate designs on their security and did not press, as the Kaiser had done, upon their nerves of empire; his interest was elsewhere. The vision of power that beckoned him was essentially land-bound, like Napoleon's, and it turned his eyes eastward. There only was the space upon which his thousand-year Reich could be built. For the sake of eastern expansion he renounced the traditional German aims that had most antagonized Great Britain. "We National Socialists consciously . . . terminate the endless German drive to the south and west of Europe and direct our gaze towards the lands in the east. We finally terminate the colonial and trade policy of the pre-war period, and proceed to the territorial policy of the future." [1]

Hitler's eastern ambitions of course involved him with Russia, but he calculated that she would not dare act alone until too late. The real key to his problem was in the West. France was committed to opposing him, as much because of her eastern satellites as of her Russian alliance, and he planned to immobilize her at the outset; if she did not move then, she would lose the initiative. As for Britain, he would give her no sufficient cause of action. He was as determined as Bismarck not to attack her interests directly; he abstained from reviving the *Drang nach Osten,* from demanding the return of Germany's overseas empire, and above all from building a great navy. He intended to undermine the foundation of Britain's security by dominating Continental Europe. But the direction of his advance — eastward, against her oldest enemy — was calculated to lull her fears until the time for effective action had passed.

His military means of aggression were actually as dangerous to Britain as the Kaiser's navy had been. The growth of the Luftwaffe into the most formidable air force in the world removed the age-old premises of British insularity, and made the Channel as archaic a defense as a castle moat. But the danger was a sudden apparition, and it was new in kind. The minor air raids of the first World War had given the islanders no inkling of what air power meant, and during the first and crucial years of German rearmament their awareness lagged behind reality. The lag was reflected in an unpreparedness, psychological as much as military, that led them to the debacle of Munich. For their imagination, like their defenses, was still concentrated on the sea rather than the air. When a traveler mentioned to his English hostess that he had arrived from South America by an unusual rout — a Zeppelin from Brazil to Germany and then a plane to London — she capped his story with the remark that her daughter had just been *"from Wapping to Edinburgh by boat!"*

Such insularity, confronted by a new dimension of danger, merely retreated into itself. The public could not be roused, and the few who attempted to rouse it condemned themselves to frustration.

---

[1] Hitler: *Mein Kampf* (New York, 1939), p. 950; quoted by permission of Houghton Mifflin Company.

Among them the most prominent was Churchill. He had the insight to read the signs abroad and the political hardihood to proclaim what he read; for years he was the Cassandra of government, and the theme of his prophecies was the terrible warning of Burke on the eve of an earlier imperial catastrophe: "a great empire and little minds go ill together." Churchill remained barred from office for the very reason that he saw too clearly.

The minds of the successive leaders of the National Government were not much larger than those of the voters. MacDonald reflected the pacifism of the Labour Party, and during his last years in office his physical strength was ebbing as rapidly as his political. Baldwin, for all his wit and shrewdness, had little taste for foreign affairs and no proclivity for the strong line; the measure of his vision was his warning that Britain's frontier was on the Rhine — an understatement that the public refused to believe and on which he himself failed to act. By the time he retired in 1937, the wind had been well sown.

The man who reaped the whirlwind was Joseph Chamberlain's son, who had little except Birmingham in common with his father. Neville Chamberlain had no religion of empire, and he was anything but a radical. He had made his name at the Exchequer and retained the rationalism of the financier — the confidence in an international order founded upon laws that bind even statesmen, the incomprehension of economic and political fanaticism, the belief that common sense must ultimately prevail. He was neither a fool nor a coward, but a competent and self-confident administrator, as wedded as Sir Robert Walpole to the ways of peace. He was confronted by masters of undeclared war, and he was no more capable than the nation at large of understanding their motives and methods.

These, then, were some of the reasons behind Britain's foreign policy in the 1930's. On the one hand a pervasive mood of retreat numbed her will to act, and manifold domestic problems distracted her attention from the storm brewing in Europe. On the other hand the nature of the storm was peculiarly difficult to grasp; the rise of new collectivist faiths was incomprehensible to a public bred on democracy and imbued with the hope of the League, and the specific menace from Germany was at once too indirect and too novel to be quickly felt. The nation could not and would not respond to Churchill. Instead it got Baldwin and Chamberlain, and to blame all the consequences on those two intelligent mediocrities is to miss the spirit of the times.

II   The Undeclared War

THE DEVELOPMENT of aggression in the 1930's is still too familiar to require more than brief mention. Three powers took the lead in refashioning the postwar settlement: in 1931 Japan embarked upon open imperialism in China; in 1935 Italy did the same in Ethiopia; simultaneously Germany violated the Treaty of Versailles, and in 1938 began the territorial expansion that led quickly to world war. These moves jeopardized, in one part of the world or another, the immediate interests of every other great power — of Britain, Russia, and the United States in the Far East, of Britain in Africa, of France and Russia in Europe. But the powers failed to combine, and in crisis after crisis their interests were assailed separately and successfully.

The first move by Japan showed the weakness of the League. Among its members Britain was the only great power seriously concerned. But she was in the most desperate phase of her economic crisis, and Mukden seemed far away; she rejected even a mild American proposal for joint action. China gained nothing from her appeal to the League, and Japan withdrew from it. Aggression in itself could not start the machinery of sanctions. The only remaining question was whether a great power would do so when aggression patently menaced its security.

This question arose in the Ethiopian crisis. When Mussolini decided to appropriate Ethiopia, the last island of native rule left from the partition of Africa, he knew that he was inviting the opposition of Britain. Her hold on Suez, already weakened by the rise of Egyptian nationalism, would be seriously endangered if the Italians seized the highlands between the Nile and the Red Sea. France was disposed to be pro-Italian, on the other hand, because of her rising fear of Germany: in the spring of 1935 Hitler reintroduced open conscription in defiance of Versailles, and revealed the formidable strength of the Nazi air force. This development was Mussolini's chance. He fortified himself by an agreement with France and sent his armies into Ethiopia.

The British government was in a quandary. The French had a

cogent argument against estranging Italy in the face of the German menace. But the argument on the other side was equally cogent: the cause of collective security had suddenly become identified with Britain's security at Suez, the defense of a great ideal with the defense of her immediate interests; this was the time, if ever, for her to insist on implementing the covenant even at the risk of war. Between these two logical courses of action the government wobbled irresolutely. First the fleet was concentrated at the ends of the Mediterranean; then an agreement was reached with Italy and promptly repudiated; then the League imposed ineffectual sanctions; then the Italians completed their conquest, and the whole matter was dropped.

Meanwhile Hitler struck. In March of 1936, at the height of the Ethiopian crisis, he sent troops into the Rhineland. This flagrant violation of Versailles and Locarno was timed to perfection. The British were too busy in the Mediterranean to be greatly disturbed that Germans had reoccupied German territory. The French saw more clearly, but they dared not fight without the certainty of British support. Their will to resist was sapped by Britain's reluctance, just as their reluctance was sapping her will to fight Mussolini; neither of the partners had the vision to see the other's interests or the resolution to act alone. Their post-war entente had reached its nadir, and the dictators profited accordingly.

Hitler's first step in immobilizing France was to control the Rhineland. His second was to fortify it, in order to preclude an attack from the West when he turned eastward. As his fortifications progressed, the strength went out of French influence in central and eastern Europe. The building of the Maginot Line had already shown that France intended to await attack if war came, and Hitler's new defenses made assurance doubly sure. The French satellites in the east began to lose hope of effective aid, and their will to resist Hitler's demands was proportionately weakened.

Britain's failure in Ethiopia had equally serious repercussions. She antagonized Mussolini as the French had feared, and in 1936 he made the pact known as the Rome-Berlin Axis. This step was a more fundamental reorientation of Italian policy than the Triple Alliance had been because it envisaged, as the alliance had not, a possible clash with Britain. Mussolini had been encouraged by his Ethiopian gamble to defy the long-established axiom that Italy, with her coastline exposed and her empire and economy dependent on the sea, must never challenge the mistress of the Mediterranean. His defiance eventually destroyed him, but for the moment it showed the depths to which British prestige had sunk.

Worse was to come. In the summer of 1936 the Spanish Civil War broke out, and it rapidly developed into an international war in miniature. Germany and Italy assisted Franco's fascists while Russia gave some help to the republicans. Britain and France were again in a quandary. For both of them a friendly Spain was vital, and foreign intervention made her friendship unlikely; a Franco victory might bind her to the Axis, a republican victory to Moscow. Yet neither Britain nor France dared take a strong line against intervention for fear of precipitating a general war. They protested and did nothing while the republic was slowly strangled. When Axis submarines established a blockade of the Spanish coast, Low's great cartoon pictured Britain watching this piracy over the caption, "Britannia waves the rules."

Meanwhile another republic went by the board. Ever since the peace conference the independence of Austria had been a cardinal tenet of France and Italy, neither of whom wished to see the Germans ensconced on the Brenner. But by the spring of 1938 Mussolini was so deeply committed in Spain that he could no longer hold out against his Axis partner. Hitler struck as suddenly as he had in the Rhineland. Again the French hesitated, and again the British felt that the Nazis had a case. Austria, after all, was populated by Germans, and her economic independence was precarious; why should she not be absorbed by the nation to which she naturally belonged? The reason was neither ethnic nor economic, but military. The French sensed it by an instinct on which they dared not act. The British missed it, and six months later Hitler brought it home to them.

His invasion of Austria was the opening move in his advance to the East. Once he controlled the Danube to the edge of Hungary, he almost surrounded the Slavic bastion of Bohemia. This was his next meal. But he was too shrewd to devour it in one gulp and thereby precipitate war; Czechoslovakia was allied with France, France was tied to Britain and possibly to Russia. He preferred a bloodless victory on the installment plan. His first demand was a modification of the Czech frontier, particularly in the Sudeten Mountains, so as to incorporate into the Reich the Germans of the area. Their position had been drastically altered by the peace settlement, which had changed them from representatives of the *Herrenvolk* in Vienna to an alien minority governed from Prague. If they wished to be part of the new Germany, had the Czechs or the French or the British the right to gainsay them? The principle of self-determination was again being turned against the democracies.

As the crisis developed, leadership devolved increasingly upon London; two years of waiting on British support seemed to have deprived Paris of the will to independence. In Britain Hitler's argument had an insidious appeal. It seemed to be based on justice, and it was backed by fleets of bombers. The nation was by now fully awake to the air menace, and the shock of waking produced a mood nearer to panic than at any other moment of recent history. The mood may or may not have been justified; it was the setting in which the government had to work. Chamberlain was convinced, along with the bulk of the British people, that war would be catastrophic for every one, including the Czechs; he believed that Hitler could be induced to compromise, and would observe whatever agreement might be reached. On these assumptions he negotiated.

Hitler steadily raised his terms, until even Chamberlain lost hope and broke off negotiations. Tension and fear grew almost unbearable; then came the sudden invitation to a conference at Munich. Hitler's psychology was masterful. His last-minute offer unloosed such a flood of popular relief and rejoicing that Chamberlain and the French Premier were not in a bargaining position by the time they reached Munich; they could no longer risk war over matters of detail, and the sum of their detailed concessions gave Hitler more than he had initially demanded. Czechoslovakia, without a shot fired, lost her defensible frontier. This was the agreement that Chamberlain hailed, in one of the most unfortunate quotations of modern history, as "peace with honor."

In the sixty years since Disraeli had applied the phrase to the Treaty of Berlin, Britain's prestige had sunk even more dramatically than her power. In 1878 she had extorted a settlement by the threat of force; it had been peace, whether honorable or not. In 1938 she yielded to the threat of force. Even Chamberlain must have doubted that the result was peace (for he accelerated the tempo of rearmament), and he could scarcely have considered it honorable. Although he believed, like Gladstone in the earlier crisis, that a measure of justice lay with the aggressor, his conduct of the negotiations showed his conviction that the Czechs also had a case. The onus of abandoning them rested technically upon France because of her treaty obligation. But Britain had assumed moral responsibility for them in assuming leadership, and at Munich she agreed to their destruction: the loss of their mountain frontier delivered them helpless into the hands of Hitler.

Whatever illusions Chamberlain brought back from Munich were dissipated within a few months. In the spring of 1939 Hitler seized what was left of Czechoslovakia. This was a logical step in his advance, and violated his pledges no more flagrantly than many of his earlier moves, but it produced a sudden shift in British opinion. Now that he had appropriated for the first time a non-German people, the most wishful thinking could no longer conceal the nature of his appetite. If it could not be sated within the limits of German nationality, a vast meal lay before him in the East from Poland to the Balkans. On that food the new caesar would grow too great to be withstood. The British realized that he was seeking not to revise the Versailles settlement but to dominate Europe, and realization gave them at long last unity and purpose. Chamberlain reversed his policy almost overnight by extending a guarantee to Poland, already marked as Hitler's next victim. In the summer of 1939, unlike that of 1914, Britain was explicitly committed to fighting if Germany attacked.

The commitment was diplomatically dangerous because it decreased the chance that the Poles would compromise. It was strategically absurd because France and Britain had no means to implement it. They were preparing for a defensive war behind the barriers of the Maginot Line and the Royal Navy, in the hope of defeating Germany a second time by attrition, and in such a war Poland would be extinguished like Serbia before her. The one hope of saving her was to avert war, and this could be done, if at all, only by securing the support of Russia. At the twelfth hour, therefore, the French and British governments opened negotiations with Moscow.

They were too late. During the Czech crisis they had extinguished what little life remained in the Franco-Soviet alliance by ostentatiously ignoring Russia, and so had translated into policy the rueful French pharse, *"mieux Hitler que Stalin."* When they tried to reverse their choice a year later in favor of Stalin, they had little to offer him. He wished to re-establish Russian influence in the territories lost in the peace settlement, if only to resist a German attack; this they could not condone without violating the very principle of self-determination for which they were ready to go to war. He naturally doubted their readiness. They had not fought for their own immediate interests, or for a treaty obligation to the Czechs; why should they do so for the Poles? If they did not, Russia might be involved alone; if they did, they were planning a defensive so static that it would leave her to bear the brunt of the onslaught. She had a vital interest in stopping Hitler, but none in aiding the democracies. If Germany turned against them instead of against her, she would have at least a breathing space. These considerations, superimposed upon decades of distrust, seem to have determined Soviet policy.

Agreement with Germany was more attractive. If the two powers partitioned the weak states between them, the Kremlin may well have argued, Russia would at worst gain space with which to cushion a German attack; the Nazi move into Poland would precipitate, if Britain and France honored their commitments, a European war in which Russia's enemies might destroy one another and pave the way for world revolution. Late in August Stalin came to terms with Hitler: two complete cynics contracted a *mariage de convenance,* and out of it came the second World War.

Hitler demanded that Poland cede much of the Corridor, for the threadbare reason that it was populated by Germans. The Poles refused to take the road the Czechs had traveled, and Chamberlain refused to force them; Britain was preparing to honor her guarantee, and France was reluctantly following her lead. Hitler's diplomacy could no longer win him bloodless triumphs. It had immobilized his Western enemies strategically, but in the process it had goaded them into challenging him on an issue they were powerless to affect. To the challenge he had only one reply. On September 1 he invaded Poland, and two days later Britain and France declared war.

The mood of the British public was wholly different from that of 1914. No one expected a short or romantic war; the flags and music and shouting were gone. Instead mothers and children were being evacuated from the great cities in a migration directed by the ubiquitous, impersonal voice of the radio; gas masks had been distributed to the civilian population, and lights were blacked out across the country against the bombers that were momentarily expected. This was war in a new guise, somber and humdrum, and the British faced it as a disaster to be endured. They had no inkling of what lay ahead. But after a decade of shortsighted confusion and false hopes they were once more gathering their strength and beginning to find themselves.

III   The Nazi Offensive in the West

FOR Britain the opening months of the war had a dreamlike quality. Instead of the prophesied air raids the skies were clear; instead of a holocaust on the Western Front the armies were inactive behind their fortifications. At sea the submarine offensive of 1917 was not renewed, and the few German surface raiders were efficiently hunted down. In the East, it is true, the Nazis destroyed Poland in a lightning campaign, and the Russians joined them for a third partition of the unhappy country. But Hitler's first experiment in blitzkrieg meant little to the West. Allied strategists had already written off Poland, and they assumed that the war as a whole would follow a different pattern. The initial inactivity in the main theater strengthened their assumption, for a stalemate was what they had expected.

In 1914 the French had been imbued with the doctrine of the offensive, but they had slowly unlearned it through years of slaughter. The lesson of modern weapons seemed to be that a front held in force could not be broken until the home front itself collapsed. This premise was particularly attractive to the British and French governments of the 1930's because it coincided with their defensive mood. They had neither the will nor the ready cash to plan a massive assault, and they therefore prepared to stand behind fixed lines. Hitler, they calculated, would be contained in central Europe and so defeated. If he sought to break out to the East, he would entangle himself with Russia. If he tried the West, his manpower would be squandered against the allied defenses. If he remained inactive, he would be doomed to the slow attrition of blockade. This was the essence of allied strategy.

It was based on a fatal error. What Hitler had called "the universal motorization of the world" had altered the balance between attack and defense. The chief innovations of the earlier war, the airplane and the tank, could now be integrated by radio into a striking force that could cut through the formerly impenetrable complex of barbed wire, trenches, and machine guns. Static defense was obsolete. This the Germans realized far more clearly than their Western enemies. For generations blitzkrieg had been the focus of German military thought; Nazism provided the climate for a strategy unencumbered by caution or moderation, and the German army and air force were fused into the most effective tactical instrument the world had seen. Hitler knew that he could not be contained. His inactivity in the West merely covered his preparations.

His first move was unexpected. In April 1940 German troops occupied Denmark and landed in Norway, partly to forestall the British and partly to gain greater access to the North Sea. A Franco-British expeditionary force, hurried to the aid of the Norwegians, was routed by the Nazis, and the completeness of the defeat shocked the British public. The Prime Minister was the victim: Chamberlain gave place to Churchill. Out of a relatively minor setback the nation acquired such a leader as it had not had since the eighteenth century.

In many ways Churchill was the child of that century. His appetite for experience, however bitter or painful, and his sense of his country's imperial mission belonged more to the exuberant Whigs of the Hanoverian era than to the nervous Tories of the National Government. But his genius for leadership was timeless. Few men have been as richly endowed with it by nature and training. His willingness to accept responsiblity had grown into a craving for it by the time he came to Downing Street, and his insight had been sharpened by long experience. If his vision, for all its magnificent clarity, was limited by old preconceptions of Britain's place in the world, its very limitation was part of his greatness for the job in hand. He personified the proud tradition of Cromwell and the Pitts, Canning and Disraeli; he believed in the British people implicitly and fearlessly because he was pervaded by a sense of their victorious past. So were they, at bottom, and in the hour of trial they drew from that sense a courage to match his own.

Their trial began the moment he took office. On May 10 Hitler launched his main offensive in the West. It poured into neutral Belgium, and this time engulfed Holland as well. The Schlieffen Plan was apparently being tried again; the enemy advance hinged on the northern end of the Maginot Line, at Sedan, and developed its thrust across the Belgian lowlands. The bulk of the allied mechanized forces advanced to meet it. The Nazis, however, were too brilliant to be repetitive. Their main drive was in fact aimed through the Ardennes at the hinge itself; the purpose was not to crush the allied armies behind an opening door, but to break their center and cut them in two. The French army guarding Sedan disintegrated under the impact, and the German tanks poured across northern France. When they reached the coast at Abbeville, almost the whole of the British contingent and some of the French were surrounded in Belgium, powerless to break through southward to the bulk of the French army. This time there was to be no retreat to the Marne.

The Germans turned first to destroying the northern segment. The Belgian army capitulated, and the Anglo-French force was driven back on the only possible port of egress, the little resort town of Dunkirk. Up and down the coast of Britain went the call for ships, and it was answered by the most motley armada that has ever played its part in modern war; everything from passenger ships to yachts and trawlers set out for Belgium, chaperoned by the navy and precariously covered by the Royal Air Force. German pressure on the exhausted troops slackened, for reasons that are not yet clear, and more than a third of a million men were evacuated. It was four years almost to the day before the Union Jack returned to northern Europe.

"The miracle of Dunkirk" was only a glimmer of hope in the dark. The German armies wheeled south, cut through the improvised defenses, and forced France to surrender. Mussolini entered the war. He was confident that the worst of the fighting was over, and that the dissolving British Empire would yield him rich spoils in Africa. The fall of Britain seemed, even to her friends, a matter only of months. She had a woefully small army salvaged from the wreck, and almost all its equipment had been left in Belgium. Her air force was scarcely tried and was heavily outnumbered by the Luftwaffe. Her navy had serious deficiencies and an appalling task. Defense of the home islands was more precarious than ever before in her modern history, and defense of the empire appeared impossible.

The British, fortunately, could not see their position for what it was. Merely because they had never lost a war they did not believe that they could lose one. "The general feeling," as one of them put

it, "seems to be, 'Thank God we've no more allies to let us down!'"
Such a people could be defeated in battle but not in spirit, and
Churchill's grim eloquence gave voice to their determination. Un-
deterred by their meager resources, they prepared methodically to
repel invasion. The same lack of imagination that had made them
shortsighted became their source of strength in calamity. Now that
they had everything to fear, they were unafraid.

Others feared for them, and particularly in Washington. There
the prospect of their defeat clarified, as nothing else could have
done, the American stake in their survival. The United States was
confronted by grave dangers both from Europe and from Asia. The
naval position in the Atlantic was worse than at the beginning of
1917 because the threat was more acute: if Britain fell, and especially if the Germans captured substantial portions of her fleet, the
United States might be forced back from the defense of South
America to the inner line of the Caribbean. And to the naval eye
Britain's fall looked imminent. Her battle fleet had less than half as
many capital ships as in 1916; much of its strength had to be concentrated in the Mediterranean to hold Suez against the Italians,
and commerce was driven to the long detour around South Africa.
The losses in the Norwegian campaign and in the evacuation from
Dunkirk, followed by the defection of the French navy, had produced a shortage of light units for anti-submarine patrol; the Germans were using U-boat bases in France for an offensive that soon
ranged to the mid-Atlantic, and even their surface raiders could
no longer be contained. The Royal Navy, in short, lacked the wherewithal to safeguard the home islands. If invasion or bombing did
not reduce them, starvation was likely to do so.

President Roosevelt, like Churchill, had the great advantage of a
training in the ways of sea power. He saw the scope of the danger,
and he acted fast. In the destroyer deal of September 1940 the
United States gave Britain fifty ancient but still serviceable destroyers, a gift the Royal Navy might once have scorned but now desperately needed. In return Britain took the unprecedented step of leas-
ing to the United States bases within the empire, and so entrusting
her with the defense of Anglo-American interests from Brazil to
Newfoundland. Thus the American government, aware of the nation's stake in the British Empire, abandoned strict neutrality in
order to decrease the chance of a British collapse and, if it came, to

370

cushion its impact on the Americas. Churchill had ample reason to say that American and British affairs "will have to be somewhat mixed up together."

They were equally mixed up in the Pacific, where the European crisis was the opportunity for Japan. Britain's erstwhile ally was now an enemy, with designs ranging from Hong Kong to Australia; to meet them Britain had strengthened Singapore, but after Dunkirk her great base was virtually without ships. She depended thenceforth, tacitly but clearly, upon the United States Pacific Fleet. Because the Philippines lay on the flank of any Japanese advance southward, an attack on the United States was an almost essential prelude to aggression. The effect of European developments was to throw upon the American navy the burden of a vast defensive in the Pacific, for which it was unprepared. Although its strength was hurriedly increased, Japan prepared with even greater intentness to exploit her chance. In September 1940, as if to underline her designs, she concluded a pact with the Axis that was a thinly disguised threat to the United States.

In Europe the fall of France had more immediate repercussions. Italy attacked the British army in Egypt and began the seesaw desert campaigns that lasted for the next two years; simultaneously she made ready to gather Balkan spoils by a war against Greece. Russia looked on uneasily. Although she pushed her frontiers westward, from Rumania to Finland, her position was unenviable. Her hopes for a war of attrition in the West had vanished, the buffer states between her and Germany were gone, and the Italians were gnawing at the Balkans. She was alone on the Continent against a triumphant Axis.

In Berlin the triumph produced a confusion of counsel. The next step was obviously the defeat of Britain, but the method was not obvious. Hitler believed that the islanders would see the strategic hopelessness of their position and ask for terms; precious time passed before he realized that they really meant to fight him, as Churchill promised, on the beaches, in the streets, and in the hills. He accepted the challenge to the point of planning an invasion, but his plans seem to have been half-hearted.

Well they might be. Unless he achieved another blitzkrieg, what might Russia do in the East? And for a cross-Channel blitzkrieg the Nazis were unprepared: they lacked experience in amphibious operations, the requisite shipping, and above all a battle fleet. Could the Luftwaffe serve instead, to destroy the Royal Navy and clear the path? Not, certainly, until the navy had been deprived of air cover by elimination of the Royal Air Force. The first prerequisite for conquest was victory in the air.

That victory was not achieved. The Battle of Britain, in the summer and early autumn of 1940, was as decisive as the Battle of the Marne; it destroyed Germany's best chance of winning the war. The Royal Air Force was a new creation, newer even than the Luftwaffe, and in its planes — particularly the Spitfire — it had a qualitative advantage; the lag in rearmament that had brought Britain to the edge of disaster now stood her in good stead. So did her last-minute development of radar and the fact that the Luftwaffe had been designed primarily for co-operation with ground forces rather than for strategic bombing. The Nazis lost so heavily in daylight raids that they were forced to substitute the more haphazard, and therefore slower, policy of night attacks. British cities took terrible punishment from fire and high explosives. But the courage of the many matched that of the few; civilians fought on the ground as stubbornly as the pilots of the R. A. F., and between them they won the battle.

The German failure scotched the invasion plan and thereby opened the way for Hitler's first great error. For the past five years he had gone from triumph to triumph, and by a skill as consummate as Bismarck's he had avoided the specter of a war on two fronts. Now his intuition produced strategic fumbling. Common prudence dictated reducing Britain to impotence before embarking on further adventures. If she could not be invaded or brought to terms by bombing, she could be crippled in the Mediterranean — by an attack through Spain on Gibraltar, by helping the Italians to capture Suez, by a drive through the Balkans and Turkey to open the Middle East. Yet instead of reaching for the prize at hand, Hitler determined to attack Russia.

This colossal blunder was the triumph of *Mein Kampf* over strategic sense. Hitler had preached for so long that communism represented the plot of "the international Jew" to dominate the world, and that Russia blocked Germany's territorial needs, that he seems to have become the dupe of his own preaching. By the autumn of 1940 he decided to turn eastward before destroying Britain's position. A projected attack on Gibraltar was abandoned, and Egypt was assigned a minor role. At the very moment when the islanders' peril seemed to be increasing, it was beginning to ebb.

In Africa Hitler was compelled to intervene, but he did so reluctantly. His mind was dominated by the great land spaces of the East; he considered the African theater as subordinate, and he intended to win Suez cheaply or not at all. Before the end he committed more than a quarter of a million men to the desert, but never in sufficient force to overcome British resistance. He grasped less clearly than Napoleon the crucial importance of Egypt, because he understood even less the workings of sea power.

In the Balkans he was also involved against his will. He feared that the British, based on Greece, might strike against his flank when he became involved in Russia, and to eject them he had to fight his way through Jugoslavia; the Serbs again, as in 1914, preferred extinction to surrender. The Nazis crushed them and poured south into Greece, where they drove the small British force back on Crete. The Luftwaffe routed the Royal Navy, and Crete was abandoned. Hitler had secured his Balkan flank. Jugoslav, Greek, and British resistance, however, had postponed his assault on Russia for a month, and he could afford delay no better than Napoleon in 1812. Campaigning had changed, but General Winter had not.

IV Counteroffensive

BRITAIN'S desperate year ended on June 22, 1941, when the German move eastward altered the whole face of the war. The effect was felt from Washington to Tokyo. The tempo of American intervention was accelerated. In the spring, after bitter debate, the United States had become an economic belligerent with the passage of Lend-Lease, and its provisions were promptly extended to the Soviet Union. Because Britain alone could not deliver Lend-Lease supplies in sufficient quantity to the Eastern Front, Iceland was occupied as an American base on the principal route, and the American navy took over the protection of the western sea lanes. In September 1941 Roosevelt ordered the fleet to sink German submarines on sight. This was open if undeclared war. Within fifteen months of the fall of France the United States had traveled the same road as in the thirty months after the Battle of the Marne, and the second time, like the first, she was driven by the logic of self-defense. "God helping her, she can do no other."

For Japan the Russo-German war brought the climax of opportunity. The need to supply Russia kept the British navy busier than ever in European waters; the American navy, also engaged in the Atlantic, was not strong enough to safeguard Anglo-Saxon interests on the other side of the world. Russia was the only land power that might oppose Japanese designs, and she was fighting for her life in the West. Japan saw in the German tanks pouring down the roads to Moscow the means of establishing her own hegemony in the Far East. When the United States government refused to capitulate to her demand for hegemony, war became inevitable. It grew out of the war in Europe by the noxious logic of aggression, which led from Poland to France to Russia to Pearl Harbor.

When Japan struck in December, she neutralized the principal force in her way. Whether the United States battle fleet could have impeded her early conquests is doubtful, but with that fleet crippled her way was clear. Britain's land power in Asia was inadequate, like American power in the Philippines, and her inability to defend her vast holdings was published to the world in the Singapore campaign. For the first time since the American Revolution she lost substantial portions of her empire. As the Japanese advanced in a matter of months to the coast of Austrialia and the Indian frontier, the ghost of the *Pax Britannica* was finally laid to rest.

This disaster ended an era in the history of the Commonwealth. All the dominions except Eire were in the war, and their military support was at least as valuable as it had been a generation earlier. In the Pacific, however, it was support primarily for the United States. She assumed, for Australia and New Zealand, the role the mother country abandoned at the fall of Singapore. Canada was equally within the American orbit. Her coasts were protected at short range by American bases, from Iceland to Virginia and from the Aleutians to San Pedro, and at long range by the fleet operating from Pearl Harbor as much as by that operating from Scapa Flow; the extension to her of the Monroe Doctrine was mere recognition of accomplished fact. Commonwealth and American affairs were also, in Churchill's understatement, "somewhat mixed up together."

The war into which the United States was precipitated had only one great land front. The Russian armies had confounded the prophets by their tenacity and skill, and maintaining their resistance was vital for the Western allies — a convenient if inaccurate phrase for the congeries of governments and governments-in-exile led by Britain and the United States. Only Russia could give the West time to prepare its counteroffensive. But supplying her was as acute a problem as in the first World War: although the Soviet state had greater industrial resources than the czarist, the demands of motorized war were also greater. By the old route around Scandinavia — which the Germans in Norway made costly but could not close — and by a new route through Iran, Russia received enough equipment to eke out her own resources. She stood, battered and reeling, and the Nazis' hoped-for battle of annihilation eluded them as it had Napoleon. By the end of October 1942 they were at Stalingrad, on the edge of Asia, but their hold on their enormous gains was precarious. They had not yet achieved decisive victory, and the Western allies had had time to gather their strength.

In the summer of 1942 the United States and Britain faced a staggering task. The Japanese advance into the Pacific had been stopped in the Coral Sea and at Midway; the counterattack was yet to be launched, and the allied high command had decided to subordinate it to victory in Europe. Japan's defeat would scarcely shake the Nazis, whereas their defeat would ruin her. Europe was the crux of the war. It could not be reconquered on the Eastern Front alone, if only because of logistics; the allies therefore had to concert a gigantic pincers movement from East and West. This meant, on the West, invasion of the Continent from outside. Such a feat on such a scale had never been attempted in the history of warfare, but there was no alternative.

A chief prerequisite for attack, in Europe as in the Pacific, was sea power. The allies had to create not only armies and air forces but the shipping to transport and supply them and the naval strength to control the sea lanes. Naval expansion affected Britain and the United States differently, because the geography of the war produced an allocation of effort: the eastern Atlantic, the Mediterranean, and the Indian Ocean were the bailiwick of the British; the rest of the Atlantic was divided between them and the Americans, with some help from the Canadians; the Pacific was primarily an American responsibility. The Pacific is as large as all the other oceans combined, and was the only one in which enemy sea power was a major factor (Italy, in the event, scarcely qualified). In consequence the floating and flying strength of the United States fleet soon far outstripped that of the Royal Navy. In terms of the seven seas, as of so much else, the war dramatized before its end the shift from British to American predominance.

In the autumn of 1942 the allies wrenched the initiative from the Axis. In the Pacific the Solomon Islands campaign began the American offensive that ended three years later in Tokyo Bay. In North Africa the British advance from Egypt and the Anglo-American landings in French Morocco and Algeria caught the Axis forces in a pincers that closed over some two thousand miles; Hitler refused to evacuate his troops, and by May 1943 he had lost them all and with them Africa. Meanwhile he had refused to withdraw before the Russian counterattack at Stalingrad and had sacrificed a quarter-million men. These defeats, after the losses of two years in Russia, blunted the striking power of his armies and forced the recruitment of men from the satellite states and even from prisoners of war. With their polyglot force the Nazis prepared to defend "fortress Europe" against the Anglo-American assault.

For breaching the fortress two bases were available, North Africa and the British Isles. From Africa an offensive might be launched against what Churchill described as "the soft underbelly of the Axis." In his eyes the conquest of Italy, followed by a drive into the Balkans, offered great rewards. Although his government had concluded a twenty-year alliance with Russia, he did not trust her; he was anxious to establish Anglo-American influence in Eastern Europe on the rock of armed occupation. But to mount the major invasion from Africa would prolong the war, because Hitler's empire had no "soft underbelly." Its vitals were protected by bone and cartilege of mountain — the Pyrenees, the Massif Central, the Alps and their Balkan outworks. Nowhere in southern Europe was there terrain for the rapid, large-scale maneuvers by which the German army in the West could be engaged and destroyed.

Only one accessible part of the Continent had the space required — the great coastal plain that stretches from the Bay of Biscay to Denmark and beyond. The British Isles, and not North Africa, therefore had to be the chief base of operations. The point of attack in the plain was largely determined by the need for air support and by logistics: the success of an invasion would hinge upon cover from the air and speed in building up supplies ashore, and to save time for planes and ships the beachheads had to be as close as feasible to the airfields and ports of the British Isles. Normandy satisfied these requirements, and it had the additional advantage that the Cotentin Peninsula, once it was occupied, could be protected on both flanks by sea power.

By 1943, when the Mediterranean theater seemed to be the focus of the European war, it was already becoming subsidiary. Sicily and southern Italy were conquered, but in the Apennines the invasion bogged down in siege operations like those of the first World War. Allied planes, however, had bases in Italy from which they could reach targets hitherto out of range; this was a solid gain, for the whole allied strategy now hinged on the air offensive. As the German hope of crossing the Channel had depended on defeating the R. A. F., so the Anglo-American hope of crossing it depended on defeating the Luftwaffe. The allies, unlike the Germans, had prepared for a systematic aerial assault on the factories and refineries, the tool shops and rail network, upon which airplane production rested. If Germany's air force were destroyed, her armies would be blind.

During the winter of 1943–4 the offensive mounted, and by spring its strategic aims were largely achieved. A concurrent tactical offensive then developed against military installations in France, and it gradually focused on the area northwest of Paris. In early June the Luftwaffe had virtually disappeared from the sky over France, and the destruction of bridges and railroads had isolated Normandy from the rest of the country. In the Channel an enormous concentration of naval strength, British and American, provided artillery support for the initial landings. Four years after Dunkirk the stage was set, and the whirligig of time had brought in his revenges.

The invasion launched on June 6 went according to plan; its unprecedented difficulties receded one by one into the quiet of accomplished fact. The beachheads were established and joined and the German counterattacks shattered; British pressure against Caen drew Nazi strength eastward until the Americans were able to break through to the west, envelop the enemy's main force, and crush it between them and the British. The allies then drove across France, and in August they also invaded the Rhine valley. The Germans extricated what they could and fell back on the Rhine defenses that

Hitler had prepared after 1936. There and in the Low Countries they stabilized their line.

Their strategic position was hopeless. The Eastern Front was crumbling before the Russians, and long resistance in the West was out of the question. Hitler had little interest in playing for time; with him the concept of *Weltmacht oder Niedergang* was carried into strategy. In December a desperate Nazi drive was contained in the Battle of the Bulge, where the last elements of German offensive strength were destroyed and victory was brought nearer. By spring the Western Front disintegrated, the Russians reached Berlin, and Hitler committed suicide. In May came the final surrender of troops that were no longer an army.

Britain then turned, for the first time since the fall of Singapore, to the war in the Far East. But there the strategic decision had already been reached. The American offensive across the Pacific, starting in the Solomons almost three years before, had cut the Japanese Empire in two by the reconquest of the Philippines, and had brought air power within effective range of Japan's home islands. Her air force had gone the way of the Luftwaffe, and her cities were being devastated. She had virtually no fleet after the battle for the Philippines. Her merchant shipping had been sunk or forced into harbor by the submarine blockade. Her government was in as hopeless a situation as Hitler's a year before, and the only question was whether it would face, as he had done, the irretrievable ruin of invasion. When Russia entered the war ruin came nearer; on August 6 the atomic bomb dropped on Hiroshima brought the threat of obliteration. The government was still sane, and it surrendered.

V   The New World

THE LONG ordeal was over, and the tide of hope set in. The fact that hope has ebbed again does not prove that it was unjustified. The organization of the United Nations during the war provided a framework for world order sufficiently strong to secure the peace if the member states would co-operate. No constitutional form can do more, just as no wedding service can ensure a successful marriage. The charter of the United Nations gave the nations opportunity, and in 1945 there was reason to hope that they would grasp it.

The war prepared the English-speaking peoples for opportunity by stretching their imagination. It was a global war to a far greater extent than the previous one, and it forced the man in the street — whether of Melbourne, Johannesburg, Winnipeg, Liverpool, or Detroit — to think in terms of vast spaces if he thought at all. Australians and New Zealanders recognized their relationship with Asia; South Africans were no longer insulated from the rest of Africa when their troops fought through Ethiopia and Libya; Canadians accepted a Battle of Midway as part of their defense in one hemisphere, and bombed Germany as part of an Anglo-Canadian offensive in the other. The British lost much of their aloofness from the outside world as their soldiers went to the far corners of it, and the millions at home learned beyond chance of forgetting that their frontiers are at the farthest range of a bombing plane. In the United States, above all, the war jolted the self-absorbed isolation that the first World War had scarcely touched. Americans became conscious of their strength when their survival depended upon it; their troops and ships and planes and supplies reached parts of the world of which few had ever heard, and they began to develop an awareness almost as wide as the ranging of their power. Mental horizons were broadened by circumstance.

This awareness, in the United States and throughout the Commonwealth, was supplemented and stimulated during the war by a new experience of co-operation. The teamwork of Americans, Australians, and New Zealanders in the Pacific, of Canadians, Americans, and British in the Atlantic and the skies over Europe, culminated in the integration of power that broke Hitler's Western defenses. Such thorough and global collaboration between sovereign states had never before been seen; it was a four-year experiment in hanging together instead of separately. The experiment evolved primarily among the English-speaking peoples partly because they understood each other better than they understood the Russians or Chinese, partly because geography forced them to a more minute co-ordination of effort. In the determination of basic policy they became a virtual unit; joint boards mapped the strategy of production and military operations, and each state exercised an influence roughly proportionate to its contribution. Because the American contribution was eventually the largest, in supplies, finance, and military power, leadership devolved in general upon the United

379

States. Each of the others was free to criticize and amend, however, and to initiate policy on matters of peculiar concern to itself, provided that it secured general agreement; the proviso was implemented by the need for support. This arrangement was informal and flexible, without benefit of treaty or covenant; it existed in fact more than in law. But it worked.

Its working was evidence of an underlying accord that had long been growing. In the nineteenth century the United States had been sheltered by British power, but in the twentieth her own began to replace it. At the same time Britain was conceding independence to the dominions and forming with them a league so loosely knit that its fabric was altered, but not torn, by the emerging force of America. As early as the first World War the United States was closely associated with the Commonwealth, and already she was becoming less a danger to it than a source of strength. The English-speaking peoples were unconsciously ending the political schism begun in 1775 and confirmed in 1812. The second World War deepened and matured their association, and trained them for working together to build the peace.

Their chance of building an immediate and stable peace was slim, despite all the high hopes. Two major factors stood in the way. In the first place the war had razed the pre-existing international structure more completely than at any time in modern history, and had concentrated power in the three great victors, Britain, the United States, and the Soviet Union; between them in Asia and Europe was a power vacuum, and on their agreement everything depended. In the second place Russia, whose power inevitably filled much of the vacuum, did not desire agreement. These factors largely determined Britain's position in the postwar world.

In the Far East the former colonial status quo had been washed away in the tide of Japanese conquest. The white man's return did not give him back his face; all southeastern Asia was seething with native unrest, and the British, French, and Dutch could not rebuild their old dominions. India had played an increasing part in the war as it reached her frontiers, and her nationalism had risen accordingly; with the world's largest volunteer army, a million and a quarter men, she patently had the means to assert her independence. China had become an even more important belligerent, with the courtesy title of a great power; although she was again torn by civil

war, she was no more likely than India to return to European tutelage. Japan, the major instrument of these changes, was herself reduced to impotence, and the occupation of her islands projected
American power one stage farther west. British influence declined
as American rose, and the complex pre-war balance of great powers
gave place to an uneasy equilibrium of the United States and
Russia.

The changes in Europe were more sweeping. There the destruction of the old order was on a scale even Napoleon had never
achieved. Where he had left his principal enemies defeated but independent, Hitler had yoked his to the service of the Reich. He had
wrenched them out of their accustomed economic, social, and political orbits, the allied air offensive had paralyzed their cities and railroads, and finally the invasion of Europe had brought back from
exile or up from the resistance movements unfamiliar and untried
regimes. In these circumstances the lesser states of Europe were in
no position to mitigate, as they had in the past, the friction between
the major powers.

The number of those powers had been more drastically cut than
ever before. After the Napoleonic Wars the Big Five of the eighteenth century had between them continued to supervise the Continent. After the first World War one of the six major pre-war states,
Austria-Hungary, had disappeared, but by the time of Locarno the
remaining five once more formed a balance of sorts. After 1945 the
situation was different in kind. Germany had not been curtailed as
a power, like the Germany of 1918; she had been wiped out for the
predictable future. Her place in the European scales could not be
filled by her old rival, France; the heritage of Richelieu and Louis
XIV, of the two Napoleons, even of Foch, had evaporated in the
debacle of 1940, and the subsequent years of Nazi rule had driven
home the truth foreshadowed years before, that the days of French
political hegemony were over. A continental balance of power, in
short, was at least for a time nonexistent.

The vacuum in Europe, as in Asia, drew into itself from opposite
directions the Soviet Union and the United States. Russia expanded
her influence beyond the fondest dreams of her pre-war imperialists;
her armies had overrun Poland, eastern Germany, Czechoslovakia,
much of Austria, and almost all the Balkans, and at the close of
hostilities her effective frontier ran from the Elbe to the Adriatic.

Britain and the United States had virtually conceded this frontier when they had determined, on military grounds, to crush the westernmost German armies before invading the Reich — to win their victory in installments rather than to race for Berlin. The scope of their concession, masked for a time by the strength of their armies in Germany, appeared as soon as they began to demobilize. Between the Soviet frontier and the British Isles was a helpless Europe, and Britain by herself lacked the economic and military strength to counterbalance Russia. The United States was forced to continue her intervention as the only alternative to Soviet dominance and the only way to make recovery possible in western Europe.

For it soon became clear that the Soviet government was opposed to recovery. It had to be, or betray the cause. Economic chaos offers the eventual means of destroying capitalism and bringing in the millennium, and only traitors in the Kremlin would work with the West to avert that consummation. A depressed and powerless Europe, furthermore, serves the immediate aim of increasing Russian power and facilitating the spread of communism. In this respect Stalin is akin to Philip II, who saw in the aggrandizement of Spain the triumph of the Roman Church, and communist methods derive from an attitude of mind in some ways similar to that of the early Jesuits — the belief in a transcendent goal, in elastic ways of reaching it, and above all in the determination of truth by infallible authority. If Moscow "teaches that what appears to us as black is white," as Loyola said of the Church, "we must go out and preach it white immediately." After 1945 Moscow taught that the Anglo-American effort to rehabilitate Europe was a cloak for imperialism, and the communists preached accordingly.

A second battle for Europe began, between the victors in the previous one, and no end is in sight. To Great Britain and the United States a viable Europe offers the only hope of preserving their own way of life; for the Kremlin it spells defeat. In consequence the second World War, unlike all the other great Continental wars of the past four centuries, has ended without producing a settlement. The struggle between Russia and the West has disunited the United Nations, which should have been the forum for settlement, and disappointed the high hopes raised by its charter.

For Britain that struggle is part of an old story, far older than communism. The Soviet threat is graver than the czarist, partly because Soviet imperialism is more dynamic and partly because Britain cannot look to the Continent for effective assistance. Since 1945 she has felt Russian pressure in the old breeding grounds of quarrels — Greece, Turkey, Iran — and has met it only with assistance from outside Europe. Her position from the Middle East to the Balkans has been buttressed and in some areas, like Greece, virtually taken over by the United States, who has simultaneously assumed the leading role in the defense of western Europe. This American intrusion means that Britain is dependent to a degree she would have found unthinkable a generation ago, but to which she has now adapted herself with little sign of rancor or humiliation. The United States, in turn, has treated her as an equal. The two powers cannot afford to antagonize each other. Their wartime partnership to destroy Hitler is being remolded into a peacetime partnership to contain Russia, and the second requires as close accord as the first.

In these circumstances the continuance of the Anglo-Soviet alliance of 1942 is a diplomatic anomaly, though of a kind often seen before. An alliance is only as important as the participants are willing to make it, and willingness depends upon their conception of their interests. The Anglo-Japanese alliance became moribund in 1918, when the defeat of Germany and the collapse of Russia removed the reasons for its existence; the Franco-Soviet pact of 1935 was vitiated from the start by the fact that neither side trusted the other. So with the Anglo-Soviet treaty. It is still nominally binding, but the victory of 1945 removed the one vital interest holding the allies together, and brought into the open the conflict of their other interests. Britain since has been committed on paper to Russia, yet at loggerheads with her. She has been uncommitted to the United States, yet deeply allied with her.

So much for the strange character of the peace. A wholly new power structure has emerged, and it contains only three great states. Russia is at war with all the world outside her own sphere, while Britain and the United States are tied to each other, to the Commonwealth, and to the states of western Europe on whose reconstruction their own survival depends. In the traditional sense this is not peace at all. It is a state of unparalleled flux, and for Britain it brings unparalleled difficulties. The elimination of the European balance of power undermines the postulates on which her statecraft has been based for centuries, and does so just when her world position and her social structure are also in metamorphosis.

The war strained her national economy to the breaking point. Her industrial plant was worked unceasingly and much of its equipment worn out; almost half a million houses were war casualties; a large fraction of her merchant marine was sunk, and overseas investments were liquidated to meet the cost of survival. After the fighting ended she found herself unable to pay for the raw materials to revivify her manufactures, and for the food to live on, except by curtailing her political and military commitments throughout the world. This disastrous possibility was averted by an American loan, but her root difficulties remain. The Industrial Revolution, which raised her to a pinnacle after 1815, has in this century dropped her slowly but inexorably into a slough. With an old plant battered by two wars she can no longer make a respectable living, let alone amass the capital to modernize her plant. This is the crux of her dilemma, and for it no permanent solution has yet appeared.

The ebbing of her economic power has been matched by an ebbing of imperial power. The dominions, with the exception of Eire, proved their loyalty in the second war even more strikingly than in the first. But Britain's traditional return for loyalty, imperial defense, was no longer within her capacity. Canada, Australia, and New Zealand took over their own protection under the aegis of American sea power, and South Africa was beholden to no one; only Eire, ironically enough, still depended on the Royal Navy. Elsewhere in the empire the same ebb tide has been more noticeable. It has taken the British from Burma, Ceylon, and Palestine, and above all from India. Before the end of the war the maturing of Hindu and Moslem nationalism destroyed the fabric of British rule, which for two hundred years had rested on native loyalty and crumbled with its foundation. After long hesitance the British government bowed to the facts, and India became two independent dominions. Once more Britain accommodated herself to the mediocrity of her circumstances.

For at least half a century the world has been witnessing the decline of the British Empire. The process has had many aspects — economic decline at the center, political decline as the dominions have grown in numbers and independence, military decline with the reduction of the Royal Navy from supremacy to second rank, diplomatic decline in the face of great new powers. The underlying causes of this recession were inherent in Britain's heyday. She was strong during the *Pax Britannica* not because she lacked potential rivals, like Rome of the *Pax Romana,* but because the states of Europe lacked the incentive to challenge her highly specialized complex of interests. By Bismarck's time the incentive was developing, and Britain's power began to weaken. Two world wars accelerated the change, and the second dramatized it.

But decline has not yet produced, despite frequent and confident prophecies, the fall of the British Empire. The colonies and dependencies that are shaking off British rule are not necessarily undermining the empire; they are emerging as members of the Commonwealth, and the Commonwealth is elastic. Material power is not the only mortar of that strange fabric. The continuance of the monarchy is a symptom of a different kind of bond: when a group of nations retains one king as their nominal governor on condition that he do no governing, and recognizes the Crown as an expression of their paradoxical unity in independence, they have outgrown the usual conventions of political science. This sophistication has made the Commonwealth possible and holds it together by subtleties — the pull of sentiment, memories of past collaboration, the ties of language. The centripetal force obviously varies among the members. Eire has seceded; South Africa holds aloof, and the attitude of the new dominions is still unpredictable. Australia, New Zealand, and Canada, the dominions most clearly within the orbit of American power, are also those that put most stress on the intangibles of the British connection. While the intangibles endure, so does the new concept of empire.

If the Commonwealth still stands firm, so does Britain herself. Her long story is far from finished, unless civilization as we know it is near its end, for there is nothing decadent about the British people of today. They are as strong as ever, and in some ways stronger. The war proved their doggedness, skill, and energy, and released in them a force that is now revolutionizing their society. They are engaged in writing their next chapter, and it promises to be both lively and significant reading.

The general election of 1945 initiated their most drastic experiment with democracy. When the voters repudiated Churchill at the moment of victory and gave their overwhelming support to Labour, they showed either ingratitude or vision, depending on the point of view. They certainly showed a boldness to match the gravity of their crisis. The Labour program is far more than the nationalization of industries; it reaches into every corner of British life. It rejects almost all the traditional liberal premises except the Bill of Rights, and endeavors to reconcile individual political freedom with an omnicompetent state. It involves rigid control of producers and consumers in the interest of the national welfare as interpreted by Whitehall, and at a time of grim austerity it demands the extension of social services beyond the fondest dreams of the pre-war years. It aims at leveling the disparity between rich and poor by stringent taxation, so that even modest fortunes disappear into the Exchequer. The result is that the state must sooner or later take over financial responsibility for hospitals, schools and universities, charities, art galleries, in short the whole field of private endowment.

These measures are not in essence new. The welfare state was foreshadowed by the Liberals after 1906; they also experimented gingerly with the egalitarian use of the taxing power, and the post-war Conservatives improved on their example. Socialism, in other words, is not a break with recent British history, but the culmination of trends apparent for at least four decades. Its novelty is less in its ideas than in the thoroughness, even ruthlessness, with which they are being applied.

Neither is socialism a peculiarly British experience. Since the depression most democracies, including the United States, have enormously tightened state controls in the interest of the general welfare rather than of individual profit. Britain has merely gone farther than others. She has carried a line of experiment to its logical conclusion, and at a critical moment. She is working out a redefinition of democracy; whatever its merits and demerits, it is of particular concern to the peoples of western Europe. For it offers them a middle road between communism, which they distrust, and the conservative, capitalistic democracy of the pre-war years, with which they are disillusioned. The British still have the vitality and resilience for political pioneering, although few would have guessed it a decade ago, and their exploration may reanimate the democratic spirit.

VI   Crystal-Gazing

DO these momentous changes justify conjecturing about the future?
Detailed conjecture is obviously a waste of time, but certain general
factors are worth considering. Their interaction, while not wholly
predictable, will shape the course of events. One factor has already
been mentioned: Britain's position as a world power has declined
sharply, and there is no reason to suppose that the decline is temporary; the void left in the Commonwealth and to a large extent in
Europe is being filled by the United States. This factor alone is misleading. It suggests, if taken by itself, that the United States is about
to dominate the world and establish on the ruins of the British Empire a *Pax Americana*. When other factors are taken into account,
the suggestion seems improbable.

One such factor is the composition of the new alignment. The
United States cannot dictate to the dominions without turning them
into enemies; they have been bred in the twin traditions of collaboration and independence, and show no signs of sacrificing the
second to the first. Neither can she dictate to Britain, who is too
powerful to be a puppet and too important to be ignored; the British Isles are the strategic keystone for any defense of western Europe, and British co-operation is essential to any league spanning the
Atlantic. Another factor is the quality of leadership required. Soviet
dominance may rest on coercion, but American cannot afford to.
Fear of Russia has tightened the Anglo-American entente, and has
extended it to western Europe in the form of the Atlantic Pact; that
fear and its converse, Russia's fear of the West, are dividing the
world into two camps as Europe was divided before 1914. But the
present division is one between principles as well as powers. On
the one hand is the principle of coercive force, on the other that of
voluntary collaboration, and the second cannot conquer the first
by force without corrupting itself.

Corruption is already under way. After two world wars Britain
and the United States have grown used to coercion, and their conscience has been correspondingly blunted — as witness the contrast
between their attitudes toward the two wars. Germany outraged
Britain in 1914 by invading a neutral, and the United States in 1917
by submarine warfare. Twenty-five years later Hitler and Mussolini
repeated the same crimes and added the wholesale bombing of civil-

ians, and after 1941 their techniques were turned against them; the American incendiary raids on Japan and the allied bombing of Germany would have been atrocities in 1918, and the explosion over Hiroshima jolted even the world of 1945. War is now hell, to a degree of which Sherman never dreamed. To wage it at all is to wage it without scruple, and Britain and the United States are inured to laying aside their scruples for the duration.

This amoral attitude toward power is particularly dangerous in an era that promises ceaseless international friction, but it is not yet the dominant attitude. Anglo-American democracy has in its marrow a sense of compromise between opposing forces. War has been a temporary recourse where compromise failed, and the communist idea of war against a way of life is alien to the democratic tradition. Although both Britain and the United States have fought civil wars, the basic issues have been resolved less by battle than by later peaceful adjustment. Although both have fought wars of aggrandizement in achieving their empires, the present status of India, Egypt, and South Africa, of Cuba and the Philippines, indicates that aggrandizement has in the long run been no match for the spirit of compromise. The more ruthless war becomes in its techniques and the more total in its scope, the more antithetical it is to that spirit. The two cannot co-exist much longer. If the spirit is tough enough to survive, it will do so by evading and eventually by eliminating war.

The task may be beyond human power. But the English-speaking peoples have a strong incentive to try it; their whole way of life is at stake. Ever since the days of the Elizabethans their society has developed and spread overseas within a cushion of sea power that has protected it against a sudden blow. They have been able to dispense with militarism in the French or German sense and to prepare for war after war began — in short, to be civilian. They have consequently developed systems of government that minimize coercive force; they have paid heavily when fighting began, but the surrounding oceans have hitherto given them time to gather their strength and bring it to bear. The margin of time has been their salvation. Now it is evaporating. New weapons are making possible a devastating surprise attack, against which the oceans of the world may soon be little more defense than the English Channel. This prospect revolutionizes the position of every Anglo-Saxon democracy.

The effects upon Britain are already evident. She is rapidly approaching, if she has not already reached, the point where a major war threatens her with annihilation. The prospect is still too novel to have revolutionized her policy, for there has always been a lag between the development of new weapons and the realization of what they imply. But development proceeds inexorably, and realization must follow. For the first time in her history Britain cannot afford to fight. At the start of the atomic era war is ceasing to be for her what Clausewitz considered it, the continuation of diplomatic policy by other means, and is becoming the negation of policy in suicide.

Events of the second World War demonstrated that the bedrock of her security is crumbling. The action off Crete, for example, had a significance out of all proportion to its bearing on strategy: German land-based planes drove away the Royal Navy and opened the island to invasion; the lesson, if Britain were substituted for Crete and France for Greece, was that the navy alone no longer offered sure defense. Three years later the invasion of Normandy showed that coastal fortifications, carefully designed and strongly manned, could be broken by a sea and air assault. The Channel became a road for successful attack, and it is not a one-way road. Britain's army and navy in conjunction are insufficient to bar it against an invader. If she ever loses control of the air, her days are numbered.

In the closing phase of the war the danger from the air grew into something she could not hope to control. The German V-1, or jet-propelled bomb, was dealt with by orthodox methods, but the V-2 could not be. A rocket traveling faster than sound and sight is immune to present defenses and must be stopped, if at all, at its point of origin. The only certain way to preclude a rocket attack is to control directly or indirectly the entire area within which it might be mounted. For Britain that area already embraces the coast and hinterland of much of northwestern Europe, and her security has ceased to be an insular problem. Before the end of the war it transcended the province of all her armed services combined, and the days of 1940 were ancient history; she could scarcely hope again to stand alone against an enemy controlling western Europe and armed with the latest weapons. If the Soviet Union acquired such control tomorrow, the urban centers of the British Isles might be devastated by guided missiles. Anglo-American air power, even when armed with atomic bombs, would presumably furnish means of retaliation more than of defense. If London or the Midlands were destroyed, the prospect of being revenged would be cold comfort for the dead.

Another contemporary development in the art of slaughter, bacteriological warfare, is perhaps even more disturbing. Its potentialities in a close-packed island population are peculiarly hideous, and the medical defensive is still problematical. But if these threats are grim, they are trifles by comparison with those that impend now that atomic explosives are no longer an Anglo-Saxon monopoly. The destruction of Hiroshima and Nagasaki, and the subsequent tests at Bikini, have terrifying implications for every state in the world. For Britain they are catastrophic.

The obvious aspect of the atomic bomb is its explosive power, against which the only present defense is the dispersion of industries and people. Dispersion requires not merely a vast refashioning of society but also physical space. Britain does not have the space. Of all the great powers she is the smallest, the most concentrated, and therefore the most vulnerable. The other aspect of the bomb is equally important. It generates a poison that is most effectively spread, as the second test at Bikini showed, by the cloud of vapor from an underwater explosion. To this form of attack Britain is particularly vulnerable. She depends upon the sea more completely than any other great power, and her chief industrial areas are within a hundred miles of the west coast, from which comes the prevailing wind. Bombs might be planted by saboteurs, laid as mines by submarines, delivered by plane and presumably by rocket; and the detonation of a single one might have paralyzing effects. The danger has the quality of nightmare. But it promises to be, before long, the waking nightmare of Britain's military planners. Her "water-walled bulwark" is becoming a death trap.

If this analysis is sound, the problem of her defense appears insoluble. The soundest defense would be to attack — to strike the first blow without warning, in order to cripple the antagonist at the start and so preclude retaliation. Such a "preventive" war, when both sides have atomic bombs in quantity, would be at best a desperate gamble, and no government responsible to the voters would be likely to take the risk; a surprise onslaught at a moment of nominal peace is out of character for a democracy. Defense through dispersion is not geographically feasible for Britain. The only remaining possibility, if she depends on her own resources, would be to amass the weapons with which to strike back and then hope that their existence would deter assault. This strategy would be at best a counsel of despair, for it would involve catastrophe if the threat of retaliation were ignored. Yet in terms of Britain's own military resources no better method is apparent.

British security, like American, is now identified with the collective security of many other states. At present the sign of identification is the Atlantic Pact, which may be the beginning of an effective coalition. Its military side is only one of its aspects, and perhaps not the most important. The amassing of armaments and the formulation of joint defensive plans is a dangerous if necessary process. The attempt to deter aggression can seem from Moscow to be aggression, and a league to prevent war defeats itself if it goads the enemy to attack.

The real effectiveness of the coalition will depend more on moral factors than on military. If its members hope to preserve what is left of the peace, they will have to draw closer together. But their chief aim cannot be to prepare for a conflict with Russia that would defeat their whole purpose, or for an agreement of which there seems no immediate hope. They must attempt to knit the non-communist nations of the world into a group with sufficent cohesive strength to give pause to Soviet aggression and sufficient wisdom to avoid provoking it. Such a group is forming, and its growth will test the democratic capacity for collaboration as it has never been tested before. If it rises to the test, a world-wide coalition will develop with Anglo-American power for its core.

But the sense of power will have to be curbed by an overriding sense of moderation. Moderation will be sorely tried. To recognize the communist's premise without accepting it, to see that his war against capitalism has no limits of time or method and yet to retain a belief in ultimate compromise, requires a degree of perception and self-control as unprecedented for Britain as for the United States. Yet nothing less can succeed.

This is only part of the challenge. Moderation in itself is a negative virtue, all too easily enlisted in the defense of the status quo. The democracies cannot afford to be static in face of the communist dynamic, or to experiment with progress in isolated laboratories of their own. They are again engaged in defending their basic values, as they did against fascism, and they can be effective only by pooling their experience as well as their power. Danish co-operatives, British socialized medicine, the Tennessee Valley Authority — these and other new departures, great and small, successful and unsuccessful, are parts of the process by which democracy widens its frontiers and generates its own dynamic. Democracies in coalition can draw upon this force wherever it exists among them, and they will have to handle it, unlike military power, with daring rather than with moderation. Perception and self-control are not enough. The crusading spirit is needed, or the Kremlin may inherit what is left of the earth.

The difficulties, even in evading war in the immediate future, seem from the present almost insuperable. Perhaps they are. To assume that the two worlds of communism and democracy will learn to adjust their conflict is rash optimism. But to assume that they will resolve it only by war is to assume that a satanic determinism is turning the nations of the atomic era into Gadarene swine.

The ground for optimism is thin but real. Fear is a powerful centripetal force in the states of the West, and promises to increase as Russia arms herself with atomic weapons; it has already helped to pull the United States into collaboration with western Europe and the Commonwealth and to prepare the way for truly united nations. They may eventually be united less by fear than by the common task of dissipating fear through agreement with Russia, as the only long-term alternative to holocaust, and agreement in the end is not inconceivable. "To suppose that any nation can be unalterably the enemy of another," in the words of the younger Pitt, ". . . is a libel on the constitution of political societies, and supposes the existence of diabolical malice in the original frame of man."

The Russian people are not the enemy, and communism evolves like all faiths. Within a generation the Stalinists may be as antiquated as Loyola's Jesuits today, and the incompatibles that sunder East and West may have gone the way of those that sundered Loyola's Europe. The Russians share the human capacity to learn, and military developments stimulate learning: a communist is as badly off as a capitalist in radioactive ruins. The point seems to be rapidly coming, if it has not already come, where no belligerent can hope to be victorious in the traditional sense, and at that point the logical grounds for fighting give way before the logic of compromise. If the democracies in general, and Britain and the United States in particular, can maintain agreement among themselves, subordinate their national sovereignties to the needs of the group, and use their corporate strength with moderation, they may maintain the surface of peace until communism, in the fullness of time, discards its dream of destroying all other forms of government. That time may never come. But to work in the hope that it will is the only antidote to despair.

Britain's role in the great experiment is likely to be crucial. Although it may be subordinate to the American from the viewpoint of power, the democracies need clear thinking at least as much as armaments. Because war would be more obviously catastrophic for the British than for any other people, they have more pressing reasons to think clearly. If their policy is dominated by the need for peace — and they can afford nothing less — they will help to set the character of the new alignment and evoke its creative energies.

Britain is its nexus. Her imperial interests have tied her to the world overseas, and her geographic position has involved her in the Continent; her sense of Europe, sharpened by the diplomatic experience of centuries, is invaluable to transatlantic nations that must now involve themselves in turn. Her socialist regime is of moment to every democracy. Her attitude toward Russia, for all its rooted distrust, may mature perforce into a realistic pacifism. For these reasons, if no others, she has the opportunity for leadership in the struggle to preserve the West.

She is caught up by the crisis, and her exposed position makes the challenge peculiarly immediate for her. But she does not face it alone. Her old aloofness is gone; she is part of a cohering federation of western Europe and America, with outposts spread across the globe. Yet she is not submerged in the new grouping. She remains herself. Her long past, climaxed by the enormous readjustments of this century, has left her far from decadent. If her material

393

resources are waning, her political vitality seems once more to be waxing. She will need it all in the years to come, and it will have to be matched with wisdom. Failure will mean death. But success will mean a prouder part in the advance of civilization than even she has ever played.

BIBLIOGRAPHICAL NOTE

A NY ONE writing a study of this sort is bound to be, as Disraeli said of Peel, a burglar of other men's ideas. I am consciously or unconsciously indebted to every historian I have read. To acknowledge the debt by listing all the books would produce only a mélange of the good and bad, the sprightly and dull, which would have far less value than the bibliographies in all the standard textbooks. But I have relied in the main on a small group of authors, and to mention them, even at the risk of seeming arbitrary, is the least return I can make for the help they have given me.

The two general textbooks of British history on which I have principally drawn are William E. Lunt, *History of England* (third edition; New York and London: Harper & Brothers; 1945) and Arthur L. Cross, *A Shorter History of England and Greater Britain* (third edition; New York: The Macmillan Co.; 1939). A stimulating text, which presupposes some knowledge of the subject, is George M. Trevelyan, *History of England* (New York and London: Longmans, Green & Co.; 1926). The evolution of British naval predominance is clearly traced in William O. Stevens and Allan F. Westcott, *A History of Sea Power* (New York: Doubleday, Doran & Co.; 1942). A classic work on the evolution of Parliament is difficult but rewarding: Charles H. McIlwain, *The High Court of Parliament and Its Supremacy* (New Haven: Yale University Press; 1910). In the economic field Ephraim Lipson, *A Planned Economy or Free Enterprise; the Lessons of History* (London: A. & C. Black, Ltd.; 1944) is a provocative essay on the subject matter of his earlier book, *The Economic History of England* (3 vols.; London: A. & C. Black, Ltd.; 1915–31).

For the development of the empire and the dominions I have made liberal use of Ramsay Muir, *A Short History of the British Commonwealth* (2 vols.; London: G. Philip & Son, Ltd.; 1920–2), which is an excellent synthesis of domestic and imperial affairs from the days of the Romans to 1914. The author, like many others, devotes scant attention to the changes on the Continent that were determinants of Britain's growth. These changes are covered, with equal brevity and brilliance, by Herbert A. L. Fisher, *A History of Europe* (revised edition; Boston: Houghton Mifflin Co.; 1939). Esmé Wingfield-Stratford has endeavored to integrate all the aspects of Britain's story, from foreign affairs to architecture, in *The History of British Civilization* (second edition; New York and London: Harcourt, Brace & Co.; 1930); if his aim is too ambitious to be fully realized, he is lively to read and penetrating in many of his comments.

For the sixteenth century Arthur D. Innes, *England under the Tudors* (London: Methuen & Co., Ltd.; 1905) is a compendium of facts enlivened by flashes of insight. For my discussion of Henry VIII's breach from Rome I have drawn also on James A. Froude, *History of England from the Fall of Wolsey to the Death of Elizabeth* (12 vols.; second edition; New York: C. Scribner's Sons; 1890). Two of the most readable and delightful books on the period, both by outstanding modern authorities, are Conyers Read, *The Tudors; Personalities and Practical Politics in Sixteenth Century England* (New York: Oxford University Press; 1936) and John E. Neale, *Queen Elizabeth* (New York and London: Harcourt, Brace & Co.; 1934). The end of the century is covered in great detail by Edward P. Cheyney, *A History of England, from the Defeat of the Armada to the Death of Elizabeth; with an Account of English Institutions during the Later Sixteenth and Early Seventeenth Centuries* (2 vols.; New York: Longmans, Green & Co.; 1914–26); the second volume is by far the best survey I know of Elizabethan local government.

The outstanding history of the Stuart period is George M. Trevelyan, *England under the Stuarts* (fourteenth edition; London: Methuen & Co., Ltd.; 1928); this book is a masterpiece, to which I am deeply indebted. A brief but invaluable study of the rise of Parliament before the Civil Wars is Wallace Notestein, *The Winning of the Initiative by the House of Commons* (London: H. Milford, Oxford University Press; 1925). For the Cromwellian period I have used particularly two major works of Sir Charles Firth, *Oliver Cromwell and the Rule of the Puritans in England* (New York: G. P. Putnam's Sons; 1900) and *Cromwell's Army: a History of the English Soldier during the Civil Wars, the Commonwealth and the Protectorate* (New York and London: Methuen & Co., Ltd.; 1902); a brief and fascinating essay by the same author is *The Parallel between the English and American Civil Wars: the Reade Lecture Delivered in the Senate House, Cambridge, on 14 June, 1910* (Cambridge: Cambridge University Press, 1910). Keith G. Feiling, *A History of the Tory Party, 1640–1714* (Oxford: The Clarendon Press; 1924) traces the origins and growth of Toryism from the Reformation to the debacle of 1714. A more basic aspect of the Reformation is examined by Richard H. Tawney in *Religion and the Rise of Capitalism; a Historical Study* (New York: Harcourt, Brace & Co.; 1926), which deals with the connection between the Protestant ethic and the commercial spirit of the rising middle class. The thesis of the book is still controversial. But, if only because its author is one of the greatest living historians, it cannot be ignored by anyone interested in the progress of ideas. Another classic of intellectual history, done on a narrower canvas, is George P. Gooch, *The History of English Democratic Ideas in the Seventeenth Century* (Cambridge: Cambridge University Press; 1898).

For the eighteenth century as a whole I know nothing better than William E. H. Lecky, *A History of England in the Eighteenth Century* (8 vols.; New York: D. Appleton & Co., 1888–91), which I used particularly for its vivid description of Methodism. An equally broad survey of social and political conditions, but confined to the reign of George III, is Sir George O. Trevelyan, *The American Revolution* (4 vols.; New York: Longmans, Green & Co.; 1905–29) and *George III and Charles Fox, the Concluding Part of the American Revolution* (2 vols.; New York: Longmans, Green & Co.; 1912–4). The Whiggism of Trevelyan has been partially offset on the political side by Keith G. Feiling, *The Second Tory Party, 1714–1832* (New York and London: The Macmillan Co.; 1938) and by Geoffrey G. Butler's delightful series of essays, *The Tory Tradition: Bolingbroke — Burke — Disraeli — Salisbury* (London: J. Murray; 1914). On the constitutional side Lewis B. Namier has upset the traditional theories of George III's experiment in his two works, *The Structure of Politics at the Accession of George III* (2 vols.; London: Macmillan & Co., Ltd.; 1929) and *England in the Age of the American Revolution* (London: Macmillan & Co., Ltd.; 1930). The outstanding treatment of British naval policy during this crucial period is still Alfred T. Mahan, *The Influence of Sea Power upon History, 1660–1783* (twenty-fourth edition; Boston: Little, Brown & Co.; 1914) and *The Influence of Sea Power upon the French Revolution and Empire,*

1793–1812 (2 vols.; Boston: Little, Brown & Co., 1892). Arthur Bryant, *The Years of Endurance, 1793–1802* (New York and London: Harper & Brothers; 1942) is a lively and sometimes gossipy account of Britain in the crisis of the Napoleonic Wars.

For the political story from 1815 to 1886 I have relied heavily on Sir John A. R. Marriott, *England since Waterloo* (third edition; New York and London: G. P. Putnam's Sons and Methuen and Co., Ltd.; 1919). A stimulating survey of the early and late nineteenth century is Elie Halévy, *A History of the English People* [1815–52] (4 vols.; London: T. F. Unwin; 1924–47) and *A History of the English People: Epilogue* [1895–1915] (2 vols.; London: E. Benn, Ltd.; 1929–34). The author approaches his subject with the wisdom and detachment of French scholarship at its best, and the only drawback of his monumental work is that it does not cover the whole period.

For the development of the empire in the nineteenth and twentieth centuries a compact and most convenient text is Paul Knaplund, *The British Empire, 1815–1939* (New York: Harper & Brothers; 1941). British economic changes in the same period are dealt with (for the serious student) in sections of Witt Bowden, Michael Karpovitch, and Alfred P. Usher, *An Economic History of Europe since 1750* (New York and Cincinnati: American Book Co.; 1937), and the evolution of political theory in Guido de Ruggiero, *The History of European Liberalism* (London: H. Milford, Oxford University Press; 1927). No reader should tackle either of these volumes without understanding that he will have to work hard for his profit. A less exacting book in the field of political theory, and one of particular value, is Carl A. Bodelsen, *Studies in Mid-Victorian Imperialism* (Copenhagen and London: Gyldendal; 1924), in which the author handles with great lucidity the different English schools of thought about the empire.

For the nature and results of Britain's military experience in the first World War I am indebted to the later chapters of Edward M. Earle (editor), *Makers of Modern Strategy* (Princeton: Princeton University Press; 1941). For my discussion of the post-war settlement I have drawn on Paul Birdsall, *Versailles Twenty Years After* (New York: Reynal & Hitchcock; 1941). Two stimulating commentaries on international affairs before and during the second World War are Edward H. Carr, *The Twenty Years' Crisis, 1919–1939; an*

Introduction to the Study of International Relations (London: Macmillan & Co., Ltd.; 1940) and *Conditions of Peace* (New York: The Macmillan Co.; 1942). These are the authors to whom I am particularly grateful. Where I have ventured to alter their ideas, the responsibility is mine.

INDEX

Afghanistan, Anglo-Russian friction in, 243, 276, 280, 281; and conclusion of Triple Entente, 313

Africa, and sixteenth-century trade routes, 47–8; in Treaty of Versailles (1783), 161; nineteenth-century European expansion in, 210, 270, 275, 276, 277, 287

Africa, North, British expansion in, 281–4, 287–8; and conclusion of Entente Cordiale, 304; and Anglo-German rivalry, 317; and Ethiopian crisis, 361; in second World War, 369, 370–3, 376

Africa, South, see Boers, Boer War; Union of South Africa

Air power, in second World War and after, 376–7, 378, 381, 388–91; see also Lutwaffe; Royal Air Force

Aix-la-Chapelle, Treaty of, (1748), 136, 139

Alabama claims, settlement of, 276–7.

Alexander I, Emperor of Russia, 189, 193, 198; death, 211.

Algeciras, Congress of, (1906), 305

Alliances: British, against Bourbon France, 117, 119, 135, 137, 139–40, against French Revolution and Napoleon, 181–2, 188, 193, in concert of Europe, 203, in Crimean War, 241–3; French, with Czechoslovakia, etc., after first World War, 340, 363, 365, with Russia (1935), 357, 359, 365–6, 383. *See also* Anglo-Japanese alliance; Anglo-Russian alliance; Atlantic Pact; Axis; Dual Alliance; Russo-German Pact; Triple Alliance

Alsace-Lorraine, annexed by Germany (1871), 270; source of Franco-German bitterness, 293, 317; surrendered by Germany (1919), 335

America, Spanish possessions in, 32, 118, 121, 196, 198; Elizabethan interest in, 41, 47–8; Jacobean colonization, 58–9; Cromwellian concern with, 90, 91–2; and rise of religious toleration, 114; British rivalry with Bourbon powers in, 133–5, 138–43;

America (*continued*)
and Monroe Doctrine, 208–10; Nazi threat to, 370–1. *See also* Revolution, American; Caribbean; United States

Amiens, Peace of, (1802), 190, 198

Anglicanism: see Church of England

Anglo-Japanese alliance (1902), formation and effects, 300, 303, 317, 326; abrogated, 341–2, 383

Anglo-Russian alliance, of second World War, 376, 383

Anne, Queen of England, heiress presumptive, 105; death of her children, 116; accession and reign, 122–7, 130.

Anne Boleyn, wife of Henry VIII, 19–23, 33

Anti-Corn-Law League, 226–8; mentioned, 253, 299

Apostolic succession, theory of, 24–5, 26, 27, 30; and Methodism, 180

Arabi, Egyptian colonel, his revolt and its effects (1882), 282–3

Aristocracy, and Tudor gentry, 8–9, 14; in Hanoverian period, 128–30; and first Reform Bill, 221–2; Disraeli's views of, 247–8, 249–50; and crisis of 1910, 309

Armada, Spanish, defeated, 42–3; effects of, 48

Armed Neutrality: of 1780, 160; of 1801, 189

Armistice of 1918, terms of, 332, 336

Army: English, sixteenth-century weakness of, 7–8, 48; of Cromwell, 82–3, 94, 96–7; of James II, 110; in settlement of Glorious Revolution, 113; and eighteenth-century patronage, 130, 151; role in Chatham's grand strategy, 139–40; in American Revolution, 157–8, 160–1, 164; in Wars of French Revolution and Napoleon, 181–2, 186, 196–7, 199–200; and Tory Reaction, 213; in mid-Victorian period, 231; in late-Victorian period, 271–2; and Irish crisis (1914), 311; reformed before first World War, 317–8; in

Index

Army (*continued*)
first World War, 321, 322–3; between wars, 358; in second World War, 367, 369
Army, Indian, 240, 243–4; in crisis of 1878, 279; in second World War, 380
Arthur Tudor, son of Henry VII, marriage and death of, 16
Articles of religion: *see* Six Articles; Thirty-Nine Articles
Asiento, conceded to Britain by Spain (1713), 121; friction over, 134–5.
Atlantic Pact, 387; potential significance, 391
Atomic weapons, first used, 378; implications, 390–1
Austerlitz, Battle of (1805), 193–4
Australia, settlement of, 232–3; in Boer War, 294; in first World War, 324, 343; after Ottawa Conference, 351; in second World War, 371, 374, 379, 384, 385
Austria, sixteenth-century dynastic alliance with Spain, 13, 14; in period of Louis XIV, 98, 117–21; eighteenth-century position of, 134–5, 136–8, 141–2; in Wars of French Revolution and Napoleon, 176, 181, 182, 188, 193, 197, 199; in Vienna settlement, 202–5; and concert of Europe, 206, 207–8; and nineteenth-century Turkey, 210, 243; and Revolutions of 1848, 239; and Italian question, 242; and Danish War (1864), 251; and German unification, 243, 269, *and see* Austria-Hungary; in settlement of 1919, 334; annexed by Germany, 363; overrun by Russia, 381
Austria-Hungary, creation of (1867), 269–70, 276; in crisis of 1878, 279; and German alliance, 279–80, 301; and origins of first World War, 314–6, 317, 318–20; in first World War, 324, 331; extinguished in settlement of 1919, 334, 381
Austrian Succession, War of the (1740), 134–6
Axis, Rome-Berlin, formed (1936), 362–3; Japanese pact with, 371. *See also* Germany, in second World War

Balance of power, nature of, 13–4; in Tudor period, 12–4, 16, 18; and

Balance of Power (*continued*)
Louis XIV, 103–4, 117–9; and Utrecht settlement (1713), 121–2, 126, 134; and Paris settlement (1763), 140–1; in Napoleonic era, 189; and Vienna settlement (1815), 201, 202, 204, 231, 276, 381; in Mediterranean, 212, 241, 243, 270; and Triple Entente, 313–4; in Europe of 1920's, 337, 381; in contemporary world, 380–2, 383–4
Baldwin, Stanley, and abdication of Edward VIII, 354–5; and Nazi menace, 360–1
Balkans, nineteenth-century Austrian interests in, 205, 243, 269–70, 279–80; nineteenth-century British interests in, 210–2, 241–3, 278–80; and origins of first World War, 313, 314–5, 317, 318–20; in first World War, 324, 331; in second World War, 371, 372, 373, 376, 381; and contemporary Anglo-Russian friction, 383
Baltic Sea, English commerce in, 4; and German sea power in first World War, 327–8
Baltic States, during American Revolution, 160; in Napoleonic era, 189, 193; after first World War, 331
Battles: *see* Austerlitz (1805); Blenheim (1704); Boyne (1690); Britain (1940); Camperdown (1797); Cape St. Vincent (1797); Copenhagen (1801); Dunbar (1650); Flodden Field (1513); Jutland (1916); Lexington (1775); Majuba Hill (1881); Marne (1914); Navarino (1827); Nile (1798); Quiberon Bay (1759); Saratoga (1777); Trafalgar (1805); Waterloo (1815); Worcester (1651); Yorktown (1781)
Beatty, Admiral Sir David, at Battle of Jutland, 327
Belgium, separation of, from Kingdom of Holland (1830), 217; in Franco-Prussian War, 276; invaded by Germans (1914), 316, 318, 319–21; and reparations, 336; French alliance with, 340; and Locarno treaties, 340–1; invaded by Germans (1940), 368–9
Berlin, Congress and Treaty of, (1878), 279–80, 293, 364; and Bosnian crisis (1908), 314

Bible, translated in reign of Henry VIII, 28

Bill of Rights (1689), mentioned, 112, 178, 386

Billeting, of troops of Charles I, 62, 63

Bishops: *see* Episcopacy

Bismarck, Prince Otto von, and Danish War (1864), 251; and unification of Germany, 269, 271; diplomacy when Chancellor of German Empire, 270–1, 279–80, 283, 286, 287; and state socialism, 297; retirement, 300–1; compared with Hitler, 359, 372; mentioned, 218, 250, 385

Black Sea, British strategic interests in (1854), 242; remilitarized by Russia (1870), 270; and crisis of 1878, 279

Blake, Robert, Cromwellian admiral, 90–1; compared with Jellicoe, 328

Blenheim, Battle of, (1704), 121

Blitzkrieg, in Austro- and Franco-Prussian Wars, 273–4, 321; failure of, in 1914–5, 321–2; by Nazis in Poland, 367, and in France, 368–9; and Battle of Britain, 371–2

Blockade: American, of Japan by submarines, 378; British, and strategy evolved in Seven Years' War, 140, 142, effect on maritime neutrals, 142, 160, in American Revolution, 158–9, 159–60, in Wars of French Revolution and Napoleon, 188–9, 191, 192, 194–6, 197–8, 326, in first World War, 326, 328, 331, in second World War, 367; German, by submarines in first World War, 326–7, 328–9, 330–1, in Spanish Civil War, 363

Blücher, Prince Gebhard von, Prussian field marshal, in Waterloo campaign, 200

Boers, early friction with British, 204, 232, 235–7; hostilities with British: *see* Boer War; in Union of South Africa, 343–4

Boer War: first (1880), 284–6, 290; second (1899), outbreak of, 288–9, 293, background, 289–93, course, 293–5, and dominion co-operation, 294, 343, and Anglo-German relations, 301, 302, 304, costs of, 308, mentioned, 300

Bolingbroke, Henry St. John, Viscount, and Tory debacle of 1714, 126–7; quoted, 138, 214; mentioned, 141

Bonaparte: *see* Napoleon

Book of Common Prayer, in reign of Edward VI, 30–1; reissued by Elizabeth, 35; imposed on Scots, 73; Anglicans' loyalty to, in Puritan Revolution, 84

Boroughs, in early Tudor period, 8–12; attempted coercion of, by Charles II and James II, 110; triumph of, in Glorious Revolution, 113; rotten, uses and abolition of, 129–30, 132, 153, 219, 221; reform of municipal government in, 222

Bosnia-Herzegovina, in Treaty of San Stefano, 278; in Treaty of Berlin, 279; and crisis of 1908, 314, 315; and outbreak of first World War, 318–9

Bosporus, in Greek revolt, 211; in crisis of 1878, 257, 281

Boston (Mass.), in American Revolution, 155, 158

Boulogne, Napoleon at, 191, 193; German drive toward (1915), 321

Bourbon, House of, accession of, in France with Henry IV, 45; marriage alliance with Stuarts, 61–2; acquisition of Spanish throne, 117–22, 134; collapse of regime of, in France, 176–8, 180–1; members of: *see* Henrietta Maria; Louis XIII; Louis XIV; Philip V

Boyne, Battle of the, (1690), 115–6; mentioned, 185, 186, 267

Brest-Litovsk, Treaty of, (1918), 330, 331, 334, 335

Bright, John, and Anti-Corn-Law League, 227; and second Reform Bill, 253

Britain, Battle of, (1940), 371–2

Brooke, Rupert, quoted, 320

Buckingham, George Villiers, Duke of, favorite of James I and Charles I, 61–4

Bulgaria, in Treaty of San Stefano, 278; in Treaty of Berlin, 279; and origins of first World War, 314, 315

Burgoyne, John, British general at Saratoga, 158–9

Burke, Edmund, political philosophy of, 147, 247, 249; and American Revolution, 157, 163, 360; and im-

Burke, Edmund (*continued*)
peachment of Hastings, 166–7; on
French Revolution, 177–8, 180; on
imperial ties, 238, 346; mentioned,
244

Bute, John Stuart, Earl of, and Peace
of Paris (1763), 141–2

Byron, George Gordon, Baron, and
Greek revolt, 211

Cabinet: British, in early Hanoverian
period, 130–2, 141, 152, 154, 165–
6, and crisis of 1914, 318, 320, reorganized during first World War,
325; Canadian, and responsible
government, 235

Calais, English acquisition of, 4; loss
of, 33; Armada at, 43; German
drive toward (1915), 321

Calvinism, and English Puritanism,
36–8; in Scotland, 39, 44, 51; in the
Netherlands, 41; in Ireland, 57–8;
of the Boers, 235, 290. *See also*
Kirk of Scotland; Presbyterianism,
Puritanism

Camperdown, Battle of, (1797), 183,
193

Canada, French settlements in, 58,
133; British attacks on, 136, 139–
40; British acquisition of, 141–4,
150; during American Revolution,
158, threatened by United States,
162, 198, 234, 235, 262, 277; development of, in early-Victorian
period, 232, 234–5, 236, 263; in
Boer War, 294; and imperial protection, 299; in first World War,
343; and abrogation of Anglo-Japanese alliance, 342; after Ottawa
Conference, 351; in second World
War, 374, 375, 379, 384, 385

Canning, George, foreign policy of,
208–9, 210; death, 211, 214; followers of (Canningites), 239, 245;
mentioned, 368

Cape Colony, acquired by Britain
(1815), 204; growth, 232; and
Great Trek, 236–7; and Zulu danger, 284; and Boer War, 289, 291,
292, 293

Cape St. Vincent, Battle of, (1797),
183, 193, 328

Capitalism, in early Tudor period, 11–
2; and abolition of monasteries, 22;
and economic position of late-Eliza-
bethan England, 47–8; and growth

Capitalism (*continued*)
of science, 146–7; and Industrial
Revolution, 171–2, 173–4, 274; and
Boer War, 289–92

Caribbean, Hakluyt on colonies near,
47; Cromwellian concern with, 91–
2; eighteenth-century rivalries in,
133–4, 142, 159, 160–1; in Napoleonic era, 190, 191–2; United States
interests in, 281, 303, 370

Carlyle, Thomas, on chartism, 224;
on second Reform Bill, 253; German influence on, 272–3

Caroline of Brunswick, Queen of
George IV, 213–4

Castlereagh, Robert Stewart, Viscount,
and concert of Europe, 206–7;
death, 208, 214, 221; mentioned,
252

Catholic emancipation, and Grattan's
reform movement, 163–4; and Act
of Union, 186–8; and crisis of 1829,
214–6, 245; compared with Home
Rule movement, 264; effect on Ulster, 266

Cavalier Parliament: *see* Parliament,
Cavalier

Cavaliers, composition of, in first Civil
War, 79–80; characteristics of, 80–
2, 87; in second Civil War, 85; return of, from exile with Charles II,
98; attitude toward Restoration
Church, 103; relationship to later
Tories, 105–6; mentioned, 112

Ceylon, acquired by Britain (1815),
204; British withdrawal from, 384

Chamberlain, Joseph, and Liberal
schism of 1886, 267–8, 299; and
Salisbury, 268, 295–6; and Boer
War, 292–3; on "Teutonic race,"
295; and protection, 298–9, 309,
350; compared with his son, 360

Chamberlain, Neville, compared with
Walpole, 135; foreign policy of,
354, 360–1, 364–6; resignation, 368

Charles I, King of England, as Prince
of Wales, 59–60; and breach with
Parliament, 61–7; character, 64, 76,
86, 99; and Laudianism, 65, 70–3;
economic and financial policies, 69–
70; in Puritan Revolution, 73–87;
mentioned, 52, 113, 151, 154, 174,
218

Charles II, King of England, with
Scots in second Civil War, 88–9;
restoration of, 95; character, 98–9;

Charles II (*continued*)
 reign, 100–9; compared with
 George III, 151–2
Charles V, Holy Roman Emperor, 17–
 8, 20, 31–2; mentioned, 118
Charles VI, Holy Roman Emperor,
 candidate for Spanish throne when
 Archduke, 118–21; dynastic problem when Emperor, 134–5
Charles Edward Stuart, the Young
 Pretender, 136
Chartism, aims and failure of, 224–5;
 mentioned, 349
Chatham, William Pitt, Earl of (elder
 Pitt), first ministry of, 138, 140–1;
 character, 138–9; strategy, 139–40,
 143, 159, 323; and American Revolution, 153–4, 157; compared with
 his son, 169, 181, and with Rhodes,
 291; mentioned, 276, 368
Chesterton, G. K., quoted 223
China, and war with Japan (1894),
 275; European attempt to partition,
 301; and Anglo-Japanese alliance,
 303; German cessions in, (1919),
 335; Japanese aggression in,
 (1931), 361; in contemporary
 world, 380–1
Church of England: in England, under Henry VIII, 23–4, 27–9, 30,
 132, under Edward VI, 29–31, under Mary, 31–3, under Elizabeth,
 34–8, 45, 50, under James I, 51–4,
 55, under Charles I, 65–6, 70–3, 76,
 77, and Cavaliers during Puritan
 Revolution, 80–1, 84, at Restoration,
 96, 100–1, 102–3, and James II,
 110–1, under Anne, 125, 126, effect
 of Hanoverian accession on, 127–8,
 130, 147, in Burke's political philosophy, 177, and Methodism, 179–
 80, Disraeli's views of, 247, 248–9,
 250, and Education Act (1870),
 258, Chamberlain's proposal to dis-
 establish, 267; in Ireland, 44, and
 "Protestant ascendancy," 115–6,
 163–4, 185–8, 214, 215–6, 267–8,
 disestablished by Gladstone, 262
Churchill, John: see Marlborough
Churchill, Winston, compared with
 Disraeli, 245; secession from Conservatives, 299; First Lord of Admiralty, 321; and strategy of first
 World War, 323–5; on Jellicoe,
 328; secession from Liberals, 349;
 and Irish naval bases, 355; and

Churchill, Winston (*continued*)
 Nazi menace, 360; Prime Minister,
 368, 370, 371, 376; defeat (1945),
 385–6; quoted, 374.
Civil War: American Revolution as,
 151, 153–4, 156–9, 161; American
 (1861), 162, 243, 251, 261–2, 269,
 271, 321; English, in Puritan Revolution, 81–3, 85; French, in sixteenth century, 14, 38, 40; Spanish
 (1936), 363
Clarendon Code, enacted, 100–1; extended by Test Act, 103; modified
 by Glorious Revolution, 113–5;
 Tory nostalgia for, 125; suspension
 of penalties of, after 1714, 127–8;
 repeal of Corporation Act (1828),
 214, 216
Clarendon, Edward Hyde, Earl of,
 minister of Charles II, 100–1, 131
Clement VIII, Pope, and marriage of
 Henry VIII, 20–1.
Cobden, Richard, and Anti-Corn-
 Law League, 227; and laissez faire,
 256; mentioned, 275
Coke, Sir Edward, Chief Justice, and
 James I, 56, 70
Colonies, Elizabethan attitude toward,
 47; Jacobean emigration to, 58–9;
 and Cromwellian imperialism, 90,
 91–2; British acquisitions in second
 Dutch War, 101, and in Treaty of
 Utrecht, 121; and Anglo-French
 rivalry in eighteenth century, 133,
 136, 138–43; British seizure of European, in Napoleonic Wars, 196,
 203; Victorian schools of thought
 about, 231–4; nineteenth-century
 European race for, 250, 270, 275–6,
 287; British acquisitions in Versailles settlement, 332, 333, 335,
 336. *See also* Revolution, American;
 Dominions; Imperialism
Commerce, in early sixteenth century,
 3–4; promotion of, by Henry VII,
 15; under Elizabeth, 41, 47–8; and
 Cromwell's wars, 90–2, 132–3; and
 War of Spanish Succession, 119,
 120; and Anglo-Scottish friction,
 123; and Spanish-American market,
 121, 133–5, 195, 208, 209; colonial,
 and American Revolution, 148–50;
 expansion of, in eighteenth century,
 162, 171; and Vienna settlement,
 203; expansion of, and Crimean
 War, 240

Common law, courts of, and James I,
55–6, 57; and ship money, 70; tenure of judges of, 77, 113; late-Victorian reform of, 259, 260

Commons, House of: *see* House of
Commons

Commonwealth, Cromwellian, 89–91,
92–4

Commonwealth of Nations, British,
foreshadowed in eighteenth century, 150; embryonic in Victorian
era, 231–8, 380; creation of, 343–4,
346; and Ottawa Conference, 350–
1; and Crown, 354–5; and Eire,
355; and collaboration with United
States in second World War, 374,
379–80; in contemporary world,
384–5, 387, 392

Communism, and eighteenth-century
rationalism, 146; and Russian Revolution, 330, 335; British fear of,
at home, 353; and Russia's position
between wars, 356–7; and Hitler's
attack on Russia, 372; and Russia's
contemporary position, 382, 388,
391–4

Concert of Europe: *see* Europe, concert of

Congress system after 1815, conflicting
views of, 206–9; collapse of, by
1878, 279; contrasted with League
of Nations, 338

Conscription, first introduced in
France, 182; copied by Prussia and
German Empire, 273; adopted in
Britain (1916), 322–3, and rein-
troduced (1939), 354; reintroduced
in Germany by Hitler, 361

Conservative Party, under Disraeli,
256–7, 259–60; under Salisbury,
265, 287–9, 292–6, 298–9, 300–2,
309, 312; split by protection, 229,
246, 256, 298–9, 305–6; and Liberal
government after 1906, 299–300,
306, 307, 308, 309–10, 311–2, 348;
and coalition of first World War,
325, 345, 348; between World
Wars, 347–50, 353–5, 357. *See also*
Conservatism; Tory Party.

Conservatism, Burke's theories of, 147,
177–8, 180; Disraeli's theories of,
245–50; and imperialism, 256–7;
and Fabians, 297

Continental System, of Napoleon I,
194–9

Contract, freedom of, and classical

Contract (*continued*)
liberalism, 220; and legalization of
trade unions, 259

Copenhagen, Battle of, (1801), 189,
193

Corn law of 1815, 213; repeal of,
225–9

Cornwallis, Charles, Earl, at Yorktown, 151, 160–1.

Cotton manufacture, origins of, 172–
3; and American Civil War, 251

Courts, English: of common law: *see*
Common law, courts of; preroga-
tive, established by Tudors, 56;
used by Charles I, 69; abolished by
Long Parliament, 77; revived in
Church by James II, 110

Cranmer, Thomas, appointed Archbishop of Canterbury, 21; relations
with Henry VIII, 28–9; in reign of
Edward VI, 30–1; execution, 33

Crete, British expulsion from, (1941),
373; implications, 389

Crimean War (1854), causes and
course, 240–3; psychological effect
of, in Britain, 269; mentioned, 279,
313, 317

Cromwell, Oliver, in Long Parliament, 78; and New Model, 82–3;
character, 83; in second Civil War,
85–6; problems of his regime, 87,
92–3; settlement of Ireland and
Scotland, 88–9; foreign and imperial policy, 90–2; domestic policy,
92–4; compared with Gladstone,
285; mentioned, 113, 142, 164, 224,
225, 235, 368

Cromwell, Richard, ("Tumbledown
Dick"), 94–5

Cyprus, British acquisition of, (1878),
279

Czechoslovakia, creation of, (1919),
334; French alliance with, 340,
363, 365; annexed by Germany,
363–5, 366; overrun by Russia, 381

Dardanelles, in Crimean War, 241; in
crisis of 1878, 281; Anglo-French
attack on, (1915), 324; mentioned,
325, 326, 343

Darwin, Charles, followers of, and
cult of force, 272

Declaration of Indulgence, by Charles
II, 102; by James II, 110

Derby, Edward Stanley, Earl of,
Prime Minister, 253

De Valera, Eamon, and Irish Free State, 345; and Republic of Eire, 355

Diggers, in Puritan Revolution, 93, 95

Disraeli, Benjamin, political philosophy of, and renascence of Toryism, 245–52, 265; and second Reform Bill, 253–4; and imperialism, 256–7, 278, 286, 312–3; and domestic reforms, 259–60; and Victoria, 260; and Home Rule, 263; imperial and foreign policy, 268, 278–82, 284–5, 354, 364; compared with Salisbury, 295; influence of, 268, 348; mentioned, 269, 305, 368

Dissenters, during Restoration, 100–1, 102–3, 106; and James II, 110; in Glorious Revolution, 112, 113–5, 116; under Anne, 125, 126; and Hanoverian accession, 127–8; in nineteenth century, 180, 214. *See also* Presbyterianism; Puritanism

Divine right, theory of, 51–2, 106

Dominions, British, genesis of, 231–5, 277–8; economic competition with Britain, 274, 350–1; Joseph Chamberlain and, 298–9; before and during first World War, 323, 343–4; in peace settlement, 332, 335, 336; and League of Nations, 338; isolationism in, 340, 352; and Anglo-Japanese alliance, 342; Irish Free State among, 345; and Statute of Westminster, 346–7; in second World War, 374, 379, 384; in contemporary world, 385. *See also* Australia; Canada; Colonies; Commonwealth of Nations, British; Eire; New Zealand; Union of South Africa

Drake, Sir Francis, and Spanish Armada, 43

Drang nach Osten, genesis of, 279–80; development of, and first World War, 301, 313, 315; Hitler's failure to revive, 359

Dryden, John, quoted, 107–8, 114

Dual Alliance, in nineteenth century, 301–2, 305; and Schlieffen Plan, 316; British attitude toward, before first World War, 317–8

Dual Monarchy: *see* Austria-Hungary

Dunbar, Battle of (1650), and its effects, 88–9

Dunkirk, British withdrawal from,

Dunkirk (*continued*) (1940), 369, 370; mentioned, 96, 377

Durham, John Lambton, Earl of, and his *Report* on Canada, 234–5; mentioned, 346

Dutch War: first, (1652), 91; second, (1665), 101–2; third, (1672), 102–3

East India Company, in eighteenth century, 129, 133–4, 165–7, 172; loss of commercial privileges, 222; and Sepoy Mutiny, 243–4

Edinburgh, Treaty of, (1560), 39–40

Education: British elementary, state financing of, 222; Gladstone's reform of, 258, 260; Indian, 244

Edward VI, King of England, birth, 23; reign, 29–31

Edward VII, King of Great Britain, accession, 295; and Entente Cordiale, 304; death, 310; mentioned, 354

Edward VIII, King of Great Britain, accession and abdication, 354–5

Egypt, Napoleon's expedition to, 184–5, 186, 188, 210, 282; and Greek revolt, 210–1; nineteenth-century French interests in, 243; Anglo-French friction over, 270; British occupation of, 281–4; and reconquest of Sudan, 288; and formation of Entente Cordiale, 304; in first World War, 331; post-war nationalism in, 337, 361; in second World War, 371, 373, 376; mentioned, 190

Eire, creation of, 355; in second World War, 374, 384, 385

Elgin, James Bruce, Earl of, and Canadian self-government, 235; mentioned, 346

Elizabeth, Empress of Russia, and Seven Years' War, 137, 141

Elizabeth, Queen of England, heiress presumptive, 23, 31; character, 33–4, 38, 46; Church settlement, 34–5, 37–8, 54, 65–6, 71, 76; foreign policy, 38–44; technique of governing, 50–1, 60–1; and ship money, 70; mentioned, 159, 174

Enclosure movement, in Tudor period, 11, 22; under Charles I, 69; in eighteenth century, 171

Enlightenment, philosophy of, 145–6. *See also* Rationalism

Entente: Cordiale, formed, 300, 304–5, extended to Russia, 312–4; Triple: *see* Triple Entente

Episcopacy, under Henry VIII, 27, 28; under Elizabeth, 34, 35, 36–8; in Scotland under James VI, 51, 73; in England under James I, 51–3, 55; under Charles I, 65, 72, 79. *See also* Church of England

Erastianism, of Henry VIII, 28, 29; and Lutheranism, 36; Laudian adherence to, 65; among English Presbyterians, 84

Ethiopia, conquered by Italy, 361–2; liberated in second World War, 379

Europe, concert of, and congress system, 205–9, 212; collapse of, by 1878, 279; compared with League of Nations, 208, 338–9

Evangelicalism, and Methodism, 180; and Victorian liberalism, 217, 230–1; and missionary movement, 232–3, 236, 237

Fabianism, its characteristics, 297; and influence, 298, 349

Fair trade, demand for, (1880's), 274–5; and Joseph Chamberlain's program, 298

Fairfax, Thomas, Baron, commander in chief under Parliament, 83; conservatism of, 86, 88

Far East, late nineteenth-century European rivalries in, 270, 275, 277, 293, 301, 302; affected by first World War, 317, 326; by Washington naval agreements, 342; Japanese aggression in, 361, 374–6, 378; in contemporary world, 380–1

Fashoda crisis (1898–9), 288, 292–3, 295, 302, 304

Fenianism, origin and course of movement, 261–2, 277; compared with Home Rule, 263, 264

Ferdinand of Aragon, mentioned, 13, 16, 17

Flodden Field, Battle of, (1513), 17

Florida, Spanish colonization of, 58; acquired by Britain (1763), 141; reacquired by Spain (1783), 161–2

Foch, Ferdinand, in first World War, 331; mentioned, 381

Forced Loan, and antagonism to Charles I, 62

Fox, Charles James, in American Revolution, 157; and impeachment of Hastings, 166–7; and George III, 169; Prime Minister, 194

France, medieval relations of, with England and Scotland, 4–5, 6; expansion under Valois, 12–13; sixteenth-century civil wars, 14, 38, 40; relations with Elizabethan England and Scotland, 38–40, 45; expansion in Canada, 58; in Thirty Years' War, 59–60; relations with Charles I, 61–2; with Charles II, 98–9, 101–4, 106; and Glorious Revolution, 103–12, 114, 115; and English wars of Louis XIV, 116–22, 125, 269; relations with Hanoverian Britain, 133–44, 148, 175; in American Revolution, 157–62, 164, 166; during French Revolution and Napoleonic Empire, 168, 169, 170, 175–8, 180–200, 282; in Vienna settlement, 202, 203–4, 205–6; and nineteenth-century Continental liberalism, 204–5; and concert of Europe, 206, 208–9, 211–2; and Revolution of 1830, 217, and of 1848, 239–40; under Napoleon III, 241–3, 269, 271, 279; under Third Republic, 270, 273, 276, 280, 281–3, 286–9; and origins of first World War, 300, 301, 304–5, 312–3, 316, 317–9; in first World War, 320–2, 324–6, 329, 331, 367; in peace settlement (1919), 332, 333, 336, 337, 338–9, 340–1; and origins of second World War, 358, 359, 361–5; in second World War, 366–9; effects of fall of, (1940), 370–4, 382; allied invasion of, 375, 376–7, 382; in contemporary world, 381

Franchise: in England, in early Tudor period, 10, in eighteenth-century boroughs, 129–30, and first Reform Bill, 218–9, and chartism, 224–5, and agitation against corn law, 225–6, Disraeli's views of, 246–8, Gladstone's views of, 252, and second Reform Bill, 253–4, and educational reform, 258, 261, and third Reform Bill, 260–1, and role of House of Commons, 265; in South Africa, and Uitlander problem, 290–3

Francis I, King of France, 17–18

Franco-Prussian War (1870), 270;

Franco-Prussian War (*continued*)
military lessons of, 273; and Belgian neutrality, 276
Frederick, Elector Palatine, son-in-law of James I, 59, 123
Frederick II, King of Prussia, 135–8, 139–42; mentioned, 202
Free trade, between England and Scotland under Cromwell, 89; genesis of nineteenth-century liberal demand for, 174–5; relation to other liberal doctrines, 220, 226; triumph after 1846, 229–30; as Victorian religious tenet, 227, 230–1; and anti-imperialism, 233–4, 246; challenged in late-Victorian era, 274–5, 298–300, 306, 309; abandoned after first World War, 348–9, 350

Gallipoli: *see* Dardanelles
Gentry, in early Tudor period, 8–12; in first Civil War, 81; and Restoration Church, 100–1, 103; loyalty to Charles II, 108; triumph in Glorious Revolution, 113; dislike of War of Spanish Succession, 125; holy orders a profession for, 128, 130; in reign of George III, 151, 174; and Tory Reaction, 213; Disraeli's views of, 248–9; and second Reform Bill, 254; and social change after first World War, 353
George I, King of Great Britain, accession and character, 126–7; position in government, 130, 131; contrasted with George III, 152
George II, King of Great Britain, position in government, 130, 131; and elder Pitt, 138, 141; contrasted with George III, 152
George III, King of Great Britain, accession and fall of Pitt, 141; domestic policy, 144, 151–4; and American Revolution, 155, 157–8, 159, 160, 161; and Ireland, 163, 187–8; after fall of North administration, 168–9, 213, 225; mentioned, 97, 132, 238
George IV, King of Great Britain, as Prince of Wales, 187–8; divorce proceedings, 213–4; death, 216, 225
George V, King of Great Britain, accession, 310; appealed to by King Albert (1914), 319–20; and for-

George V (*continued*)
mation of National Government, 350; death, 354.
George VI, King of Great Britain, accession, 356
Germany, in Vienna settlement, 202, 204; rise of liberalism in, 205, 206, 239; unification of, 239, 240, 243, 269, 271; Empire (1871) and Balkan question, 270, *and see Drang nach Osten*; as challenge to Victorian liberalism, 271–4, 276, 295; and Congress of Berlin, 279–80; in South Africa, 289, 292, 293; and Salisbury, 295; economic competition with Britain, 270–1, 296; role in formation of Triple Entente, 300–3, 304–5, 313–4; and origins of first World War, 314–20; in first World War, 320–2, 324–31, 345; and peace settlement, 332, 333, 336, 337, 340–1, 356, 382; and origins of second World War, 358–9, 360, 361, 362–6; in second World War, 367–9, 371–4, 375–8; in contemporary world, 381
Gibraltar, acquired by Britain, 120–1, 122; besieged during American Revolution, 160, 161; in Napoleonic era, 196; and formation of Entente Cordiale, 304; in second World War, 372–3; mentioned, 207
Gladstone, William, and transformation of liberalism, 252–3, 256–8, 268; domestic reforms, 257–9, 260–1; and Victoria, 260; and Ireland, 261–8, 286–7; imperial and foreign policy, 267, 275, 276–8, 282–4, 285–6, 293; death, 287; influence, 299, 300, 312–3, 358; and House of Lords, 308; mentioned, 218, 235, 269, 273
Gordon, Charles, and Egyptian Sudan, 283–4, 288
Grattan, Henry, and Irish autonomy, 163–4, 215
Great Contract, of James I, 55, 99
Greece, revolt against Turks, 210–2, 215; in peace settlement after 1919, 337; in second World War, 371, 373; contemporary Anglo-Russian friction in, 383
Grey, Charles, second Earl, and first Reform Bill, 217–8, 221; mentioned, 226

Grey, Sir Edward, British Foreign Secretary (1914), 319

Grey, Henry, third Earl, and Canadian self-government, 235

Hakluyt, Richard, quoted on colonization, 47

Hampton, John, and ship money, 70

Hampton Court Conference (1604), 53

Hanover: Electorate of, allegiance of George I and George II to, 131, in British foreign policy, 137–8, 141, 203, 207, alienated from British Crown (1837), 240; House of, accession to British throne, 123, 124, 126–7; sovereigns of: *see* Edward VII; Edward VIII; George I; George II; George III; George IV; George V; George VI; Victoria; William IV

Hapsburg, House of, sixteenth-century dynastic state of, 13, 14, *and see* Charles V; possessions of, after Charles V: *see* Austria; Austria-Hungary; Spain; Austro-Spanish family alliance of, 60–1; and War of Spanish Succession, 117–21; eighteenth-century dynastic misfortunes of, 134; sovereigns of: *see* Charles V; Charles VI; Maria Theresa; Philip II

Hastings, Warren, career in India and impeachment, 166–8

Henrietta Maria, wife of Charles I, married, 61; during Puritan Revolution, 77; and Charles II, 99

Henry VII, King of England, accession, 7; situation confronting, 11–2; reign, 15–7

Henry VIII, King of England, first marriage, 16–7; reign, 17–24, 27–9, 30

Henry IV, King of France (Henry of Navarre), 45

Hitler, Adolf, compared with Napoleon, 184, 190, 358, 373, and with Bismarck, 359; abrogation of Versailles settlement by, 338, 358–9, 362–6; in second World War, 367–9, 371–3, 376, 378, 381. *See also* Nazism

Holland, Kingdom of, created (1815), 204; loss of Belgium (1830), 217; Kaiser's flight to, 331; invaded by

Holland (*continued*)
Germany (1940), 368–9. *See also* Netherlands, Dutch

Holy Roman Empire, Henry VIII as candidate for emperor of, 17; Napoleon's abolition of, (1806), 193

Home Rule, causes and growth of movement for, 261–8; first Bill, (1886), 266, 267; second Bill, (1892), 286–7; third Bill, (1912), 307, 310–2, 318, 320, 345; fourth Bill, (1920), 345; mentioned, 269, 299

House of Commons, English, in early Tudor period, 9–11; under Henry VIII, 18; under Elizabeth, 37, 50; under James I, 50, 54–5, 59; under Charles I, 61–7, 74, 75–9, 84, 86; under Charles II, 99–101, 102–3; under James II, 110; and settlement of Glorious Revolution, 113, 115–6; under Anne, 124–5; in Hanoverian government, 129–32; and elder Pitt, 138–9; and George III's experiment, 152–3; under younger Pitt, 168–70; and Catholic emancipation, 215–6; and first Reform Bill, 216–9, 221–2; and chartist program, 224; and repeal of corn law, 226, 228–9; Disraeli's views of, 247–8, 250; and second Reform Bill, 253–4; and Home Rule, 264–5; emergence of Labour Party in, 298, 307; payment of members, 307; struggle with House of Lords, 308, 309–10; and crisis of 1914, 318. *See also* Parliament; Union, Acts of

House of Lords, English, in early Tudor period, 10; clerical members of, 27; and trial of Strafford, 76–7; eclipse of, during Puritan Revolution, 84, 86; packed by Anne, 125; and first Reform Bill, 221–2, 308; and repeal of corn law, 229; Disraeli's views of, 247, 250; and reform of judiciary, 259; and second Home Rule Bill, 287, 308; and legal assault on trade unions, 297–8; and Liberal government after 1906, 308, 309, 310, 311. *See also* Parliament

Housman, A. E., quoted, 322

Hudson Bay territory, acquired by Britain (1713), 121

Hudson River Valley, in American Revolution, 158, 160

Huguenots, French, and Charles I, 61–3, 67; and Louis XIV, 111; mentioned, 37

Hundred Years' War, and effect upon England, 4–5, 8; upon Scotland, 6

Hungary, in creation of Dual Monarchy (1867), 269–70; in settlement of 1919, 334; and Hitler's aggression, 363. *See also* Austria-Hungary

Imperialism, of Cromwell, 88–92; in Walpole era, 133–4; of elder Pitt, 139, 140–1; and reform of colonial system after 1763, 147–51; effect of American Revolution upon, 163–8; liberal opposition to, 220–1, 233–4; transformation of, in early Victorian era, 231–9, 278, 294; and Disraeli, 246; in late nineteenth-century Europe, 250, 269, 275, 301; renascence of, in late-Victorian Britain, 255, 256–7, 268, 273, 275–6, 287, 291, 298–300, 355; in France, 270, 276, 282; in United States, 277; among Boers, 290, 294; and Russian Revolution, 335; and contemporary Russian policy, 382

Independents, and New Model, 83; opposition of, to English Presbyterians, 84–6; government of, 86–95; and Clarendon Code, 100–1

India, eighteenth-century British expansion in, 133–4, 138, 140, 141; British policy toward, before 1793, 165–8; in Napoleonic era, 184, 190; and Sepoy Mutiny, 240–1, 243–4; government of, after 1858, 244, 260, 283; before and during first World War, 331, 344; in second World War, 374; British withdrawal from, 384, 388. *See also* East India Company

Indulgence, Declaration of: *see* Declaration of Indulgence

Instrument of Government (1653), 94

Iran: *see* Persia

Ireland, Tudor government of, 3, 5–6; under Elizabeth, 44–5, 346; Jacobean colonization, 57–8, 346; under Strafford, 74; rebellion (1641), 78; Cromwellian conquest and settlement, 88, 92, 346; settlement after Glorious Revolution, 115–6, 346; during American Revolution, 163–5;

Ireland (*continued*)
during French Revolution and Napoleonic era, 183, 185–8; and enactment of Catholic emancipation, 214–6; famine in, and repeal of corn law, 228, 229, 232; effects of Home Rule crisis, 252, 255, 257, 260, 275–6, 283, 286, *and see* Home Rule; creation of Free State, 344–7, 351; British naval bases in, 345, 355; creation of Republic of Eire, 355, *and see* Eire

Irish Free State: *see* Eire; Ireland

Ironsides, Cromwell's creation of, 83; mentioned, 88

Isabella of Castile, mentioned, 13, 16, 18

Ismail, Khedive of Egypt, 281–2, 283

Italy, commercial importance of, in sixteenth century, 3; in War of Spanish Succession, 119, 120, 121; in Wars of French Revolution and Napoleon, 181, 182, 190, 193, 195, 198; and Vienna settlement, 202, 204; rise of liberalism in, 205, 206, 208, 239; unification of, 239, 240, 242, 251, 269; Kingdom of, (1861), 269, 301; in first World War, 326, 331; and settlement of 1919, 335, 337, 340, 356; and origins of second World War, 361–3; in second World War, 369, 371, 372, 376, 377

Jacobinism, and Methodism, 179, 180; and change in warfare, 182; and nineteenth-century Continental liberalism, 205; absence of, in French Revolution of 1830, 217; compared with communism, 356, 357

Jacobites, genesis of, 122; and rising of 1715, 127; and Walpole's policy, 133; and rising of 1745–6, 136

James I, King of England (James VI of Scotland), birth, 40; claim to English throne, 46; character, 50–1, 60–1; Scottish background, 51–2, 72–3; ecclesiastical policy, 53–4, 65; financial policy, 54–7; foreign policy, 59–60; and royal suspending power, 102

James II, King of England, as Duke of York, 104–6, 107–9; character, 109; reign, 109–12; in Ireland, 115; championed in exile by Louis XIV, 116; death, 118; and Toryism, 122; mentioned, 97, 123, 154, 320

James "III," the Old Pretender, championed by Louis XIV, 116, 118, 126; emotional appeal of, to Tories, 123, 126; and Jacobite risings, 127, 136

James IV, King of Scotland, married to Margaret Tudor, 16, 17

Jameson Raid (1895), 292

Japan, and revolution of 1867–8, 269; and war with China (1894), 275; and British alliance (1902), 300, 303, 317, 326, 341–2; naval competition with Britain, 303, 341–2; war with Russia (1904), 305, 313; gains in Versailles settlement, 335; and Washington naval treaties, 341–2; economic competition with Britain, 347, 351; and nationalism, 356; in second World War, 371, 374–6, 378; in contemporary world, 381

Jefferson, Thomas, and promulgation of Monroe Doctrine, 209–10

Jellicoe, Admiral Sir John, and Battle of Jutland, 327–8

Jenkins's Ear, War of, (1739), 134–5, 136

Jervis, Sir John: see St. Vincent

Jesuits, founding of, 32; during Restoration, 105–6, 107; and communists, 382, 392–3

Jugoslavia, created (1919), 334; French alliance with, 340; overrun by Germans (1941), 373

Julius II, Pope, and marriage of Henry VIII, 17, 19–20

Junius, *Letters* of, quoted, 153–4, 154–5

Jutland, Battle of, (1916), 327–8

Katharine of Aragon, wife of Henry VIII, 16–7, 18–9, 31

Khartum, Gordon at, 283; Kitchener at, 288

Kipling, Rudyard, quoted, 168, 295, 303

Kirk of Scotland, and James I, 46, 51–2; and Charles I, 73; and Cromwell, 88–9; and union with England, 123; mentioned, 37. *See also* Presbyterianism

Kitchener, Sir Herbert, (later Earl Kitchener), and reconquest of Sudan, 288; in Boer War, 294; in first World War, 321

Klosterzeven, capitulation of, (1757), 138; mentioned, 96

Kruger, Paul, and Boer War, 290–4; tradition of, 343

Labour Party, genesis of, 296–8; and Liberal triumph of 1906, 307, 348; and Parliament Bill (1910), 310, 311; during first World War, 348; between wars, 348–50, 353–4, 360; triumph of, in election of 1945, 349, 385–6, 393

Laissez faire, foreshadowed in reign of Charles I, 69; development with Industrial Revolution, 174–5, 219–20; and factory acts, 222; and chartism, 224; and Tory democracy, 249; and Gladstonianism, 256, 258; abandoned by Liberals after 1906, 307–8, 348

Land, ownership of: in England, relationship to taxation, 125, social and political importance in eighteenth century, 128–9, and agrarian revolution, 171, and first Reform Bill, 218–9, and corn law, 213, 226–8, and Liberal legislation after 1906, 308, and social changes after first World War, 353, *and see* Gentry; in Ireland, and problem of absenteeism, 88, 214–5, and Gladstone's reform of land law, 262–4

Land Acts, Irish, (1870, 1881), 263–4

Land League, Irish, (1879), 263–4

La Rochelle, siege of, by Richelieu, 62–3

Laud, William, Archbishop of Canterbury, 66, 70–3; death, 76; mentioned, 113

League of Augsburg, War of the, (1688), 117

League of Nations, and problem of coercion, 208; early years of, 338–41; dominions' membership in, 344; compared with British Commonwealth, 346; British faith in, 353–4, 357–8, 360; British policy toward, 354, 361–2

Levellers, opposed to Cromwell, 93–4; survival of theories of, 95; compared with chartists, 224, 225

Lexington, Battle of (1775), 156

Liberal Party, adoption of name, 229–30; heretics in, 244; mid-Victorian monopoly of power by, 245, 247; and second Reform Bill, 252–4; under Gladstone, 256–9, 260–8, 276–8, 280–6; and schism of 1886, 229,

Liberal Party (*continued*)
256, 266–8, 273, 284, 286, 312; reconstructed after Gladstone, 268, 299–300, 306; policies after 1906, 307–20, 348, 355, 386; and coalition of first World War, 325, 345; post-war extinction of, 348–9, 351. *See also* Whig Party

Liberalism, economic, in younger Pitt's ministry, 174–5; political, in Restoration Europe, 205, 206, 207, 212; and Greek revolt, 211; and Whiggism of 1830's, 217–25; and corn-law crisis, 225–8, 229–30; and early-Victorian imperialism, 231–9, 278, 280; threats to, foreign and domestic, 244–51, 271, 272; Gladstonian transformation of, 252–4, 256, 257, 263, 268, 286; subsequent transformation of, 268, 299–300; and Fabianism, 297; and return of protection, 350, 351; and contemporary British socialism, 386

Lilburne, John, Leveller leader, 93–4

Lloyd George, Chancellor of Exchequer, 309–11; in first World War, 323, 325, 330, 348; at Paris Conference, 333, 336; and Irish Free State, 345; fall of, 347, 348; mentioned, 218

Localism, and character of Tudor local government, 9, 50; effect on Charles I's personal rule, 68–9, 70, 80; in opposition to Cromwell's regime, 94, and to James II's, 110; triumph in Glorious Revolution, 113, 116; in American colonies, 148, 150; undermined by poor law of 1834, 223–4

Locarno, Treaties of, (1925), 340–1; violated by Hitler, 362; mentioned, 381

Long Parliament: *see* Parliament, Long

Lords, House of: *see* House of Lords

Louis XIII, King of France, mentioned, 61

Louis XIV, King of France, his system, 98; relations with Charles II, 99, 101–4, 106, 107–9, with James II, 109, 111–2; wars against England, 116–22; champion of James "III," 116, 118, 126; mentioned, 182, 201, 313, 320, 381

Louis XV, King of France, mentioned, 61, 140

Louis-Philippe, King of France, regime of, 217, 239–40

Louisburg, captured from French and restored (1748), 136; recaptured, 140

Louisiana, transferred from France to Spain (1763), 141; weakness of Spanish control, 162; in Napoleonic era, 190

Low Countries, acquired by Philip II, 32–3; revolt of, 40–1, 42; in Vienna settlement, 204; nineteenth-century British policy toward, 204, 274; in second World War, 368–9, 378; mentioned, 207. *See also* Belgium; Holland; Netherlands

Loyalists, in American Revolution, 156

Luftwaffe, before second World War, 359, 361, 364, 366–7; in Battle of Britain, 369, 371; and Crete, 373, 389; and allied air offensive, 377

Luther, Martin, quoted, 26; mentioned, 20

MacDonald, Ramsay, and formation of National Government, 350; resignation, 354; and Nazi menace, 360

Machiavelli, Nicolo, mentioned, 34, 64, 272, 291

Maginot Line, begun by France, 340, 362; in Anglo-French strategy, 365, 367; and fall of France, 368–9

Magna Carta, mentioned, 55–6, 178

Mahan, Alfred T., and German naval expansion, 302

Mahdi, the, and Sudanese rebellion, 283–4, 286; followers of, 287–8

Majuba Hill, Battle of, (1881), 285

Malta, acquired by Britain in Napoleonic Wars, 189, 196, 204

Maoris, friction of New Zealand settlers with, 232–3, 277

Margaret Tudor, sister of Henry VIII, and Stuart marriage, 16

Maria Theresa, accession to Austrian throne, 134, 135; duel with Prussia, 135–7; mentioned, 202

Marlborough, John Churchill, Duke of, in War of Spanish Succession, 120–21; relations with Tories and Whigs, 122–3, 125; compared with George Washington, 159, and with Wellington, 197

Marne, Battle of, (1914), 321, 322, 331; mentioned, 369, 372, 373.

Marriage policy, of Henry VII, 16; of Henry VIII, 18–23; of Mary, 31–3; of Elizabeth, 46; of James I, 59–60; of Charles I, 61–2; of Stuarts after Restoration, 105

Marxism: *see* Socialism, Marxian

Mary, Queen of England, daughter of Henry VIII, birth and childhood, 18–9, 23; reign, 31–3; compared with James II, 109, 110; mentioned, 114

Mary II, Queen of England, daughter of James II, as heiress presumptive, 105, 106, 110–1; accession, 111–2; death, 122

Mary Stuart, Queen of Scots, reign and dethronement in Scotland, 39–40, 53, 72; claimant to English throne, 41, 42, 46

Mary Tudor, sister of Henry VIII, 16, 23, 46

Massachusetts, settlement of, 58; in American Revolution, 155–6

Mediterranean, British concern with, under Cromwell, 90–2; in War of Spanish Succession, 119, 120–2; in Wars of French Revolution and Napoleon, 183, 184, 191–2; in Greek revolt, 210–2; in Crimean War, 241–3; in late-Victorian era, 270, 278–80, 281; in first World War, 326; and Ethiopian crisis, 361–3; in second World War, 370, 372, 375, 376–7

Mercantilism, and policy of Charles I, 69; and Cromwell's trade wars, 90–2; and English hostility to Louis XIV, 104, 111; and eighteenth-century colonial rivalries, 133, 139, 142–3; and American Revolution, 148, 163; and Industrial Revolution, 174–5; rejected in Britain after 1846, 225–30, 233; revival of, in late nineteenth century, 274–6

Methodism, origin and effects of, 178–80

Metternich, Prince Clemens von, and concert of Europe, 205–6, 207–8, 211, 212, 239, 338; mentioned, 250, 269

Middle class, in Tudor period, 8–12, 14; and abolition of monasteries, 21–3; under Elizabeth, 37, 50; in Stuart local government, 68–9; enfranchised (1832), 221; loyalty of, to Victoria, 225; Disraeli's views of,

Middle class (*continued*) 247–8; and second Reform Bill, 254

Midlothian campaign (1880), 280, 286; and first Boer War, 285

Milton, John, quoted, 84, 230; and *Paradise Lost,* 115; mentioned, 113

Minorca, acquired by Britain (1708), 120–1, 122; captured by French (1756), 138; ceded to Spain by Britain (1783), 161; and Peace of Amiens, 189

Missionary movement: *see* Evangelicalism

Monasteries, abolition of, by Henry VIII, 21–2, 32

Monk, George, Cromwellian general and admiral, in first Dutch War, 91; and end of Protectorate, 95, 97

Monmouth, James Scott, Duke of, and claim to throne, 104, 106; rebellion and death, 110

Monroe Doctrine, formulated (1823), 209–10; and German expansion by 1914, 317; extended to Canada, 374

Montenegro, in Treaty of San Stefano, 278; in Treaty of Berlin, 279

Morocco, French designs on, 304–5; international crises over, 305, 312, 315, 316, 317–8; in second World War, 376

Munich, Peace of, (1938), compared with Peace of Amiens, 190, and with Peace of Tilsit, 199; origins and conclusion of, 359, 363–5

Mussolini, and pre-war Italian aggression, 357, 361–3; in second World War, 369

Napoleon I, Emperor of the French, and Egyptian expedition, 184–5; First Consul, 188, 190; Emperor, 191–7, 198–200, 203; compared with Napoleon III, 240, and with Hitler, 184, 190, 358, 373; mentioned 326, 381

Napoleon III, Emperor of the French, accession, 239–40; and Crimean War, 241–3; mentioned, 381

Natal, settled by Boers, 236; annexed by Britain, 237; and Zulu danger, 284; and first Boer War, 285; and second Boer War, 289, 293

National Government, formed (1931), 350; quality of leadership in, 353, 354, 360, 364–6, 368

Nationalism, and Anglo-Scottish friction, 123–4; Irish, and Grattan, 164, and O'Connell, 215; in Napoleonic Europe, 189–90, 196–7; in Restoration Europe, 204–5, 210, 334; in British dominions, 234, 344; in India, 244, 344, 380, 384; in late-Victorian Britain, 267, 268, 272; in world of late nineteenth century, 269, 271, 274, 275, 279, 282; among Boers, 285, 292, 343; in Balkans, 314–5; after first World War, 334, 335, 337; and rise of dictatorships, 356–7, 358–9

Navarino, Battle of, (1827), 211

Navigation Act, and first Dutch War, 91; liberalized (1822–5), 214; repealed, 230

Navy, British: *see* Royal Navy

Navy, Dutch, in seventeenth and eighteenth centuries, 91, 117; in Wars of French Revolution and Napoleon, 183

Navy, French, in seventeenth century, 104, 117; in eighteenth century, 119, 120–2, 135–6, 138, 140, 142, 159–61; in Wars of French Revolution and Napoleon, 183, 184–5, 191–3; in later ninetenth century, 211, 241–2, 282; in twentieth century, 318, 370

Navy, German, and first World War, 302–3, 316, 318, 327–8; in second World War, 359, 370. *See also* Blockade, German

Navy, Japanese, and British alliance, 303, 326; and Washington treaties, 341–2; and second World War, 371, 374–6, 378

Navy, Spanish, under Philip II: *see* Armada; in eighteenth century, 119, 120–2, 135, 160; in Wars of French Revolution and Napoleon, 183, 191–2

Navy, United States, and first World War, 303, 329, 330; and Washington treaties, 341–2; and second World War, 370–1, 373, 374, 375–6, 377, 384

Nazism, incomprehensible to British, 357, 358–9, 360; and second World War: *see* Germany; and blitzkrieg, 368

Nelson, Horatio, Viscount, at Cape St. Vincent, 183; at the Nile, 184; at Copenhagen, 189; and Trafalgar

Nelson, Horatio (*continued*) campaign, 191–2; compared with Jellicoe, 328; mentioned, 193, 197

Netherlands, Austrian, acquired in 1713, 121; menaced by France in eighteenth century, 134, 136, 137–8; in Wars of French Revolution and Napoleon, 181, 182; surrendered in 1815, 203–4, *and see* Belgium. *See also* Low Countries

Netherlands, Dutch, revolt against Philip II, 40–1, 42, 45, 159; American colonies of, 58; and Anglo-Dutch Wars: *see* Dutch Wars; and Louis XIV's designs, 101–2, 107, 117; naval decline of, 117; in War of Spanish Succession, 119, 121; in American Revolution, 160; in Wars of French Revolution and Napoleon, 181, 182, 190, 193; in Vienna settlement, 203–4, *and see* Holland; mentioned, 314. *See also* Low Countries

Netherlands, Spanish, revolt against Philip II, 40–1; attacked by Louis XIV, 101–2, 118–9; transferred to Austria in 1713, 121, *and see* Netherlands, Austrian. *See also* Belgium; Low Countries

Newcastle, Thomas Pelham-Holles, Duke of, and elder Pitt, 138, 141

Newfoundland, acquired by Britain (1713), 121; French fishing rights off, 141–2, 304; and Dominion of Canada, 235

New York, acquired by Britain (1667), 101; in American Revolution, 158, 160

New Zealand, settled, 232–3; and Maori crisis, 277–8; in Boer War, 294; in first World War, 324, 343; in second World War, 374, 379, 384, 385

Nicholas I, Emperor of Russia, and Greek revolt, 211–12; and Crimean War, 241–2

Nile, Battle of, (1798), 184, 188, 193

Nile Valley, Anglo-French friction over, 270, 284; British expansion in: *see* Egypt; Sudan; and formation of Entente Cordiale, 304; and Ethiopian crisis, 361–2; mentioned, 184, 257

Nonconformists: *see* Dissenters

Norman Conquest: of England, 4; of Ireland, 5

North, Lord (Earl of Guilford), Prime Minister, 154–6, 161, 164, 169; mentioned, 238

North Sea, German bid for naval supremacy in, 303, 313, 316, 321, 327–8; and German invasion of Scandinavia (1940), 368

Northumberland, John Dudley, Duke of, Regent for Edward VI, 30–1

Nova Scotia, acquired by Britain from France (1713), 121

Oates, Titus, and Popish Plot, 107–8; mentioned, 213

O'Connell, Daniel, and Catholic emancipation, 215; compared with Parnell, 264

Orange Free State, settled by Boers, 236; granted autonomy (1854), 237; relations with South African Republic, 285, 292; annexed by Britain, 294

Orthodox Church, origin of, 25; in Turkey, and Crimean War, 241, 242

Ottawa Conference (1932), 350–1; mentioned, 352

Ottoman Empire: *see* Turkey

Palatinate, in Thirty Years' War, 59, 62

Pale, Irish, 3, 5–6; under Elizabeth, 44; under James I, 57–8

Palestine, in Crimean War, 241; in first World War, 331; and Zionism, 337; British withdrawal from, 384

Palmerston, Henry Temple, Viscount, and *Pax Britannica*, 239, 271, 276; and Crimean War, 241; influence on Disraeli, 246, 257, 286; last ministry, 251; effect of death, 252

Panama Canal, American interest in, compared with British interest in Suez, 281; British abandonment of rights in, (1901), 303

Papacy, relations of, with Henry VIII, 19–24; claims of, 24–7; relations of, with Mary, 31–3; in Elizabethan Ireland, 44; English antipathy to, 33, 35, 45, 60, 65, 71–2, 103, 104–5, 107–9, 110. *See also* Recusants

Paris: Peace of, (1763), 141–4, 149, 160, 162; Peace of, (1856), 242–3, amended by Russia, 270, 276, 278; Conference and Peace of, (1919), and resultant settlement, 332–7,

Paris: Peace of (*continued*) 339, 356, *and see* Versailles, Treaty of

Parliament, British, in early Tudor period, 9–11; and Henry VIII, 20–1, 22, 27, 28; and Mary, 32; and Elizabeth, 34–5, 46; and James I, 54–6, 59–60; and Charles I, 61–7, 74, 75–9, 84, 86; of Commonwealth and Protectorate, 91, 94; and Charles II, 95–6, 99–101, 102–3, 106, 108; and James II, 110; and settlement of Glorious Revolution, 113, 115–6; and union with Scotland, 123–4; under Hanoverians, 129–32, 138, 174; and American Revolution, 148, 150, 152, 153, 154–5; and India, 165–7; movement to reform, 169–71, 175, 176–8, 216–9, 221–2, 245, 253–4; and repeal of corn law, 228–9; Disraeli's views of, 246–9, 250; Parnell's attempt to discredit, 265–6; and Liberal reforms after 1906, 307, 308, 309, 310; and National Government of 1930's, 354. *See also* House of Commons; House of Lords; Union, Acts of

Parliament, Cavalier, (1661), early years of, 100–1, 113; dissolution (1679), 108

Parliament, Irish, 163–4, 186–7, 188

Parliament, Long, (1642), and destruction of monarchy, 75–9, 84, 86; restored and dissolved, 95; acts of, at Restoration, 99

Parliament, Rump, created (1648), 86; and Navigation Act, 91; dissolved by Cromwell (1653), 94; reconvened, 95

Parliament, Short, (1640), 74, 75

Parnell, Charles, and Home Rule, 264–6; death, 286

Paul, Emperor of Russia, 189

Peel, Sir Robert, and Catholic emancipation, 215, 216; and repeal of corn law, 228–9; followers of, (Peelites), 229, 245, 252, 256, 268; and franchise, 247; compared with Gladstone, 266

Peerage, Tudor, 8–9, 10; as source of Hanoverian patronage, 130; condition of, by 1906, 308; threat to, in 1910, 310

Peninsular War (1808), 196–7

Persia (Iran), Anglo-Russian friction over, 243; and Triple Entente, 313;

Persia (Iran) (*continued*)
in second World War, 375; and contemporary Anglo-Russian friction, 383
Petition of Right (1628), 63, 67
Petrine supremacy, theory of, 25–6, 27
Philip II, King of Spain (Philip I of England), inheritance and marriage of, 31–2, 33; relations with Elizabethan England, Scotland, and Ireland, 38–9, 40–4, 45; compared with Stalin, 382; mentioned, 192
Philip V, King of Spain, in War of Spanish Succession, 118, 120, 121
Philippines, before and during second World War, 341–2, 371, 374, 378
Pitt, William, the elder: *see* Chatham
Pitt, William, the younger, beginning of ministry, 168–9; and reform, 175–6, 180; wartime ministry, 181–8, 193–4; quoted, 392; mentioned, 214, 245, 368
Poland, early partitions of, 202–3; reconstituted after first World War, 334, 335, 336; French alliance with, 340; and outbreak of second World War, 365–6; in second World War, 367, 381; mentioned, 352, 374
Polish Corridor, created (1919), 334; and German revisionism, 335; and outbreak of second World War, 366
Poor relief, and Industrial Revolution, 173–4, 178; reform of, (1834), 222–4; and unemployment of 1930's, 350, 352–3
Popish Plot (1678), 107–8; mentioned, 114
Portugal, in early sixteenth century, 4, 48; in War of Spanish Succession, 120; in Napoleonic era, 193, 196–7
Potato, and Irish discontent, 215, 228–9
Predestination, theory of, 36
Presbyterianism, in Scotland, 37, 51–2, 88–9, 123; in England, 53, 84–6, 96 100–1, 113; in Ulster, 58, 115–6, 164, 185–6, 188, 215. *See also* Dissenters
Prime minister, genesis of office of, 131
Primogeniture, social effects of, 8–9, 128
Protection, economic, and Pitt's commercial treaty with France (1786),

Protection (*continued*)
174–5; of domestic grain: *see* corn law; and classical liberalism, 220; and Disraeli's imperialism, 246; and fair trade movement, 274–5; Joseph Chamberlain's program for, 298–300, 306, 309; triumph of, in Britain of 1930's, 348–9, 350, and effects, 350–1, 352–3, 355
Protectorate, Cromwellian, 94–5
Protestantism, origins of, 20, 26–8; in reign of Edward VI, 30–1, 35–6; in reign of Mary, 32–3, 36; in Elizabethan Church, 34–8; and divine right, 51–2; and English foreign policy, 59, 65, 91, 105; and Laudian movement, 65–6, 71; and eighteenth-century enlightenment, 146
Prussia, East, and origins of second World War, 334, 335, 366
Prussia, eighteenth-century rivalry with Austria, 134–8, 139–42; in Wars of French Revolution and Napoleon, 176, 181, 182, 189, 193, 199–200; in Vienna settlement, 202–4, 206; and Revolution of 1848, 239; and Danish War (1864), 251; and unification of Germany, 269, 273, 321, *and see* Germany; and German nationalism, 271; as guarantor of Belgium neutrality, 316; mentioned, 159
Puritanism, in Elizabethan Church, 36–8, 45, 46; under James I, 53–4; under Charles I, 64, 65–6, 71, 72; characteristics of, in first Civil War, 81, 82–3; Lilburne as representative of, 93–4; and Clarendon Code, 100–1; and Restoration Whigs, 106; and nineteenth-century liberalism, 219. *See also* Dissenters

Quiberon Bay, Battle of, (1759), 140

Radicalism, English, among Independents, 85, 93–4; prevention of, in Glorious Revolution, 112; and American Revolution, 155, 169; and French Revolution, 176–8, 179, 180–1; among Liberals of 1860's, 253, and of 1880's, 267, 268; among Chamberlain's Unionists, 298
Railroads, and British industrialization, 173; and inland expansion of dominions, 238; and unification of

Railroads (*continued*)
India, 244; and decay of Irish agriculture, 263; and Boer War, 291–2, 294

Raleigh, Sir Walter, and theories of colonization, 47

Rationalism, and religious toleration, 114–5; revolutionary implications of, in late eighteenth century, 145–9, 156; and George III's experiment, 151; and French Revolution, 176–8; and classical liberalism, 217, 219–20, 227, 230–1, 234; and Gladstonianism, 256, 257, 272; and Neville Chamberlain, 360

Recusants, under Elizabeth, 35, 40, 42, 45; under Charles I, 61–2; under Charles II, 99, 101, 102, 104–5, 106; under James II, 110; after Glorious Revolution, 114, 115–6, 126; enfranchised in Ireland (1793), 185, *and see* Catholic emancipation.

Reform Bill: first (1832), 217, 221–2, 229, 252, results of, 222–4, Disraeli's views of, 247–8; second (1867), 253–4, 255, 261, and trade unionism, 259, mentioned, 261, 278; third (1884–5), 269–1, 265

Reformation, Catholic: *see* Papacy; Spain; Trent, Council of

Reformation, Protestant, 20, 146, *and see* Protestantism

Renaissance, spread of, in sixteenth century, 4; and eighteenth-century enlightenment, 146

Revenues, governmental, early nature of, 10; under Henry VII, 15–6; under Henry VIII, 18; under James I, 54–5, 56–7; under Charles I, 62, 70, 77; at Restoration, 99; problem of, created by Peace of Paris (1763), 143, 144, 147–50, 151, 154–5; problem of, created by Liberal triumph of 1906, 308–9

Revolution, American, causes, 142–4, 147–51, 154–6; in British politics, 153, 155, 157, 161, 169; War of the, 156–61, 188–9, 194; and Ireland, 163; mentioned, 177, 374, 380

Revolution, Diplomatic, of 1756, 137; of 1902–7, 300–6, 312–20

Revolution, French: first (1789), outbreak, 176–7, opposition of British conservatism to, 177–8, 180–1,

Revolution, French (*continued*)
Wars of the, and Napoleon, 168, 169, 170, 175, 178, 181–6, 188–200, 232, 323, aftereffects of, 200–1, 204–5, 210, 273, and educational reform, 258; second (1830), 217; third (1848), 239–40

Revolution, Glorious, (1688), course and characteristics, 110–1; settlement following, 112–6; and Hanoverian accession, 126–7; mentioned, 139, 222, 229

Revolution, Industrial, and relation to rationalism, 147; advent and problems of, 170–6; affected by Wars of French Revolution and Napoleon, 176, 195, 201; and Tory Reaction, 212–3; and economic liberalism, 219, 220, 222–3, 226–8, 230; and growth of Victorian empire, 232, 237–8; and second Reform Bill, 254; worldwide spread of, in late nineteenth century, 274–5, 296, 305; and British depression of 1930's, 347, 349–50, 352–3; and Britain's contemporary position, 384

Revolution, Puritan, Charles I's personal rule as preliminary phase of, 68–75; reforms of Long Parliament in, 75–9; first Civil War in, 81–3; triumph of Independents in, 83–7; Commonwealth and Protectorate as climax of, 87–95; aftereffects of, 95–7, 99–100, 132; compared with Glorious Revolution, 112, with American Revolution, 156, and with chartism, 225

Rhineland, in armistice and peace settlement (1918–9), 332, 335, 336, 338, 340; and Locarno treaties, 340–1; reoccupied and fortified by Hitler, 362; in second World War, 377–8

Rhodes, Cecil, and origins of Boer War, 291–2

Rhodesia, creation of, 291

Richard III, King of England, despotism of, 7, 12

Richelieu, Cardinal, and French foreign policy, 61–2, 98; mentioned, 381

Romanticism, and Jacobitism, 123; and eighteenth-century imperialism, 139, 167–8; and Greek revolt, 211; and popular loyalty to Victoria, 225; of Disraeli, 245–6

Roosevelt, President Franklin, and American sea power in second World War, 370–1, 373

Roses, Wars of the, effects of, 5, 8; and Tudor accession, 7

Roundheads, composition of, in first Civil War, 79–80, 81–2; mentioned, 112

Royal Air Force, and retreat from Dunkirk, 369; and Battle of Britain, 369, 371; and allied counter-offensive, 376–7, 381

Royal Navy, Elizabethan, 41–3, 47, 48–9; early Stuart, 58–9, 70; Puritan, 89–92, 97; in wars against Louis XIV, 117, 119, 120–2; and eighteenth-century patronage, 130, 151; in wars of mid-eighteenth century, 135–6, 137–41, 142; in American Revolution, 149, 156, 158–61; and infant United States, 162–3; in Wars of French Revolution and Napoleon, 181–2, 182–4, 188–9, 191–3, 194–5, 197–8; in crisis of 1823, 209–10; and mid-Victorian empire, 231; and Crimean War, 240, 241–2, 243; in late-Victorian era, 274, 278, 288, 293; and German competition, 302–3, 305, 308, 316; and Anglo-French agreement of 1912, 318, 320–1; in first World War, 324, 325–8, 329–32; provisions for, in post-war settlement, 332, 336; and Washington treaties, 341–2, 347, 351; and Irish bases, 345, 355; and Ethiopian crisis, 362–3; and British strategy for second World War, 365; in second World War, 367, 368, 369, 370–1, 372, 374, 375–6, 377, 384, 389

Rumania, in Crimean War, 241, 242; in Treaty of San Stefano, 278; in Treaty of Berlin, 279; in Peace of Paris (1919), 334; French alliance with, 340; in second World War, 371

Rump Parliament: *see* Parliament, Rump

Rupert, Prince, nephew of Charles I, as cavalry leader, 82; at sea, 90

Russell, Lord John, (later Earl Russell), and repeal of corn law, 228; Prime Minister, 252–3

Russia, in Seven Years' War, 137, 141; in Wars of French Revolution and

Russia (*continued*)

Napoleon, 188, 189, 193, 198–9; in Vienna settlement, 202–4, 206; and Greek revolt, 210–2; and Crimean War, 239, 240-2, 244; and Sepoy Mutiny, 243; and Polish revolt (1863), 251; and Balkans, 270, 278–80, 284, 286, 293; and formation of Triple Entente, 300, 301; rivalry with Japan, 303, 304, 305, 313; and origins of first World War, 312–6, 317, 319; in first World War, 321, 322, 324, 328, 374; Revolution (1917), 330; in peace settlement, 334, 335, 336, 337, 358; and international communism, 356–7; and origins of second World War, 359, 361, 363, 365–6; and partition of Poland (1939), 367, 371; in second World War, 372–4, 375–6, 378; in contemporary world, 380, 381–2, 387, 390–3

Russo-German Pact (1939), 366; mentioned, 199

St. Vincent, John Jervis, Earl of, naval victory (1797), 183; First Lord of Admiralty, 191; compared with Jellicoe, 328

Salisbury, Robert Gascoyne-Cecil, Marquis of, and Irish question, 265; and Joseph Chamberlain, 268, 295–6; and Boer War, 292; retirement, 295–6, 298

San Stefano, Treaty of, (1878), 278, 279; mentioned, 305

Saratoga, Battle of, (1777), and effect on American Revolution, 158–9

Sardinia, Kingdom of, in Wars of French Revolution and Napoleon, 181, 190; and Vienna settlement, 204; and unification of Italy: *see* Italy

Savoy, Kingdom of, *see* Sardinia

Schlieffen Plan, genesis of, 316; operation and collapse of, (1914), 319–21; apparent repetition of, (1940), 368–9

Science, and Restoration society, 115; and eighteenth-century enlightenment, 145, 146, 147; and mid-Victorian optimism, 230; and late-Victorian imperialism, 275

Scotland, relations of, with Tudor England, 6, 16, 18, 23, 39–40, and

Scotland (*continued*)
with France, 6, 39; in late sixteenth century, 51–2; and plantation of Ulster, 57–8; rebellion against Charles I, 72–5; in second Civil War, 85–6, 88–9; Cromwellian settlement of, 89, 92; union with England (1707), 123–4, 164; and Jacobite risings, 127, 136

Sea dogs, Elizabethan, 41–3, 48

Sea power: *see* Navy; Royal Navy

Selden, John, quoted, 80

Sepoy Mutiny (1857), 243–4

Serbia, revolt of, against Turks, 210; in Treaty of San Stefano, 278; in Treaty of Berlin, 279; and origins of first World War, 314, 315, 318–9; in first World War, 324, 365; and settlement of 1919: *see* Jugoslavia

Settlement, Act of, (1701), 123

Sevastopol, siege of, in Crimean War, 242

Seven Years' War (1756), 137–43; mentioned, 157, 167, 188, 302

Seymour, Jane, wife of Henry VIII, 23

Shakespeare, William, quoted, 10, 25, 28, 49, 86, 194

Ship money (1634), 70, 90; mentioned, 154

Short Parliament: *see* Parliament, Short

Silesia, Austro-Prussian rivalry over, 134, 135, 136, 137

Singapore, and fall of France (1940), 371; captured by Japanese, 374, 378

Sinn Fein, and rebellion of 1916, 345. *See also* Ireland, creation of Free State

Six Articles, of Henry VIII, 27, 28

Slavery, and slave trade with Spanish America, 121; abolition of, throughout British Empire, 180, 222, 236; and British opinion of American Civil War, 251

Smith, Adam, on imperial reform, 149, 163

Socialism: British, and classical liberalism, 218, and Tory democracy, 249, and Fabians, 297, and party realignments before 1906, 298–300, and Liberal policies after 1906, 307–9, 310–1, and Labour program of 1920's, 348–9, and contemporary Labor program, 386, 393; Marxian,

Socialism: British (*continued*)
and cult of force, 271–2, and British trade unionism, 296–7

Somerset, Edward Seymour, Duke of, Regent for Edward VI, 29–31, 35

Sophia, Electress of Hanover, 123, 126

South Africa Company, and origins of Boer War, 291–2

South African Republic, creation of, (1881), 285; in Boer War, 289–94. *See also* Transvaal

Spain, sixteenth-century dynastic alliance of, with Austria, 13–4, with early Tudors, 16–7, 18–23, with Mary, 31–3; and partition of Charles V's empire, 31–2; role of, in Catholic Reformation, 32, 382; relations with Elizabethan England, 38–9, 40–4, 45, and with James I, 58–60; war with Charles I, 61–2, and with Cromwell, 91–2; in era of Louis XIV, 98, 117–22; relations with Hanoverian Britain, 134–6, 141; in American Revolution, 157, 159, 161–2, 164; in Wars of French Revolution and Napoleon, 176, 182–3, 191–2, 193, 196–7; and crisis of 1823, 206, 208–10, 212; war with United States (1898), 275, 302; rights of, in Morocco (1904), 304; Civil War (1936), 363; in second World War, 372

Spanish Succession, War of the, (1702), 117–22; and Act of Union with Scotland, 123–4

Squirearchy: *see* Gentry

Stalin, Joseph, and outbreak of second World War, 365–6; compared with Philip II, 382

Strafford, Thomas Wentworth, Earl of, and attempt to preserve Charles I's personal rule, 74–5; attainted, 76–7, 108; mentioned, 78

Stuart, House of, and claim to English throne, 16, 18, 23; and Palatinate, 59–60; post-Restoration dynastic problem of, 104–5; and Anglo-Scottish union, 124; sovereigns of: *see* Anne; Charles I; Charles II; James I; James II; Mary II; William III

Submarines, in first World War, 326–7, 328–9, 330–1; in Spanish Civil War, 363; in second World War, 367, 370, 373, 378, 384

Sudan, French designs on, 270, 284; British policy toward, 283–4, 285–6, 287–8; mentioned, 304

Suez, British strategic interest in, 210, 281, 284; Canal opened, 278, 282; and *Drang nach Osten*, 315; and Ethiopian crisis, 361–2; in second World War, 370, 372, 373

Tanks, in first World War, 324–5, 331; and blitzkrieg of second World War, 367–8

Tariffs: *see* Protection

Taxation, early nature of, 10; under Henry VII, 15–6; under Henry VIII, 18; under James I, 54–5; under Charles I, 62, 69–70, 74; under Anne, 125; and Walpole's policy, 133; and American Revolution, 143, 149–50, 153, 155, 157–8; and franchise of 1832, 218; and poor law of 1834, 223; and Victorian imperialism, 233–4; Chamberlain's proposal for, (1885), 267; in South African Republic, 290–1; by Liberal government after 1906, 306–9, 347; and party programs of 1920's, 347, 386; social effects of, 353; and contemporary British socialism, 386

Tennyson, Alfred, Baron, quoted, 230

Test Act passed (1673), 103; defied by James II, 110; modified by Glorious Revolution, 113–5; evaded under Anne, 125; suspended against dissenters after 1714, 128; repealed (1828), 214, 216

Theocracy, in Scotland, 51

Thirty-Nine Articles, of Elizabethan Church, 35, 37

Thirty Years' War (1618), and English wool trade, 57; and English colonization in America, 58–9; English policy toward, 59–60, 61–2, 68; and rise of France, 98

Tilsit, Peace of, (1807), 193, 198

Toleration in religion, in reign of Edward VI, 30–1; attempted by Independents, 84, 96, 113; partially secured by Toleration Act, 113–5; unpopular in rural England, 125; established after 1714, 127–8; mentioned, 268

Torres Vedras, Lines of, defended by Wellington (1810), 197, 199

Tory Party, in reign of Charles II,

Tory Party (*continued*)
105–9; of James II, 110–1, 320; and settlement of Glorious Revolution, 112–3, 116, 122–3, 124–7; after Hanoverian accession, 132, 141, 251; renascence under younger Pitt, 169–70, 175–6, 177–8; opposition to reform movement, 201, 212–4, 357; encouragement of Continental liberals, 207–9, 210–2; domestic policies after 1815 ("Tory Reaction"), 212–4, 215–6; and first Reform Bill, 216–9, 221–2, 256; and repeal of corn law, 226–9, 265; renascence after 1846, 218, 224, 225, 239, 244, 245–9, 253–4, 354; and Tory democracy, 249–51, 298; after second Reform Bill (1867): *see* Conservative Party

Tory Reaction: *see* Tory Party, domestic policies after 1815

Trade, acts of, 148–9, *and see* Commerce; Navigation Act

Trade unions, in early nineteenth century, 214, 220; and Tory democracy, 248; legalized by Gladstone and Disraeli, 259, 260; changing character of, in Salisbury era, 296–8; and protection, 299; Liberal legislation for, after 1906, 307–8; and Labour Party, 349–50

Trafalgar, Battle of, (1805), 192–3

Transvaal, settled by Boers, 236; granted autonomy (1852), 237; and first Boer War, 284–6, 287; after 1881: *see* South African Republic

Treaties: *see* Aix-la-Chapelle, Treaty of, (1748); Alliances; Amiens, Peace of, (1802); Berlin, Congress and Treaty of, (1878); Brest-Litovsk, Treaty of, (1918); Edinburgh, Treaty of, (1560); Locarno, Treaties of, (1925); Munich, Peace of, (1938); Paris, Peace of, (1763; 1856; 1919); San Stefano, Treaty of, (1878); Tilsit, Peace of, (1807); Utrecht, Treaty of, (1713); Vereeniging, Treaty of, (1902); Versailles, Treaty of, (1783; 1919); Vienna, Congress and Treaty of, (1815); Washington, Conference and naval treaties of, (1922)

Trent, Council of, (1545), and Catholic Reformation, 32

Triple Alliance, 301, 304; deserted by Italy in first World War, 326

Triple Entente, genesis of, 312–4; and first World War, 314–6, 317–20; possibility of reviving in late 1930's, 357

Tudor, House of, problems confronting, 5–12; governmental system of, 14–5, 20, 50, 66–8; sovereigns of: *see* Edward VI; Elizabeth; Henry VII; Henry VIII; Mary

Turkey (Ottoman Empire), in Napoleonic era, 196; and Greek revolt, 210–2; and Crimean War, 241–3, 244; and crisis of 1878, 278–80; and British occupation of Egypt, 281–4; and origins of first World War, 313–5; in first World War, 324, 331; and peace settlement, 336–7; in second World War, 372; contemporary Anglo-Russian friction over, 382

Uitlanders, role of, in precipitating Boer War, 289–93

Ulster, Jacobean plantation of, 57–8; restrictions on Protestants of, 164, 185–6; and Catholic emancipation, 187, 215; and first Home Rule Bill, 266; and third Home Rule Bill, 311–2; and creation of Irish Free State, 345, 346

Union, Act of: with Scotland (1707), 124; with Ireland (1800), 186–8, 214–6, 267, and movement to repeal: *see* Home Rule; Ulster; Unionists

Union of South Africa, created (1910), 343; in first World War, 344; in second World War, 379, 384; in contemporary world, 385, 388

Unionists, genesis of, 267–8; fusion with Conservatives, 286–7, 295; split by Joseph Chamberlain, 299–300

United Nations, and problem of coercion, 208; origins of, 378; and Anglo-American struggle with Russia, 382

United States, role of judiciary in, 56, 70, 308; achievement of independence, 159–61; nineteenth-century position, 162–3, 329, 380; and War of 1812, 195–6, 197–8; and Monroe Doctrine, 209–10, 317;

United States (*continued*)
Civil War, 243, 251, 261–2, 269, 271, 321; Spanish-American War, 135, 275, 302; economic competition with Britain, 274, 296, 347, 351; and *Alabama* claims, 276–7; and Panama Canal, 281, 303; Salisbury's policy toward, 295; naval competition with Britain, 303, 329, 341–2; during first World War, 325, 326–7, 328–31, 345; withdrawal from peace settlement, 330, 332, 336, 338–9, 340, 379; and reparations, 341; in 1930's, 308, 350; and origins of second World War, 361; in second World War, 355, 370–1, 373–80, 381; in contemporary world, 380, 381–3, 386; present relationship with British Commonwealth, 384–5, 387–93

Utrecht, Treaty of, (1713), 121–2, 125–6; instability of peace settlement, 133–5; mentioned, 140

Valois, House of, in sixteenth-century France, 12–3, 38–40

Venezuela, Anglo-American friction over, 277

Vereeniging, Treaty of, (1902), 294–5; mentioned, 300

Verona, Congress of, (1822), 206

Versailles, Treaty of: (1783), 161–2, mentioned, 168; (1919), 333, 341, Nazi abrogation of, 338, 358–9, 361–2, 365

Victoria, Queen of Great Britain, character and initial problems, 225; and alienation of Hanover from British Crown, 240; relations with Disraeli, 260; and relief of Gordon, 283; death, 256, 295

Vienna, Congress and Treaty of, (1815), 202–6, 276, 332

Villeneuve, Pierre Charles de, French admiral in Trafalgar campaign, 192, 199

Villiers, George: *see* Buckingham

Virginia, in early Stuart period, 58, 69; and Cromwellian Commonwealth, 90; in American Revolution, 160–1

Voltaire, François Marie Arouet, quoted, 167; mentioned, 147

Wales, English conquest of, 7; in Industrial Revolution, 173

Walpole, Sir Robert, constitutional importance of, 131; policies, 133, 134–5; compared with Neville Chamberlain, 360; mentioned, 175, 179, 187
War of 1812, 162, 195–6, 197–8; mentioned, 380
Warfare, effect of French Revolution on, 182; significance for Britain of recent developments in, 388–91
Wars: *see* Austria Succession, War of the, (1740); Boer War (1880; 1899); Civil War; Crimean War (1854); Dutch War (1652; 1665; 1672); Franco-Prussian War (1870); Hundred Years' War; Jenkins's Ear, War of, (1739); League of Augsburg, War of the, (1688); Peninsular War (1808); Revolution, American, War of the; Revolution, French, Wars of the, and Napoleon; Roses, Wars of the; Seven Years' War (1756); Spanish Succession, War of the, (1702); Thirty Years' War (1618); War of 1812; World War (1914; 1939)
Washington Conference and naval treaties (1921–2), background and implications, 341–2, 351
Washington, George, in War of American Revolution, 159
Waterloo, Battle of, (1815), 199–201
Wellesley, Sir Arthur: *see* Wellington
Wellington, Arthur Wellesley, Duke of, in Peninsular War, 197; in Waterloo campaign, 199–200; in post-war politics, 201; at Congress of Verona, 206; Prime Minister, 211–2, 214, 215, 216–7; and first Reform Bill, 221, 247, 252; and corn law crisis, 229; compared with Salisbury 295
Wentworth, Peter, Elizabethan Puritan, 37, 66
Wentworth, Thomas: *see* Strafford
Wesley, Charles and John, and Methodism, 179–80
West Indies: *see* Caribbean
Westminster, Statute of, (1932), 346, 347, 355
Whig Party, in reign of Charles II, 105–9, and of James II, 110–1, 320; and settlement of Glorious Revolution, 112–4, 122–3, 124–7, 205; after Hanoverian accession, 132, 133, 141, 144, 174, 368; and George III's experiment, 151–5, 157; under younger Pitt, 168, 169–

70, 176; during Tory Reaction, 214, 215; and triumph of liberalism, 216–38, 247, 256; tradition of, in late nineteenth century, 267–8, 272. *See also* Liberal Party
Whitefield, George, Methodist leader, 179
William II, German Emperor, and telegram to Kruger, 292; and Mahan, 302; at Tangier, 305; and crisis of 1914, 319; flight to Holland, 331, 332; mentioned, 301, 313, 329, 358, 359
William III, King of England, and claim to English throne, 105–7; accession, 111–2; and Toleration Act, 113; in Ireland, 115–6; dealings with Louis XIV, 116–20; character, 119; relations with Tories, 122; death, 119–20; mentioned, 123, 235
William IV, King of Great Britain, and first Reform Bill, 216–7, 221; death, 225
Wilson, President Woodrow, in first World War, 328–30; at Paris Conference, 332–3, 334, 339; quoted, 374
Wolsey, Thomas, Cardinal, and Henry VIII, 17–8, 21, 50
Wool trade, in Tudor period, 9, 11; and revolt of Netherlands, 41; and James I, 57; and Charles I, 69; and British treatment of Ireland after 1690, 116; and Industrial Revolution, 171, 172
Worcester, Battle of, (1651), 89; flight of Charles II from, 99
World War: first (1914), origins of, 205, 280, 312–20, and Irish crisis, 311–2, 345, course of, 320–32, 389, settlement following, 332–7, and British dominions, 323, 343–4, effects of, on Britain, 346, 347, 353, 358, 359, 385, and stimulus to nationalism, 334, 356, and strategy of second World War, 367–8, mentioned, 377, 379; second (1939), origins of, 330, 356–66, course of, 366–78, effects of, on English-speaking peoples, 379–80, 384, effects of, on Britain, 384–5

Yorktown, surrender of Cornwallis at, (1781), 151, 160–1

Zulus, danger from, to white settlers in South Africa, 234, 284–5

A NOTE ON THE

T Y P E

IN WHICH THIS BOOK IS SET

THE TEXT *of this book is set in* Caledonia, *a Linotype face which belongs to the family of printing types called "modern face" by printers — a term used to mark the change in style of type-letters that occurred about 1800. Caledonia borders on the general design of Scotch Modern, but is more freely drawn than that letter.*

The book was composed, printed, and bound by The Plimpton Press, Norwood, Massachusetts. The typography and binding design are by W. A. Dwiggins.

WAD

15- 6995 34